Steps to College Reading

Steps to College Reading

Third Edition

Dorothy U. Seyler
Northern Virginia Community College

PEARSON
Longman

New York San Francisco Boston
London Toronto Sydney Tokyo Singapore Madrid
Mexico City Munich Paris Cape Town Hong Kong Montreal

Vice President and Editor in Chief: Joseph Terry
Senior Acquisitions Editor: Steven Rigolosi
Senior Marketing Manager: Melanie Craig
Senior Supplements Editor: Donna Campion
Production Manager: Joseph Vella
Project Coordination, Text Design, and Electronic Page Makeup: Electronic Publishing Services Inc., N.Y.C.
Cover Designer/Manager: Wendy A. Fredericks
Cover Art: Leger, Fernand (1881–1955) "Le Disque" 1918. (Detail) The Art Archive/Thyssen-Bornemisza
        Collection/Dagli Orti. © 2003 ARS, Artists Rights Society, New York, New York
Manufacturing Manager: Dennis J. Para
Printer and Binder: R.R. Donnelley & Sons Company
Cover Printer: Coral Graphics Services

For permission to use copyrighted material, grateful acknowledgment is made to the copyright holders on
pp. 477–479, which are hereby made part of this copyright page.

Library of Congress Cataloging-in-Publication Data

Seyler, Dorothy U.
    Steps to college reading/Dorothy U. Seyler.—3rd ed.
        p. cm.
    Includes bibliographic references and index.
    ISBN 0-321-10467-6
     1. Reading (Higher Education) 2. Reading (Higher Education)—Problems, exercises, etc.
    I. Title

    LB2395.3.S49 2004
    428.4´071´1—dc21

                                                                    2003041022

Visit us at www.ablongman.com

ISBN 0-321-10404-8

1 2 3 4 5 6 7 8 9 10—DOH—06 05 04 03

Brief Contents

Detailed Contents

Part III Topics, Main Ideas, and Supporting Details

Part IV Strategies and Structures

■ Chapter 9

Part V Critical Reading

■ Chapter 10

▪ **CHAPTER 11**

Understanding Graphics and Separating Fact and Opinion 353

Preface

Are you reading to improve your reading? *Steps to College Reading* is ready to be your guide, to take you step by step to better reading skills. If you have the desire, *Steps* has the strategies. But understand. There is no magic wand in these pages. The only way to improve is to *read*! If you just start reading more, your skills will improve. But if you want to prepare for your college classes, you need advice and guided practice. Your instructor and this text will give you both. So, turn the page and let's get to work.

Steps has been created on several key ideas:

- The best way to improve a skill is to understand the "subskills" that make it up and to practice those subskills separately first.
- Reading is a process that can be divided into the three basic steps of **Prepare–Read–Respond**.
- Reading happens only when an active reader makes meaning from the words.
- Reading needs a context. Readers need to know the author and the author's purpose as well as their own purpose in reading.

FEATURES OF *STEPS TO COLLEGE READING*

The following features give you a great "tool kit" for improving your reading skills:

- A simple, clear reading strategy that works.
- An emphasis throughout on understanding your reading context.
- Clear explanations supported by many examples.
- Lots of exercises offering plenty of practice.
- Interesting, varied readings combining textbook selections and essays.
- Detailed comprehension and vocabulary exercises.
- Questions that engage readers and encourage critical thinking.

NEW FEATURES IN THE THIRD EDITION

This new edition of *Steps* keeps the key features of the text while providing some changes and some new features that make the third edition even stronger, more helpful, than the second edition. Here are the key changes:

- A neater organization that groups all chapters under six clear headings: an Introduction that gets readers thinking about reading and learning a reading strategy; Vocabulary that groups two chapters that study context clues, word parts, and using the dictionary; Topics, Main Ideas, and Supporting Details (that expands work on main ideas to three chapters); Strategies and Structures (that expands recognizing patterns to three chapters); Critical Reading that includes both drawing inferences and reading graphics; and College Success (with work on writing-to-learn strategies and preparing for testing).
- An appendix of additional readings complete with comprehension and vocabulary exercises.
- An appendix on more efficient reading that explains how to determine reading rate.
- Pages that easily tear out for turning in exercises from the text.
- Many more exercises—putting the most emphasis on reading for main ideas and recognizing a writer's structures and strategies.
- More end-of-chapter readings, and readings that are related in topic or theme and allow for "Making Connections" questions.
- A new vocabulary exercise (Word Power) at the end of each chapter.
- At least one Workshop (Collaborative) exercise in each chapter.
- "E" Connections at the end of each chapter that provide an Internet search activity connected to one or more of the chapter's readings.
- Guidelines for Internet searches.

THE LONGMAN BASIC SKILLS PACKAGE

A combined instructor's manual and test bank to accompany *Steps to College Reading* is available. The instructor's manual provides answers to exercises and to the questions following each of the text's reading selections. It also contains sample syllabi, tips for teaching each chapter, and grade reading levels for all reading selections. The test bank includes preformatted tests for all key reading skills. Please ask your Longman sales representative for ISBN 0-321-10406-4.

In addition, many other skills-based supplements and testing packages are available for both instructors and students. All of these supplements are available either free or at greatly reduced prices.

For Additional Reading and Reference

The Dictionary Deal. Two dictionaries can be shrinkwrapped with this text at a nominal fee. *The New American Webster Handy College Dictionary* is a paperback reference text with more than 100,000 entries. *Merriam Webster's Collegiate*

Dictionary, Tenth Edition, is a hardback reference with a citation file of more than 14.5 million examples of English words drawn from actual use. For more information on how to shrinkwrap a dictionary with your text, please contact your Longman sales representative.

Penguin Quality Paperback Titles.   A series of Penguin paperbacks is available at a significant discount when shrinkwrapped with this text. Some titles available are Toni Morrison's *Beloved*, Julia Alvarez's *How the Garcia Girls Lost Their Accents*, Mark Twain's *Huckleberry Finn, Narrative of the Life of Frederick Douglass*, Harriet Beecher Stowe's *Uncle Tom's Cabin*, Dr. Martin Luther King, Jr.'s, *Why We Can't Wait*, and plays by Shakespeare, Miller, and Albee. For a complete list of titles or more information, please contact your Longman sales consultant.

Penguin Academics: *Twenty-Five Great Essays, Fifty Great Essays*, **and** *One Hundred Great Essays*, **edited by Robert DiYanni.**   These alphabetically organized essay collections are published as part of the "Penguin Academics" series of low-cost, high-quality offerings intended for use in introductory college courses. All essays were selected for their teachability, both as models for writing and for their usefulness as springboards for student writing. For more information on how to shrinkwrap one of these anthologies with your text, please contact your Longman sales consultant.

The Longman Textbook Reader.   This supplement, for use in developmental reading courses, offers five complete chapters from Addison-Wesley/ Longman textbooks: computer science, biology, psychology, communications, and business. Each chapter includes additional comprehension quizzes, critical thinking questions, and group activities. Available FREE with the adoption of this Longman text. For information on how to bundle *The Longman Textbook Reader* with your text, please contact your Longman sales representative. Available in two formats: with answers and without answers.

Newsweek Alliance.   Instructors may choose to shrinkwrap a 12-week subscription to *Newsweek* with any Longman text. The price of the subscription is 59 cents per issue (a total of $7.08 for the subscription). Available with the subscription is a free "Interactive Guide to *Newsweek*"—a workbook for students who are using the text. In addition, Newsweek provides a wide variety of instructor supplements free to teachers, including maps, Skills Builders, and weekly quizzes. For more information on the Newsweek program, please contact your Longman sales representative.

Electronic and Online Offerings

Longman Reading Road Trip Multimedia Software, CD Version and Web Version.   This innovative and exciting multimedia reading software is available either on CD-ROM format or on the Web. The package takes students on a tour of 16 cities and landmarks throughout the United States. Each of the 16 modules corresponds to a reading or study skill (for example, finding the main idea, understanding patterns of organization, and thinking critically). All modules contain a tour of the location, instruction and tutorial, exercises, interactive feedback, and mastery tests. To shrinkwrap the CD or the access code to the Website with this textbook, please consult your Longman sales representative. Also ask about the CourseCompass version, which contains classroom management functions.

Longman Vocabulary Website. For additional vocabulary-related resources, visit our free Vocabulary Website at **http://www.ablongman.com/vocabulary.**

The Longman Study Skills Website. This Website is the perfect accompaniment to any freshman orientation, study skills, or reading course. It offers a wealth of resources, exercises, and Weblinks to help students make the most of their college courses and college experience. Visit the Website at **http://www.ablongman.com/studyskills.**

The Longman Electronic Newsletter. Twice a month during the spring and fall, instructors who have subscribed receive a free copy of the Longman Developmental English Newsletter in their e-mailbox. Written by experienced classroom instructors, the newsletter offers teaching tips, classroom activities, book reviews, and more. To subscribe, visit the Longman Basic Skills Website at **http://www.ablongman.com/basicskills**, or send an e-mail to **BasicSkills@ablongman.com.**

For Instructors

Electronic Test Bank for Reading. This electronic test bank offers more than 3,000 questions in all areas of reading, including vocabulary, main idea, supporting details, patterns of organization, language, critical thinking, analytical reasoning, inference, point of view, visual aids, and textbook reading. With this easy-to-use CD-ROM, instructors simply choose questions from the electronic test bank, then print out the completed test for distribution. CD-ROM: 0-321-08179-X; Print version: 0-321-08596-5.

Teaching Online: Internet Research, Conversation, and Composition, Second Edition. Ideal for instructors who have never surfed the Net, this easy-to-follow guide offers basic definitions, numerous examples, and step-by-step information about finding and using Internet sources. Free to adopters. 0-321-01957-1

The Longman Instructor's Planner. This all-in-one resource for instructors includes monthly and weekly planning sheets, to-do lists, student contact forms, attendance rosters, a gradebook, an address/phone book, and a mini-almanac. Ask your Longman sales representative for a free copy. 0-321-09247-3.

For Students

Researching Online, Fifth Edition. A perfect companion for a new age, this indispensable new supplement helps students navigate the Internet. Adapted from *Teaching Online*, the instructor's Internet guide, *Researching Online* speaks directly to students, giving them detailed, step-by-step instructions for performing electronic searches. Available free when shrinkwrapped with this text. 0-321-09277-5.

Ten Practices of Highly Successful Students.   This popular supplement helps students learn crucial study skills, offering concise tips for a successful career in college. Topics include time management, test-taking, reading critically, stress, and motivation. 0-205-30769-8.

The Longman Student Planner.   This daily planner for students includes daily, weekly, and monthly calendars, as well as class schedules and a mini-almanac of useful information. It is the perfect accompaniment to a Longman reading or study skills textbook, and is available free to students when shrinkwrapped with this text. 0-321-04573-4.

The Longman Reader's Journal,   by Kathleen T. McWhorter. The reader's journal offers students a space to record their questions about, reactions to, and summaries of materials they've read. Also included is a personal vocabulary long, as well as ample space for free writing. For an examination copy, contact your Longman sales consultant. 0-321-08843-3.

[NEW] The Longman Reader's Portfolio.   This unique supplement provides students with a space to plan, think about, and present their work. The portfolio includes a diagnostic area (including a learning style questionnaire), a working area (including calendars, vocabulary logs, reading response sheets, book-club tips, and other valuable materials), and a display area (including a progress chart, a final table of contents, and a final assessment). Ask your Longman sales representative for ISBN 0-321-10766-7.

State Specific Adoptions

[For Florida Adoptions] *Thinking Through the Test,* **by D.J. Henry.** This special workbook, prepared specially for students in Florida, offers ample skill and practice exercises to help student prep for the Florida State Exit Exam. To shrinkwrap this workbook free with your textbook, please contact your Longman sales representative. Available in two versions: with answers and without answers. Also available: Two laminated grids (one for reading, one for writing) that can serve as handy references for students preparing for the Florida State Exit Exam.

[For New York Adoptions] Preparing for the CUNY-ACT Reading and Writing Test, edited by Patricia Licklider. This booklet, prepared by reading and writing faculty from across the CUNY system, is designed to help students prepare for the CUNY-ACT exit test. It includes test-taking tips, reading passages, typical exam questions, and sample writing prompts to help students become familiar with each portion of the test.

[For Texas Adoptions] *The Longman TASP Study Guide,* **by Jeanette Harris.** Created specifically for students in Texas, this study guide includes straightforward explanations and numerous practice exercises to help students prepare for the reading and writing sections of the Texas Academic Skills Program Test. To shrinkwrap this workbook free with your textbook, please contact your Longman sales representative. 0-321-20271-6

THE LONGMAN SERIES OF MONOGRAPHS FOR DEVELOPMENTAL EDUCATORS

Ask your Longman sales consultant for a free copy of these monographs written by experts in their fields.

#1: The Longman Guide to Classroom Management

Written by Joannis Flatley of St. Philip's College, the first in Longman's new series of monographs for developmental English instructors focuses on issues of classroom etiquette, providing guidance on dealing with unruly, unengaged, disruptive, or uncooperative students. Ask your Longman sales representative for a free copy. 0-321-09246-5.

#2: The Longman Guide to Community Service-Learning in the English Classroom and Beyond

Written by Elizabeth Rodriguez Kessler of California State University–Northridge, this is the second monograph in Longman's series for developmental educators. It provides a definition and history of service-learning, as well as an overview of how service-learning can be integrated effectively into the college classroom. 0-321-12749-8.

ACKNOWLEDGMENTS

Fortunately for both authors and readers, no book is created alone. Many colleagues and friends have helped me think about how we read and how we learn. To all of them I am grateful. Specifically, I wish to acknowledge Evonne Jones, Barbara Wilan, Pam Legatt, Pat Hodgdon, Priscilla Howard, Daphne Keys, and Carol Ischinger for lending books and sharing ideas. I can never complete a textbook without the support of our reference librarians, especially Marian Delmore and Ruth Stanton. I also want to thank, once again, my most important "first reader," my daughter Ruth. In addition I want to thank Joe Opiela for asking me to do two developmental reading texts and guiding me through two editions of each one. I am much in debt to my editor for this third edition, Steven Rigolosi, who helped me immensely in the reshaping of the chapters and in suggestions for new features.

Finally, and important, the following reviewers have contributed excellent suggestions for this third edition: Kathleen A. Celaya, St. Philip's Community College; David Elias, Eastern Kentucky University; Marian Helms, College of Southern Idaho; Annie Maeda, Hawaii Community College; Marilee McGowan, Oakton Community College; Marlene Merritt, Seminole Community College; Linda Streb Gannon, Horry-Georgetown Technical College; and Pam Williamson, Odessa College.

DOROTHY V. SEYLER
NORTHERN VIRGINIA COMMUNITY COLLEGE
ANNANDALE, VIRGINIA

Steps to College Reading

| CHAPTER 1 | Developing a Reading Strategy |

LEARNING OBJECTIVES

- To know what reading is

- To understand why you need commitment and concentration to read well

- To know how a reading plan will improve reading

- To learn the steps in your reading strategy

In his *Autobiography*, Ben Franklin lists 13 virtues that he wants to develop. He then explains his specific plan for success: Work on one at a time until it becomes a habit and then move on to the next. Franklin knew that we act more on habit than principle.

Stephen R. Covey, in his popular best-seller *The 7 Habits of Highly Effective People*, asks readers to imagine that they have come to a funeral—their own! They will listen to eulogies—talks praising a dead person—about themselves. Sounds weird? Well, if this were happening to you, what would you like to hear others saying about you?

| EXERCISE 1-1 | **Who Do You Want to Be?** |

I. What do you want others to say about you at the end of your life? Write a paragraph "eulogy" for yourself—what you hope others would say about you.

_____

_____

_____

1

_____

_____

_____

_____

_____

_____

_____

II. Have you written something about career? About money and possessions? About education? Family life? Personal fulfillment? Organize what you have written by grouping specific details under appropriate headings.

Heading 1. _____

_____

_____

_____

Heading 2. _____

_____

_____

_____

Heading 3. _____

_____

_____

_____

Do you see your goals and values more clearly now? We cannot take charge of our lives until we know what kind of life we want to have. The next step—and an important one—is to figure out the steps to achieve those goals.

| EXERCISE 1-2 | **What Steps Do You Need to Take?** |

WORKSHOP

How can you become the person you have written about? List specific steps you need to take to reach some of the goals you listed in Exercise 1-1. (You may want to work with a class partner and help each other with your lists of steps.)

_____

_____

_____

_____

_____

_____

■ ■ ■ ■ ■

Have you listed education in these exercises? If the career you hope for requires a college degree, you will be studying for several years. Suppose you want to start your own business. You will need to study tax forms and government regulations. Do you want to be (or are you already) a parent? There are guides to parenting and to making marriage work. Learning is a lifelong activity. It does not end when you finish formal schooling. One way to keep learning and moving toward your goals is through **reading**. You are a key part of the reading process. To do your part, here are three important reading habits to develop.

THREE HIGHLY EFFECTIVE HABITS OF GOOD READERS

Commit to reading:

Develop an *active* desire to read well and benefit from reading. *Visualize* your success as a reader. Believe in yourself. Attitude does matter.

Concentrate:

Give *active* attention to reading. Use specific strategies for improving concentration.

(continued on next page)

(continued from previous page)

Read actively:

Understand the reading process. Have a reading strategy. Use your knowledge and your strategy to be an active reader *every time you read.*

■ COMMIT

Only you can improve your reading skills. And reading is a skill—just like driving a car. How do you improve at any skill? Through a desire to learn, good instruction, and practice, practice, practice! Your instructor will provide instruction and opportunities for practice. The commitment must come from you. Your desire to improve will show in how much time you spend reading and building your vocabulary. Commitment shows itself in action.

Commit to the behaviors of successful people. Successful people use their time wisely. They don't talk endlessly on cell phones or watch hours of TV. They don't talk about how much work they have, or fret over the workload. When it is work time, they sit down and do it.

Connect your desire to improve reading skills to your goals in life. Use your plans for the future as motivation to keep working when you become anxious or frustrated. Do what successful athletes do: visualize yourself achieving your goals. Throw away negative feelings. They only get in the way of positive actions.

■ CONCENTRATE

If you do not concentrate well when you read, then developing greater concentration will be a necessary step to better reading. Concentration, like commitment, requires action. Here are some specific steps you can take to improve your concentration.

Steps to Improved Concentration: Before You Begin Reading

1. *Reduce Distractions.* Find a quiet place to read. Turn off the television. Sit comfortably, but don't get too relaxed. If your house or dorm is rarely quiet, learn to read in the library at an individual desk in a quiet zone, not at a large table in a busy area.

2. *Choose Good Times to Read.* Do not read late at night or when you are very tired. If you must study late, save work that requires writing as well as reading, such as completing exercises. Many successful people will argue that we are most productive in the morning. Consider reading in the morning before classes, and in the library between classes.

3. *Let Others Know Your Reading Schedule.* Let roommates or family members know that you will be reading and should not be disturbed. Ask friends not to call or come by during your study times. Post a Do Not Disturb sign on your door. Then ignore those who try to interrupt.

4. *Keep Your Body in Shape.* Willpower alone cannot keep us going. If you are abusing your body, the body will say "enough," often in the form of a cold or flu. So, get enough rest. Eat properly, and that means—beginning with breakfast—plenty of fruits and vegetables. (A bag of chips is *not* a fruit!) Also schedule time for exercise. You will get more done during the day if you get at least 30 minutes of aerobic exercise every day.

5. *Set Up a Work Plan.* Plan the time you will spend on each reading assignment. Consider writing out a schedule for each day. Divide your time among your courses, with a short break in between. But be sure to read in complete units: an entire article, a complete chapter, or several related sections within a long chapter. If you read only a few pages at one sitting, you will have to reread them when you return to that assignment.

6. *Start Using a To-Do List.* Counselors often advise students to make a to-do list for each day—because many successful people organize their time this way. You can make your list in a special notebook or in an electronic notepad. The key is to list all the tasks needing action on a given day, carry the list with you, and check off each task as you complete it. Often these lists contain more than anyone can do in a day. So, first you must highlight the most important tasks and be sure to get those done. Second, carry on to the next day the tasks not completed along with new tasks. Again, be sure to prioritize your list—put the most important items first or highlight them in some way. When you make your daily list, think about the most efficient way to get the tasks done. For example, if you need to pick up a book at the library, plan to drop off your cleaning at the same time because it is on the way. Include in your list your class times and study times.

7. *Free Your Mind.* Before reading, try to free your mind from distracting details. Your to-do list can help you set aside time to pay bills, exercise, or make phone calls. Then, when you are ready to read and study, focus just on that activity.

Steps to Improved Concentration: While You Are Reading

1. *Think Positively.* Try to turn to each reading assignment with enthusiasm. Think about what you may learn. Note the progress you are making through a difficult textbook.

2. *Use Previous Knowledge.* As you begin to read, think about what you already know about the topic. When beginning a new chapter in a text, take time to recall last week's reading and class discussion. Make connections to keep your focus and get more from your reading.

3. *Read Actively to Keep Focused.* To read actively, ask yourself questions as you go. Try to picture what you are reading about. Mark the text—if it is yours—or take notes as you read. Reading with a pencil in hand and connections in your head will keep you involved.

4. *Take Breaks.* You may concentrate better if you take a short break from reading every hour or so. Reading should not be physical torture. Just be sure

that the breaks come at logical places to pause—and that the breaks do not last longer than the reading periods!

5. *Monitor (Check) the Loss of Concentration.* When your attention wanders, try to understand why. Are you thinking about errands you need to run? If so, then you have not followed the steps for improved concentration before reading. Commit to following those steps more faithfully. When the reading gets hard, give yourself a "commitment booster" and keep working.

READ ACTIVELY: UNDERSTAND READING AND USE A READING STRATEGY

What is reading? A good answer is that *reading is the process of making meaning from a word or cluster of words.* This definition gives us three key ideas about reading.

1. We can find meaning in clusters of words that do not necessarily make a complete sentence. For example:

> Hilda locked her keys in her locker. And her bookbag. Her purse too.

The first statement is a complete sentence, but "And her bookbag" is a fragment. All by itself it would not make much sense. But when read with the first statement, each cluster of words provides meaning. We understand that Hilda's keys, bookbag, and purse are in her locker, and she cannot get them out.

2. Reading involves getting meaning from the words. Reading means *understanding* the information or ideas or feelings expressed by the words. Reading is a thinking activity. If you are not getting a message, you are not really reading.

3. We do not just understand a writer's meaning; we, the readers, *make* meaning. Readers must use their knowledge of vocabulary, sentence structure, and the subject to *construct* meaning. The more we know, the easier reading is.

> Reading is a complex thinking activity. To make meaning, readers draw on their vocabulary, previous knowledge, feelings, and visual skills. That's why readers need to commit to reading and concentrate to read effectively.

Reading is intellectual work, and for work to be productive, most people need a plan. A good reading strategy is one that:

- Guides you to prepare before reading
- Improves your comprehension from reading
- Helps you retain information and ideas
- Allows you to fulfill your purpose in reading

If you make a habit of using the three-step plan of **Prepare–Read–Respond**, you will become a better reader.

Part of following a reading plan or strategy is being *aware* that you are using a plan. This means that you are not just reading but paying attention to how you are reading. When you are having trouble comprehending, check to see if you are completing all the steps in your strategy, locate the source of the trouble, and go back to fix the problem. For example, perhaps you realize, when the reading becomes confusing, that you started to read without preparing. You just skipped the first step in your reading strategy. Completing the first step may help you sort out the earlier confusion.

PREPARE–READ–RESPOND: HOW THE STEPS CONNECT

Figure 1.1 shows how the three steps in your reading plan divide into three stages: before reading, during reading, and after reading. Each major step includes several important activities. The activities included in **preparing** to read make you an active reader. As you **read** actively, you become engaged with the text while monitoring (checking) your comprehension. You are not finished with the reading process until you **respond**, a step that includes reviewing to reinforce learning and reflecting to give your reading significance or value.

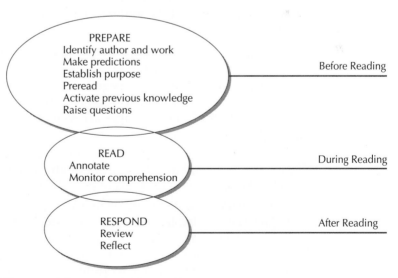

■ FIGURE 1.1   **Steps in the Reading Process**

Notice in the diagram that the first and third steps overlap the middle step. The diagram shows that the three steps are not completely separate activities. As you read, you may raise more questions or have to make new predictions about what is coming. You may also pause in your reading to reflect on what you have just learned. So, your reading strategy is both an organized plan to follow but also an interconnected process.

PREPARE

Good readers prepare in some way before they read. When you are facing new—and sometimes difficult—material to be learned for class, you need to rely heavily on the prepare stage. Don't rush through or skip this key step if you want to read efficiently and get the most out of your reading.

Identify the Author, Type of Work, and Subject to Make Predictions

Learn About the Author. Begin by learning all you can about the author (or authors). Learn about each writer's education, position, or experiences, the facts that explain why this writer has been published. Most books and magazines provide some information about each author. *Note: In this textbook, information about authors precedes each selection.*

Learn About the Work. Take a minute to look over the reading to get an idea of the kind of work it is and the way the material will be presented. When you know the kind of work you are about to read, you can **predict** both how the work will be presented and what the writer's purpose is.

- *Poems*
  Lines are arranged differently from prose works (all other kinds of writing). They may be short; they may be grouped in stanzas that have rhyme. Often each new line begins with a capital letter even though it does not start a new sentence. Sometimes no words are capitalized, or the lines "dance" in odd shapes across the page.

- *Novels*
  In prose: Lines of sentences flush with both the left and right margins. Usually presented in chapters, although chapters are often numbered but not titled. Rarely uses headings/subheadings or graphics.

- *Nonfiction books, including textbooks*
  In prose and in chapters: Chapters are usually titled. Often, especially in textbooks, there are many headings and subheadings to divide and organize the material. Color is usually found to highlight key passages and to separate, visually, one part from another. Often many graphs and charts and pictures are used.

- *Magazine articles*
  Each article/essay is separately authored and titled. Each is usually shorter than a chapter in a book and is focused on one topic. Articles in popular magazines frequently use color, headings/subheadings, and graphics much like textbooks. (This textbook reprints a number of articles that originally appeared in magazines.)

- *Newspaper articles*
  Contains several kinds of articles: news stories, feature stories, editorials, and columns of opinion. The importance of each article is signaled by the size of the headline type, by its location in the paper (most important news stories are on the front page), and by the length of the article. News stories provide the facts; feature stories go into greater depth and may state or imply a point of view on the topic; editorials and opinion pieces are brief arguments, taking a position on a current event.

Learn about the Subject. As part of your preparation, you need to **preview** or **preread** the selection. Prereading gives you an idea the author's topic and approach, a **context** that will let you get more out of your reading. The less you know about the subject, the less context for understanding you have—the more important prereading is. Each time you start to use a new textbook, or to read any nonfiction book, follow these guidelines.

Guidelines for Prereading a Textbook

1. **Read and think about the title. Learn about the author(s) and observe the date of publication.**

2. **Read the preface or introduction.** Here the author explains the book's focus and gives some key ideas that have guided his or her approach to the subject.

3. **Study the table of contents.** This will give you an idea of the specific topics covered. It will also give you an overview of the course you are about to take. Write down questions or thoughts about the topics as you read.

4. **See if the book has any appendices, notes, bibliography, or a glossary.** Many textbooks will have all of these additional sections at the end of the book. Appendices contain additional information; notes document borrowed information; a bibliography guides you to other works on the same subject; the glossary lists and defines key terms used in the book.

Each time you read a textbook chapter or an article, you also need to pre-read. For chapters and articles follow these guidelines.

Guidelines for Prereading a Chapter or Article

1. **Read and think about the title.** Also read the subtitle, if there is one. Sometimes authors choose catchy titles and then explain their subject in a subtitle. The title contains the author's first words to you; pay attention to them.
2. **Read the opening and concluding paragraphs.** Authors usually state their main points at the beginning and then again at the end of their writing. Glance at the opening sentences of each paragraph. Often the main idea of a paragraph is stated in the first sentence.
3. **Look through the chapter or article to note headings, subheadings, and words in italics or bold type.** Many books and articles guide readers through the material with visual signals that reveal organization and the subjects covered.
4. **Also look at any graphics—diagrams, charts, pictures.** The author has carefully chosen accompanying graphics not only to add interest but also to clarify the topic. Looking at the graphics will give you a good sense of the work's subject.

Make Predictions. After learning about author, work, and subject, talk to yourself about the work, reflecting on the writer's subject and purpose and approach. Here is an example.

Your speech class text is *Mastering Public Speaking* (by George L. Grice and John F. Skinner). Your observe from the title page that both authors are college professors. You conclude that the text has been well received because it is in a second edition—and your instructor has assigned it. You read the preface, look through the table of contents to see what is covered, and note that there are several appendixes. You then turn to the first chapter to preview. Here are the chapter's title and some headings and subheadings. What do they tell you about the chapter's content? Note your thoughts and questions—perhaps as you see below.

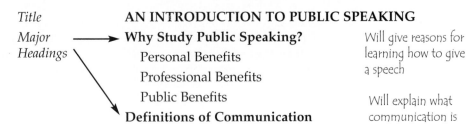

Title	**AN INTRODUCTION TO PUBLIC SPEAKING**
Major Headings ⟶	**Why Study Public Speaking?** — Will give reasons for learning how to give a speech
	Personal Benefits
	Professional Benefits
	Public Benefits — Will explain what communication is
	Definitions of Communication

Levels of Communication

Subheadings {
Intrapersonal Communication
Interpersonal Communication
Group Communication
Public Communication
Mass Communication

Will talk about different kinds—going from one person to larger groups

...

Your First Speech

Section gives steps to get you through a speech

Understand the Assignment
Develop Your Speech Content
Organize Your Speech

Second-level Headings {
Organize Your Speech Introduction
Organize the Body of Your Speech
Organize Your Speech Conclusion

Word Your Speech
Practice Your Speech
Prepare Your Notes
Practice Productively

...

The Public Speaker as Critical Thinker   *What does this mean?*

Note two key parts in this student's predictions about the chapter. First, the student does not just repeat headings. The student states the *idea* of the various sections. Second, the student notes new terms or concepts with questions—but also understands the way many of the sections are organized

EXERCISE 1-3	Workshop on Prereading and Predicting

WORKSHOP

Read the title and headings of Chapter 4 of Mastering Public Speaking *and make notes or questions about the chapter's contents. Then, with a class partner or in small groups, answer the questions that follow.*

LISTENING
The Importance of Listening
Listening versus Hearing
Listening Is Intermittent
Listening Is a Learned Skill
Listening Is Active
Listening Implies Using the Message Received

The Process of Listening

Receive

Select

Interpret

Understand

Evaluate

Resolve

Obstacles to Effective Listening

Physical Distractions

Physiological Distractions

Psychological Distractions

Factual Distractions

Semantic Distractions

Promoting Better Listening

Desire to Listen

Focus on the Message

Listen for Main Ideas

Understand the Speaker's Point of View

Withhold Judgment

Reinforce the Message

Provide Feedback

Listen with the Body

Listen Critically

1. Briefly explain what each of the five major sections will cover. Use your own words, and use questions when you are confused.

_____

_____

_____

_____

_____

_____

_____

_____

_____

_____

2. Why do you think the author has included a chapter on listening in a text on public speaking?

_____

_____

3. Which is the more important skill, hearing or listening? In what key way do hearing and listening differ?

_____

_____

4. How might someone "listen with the body"?

_____

_____

■ ■ ■ ■ ■

Identify What You Already Know

Studies have shown that the more you know about the topic, the better you read. This makes sense when you remember that reading is a thinking skill. But interest in learning about new subjects also helps. You will remember more from your reading and build on your knowledge if you are eager to learn.

You may actually know more about a topic than you think you do. If you can apply the knowledge you already have, you will understand and remember more of what you read. You want to *activate* your knowledge so that you have a context in which to read.

EXERCISE 1-4	What Do I Already Know?

I. You have just preread a chapter on listening. Write down what you already know about listening.

_____

_____

_____

_____

_____

_____

_____

II. Write down what you know about the subjects of each of the following textbook chapter or section titles.

a. "Ethics and Public Speaking" (from *The Art of Public Speaking*)

_____

_____

_____

_____

b. "Advertising Controversies" (from *Making Sense of Media*)

_____

_____

_____

_____

c. "Energy Balance and Weight Control" (from *Nutrition: Concepts and Controversies*)

_____

_____

_____

_____

■ ■ ■ ■ ■

Raise Questions to Fulfill Your Purpose in Reading

Why are you reading? That's a good question to ask yourself before you start. You read a novel for pleasure but also for insight into human life and experience. You read the newspaper to keep informed on current events—and to see what's on sale. When approaching new or difficult material, remind yourself of your reading purpose. If you are reading a textbook, remember that your purpose is not just to complete an assignment. Your purpose is to learn the material for testing—and to master the knowledge you will need on the job.

One important **Prepare** strategy to help you fulfill your reading purpose is to raise questions that can be answered by the reading. If you seek answers to questions, you will read more purposefully. Ask yourself what you will be learning by turning titles and section headings into questions. So, instead of just reading the heading "Obstacles to Effective Listening," create questions such as:

What are some obstacles to effective listening?

What are some ways to remove obstacles to effective listening?

| EXERCISE 1-5 | **Turning Headings into Questions** |

Turn each of the following titles or section headings into at least two questions.

1. "Computer Crime" (from Fuller and Manning's *Computers and Information Processing*)

_____

_____

_____

2. "The Roles of Proteins in the Body" (from Sizer and Whitney's *Nutrition: Concepts and Controversies*)

_____

_____

_____

3. "Sources of Stress: The Common and the Extreme" (from Wood and Wood, *The World of Psychology*)

_____

_____

_____

4. "The Effects of the Automobile" (from Henslin, *Sociology*)

_____

_____

_____

5. "The West in the Global Community" (from Kishlansky et al., *Civilization in the West*)

_____

_____

_____

■ READ

This entire book is about ways to become a more skilled reader. So here we will examine two activities you need to include with your reading step—annotating and checking comprehension.

Annotate

Studies have shown that writing aids reading comprehension. When you write, you are more likely to concentrate and be an active reader. Also, writing pushes you to note what is important and to think about the material.

When you **annotate**, you mark up the text, underlining and making notes in the margins. Now, before you say to yourself that you cannot write in books, let's stop and think about this. Of course you cannot mark up the books that are not yours, but you can annotate your textbooks and other books and magazines that belong to you. What have you gained by keeping your texts spotless if you end up not doing well in the course? You need to learn to annotate and to use this strategy regularly when reading. Here's how to do it.

Guidelines for Annotating

1. After you read a section, underline key sentences (or important parts of sentences). Underline what seems to be the most important idea in each paragraph.

2. Remember: Underlining highlights by contrast, so underline only what is important.

3. When you look up a word's definition, write the definition in the margin next to the word.

4. Try to separate ideas from examples. Write "ex" in the margin next to an example. If several examples (or points or reasons) are given, label them and then number each one in the margin. This will help you see how many examples (or points or reasons) the author provides.

5. If the selection provides a list, note what the list is about and then circle or number each item in the list.

6. Draw arrows to connect each example to the idea it illustrates. Draw pictures to illustrate concepts—whatever will help you understand and remember.

7. Add any other notes that will help you concentrate on your reading.

An Example of Annotating

As you read the following selection, observe the extent of the reader's involvement.

Long-Term Memory: As Long as a Lifetime Some information from short-term memory makes its way into long-term memory. **Long-term memory** (LTM) is our vast storehouse of permanent or relatively permanent memories. There are no known limits to the storage capacity of long-term memory, and long-term memories last a long time, some of them for a lifetime.

Characteristics
1. no limits to storage
2. lasts a long time

Def—LTM

When we talk about memory in everyday conversation, we are usually referring to long-term memory. Long-term memory holds all the knowledge we have accumulated, the skills we have acquired, and the memories of our past experiences. Information in long-term memory is usually stored in semantic form, although visual images, sounds, and odors can be stored there as well.

What is in long-term memory?

But how does this vast store of information make its way from short-term memory into long-term memory? We seem to remember some information with ease, almost automatically, but other kinds of material require great effort. Sometimes, through mere repetition or rehearsal, we are able to transfer information into long-term memory. Your teachers may have used drills to try to cement the multiplication tables and other material in your long-term memory. This rote rehearsal, however, is not necessarily the best way to transfer information to long-term memory (Craik & Watkins, 1973). When you relate new information to the information already safely tucked away in long-term memory and then form multiple associations, you increase the chance that you will be able to retrieve the new information.

How to:
1. rehearsal
2. relate new info to old & make connections— the best way

Wood and Wood, *The World of Psychology*

EXERCISE 1-6	**Annotating a Selection**

Read the following excerpt, another selection from Wood and Wood's The World of Psychology, *and, using the Guidelines for Annotating, annotate the selection. Compare your work with that of classmates and discuss any differences.*

The Three Processes in Memory: Encoding, Storage, and Retrieval

What must occur to enable us to remember a friend's name, a fact from history, or an incident from our past? The act of remembering requires the successful completion of three processes: encoding, storage, and retrieval. The first process, **encoding,** involves transforming information into a form that can be stored in memory. Sometimes we encode information automatically, without any effort, but often we must do something with the information in order to remember it. For example, if you met someone named George at a party, you might associate his name with George Washington or George Bush. Such simple associations can markedly improve your ability to recall names and other information. The careful encoding of information greatly increases the chance that you will remember it.

The second memory process, **storage,** involves keeping or maintaining information in memory. For encoded information to be stored, some physiological change in the brain must take place—a process called **consolidation.** Normally consolidation occurs automatically, but if a person loses consciousness for any reason, the process can be disrupted and a permanent memory may not form. That is why a person who has been in a serious car accident could awaken in a hospital and not remember what has happened.

The final process, **retrieval,** occurs when information stored in memory is brought to mind. Calling George by name the next time you meet him shows that you have retrieved his name from memory. To remember, we must perform all three processes—encode the information, store it, and then retrieve it. Memory failure can result from the failure of any one of the three.

■ ■ ■ ■ ■

Monitor (Check) Comprehension

As you read, you also need to be thinking about how well you are reading. Are you comprehending? And if not, what are you going to do about it? As an active reader, you need to be both player and coach. You are participating in the reading activity, but at the same time you are **monitoring** how well the activity is going. When you monitor your reading, you can step in and redirect your attention when problems develop.

What are some clues that warn us of trouble with reading? First, here are some behavior clues to watch for:

You find yourself gazing out the window.

You keep going back to reread passages.

You take a second break in only ten minutes.

You realize that you are frowning as you read.

Can you think of other behavior clues? What do these actions tell you? First, that you have lost concentration. Second, that you are struggling with comprehension.

Now think about the conversations we have with ourselves that signal problems. What do the following verbal clues tell you?

"I've just read three pages, but I don't know what I've read."

"None of this makes any sense."

"I'll never understand this stuff!"

Can you think of other verbal clues?

If you are monitoring your reading, you can tell when all is not going well. The first step is recognizing that just continuing to turn pages will not work. The next step is to find a way to remove the difficulty so that you can once again make progress. Here are some suggestions for fixing comprehension problems. Find the solutions that work for you.

Guidelines for Fixing Comprehension

1. **Monitor your concentration.** Your comprehension problem may be the result of a loss of concentration. Review the guidelines for concentration and respond appropriately. (For example, move from a noisy room to a quiet place to complete the reading.)

2. **Redo the *Prepare* steps.** Perhaps you forgot to **Prepare,** only to become confused. If so, go back and identify the work and subject, preread, identify what you know, and raise questions about the material.

3. **Connect the material to previous reading.** If your comprehension problems occur in the middle of a section or chapter, go back and review the material in the previous section or chapter. You may need to review a good bit to activate your knowledge before moving forward.

4. **Fill in the gaps.** A specific passage may be a problem because there are key words you do not know. If you cannot figure out the meaning from context, you will need to obtain the definitions before continuing to read. Perhaps the definitions can be found in a previous section of the text. Next, try the text's glossary, if there is one. Finally, use your dictionary.

5. **Reread the material.** Accept that some material is difficult and may require a second reading for full comprehension. Be sure that you are annotating as you read.

6. **Go to additional sources for help.** If these solutions don't work, you may need to find help. Try the library for other, simpler books on the subject, or ask your instructor to recommend other books or study guides. Find a classmate to study with or obtain a college-sponsored tutor.

| EXERCISE 1-7 | Monitoring Reading Comprehension |

Read the following selection, monitoring your comprehension. Then list strategies you would use to fix any comprehension problems you had or that you think other readers might have. Discuss your list of strategies with classmates.

The sequences of amino acids that make up a protein molecule are specified by heredity. For each protein there is only one proper amino acid sequence. If a wrong amino acid is inserted, the result may be disastrous to health.

Sickle-cell disease, in which hemoglobin, the oxygen-carrying protein of the red blood cells, is abnormal, is an example of an inherited mistake in the amino acid sequence. Normal hemoglobin contains two kinds of chains. One of the chains in sickle-cell hemoglobin is an exact copy of that in normal hemoglobin. But in the other chain, the sixth amino acid, which should be glutamine, is replaced by valine. The protein is so altered that it is unable to carry and to release oxygen. The red blood cells collapse into crescent shapes instead of remaining disk shaped, as they normally do. If too many abnormal, crescent-shaped cells appear in the blood, the result is illness and death.

Sizer and Whitney, *Nutrition: Concepts, and, Controversies*

_____

_____

_____

_____

_____

_____

_____

■ RESPOND

Responding to your reading is just as important as preparing to read. You need both to review and reflect.

Review

You need to review *immediately* and then several more times thereafter.

The best time for your first review is immediately after you finish reading. How does reviewing aid learning? Consider: If you want to remember the names of people introduced to you, repeat their names when you greet them. This repetition is called *rehearsing*. After this initial repetition, say the names to yourself several times, and then use them again in conversation. Chances are good that you will remember the names.

Note that you reviewed the names immediately and then periodically thereafter. Even with an immediate review, some information will not be remembered unless you continue to go over it. You need to review several times rather than just prior to a test. When studying for your courses, review Chapter 1 before reading Chapter 2, review Chapter 2 before reading Chapter 3, and so on. Each time you relearn the material, you will remember more of it.

Your immediate review may include several strategies. First, redo the prereading step. Second, look over your annotations. Third, answer the questions you raised as a part of your **Prepare** step. Also, if you are reading a textbook, answer any discussion or review questions in the text. Finally, include reflection with reviewing.

Reflect

If you can connect what you are reading to something else in your life, the material will be easier to remember. Reflect on how new information and ideas connect to what you already know and to what is important in your life.

Take, for example, information about memory. We do not have to be psychologists to be interested in how our memories function. Just wanting to understand how your own brain works is a good reason to reflect on the passages in this chapter.

If you develop the habit of reflecting as a strategy for improving reading skills, you may become a more reflective person generally. This new dimension to your life will bring you pleasure.

What kinds of questions can you ask to aid reflection? Here are some general questions that can be applied to many different readings.

Questions to Aid Reflection

- How does the selection relate to the course? Why has the instructor assigned (or recommended) it?
- How does this work relate to other courses I'm taking? Am I studying a similar time period? Similar ideas? Subjects that are closely related?
- How can I use this information in my career? Will it make me better trained? Or better informed? Or more understanding of people with whom I will be working?
- How does this material help me better understand myself? My family relationships? People who are different from me? The natural world of which I am a part? How do I feel about this new knowledge?

| EXERCISE 1-8 | **Reflecting on What You Read** |

Reread the two selections on memory (pp. 18–19) and then reflect on their connections with your courses, your career plans, and your learning about life. Write some of your reflections in the space below.

_____

_____

_____

_____

_____

_____

_____

Now, practice your **Prepare–Read–Respond** strategy on the following selections.

■ ■ ■ ■ ■

SHE GIVES THEM A HAVEN

Elizabeth Shepard

Elizabeth Shepard is a freelance writer and editor, and the editor-in-chief of *Epicurious*. Her novel, *H*, was published in 1995. She wrote the following article for *Parade* magazine's February 24, 2002, issue.

Prepare

1. Identify the author and the work. What do you expect the author's purpose to be?

_____

_____

2. Preread to identify the subject and make predictions. What do you expect to read about?

_____

_____

3. What do you already know about the subject?

_____

_____

_____

4. Raise two questions that you expect the article to answer.

_____

_____

_____

_____

Vocabulary Alert: Do You Know These Words?

Here are four words you need to know to read the following article with understanding.

haven place of refuge or rest

sanctuary place of refuge, protection

habitat area in which an animal normally lives

preserve area maintained for wildlife protection

■ ■ ■ ■ ■

1   On 800 acres of secluded pastures and forests in Hohenwald, Tenn., six female Asian elephants—retired from zoos and circuses—are as free as they can be. Unchained, unrestricted and not required to perform tricks for the first time in decades, "the girls" roam the grounds, play with each other in the pond and graze in the grass.

2   Welcome to The Elephant Sanctuary, the country's only protected natural habitat for Asian elephants. The preserve is the brainchild of Carol Buckley, 47, a for-

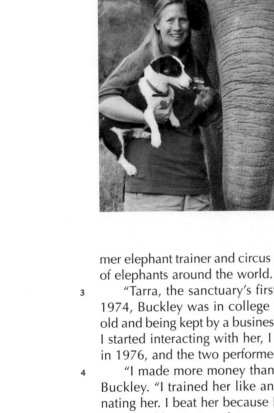

■ Carol Buckley,
her dog, and
Tarra

mer elephant trainer and circus performer who is on a crusade to improve the fates of elephants around the world.

3   "Tarra, the sanctuary's first resident, was my inspiration," Buckley says. In 1974, Buckley was in college in California when she met Tarra, then 6 months old and being kept by a businessman as an attraction in the back of a truck. "Once I started interacting with her, I was hooked," says Buckley. She purchased Tarra in 1976, and the two performed throughout the world.

4   "I made more money than I could spend from performing with Tarra," says Buckley. "I trained her like any traditional elephant-handler would—by dominating her. I beat her because I was taught that hitting an elephant was the only way she'd listen. It took me years to figure out that what I was doing was wrong, that what all elephant-handlers are doing is wrong. We're killing the elephants' spirit to make them obedient for our benefit.

5   "I finally decided that I couldn't do that to Tarra anymore. When I realized she was becoming a broken creature, I decided to dedicate my life to changing hers." In 1995, after 20 years as a circus performer, Buckley founded The Elephant Sanctuary with Scott Blais, 29, a former elephant-keeper. Their goal: to rescue elephants who have been beaten into submission. "Here, we use passive control

to manage our girls," says Buckley. "Positive reinforcement, like food and praise, encourages them to respond."

6   The idea of the sanctuary took root when Buckley saw an ad for land in Tennessee. She bought the former cow pasture and built a heated barn on the property for $500,000. Today, donations from private individuals and corporations provide funding. With an additional $5 million, Buckley says, she could care for almost 100 elephants. Although the sanctuary works to relocate sick or retired male elephants, it only accepts females, who remain in herds as adults and adapt better to confinement than males do.

7   Buckley says she knows the sanctuary is not perfect: "The elephants are still captive here, but we can't release them back in the wild, because there is no wild to release them to. Their natural habitat has been destroyed. There isn't even enough room for the elephants that still live in the wild. So this is the best we can do for these girls for now."

8   Some of the elephants arrived at the sanctuary because they were too old or expensive to care for. Others came as a result of public outrage over their mistreatment. Whatever their circumstances, the reception is the same: "Every time we bring in a new resident," Buckley says, "the other elephants gather around and fondle her with their trunks. They touch her scars and pause there, caressing the wounds. It's extraordinary."

550 words

Comprehension Check

Answer the following with a, b, c, or d to indicate the phrase that best completes each statement.

_____   1. The essay's topic is

a. circus elephants.

b. where elephants live.

c. a home for abused elephants.

d. abusing elephants.

_____   2. The elephant sanctuary is located in

a. Tennessee.

b. Asia.

c. Africa.

d. the circus.

_____   3. The owner of the Elephant Sanctuary is

a. Tarra.

b. a former circus performer.

c. Elizabeth Shephard.

d. the state of Tennessee.

_____ 4. The Elephant Sanctuary is

    a. the United States' only preserve for Asian elephants.

    b. one of several preserves in this country.

    c. the only preserve for African elephants.

    d. a preserve for all kinds of elephants.

_____ 5. Carol Buckley used to train elephants by

    a. dominating them.

    b. encouraging them.

    c. using Zen.

    d. showing them on the road.

_____ 6. Buckley decided to start the Elephant Sanctuary when

    a. she was too old to be in the circus.

    b. Tarra was too old to perform in the circus.

    c. she decided to help Tarra recover from abuse.

    d. she had earned enough money to retire from the circus.

_____ 7. When we read that Tarra, at six months, was kept in a truck, the author wants us to conclude that

    a. Tarra was eager to join the circus.

    b. Tarra was being abused.

    c. Tarra was ready to be trained.

    d. elephants are big business.

_____ 8. The elephant sanctuary accepts

    a. only female elephants.

    b. both male and female elephants.

    c. only baby elephants.

    d. only circus elephants.

_____ 9. Buckley needs $5 million to

    a. create more sanctuaries.

    b. care for 100 elephants.

    c. travel again with Tarra.

    d. take male elephants.

_____ 10. The main idea of the essay is that we need to

    a. care for rather than abuse elephants for our benefit.

    b. return circus and zoo animals to the wild.

    c. start a sanctuary for male elephants.

    d. let elephants retire at 20 years.

Expanding Vocabulary

Answer the following with a, b, c, or d to indicate the best definition of the word in **bold** *as it was used in the selection. The number in parentheses is the number of the paragraph in which the word appears.*

_____ 1. "acres of **secluded** pastures" (1)

      a. seasonal

      b. set apart

      c. secret

      d. sectional

_____ 2. "**roam** the grounds" (1)

      a. rob

      b. rival

      c. wander

      d. withstand

_____ 3. "on a **crusade** to improve" (2)

      a. committed action for a cause

      b. challenge

      c. cure-all

      d. connection

_____ 4. "make them **obedient** for our benefit" (4)

      a. capable

      b. obstinate

      c. odious

      d. complying with authority

_____ 5. "decided to **dedicate** my life" (5)

      a. commit to a course of action

      b. cooperate with others

      c. defend

      d. destroy

_____ 6. "beaten into **submission**" (5)

      a. subversiveness

      b. substitution

    c. surrendering one's will

    d. surrendering one's stronghold

_____ 7. "use **passive** control" (5)

    a. natural

    b. nonaggressive

    c. nonchalant

    d. partial

_____ 8. "works to **relocate**" (6)

    a. place somewhere else

    b. rearrange

    c. reestablish

    d. plan new activities

_____ 9. "**fondle** her with their trunks" (8)

    a. fool

    b. fizzle

    c. stroke lovingly

    d. stop forcefully

_____ 10. "**caressing** the wounds" (8)

    a. touching carefully

    b. touching fondly

    c. caring for

    d. covering

Reflection and Discussion

1. What is your reaction to Carol Buckley and her Sanctuary? Do you admire her? Think she is wasting her time and money? Something else? Explain.

2. If you had money, what animals would you most want to help? (Consider those that are endangered and those that are abused to make your choice.) Why did you choose as you did? How would you seek to help your chosen animal?

3. Do you think that animals are abused in circuses? Why or why not? If you think they are abused, what changes would you like to see?

Your Reading Assessment

Make it a habit! Use these five questions to judge your reading each time you finish an end-of-chapter selection. Compare assessments to check your progress throughout the course.

1. How many of the comprehension questions did you answer correctly?

   _____

2. How many vocabulary words could you identify?   _____

3. How well did you predict what you would read about?

   _____

4. Did the article answer your questions? If not, why do you think that it

   did not? _____

   _____

5. What parts of your reading need the most work?

   Predicting what the reading will be about?   _____

   Comprehension? _____

   Vocabulary? _____

   Reflection? _____

■ ■ ■ ■ ■

DR. FRANKLIN'S TIPS FOR STAYING WELL

Thomas V. DiBacco

Thomas DiBacco is a historian at American University. He wrote the following article for the *Washington Post*'s Health Section. The article was published January 30, 1996.

Prepare

1. Identify the author and the work. What do you expect the author's purpose to be?

   _____

   _____

2. Preread to identify the subject and make predictions. What do you expect to read about?

_____

_____

3. What do you already know about the subject?

_____

_____

_____

4. Raise two questions that you expect the article to answer.

_____

_____

_____

_____

■ ■ ■ ■ ■

1   The more things change, the more they stay the same. One of colonial America's most senior citizens, Benjamin Franklin (1706–1790), whose birthday is celebrated in January, had medical views regarding a long life that in many cases agree with contemporary professional advice.

2   Of course, Franklin was not a medicine man. But the self-educated American became a scientist noted for practical accomplishments (such as devising bifocals and a catheter and employing electrical treatments for paralysis). He was awarded a doctor of laws degree from Scotland's University of St. Andrews at age 53. Therefore it was not unusual that "Dr. Franklin," as he was henceforth addressed, would continually dabble in medical science, often by coping with his own blues and blahs.

3   Franklin was better known to his contemporaries for fighting colds than for his role in the American Revolution. He advised staying away from people with the malady: "People often catch cold from one another when shut up together in close rooms, coaches, etc., and when sitting near and conversing so as to breathe in each other's transpiration; the disorder being in a certain state."

4   Franklin also believed that colds and "too full living, too little exercise" went hand in hand. To be sure, he wasn't a diet or fitness freak (as the contour of his paunch would attest). But he was still using dumbbell weights at age 66, taking 40 hoists at a time. He walked a lot and recognized that a "greater quantity of some things may be eaten than of others, some being of lighter digestion than others."

5   Franklin took issue with a widespread belief at the time that cold weather and high humidity increased the likelihood of catching colds. "Traveling in our severe winters," he wrote fellow American Benjamin Rush, a physician, on July 14, 1773, "I have suffered cold sometimes to an extremity only short of freezing, but this did not make me catch cold. And, for moisture, I have been in the river every evening two or three hours for a fortnight together, when one would suppose I might imbibe enough of it to take cold if humidity could give it; but no such effect ever followed.

6   "Boys never get cold by swimming. Nor are people at sea, or who live at Bermudas, or St. Helena, small islands, where the air must be ever moist from the dashing and breaking waves against their rocks on all sides, more subject to colds than those who inhabit part of a continent where the air is driest."

Did Franklin agree or disagree with the idea that cold and humidity increase the chance of catching a cold?

7   Franklin delighted in a form of indoor streaking: "I rise almost every morning and sit in my chamber without any clothes on whatever, half an hour or hour, according to the season, either reading or writing. This practice is not in the least painful, but, on the contrary, agreeable...."

What is streaking?

8   He would have agreed wholeheartedly with recent medical studies that advocate moderation in drink. He was one of the first Americans to make a study of the effects of excessive drinking on people. Quiet individuals, he noted, often became extroverts, the religious sometimes used profanity, and people of modest learning were not infrequently experts on "all arts and sciences."

9   On choosing eyeglasses: "I send you," he wrote to Mrs. Jane Mecom on July 17, 1771, "a pair of every size [lens] from 1 to 13. To suit yourself, take out a pair at a time, and hold one of the glasses first against one eye, and then against the other, looking on some small print.... I advise your trying each of your eyes separately, because few people's eyes are fellows, and almost everybody in reading or working uses one eye principally, the other being dimmer or perhaps fitter for distant objects...."

10   Short cures (from Franklin's "Poor Richard's Almanack"):

- "Don't go to the doctor with every distemper, nor to the lawyer with every quarrel, nor to the pot with every thirst."
- "He's a fool that makes his doctor his heir."
- "Pain wastes the body; pleasures, the understanding."
- "Discontented minds, and fevers of the body, are not to be cured by changing beds or business."
- "He that would travel much, should eat little."
- "He's the best physician that knows the worthlessness of the most medicines."

▪ **Benjamin Franklin**

11   Franklin slept soundly in his four score plus four years.

How many years did Franklin live?

12   He knew good sleep and heavy suppers don't mix ("Nothing is more common in the newspapers than instances of people who, after eating a hearty supper, are found dead abed in the morning"). And that fresh air in the bedroom is a must.

13   He even had a remedy for the person who wakes in the middle of the night. Get out of bed, first of all, and turn the pillow. Then take off your nightgown and shake it about 20 times. Draw back the covers to cool the bed. Walk around the bedroom naked for several minutes. "When you begin to feel the cold air unpleasant, [put on your bedclothes], then return to your bed, and you will soon fall asleep, and your sleep will be sweet and pleasant. All the scenes presented to your fancy will be, too, of the pleasing kind. I am often as agreeably entertained with them as by the scenery of an opera."

14   Of course, good sleeping, according to Franklin, is ensured by one other ingredient. He called it "a good conscience."

888 words

Comprehension Check

Answer the following with a, b, c, or d to indicate the phrase that best completes each statement.

_____ 1. Ben Franklin was called Dr. Franklin because he
    a. was a medical doctor.
    b. liked the title.
    c. was given an honorary doctor of laws degree.
    d. was a good swimmer.

_____ 2. Ben Franklin was the inventor of
    a. bifocal glasses.
    b. medicine.
    c. the Polaroid camera.
    d. the radio.

_____ 3. Franklin believed that people can catch colds from
    a. swimming.
    b. overeating of rich foods and getting little exercise.
    c. open windows.
    d. wearing glasses.

_____ 4. As an older man, Franklin continued to work at his fitness by
    a. lifting weights and walking.
    b. eating and drinking.
    c. developing a paunch.
    d. visiting doctors regularly.

_____ 5. Franklin argued that people do not get colds from
    a. swimming.
    b. cold weather.
    c. both a and b.
    d. neither a nor b.

_____ 6. Franklin understood that people often
    a. benefit from eating late at night.
    b. benefit from excessive drinking.
    c. have one eye that sees better than the other.
    d. act much the same whether sober or consuming alcohol.

_____ 7. Franklin believed that the best way to get back to sleep at night is

  a. read for an hour.

  b. walk around the room undressed until you are chilly.

  c. put more covers on the bed.

  d. eat some rich foods.

_____ 8. The best way to be sure to have a good night's sleep, according to Franklin, is to have

  a. a big dinner.

  b. a few drinks before bedtime.

  c. a good conscience.

  d. bifocals.

_____ 9. The author thinks that Franklin

  a. had some crazy ideas.

  b. understood a great deal about health.

  c. was not important to the American Revolution.

  d. should not have been in favor of streaking.

_____ 10. The best statement of the main idea of this selection is

  a. Franklin was an important inventor.

  b. Franklin did not understand medicine.

  c. Franklin's views on health are similar to what doctors would advise today.

  d. since Franklin was not a medical doctor, he should not have been called Dr. Franklin.

Expanding Vocabulary

Answer the following with a, b, c, or d to indicate the best definition of the word in **bold** _as it was used in the selection. The number in parentheses is the number of the paragraph in which the word appears._

_____ 1. "he was **henceforth** addressed" (2)

  a. forever

  b. from now on

  c. helpfully

  d. heartedly

_____   2. "**dabble** in medical science" (2)
   a. dangle
   b. analyze in detail
   c. undertake without great depth
   d. deliberate

_____   3. "away from people with the **malady**" (3)
   a. illness
   b. malice
   c. accent
   d. meanness

_____   4. "**contour** of his paunch" (4)
   a. contrast
   b. control
   c. outline of a body
   d. observance

_____   5. "contour of his **paunch**" (4)
   a. pavement
   b. brain
   c. patio
   d. belly

_____   6. "his paunch would **attest**" (4)
   a. attract
   b. give evidence of
   c. auction
   d. equal

_____   7. "I might **imbibe** enough" (5)
   a. drink
   b. initiate
   c. imitate
   d. dupe

_____   8. "medical studies that **advocate** moderation" (8)
   a. accommodate
   b. announce
   c. alienate
   d. argue in favor of

_____ 9. "the religious sometimes used **profanity**" (8)

    a. promises

    b. proof

    c. bad language

    d. profuseness

_____ 10. " 'a good **conscience' " (14)

    a. awareness of right conduct

    b. conscious

    c. consensus

    d. constitution

For Reflection and Discussion

Reflect on these questions and have answers ready for class discussion.

1. What is the most interesting information or idea you learned from this article? Why do you find it interesting?

2. Do you think Franklin would have been a fascinating person to know? Why or why not?

MAKING CONNECTIONS

1. What do Carol Buckley of the Elephant Sanctuary and Ben Franklin have in common? On your own or with your class partner, make a list of several points in common.

2. Why might articles on these two people have been included in this chapter? What connection may they have with the chapter's introductory material?

3. If Ben Franklin were to return and meet Carol Buckley at her Sanctuary, what do you think he might say to her, or what questions might she ask him? Be either Buckley or Franklin and imagine what "you" would say to the other person.

"E" CONNECTIONS

At the end of the readings in each chapter, you will find this section—a suggested electronic search activity connected to the chapter readings. But first, what about searching the Web? Most students can e-mail or chat online. Not all, though, know how to find and use electronic sources for research. Here are brief points of advice for electronic searching.

A BRIEF GUIDE TO ELECTRONIC SEARCHING

- *If your college offers access to library holdings online, get your PC hookup immediately.* You can then access the book catalog and many online databases from your own computer.
- *Become familiar with your library's online offerings.* They will have many databases providing articles that can be searched using author, title, or keyword(s) (e.g., *space* or *dinosaurs*) plus reference materials such as encyclopedias and *Book Review Digest*. They may also list the best search engines and have a "Best of the Internet" link as well. Rely on your library's online sources and guidance.
- *When you turn to the Internet, remember:*
    1. No search engine searches the entire Web. If you cannot find what you need with one engine, try another.
    2. Anybody can have a Web page. Many are not worth your visit.
    3. Pay attention to the domain in the site's URL (Uniform Resource Locator) or "address." One part of a URL will indicate the *type* of site—a commercial site (.com), a governmental site (.gov), an organization (.org), or an educational site (.edu). Look for "gov" and "edu" sites, or respected organization Websites, such as the American Psychological Association or the Sierra Club.
- *Bookmark useful sites*—or carefully copy the URL—or print out a page with the URL at the top. You may need to return to a site, and your instructor may require this information as part of your citing of sources used.
- *Scan sites but print out material that looks helpful to your search.* It is easier to study several pages of print than to read several screens.
- *Scan each site's homepage to see how the site is organized, what is included, and what useful links are available.* Many Websites invite our eyes to jump from item to item. These lively sites may be visually more interesting than a typical page of print, but at times the end result is visual confusion, especially when you add the advertisements. Remember that most homepages contain a list of options down the left side of the screen. Study that list to find what you need.
- *Compare information and evaluate sources.* Commercial sites are in business; most organizations have a goal or purpose beyond providing information. Individuals without credentials can prepare sites that look professional, but are filled with incorrect or misleading facts. So, always judge the quality of each source you use. Never take information or ideas from a site that does not clearly indicate who maintains it.
- *Plan your search to avoid wasting time.*
    1. Think about what you already know about your topic and therefore what you can guess about possibly useful Websites.
    2. Narrow your search to reduce the number of "hits." If you want to learn about dinosaur extinction, for example, type in "dinosaurs and extinction," not just "dinosaurs."

THIS CHAPTER'S EXERCISE:

Learn more about the Elephant Sanctuary by visiting its Website at <www.elephants.com>. Then seek to answer this question: Is anyone helping elephants in their natural habitats in Africa or India? See if you can answer that question by conducting your own search, or begin by visiting one of these sites:

<http://www.wildlifeadvocacy.org>

<http://www.worldwildlife.org>

<http://eces.org>

CHAPTER REVIEW

Complete each of the following statements.

1. Three steps to take to improve concentration *before* reading include:

   a. _____

   b. _____

   c. _____

2. Three steps to take to improve concentration *while* reading include:

   a. _____

   b. _____

   c. _____

3. Reading is a _____ activity.

4. The three steps in your reading strategy are:

   a. _____

   b. _____

   c. _____

Take a Reading Road Trip!

For additional practice with your reading skills, use the Reading Road Trip CD-ROM or visit Reading Road Trip on the Web at **<http://www.ablongman.com/readingroadtrip>** (password required).

CHAPTER 2

Using Context Clues and Building Vocabulary

LEARNING OBJECTIVES

■ To know why building vocabulary is important

■ To understand the meaning of unfamiliar words by using context clues

■ To find strategies for building your vocabulary

■ Know some good magazines and books to read

PREPARE TO READ

Read and reflect on the chapter's title and objectives. Glance through the chapter, observing headings to see what is covered. Now answer these questions:

1. What do you expect to learn from this chapter?

   _____

   _____

2. What do you already know about the chapter's topic?

   _____

   _____

3. What two or three questions do you want answered from reading this chapter?

   _____

   _____

_____

_____

What would happen if you tried to play a piano that was missing some of its keys? You would make more noise than beautiful music. You would probably become frustrated and annoyed. Trying to read without a good vocabulary is much the same. You may use active reading strategies and still become frustrated because too many words are "missing."

Studies show a strong connection between career success and a good vocabulary. Let's face it: Everyone needs a strong vocabulary. The best way to build a strong vocabulary is through reading—or, more precisely, through the study of new words you come across in your reading.

■ CONTEXT CLUES

Suppose you were to read the following sentence:

> Although they clapped after each speech, the audience gave the most applause to the president's _oration_.

Perhaps _oration_ is a word somewhat unfamiliar to you. If you think about how it is used in the sentence, you might guess that it is another word for _speech_. How? The sentence tells you that the audience listened to more than one speech and liked the president's _speech (oration)_ the best. You have guessed the word's meaning from its _context_, from the words in the sentence (or sentences) surrounding the unfamiliar word.

Often, you can guess at the meaning of an unfamiliar word by studying context clues. Using context clues means that you can continue to read. You don't have to stop to use the dictionary each time you come to a new word. The key is to look for clues, to think about how the word is used.

EXERCISE 2-1	Workshop on Understanding Words in Context

With your class partner or in small groups, study the context for each word in **bold** type. Then circle the word that comes closest to the meaning of the **bold** type word. Also, briefly explain your reasoning from the context. The first one has been completed for you.

1. When the judge told the prosecutor to continue her **inquiry**, the prosecutor asked more questions of the witness.

   a. lecture

   b. questioning

   c. speech

   d. argument

Your reasoning: _What does the prosecutor do when told to continue her inquiry? She questions the witness. So an inquiry must have something to do with questioning._

2. Some elderly people live in such **abject** poverty that they go without meals.
   a. little
   b. jaded
   c. miserable
   d. charming

   Your reasoning: _____

   _____

   _____

3. The librarian directed the student to the **periodicals** section to find *Time* and the *Wall Street Journal*.
   a. newspapers/magazines
   b. books
   c. periods of history
   d. microfilm

   Your reasoning: _____

   _____

   _____

4. Although George was a great basketball player, he felt **inept** at parties.
   a. injured
   b. unskilled, awkward
   c. quiet
   d. noisy

   Your reasoning: _____

   _____

   _____

5. The professor **clarified** the idea by giving several examples.
    a. made essential
    b. challenged
    c. undercut
    d. made clear

    Your reasoning: _____

    _____

    _____

6. Sandra tried to **facilitate** the election process by handing out the ballots.
    a. assist
    b. control
    c. alter
    d. falsify

    Your reasoning: _____

    _____

    _____

7. Feeling trapped when in crowds, Maria stayed on the **periphery** of the group.
    a. angle
    b. inside
    c. outside
    d. personality

    Your reasoning: _____

    _____

    _____

■ ■ ■ ■ ■

How well did your group do? Were you able to reason from the context to select the correct word? Most readers can understand more words in context than they can actually define. Writers also help us, using several strategies to clarify words in context. Let's examine them, one at a time.

Definition

Textbooks and other readings are filled with new terms. In psychology you will learn about *cognition* and *paranoia*. In biology you will learn about the *ecosystem* and *organisms*. Fortunately for students, writers usually give definitions of key terms. In the following textbook passage, two terms are defined.

> Energy passes from one organism to another along a particular food chain. A *food chain* is a sequence of organisms related to one another as prey and predator. The first is eaten by the second, the second by the third, and so on, in a series of *trophic levels*, or feeding levels.
>
> Helena Curtis, *Biology*

Direct Definition: The first type of definition, for *food chain*, is clearly announced as a definition. The term is used in the first sentence of the passage. The second sentence states the meaning of the term, and the third sentence further explains the definition.

There are several signal words and visual signals that announce a direct definition. Usually the defined term is printed in *italics* or in **bold** type. Sometimes the definition is repeated in the margin of the page. Direct definitions are often introduced by expressions such as "is" or "means," "refers to," or "consists of."

Indirect Definition: The second term defined in the passage above is *trophic levels*. This term is defined informally, in the phrase "or feeding levels." Even though the purpose of the sentence is to further define *food chain*, the sentence also explains the new term, *trophic levels*. Be alert to these helpful indirect definitions. Sometimes indirect definitions follow a comma after the term, as in the example above. Sometimes they are placed in parentheses (like this), or they follow a dash—like this.

EXERCISE 2-2	Identifying Passages That Define

*In each of the following sentences, underline the words that provide a definition of the word in **bold** type. Circle all signals. Then state whether the definition is direct or indirect. The first one has been completed for you.*

1. (**Advertising**) is paid nonpersonal communication from an identified sponsor using mass media to persuade or influence an audience.

Wells, Barnett, and Moriarty, *Advertising*

direct definition

2. One of the properties of ecosystems is **productivity**, the total amount of energy converted to organic compounds in a given length of time.

Helena Curtis, *Biology*

———————————————————————————————

3. **Fossils**, the remains or traces of prehistoric life, were also essential to the development of the geologic time scale.

Tarbuck and Lutgens, *The Earth*

———————————————————————————————

4. A **corporate culture** consists of the shared values, norms, and practices communicated to and followed by those working for a firm.

Evans and Berman, *Marketing*

———————————————————————————————

5. [Some] psychologists see learning as a **generative** process—that is, the learner **generates** (constructs) meaning by building relationships between familiar and unfamiliar events.

Lefton and Valvatne, *Mastering Psychology*

———————————————————————————————

6. **Insomnia**, a prolonged inability to sleep, is a common sleep disorder often caused by anxiety or depression.

Lefton and Valvatne, *Mastering Psychology*

———————————————————————————————

7. A **metaphor** is a comparison of two unalike things.

———————————————————————————————

8. Sontag saw a valuable service being performed by artists who both understood high culture and could "translate" it for unsophisticated audiences, a process known as **popularization**.

John Vivian, *The Media of Mass Communication*, 6th ed.

———————————————————————————————

9. Some have said that the Iroquois are an example of a **matriarchy**, or a society in which women are dominant in terms of economics, politics, and ideology.

Barbara Miller, *Cultural Anthropology*, 2nd ed.

_____

10. A **calorie** is a measure of the amount of energy or heat required to raise the temperature of one gram of water one degree Celsius.

Bishop and Aldana, *Step Up to Wellness*

_____

▪ ▪ ▪ ▪ ▪

Examples

When not providing direct or indirect definitions, writers often clarify words by giving examples. For instance, you may not know the word *malapropism* before reading this sentence:

> A common **malapropism** in student writing is the use of "conscious" when the writer needs "conscience."

From the example, you may be able to conclude that a malapropism is an incorrect word accidently used instead of the correct word. Here is another example of this type of context clue. After reading the sentence, write a brief definition or synonym for the word in italics.

> A writer's **diction** may range from the formality of Lincoln's "Gettysburg Address" to the slang of rap artists.

_____

From the two examples in the sentence you may be able to conclude that the term *diction* is a synonym for *word choice*. The type of language a writer usually uses is that writer's diction. Examples are sometimes introduced by words such as "for example," "such as," and "including." Not all examples are introduced by signal words, though; they are just part of what the sentence is about.

EXERCISE 2-3	Using Examples as Context Clues

*Write a definition or synonym for each word in **bold** type in the following sentences. Then list the example clues. The first has been started for you.*

1. Working in the library and waiting tables at nearby restaurants are two ways to **augment** college scholarships.

a. **augment** means: <u>add to, increase</u>

b. clues: _____

_____

2. The Department of Motor Vehicles keeps several **databases**, including a driver's license file and a file on vehicle registration.

a. **databases** means: _____

b. clues: _____

_____

3. **Autocratic** rulers from Napoleon to Hitler have changed the course of history.

a. **autocratic** means: _____

b. clues: _____

_____

4. By painting the outside and building a deck in the back, the owners **enhanced** their new home.

a. **enhanced** means: _____

b. clues: _____

_____

5. The cotton gin and the steam engine were two inventions that **spurred** the Industrial Revolution.

a. **spurred** means: _____

b. clues: _____

_____

6. Several **phobias**, including fear of heights, fear of flying, and fear of crowds, limited Michael's social life.

a. **phobias** means: _____

b. clues: _____

_____

7. Jane was quite **frugal**; she used coupons at the grocery store and bought all her clothes on sale.

   a. **frugal** means: _____

   b. clues: _____

   _____

8. **Inanimate** objects include rocks and minerals.

   a. **inanimate** means: _____

   b. clues: _____

   _____

9. Laser surgery and computer-assisted surgery are important **innovations** in medicine.

   a. **innovations** means: _____

   b. clues: _____

   _____

10. The oceans **sustain** many forms of life, from algae to whales.

   a. **sustain** means: _____

   b. clues: _____

   _____

■ ■ ■ ■ ■

Comparison and Contrast

Writers often use comparison or contrast to organize a passage or an entire essay. They can also use these patterns to organize a sentence. You can use your recognition of these patterns to help understand the meaning of a new word. Suppose you read the following sentence:

All winter the trees in my neighborhood were without leaves, but now that spring is here they are covered with new **foliage**.

If you do not know the word *foliage*, you may be able to guess from the contrast structure of the sentence that *foliage* means the opposite of "without leaves."

The contrast of winter and spring also helps readers conclude that *foliage* refers to the leaves that have come out in the springtime. Here is another example:

> It is incorrect to speak as if all secretaries or nurses are women; it is also **erroneous** to speak as if all lawyers or pilots are men.

Although the first part of the sentence is about women and the second part about men, the two parts of the sentence have the same structure. The writer says that each type of reference to jobs is incorrect—or **erroneous**. The word "also" tells us that both kinds of speech are incorrect, so readers can conclude that the word **erroneous** also means incorrect.

Comparisons are sometimes introduced by "just as," "the same as," "alike," "equate," "also," and "similarly." Contrasts may be signaled by words such as "unlike," "differ," "disagree," "although," "but," "while," "yet," and "on the other hand."

EXERCISE 2-4	Using Comparison and Contrast Clues

*Write a definition or synonym for each word in **bold** type in the following sentences. Then list any signal words that help to reveal the comparison or contrast structure. The first has been started for you.*

1. Abigail wore a neat, professional-looking suit to her interview, while Susan's clothes were **tawdry**; Abigail was given the job.

   a. **tawdry** means: not neat; flashy or cheap _____

   b. clues: _____

   _____

2. Although Haruko never doubted or questioned her professors' lectures, Sawa was often **skeptical**.

   a. **skeptical** means: _____

   b. clues: _____

   _____

3. The history teacher encouraged his students to **emulate** the leaders of the past rather than try to be like Michael Jordan.

   a. **emulate** means: _____

   b. clues: _____

   _____

4. A good doctor will tell you honestly and directly what you need to do to get well. Wouldn't it be nice if politicians always spoke just as **candidly**?

a. **candidly** means: _____

b. clues: _____

_____

5. Although Bob was quick to give up on difficult tasks, Boris remained **tenacious**, no matter how hard the assignment.

a. **tenacious** means: _____

b. clues: _____

_____

6. Although it is not smart to ignore problems or pretend they don't matter, it is just as unwise to **brood** endlessly over every little problem.

a. **brood** means: _____

b. clues: _____

_____

7. The twins were so different at feeding time. Jill ate everything and liked to try new foods, but Jake was a **finicky** eater.

a. **finicky** means: _____

b. clues: _____

_____

8. The young candidate's speeches were loud and challenging, whereas the mature candidate's style was softer and more **subtle**.

a. **subtle** means: _____

b. clues: _____

_____

9. To make decisions, some business managers study sales figures and other available facts, while others rely more on their **intuition**.

a. **intuition** means: _____

b. clues: _____

_____

10. Most of the first graders clapped and cheered the silly clown, but a few remained **passive**.

a. **passive** means: _____

b. clues: _____

_____

■ ■ ■ ■ ■

Experience/Logic

Not all sentences contain specific clues such as examples or contrast. Still, you can often guess at a word's meaning by using your experience or by reasoning from the information in the sentence. For example, suppose you read the following sentence:

He wished that he could write speeches that were as **eloquent** as Martin Luther King, Jr.'s.

If you have read King's "I Have a Dream" or have heard about his speeches, you can draw on your experience to conclude that *eloquent* means expressive and moving. Another approach is to reason from the context of the sentence. The writer wants to write speeches like King's, so we can guess that King's speeches must be very good. Very good or *eloquent* speeches are effective or moving works.

EXERCISE 2-5	Using Experience or Logic to Understand New Words

*Write a definition or synonym for each word in **bold** type in the following sentences. Then briefly explain how you decided on the word's meaning. The first one has been started for you.*

1. The judge told the jury to continue talking to try to reach **consensus** on a verdict.

a. **consensus** means: agreement _____

b. your reasoning: _____

_____

2. When the family entered the kitchen, they were nearly overcome by the horrible smell that **pervaded** the room.

    a. **pervaded** means: _____

    b. your reasoning: _____

    _____

3. Although John was somewhat **intimidated** by his new boss, he tried not to show any anxiety in the office.

    a. **intimidated** means: _____

    b. your reasoning: _____

    _____

4. Martha's mother worried about her living in New York City, but Martha loved the excitement of **urban** living.

    a. **urban** means: _____

    b. your reasoning: _____

    _____

5. When the doctor could not **alleviate** Dorothy's pain with medication, he recommended surgery for the tennis star.

    a. **alleviate** means: _____

    b. your reasoning: _____

    _____

6. The students wondered if their backpacks received more **scrutiny** than the other travelers' suitcases because the students were young and wearing jeans.

    a. **scrutiny** means: _____

    b. your reasoning: _____

    _____

7. The crowd's excitement grew as they **anticipated** their team's entrance into the stadium.

   a. **anticipated** means: _____

   b. your reasoning: _____

   _____

8. To express his **adoration**, the young man brought flowers to his lady.

   a. **adoration** means: _____

   b. your reasoning: _____

   _____

9. Juan remained **disconsolate** because he had dropped his ice cream cone, even though his sister offered to share hers.

   a. **disconsolate** means: _____

   b. your reasoning: _____

   _____

10. Volunteers used many strategies—phone surveys, e-mail messages—to promote the senator's candidacy. As a result, they **disseminated** the senator's views at relatively little cost.

    a. **disseminated** means: _____

    b. your reasoning: _____

    _____

| EXERCISE 2-6 | **Using Context Clues When Reading Paragraphs** |

*Select the word(s) from the box below that best defines each word in **bold** type in the following paragraph.*

President Jefferson supported the Lewis and Clark **expedition** to explore the country west of the Mississippi River. Jefferson believed that our **exploding** population would soon fill the entire **continent**. In August 1893, Lewis

embarked on one of the most demanding **exploits** in American history. Lewis picked up Clark and **recruits** for their adventure in October. Working well together, Lewis and Clark **complemented** one another's personalities. Surviving their trip, they returned to **recognition** but not to **fortune**. Lewis was **inept** as governor of the Louisiana Territory and eventually killed himself. Clark was finally able to get their *Journals* published, but without all their descriptions of new animals and plants.

completed	set out	new members of the group
heroic acts	a principal landmass	wealth journey
increasing suddenly	not skilled	favorable notice

1. **expedition** _____   6. **recruits**   _____

2. **exploding** _____   7. **complemented** _____

3. **continent** _____   8. **recognition**   _____

4. **embarked** _____   9. **fortune**   _____

5. **exploits** _____   10. **inept**   _____

EXERCISE 2-7

Using Context Clues When Reading Paragraphs

*Write a brief definition or synonym for each word in **bold** type in the following paragraphs. Use context clues to help you.*

Paragraph 1

In time, your college experiences and activities will change you as well as your life. They will increase your knowledge and **competence,** and influence your attitudes and values. They will add **conspicuously** to your career opportunities and **modify** your **avocational** interests. Your plans for the future will change. The experiences you **encounter,** the **diverse** persons you meet, all will have an impact on the kinds of friends and types of relationships you enjoy.

Chickering and Schlossberg, *How to Get the Most Out of College*

1. **competence** _____

2. **conspicuously** _____

3. **modify** _____

4. **avocational** _____

5. **encounter** _____

6. **diverse** _____

Paragraph 2

Broadly speaking, **offensive** language is that which **denigrates** people because of gender, race, **ethnicity,** class, sexual preference, age, or **disability**. It also includes **obscene** or sexually **explicit** language. Common to all offensive language is intent: to put down those who are different or less fortunate than others. Whether a racial **slur,** a **sexist** statement, or a **demeaning stereotype,** most people agree that such language is obvious and ugly.

Gary Goshgarian, *Exploring Language*, 7th ed.

1. **offensive** _____

2. **denigrates** _____

3. **ethnicity** _____

4. **disability** _____

5. **obscene** _____

6. **explicit** _____

7. **slur** _____

8. **sexist** _____

9. **demeaning** _____

10. **stereotype** _____

WORDS WITH MORE THAN ONE MEANING

Many common words have more than one meaning. If you know only one meaning of the word, you may be confused when you find that word in your reading. For example:

Please **ship** the shoes to me by UPS.

In this sentence, **ship** means send or mail. Now you write a sentence in which the word **ship** has a different meaning:

_____

What does the word **ship** mean in your sentence? _____

Be alert to the possibility of a word being used with an unfamiliar meaning to you and use context clues to help you decide on the word's meaning.

EXERCISE 2-8	Practicing with Words Having More Than One Meaning

*For each sentence, give the meaning of the word in **bold** type. Then, on the following line, write a sentence using the word in a different meaning.*

1. I would like you to **book** me for three nights in a double room.

   book means: _____

   _____

2. **State** your business and be quick about it!

   State means: _____

   _____

3. The Federal **Bureau** of Investigation has its national headquarters in Washington, D.C.

   Bureau means: _____

   _____

4. The fresh tulips will **last** about one week.

   last means: _____

   _____

5. The **rest** of the group is on the second bus.

   rest means: _____

   _____

6. Religious paintings in the 15th century were often prepared on three connected **panels**.

   panels means: _____

   _____

7. He believed that failure was his **lot** in life.

   lot means: _____

   _____

8. Most of the houses in the county have **appreciated** at least 30 percent in the last five years.

   appreciated means: _____

   _____

9. The factory whistle gave a loud **blast** to signal the end of the work day.

   blast means: _____

   _____

10. The gangster **finished** his chief competitor with one shot to the back of the head.

    finished means: _____

    _____

◢ LEARNING NEW WORDS

Using context clues to aid understanding of a word helps make reading easier, but context can't help readers all the time. To really know a word, you have to *overlearn* it. How can you build your word power? Here are some strategies to use.

Keep a Vocabulary Notebook

To expand your working vocabulary, you need to study new words in an organized way. One method is to make a list of new words either in a section of your notebook for this class or in a separate vocabulary notebook. To make your notebook list a useful study tool, follow these steps.

Guidelines for a Vocabulary Notebook

1. Use a looseleaf (not a spiral) notebook so that you can remove pages for studying.
2. Draw a line down each page about one-third of the way from the left margin.

(continued on next page)

(continued from previous page)

3. Write each word to be learned in a list down the left side of the page. If you are not sure how to pronounce the word, write the phonetic spelling under the word. (You will find the phonetic spelling in a dictionary immediately after the initial entry word.)

4. On the right side of the page, across from each vocabulary word, write the word's definition(s). Include a sentence in which the word is used, but draw a line where the word would go instead of writing it in the sentence. You may also want to include a synonym of the word. You will need several lines on the right side of the page for each word listed on the left. (See Figure 2.1 for a sample.)

5. Now study the words in one of two ways. First, fold back the right side of the page so that you can see only the words. Try to state each word's definition and use each one in a sentence. Sometimes, study the words by folding back the left side of the page. By looking at the definition, can you name the word? Whenever you are stuck, check the information on the folded-back part of the page.

Make Vocabulary Cards

You can make your own flash cards to learn new words by using a set of 3" × 5" index cards. Follow these guidelines.

Guidelines for Vocabulary Cards

1. Make one card for each new word. Start the cards either when you come across new words or later from the words you have circled in your reading.

2. Write each word on one side of a card. If you have trouble pronouncing the word, add the word's phonetic spelling to this side of the card.

3. Find the meaning(s) of the word in your dictionary and write the definition(s) on the other side of the card. Also include examples or synonyms of the word and a sentence in which you use the word (but put a line in the sentence where the word would go).

4. Now you can test yourself in one of two ways. Look at the word on the front of the card and say its definition to yourself. Also try to use it in a sentence. Then turn to the back of the card to see if you have defined and used the word correctly. You can also study the definitions and sample sentences on the back to see if you can name the word on the front of the card.

(continued on next page)

(continued from previous page)

5. After you think you have really learned some of the words, divide your stack of cards into two piles: one for the words you have learned and one for the words you still need to study. Continue to practice with the words you do not know and with the new cards you keep adding to your stack.

6. Shuffle the cards after each practice so that you do not go through the words in the same order each time.

7. Every week or so, review the stack of cards you have set aside, just to make sure that you continue to know them. (Sample vocabulary cards are shown in Figure 2.2.)

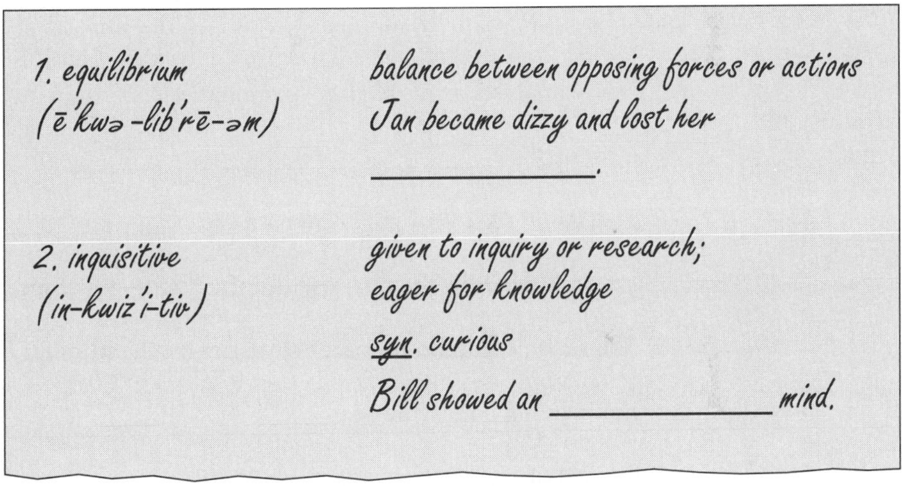

1. *equilibrium*
   (ē'kwə-lib'rē-əm)

   balance between opposing forces or actions
   Jan became dizzy and lost her
   _____.

2. *inquisitive*
   (in-kwiz'i-tiv)

   given to inquiry or research;
   eager for knowledge
   syn. curious
   Bill showed an _____ mind.

■ **FIGURE 2.1** **Sample Vocabulary Notebook Page**

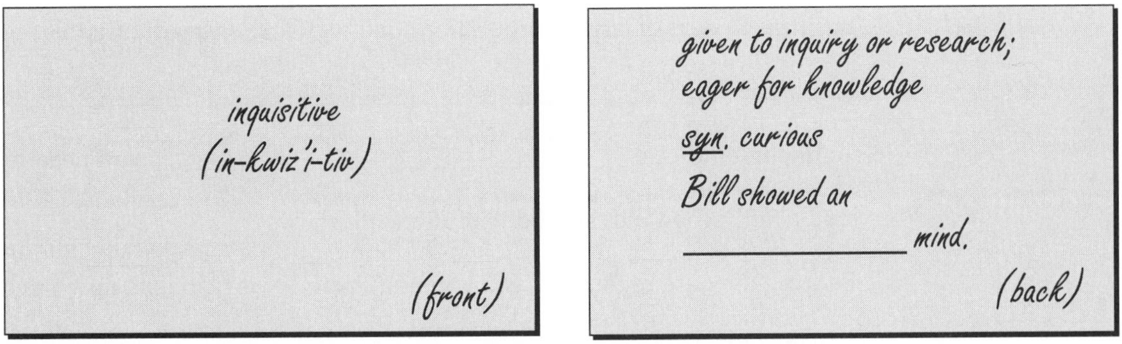

inquisitive
(in-kwiz'i-tiv)

(front)

given to inquiry or research;
eager for knowledge
syn. curious
Bill showed an
_____ mind.

(back)

■ **FIGURE 2.2** **Sample Vocabulary Cards**

Learn New Words from Textbook Reading

Only you can build your word power. You can begin by circling every word in this chapter that is not now a part of your working vocabulary. Then start a vocabulary notebook or make cards for these words.

Part of your study will involve learning the vocabulary of each discipline. Each area of study (for example, business or psychology) uses terms that have special meanings for that discipline. Use your textbook's glossary to learn the definitions of terms for that course. Study some terms from sociology on the sample glossary page from *Living Sociology* (Renzetti and Curran, 2nd ed.). An exercise follows to give you practice with glossaries.

| EXERCISE 2-9 | Practice with Glossaries |

Fill in each blank with a term from the Glossary that best completes each sentence.

1. Many analysts argue that government decisions are heavily influenced by

   a country's _____.

2. Special interest groups, known as _____,

   are organized for the purpose of influencing government decisions.

3. The Census Bureau prepares statistics on the number of American house-

   holds living below the _____.

4. Typical of _____ are

   receptionists and secretaries; most workers in these jobs are women.

5. Business leaders of larger corporations and well-known media figures are

   part of the _____.

6. To understand our _____ you need to

   study Hollywood movies and television talk shows.

7. Because they are organized and vote regularly, senior citizens now have

   considerable _____.

615 Glossary

Piaget, Jean (1892–1980): the social psychologist who focused his life's work on examining how children think and interpret the world around them

pink-collar jobs: jobs primarily in the service sector with a high concentration of women workers, which got their name not because of the way workers dress for work, but because the jobs are associated with females and femininity

play stage: the second stage of socialization in Mead's theory, during which children distinguish a variety of social roles and spend time in play that involves role taking

plea bargaining: a process whereby the accused agrees to plead guilty in exchange for a reduction in the charges or the sentence

pluralism: the diffusion of political influence among numerous interest groups with no single group dominating; the maintenance of racial and ethnic diversity in a society

political action committees (PACs): special interest groups dedicated to fundraising and distributing contributions on political campaigns, making them a powerful force on the political scene

political party: an organization that supports and promotes particular principles and candidates for public office

political power: the decision-making component of stratification, referring to an individual's relationship to government and the ability to influence political decisions

political socialization: the development of political values and attitudes over time in response to various environmental influences, including one's social locations and experiences of political events

politics of research: the ways in which research may be used to promote or support a particular interest or partisan position

polyandry: a marriage in which one woman is married concurrently to two or more men

polygamy: marriage to multiple partners concurrently

polygyny: a marriage in which one man is married concurrently to two or more women

polytheism: belief in many gods

popular culture: the beliefs, values, expectations, and artifacts of a society's masses

population: the entire group that a researcher is interested in studying; all possible subjects of relevance to a study

population pyramid: a device used by demographers to make a visual presentation of population variation

positional mobility: movement through the stratification hierarchy as a result of individual causes, such as hard work and luck

positivism: the position that knowledge must be derived from observable facts, not from superstition, fantasy, or some other nonempirical (nonverifiable) source

postconventional morality: the highest level of moral development in Kohlberg's theory, during which people evaluate behavior in terms of whether they consider it to be in the best interests of their community or their society

postindustrial economy: a system for producing, managing, and distributing services and information, with the help of electronic technology, especially computers

postindustrial society: a society in which work is devoted primarily to the production of services and information rather than to the physical production of goods

poverty line: the federal government's measure of poverty, calculated by multiplying by three the amount of money needed for a minimally nutritional diet, while also taking into account factors such as size of the family and age of the household head

power: the ability to get others to do one's will even if they do not want to do it

power elite: a term coined by C. Wright Mills to describe the segments of society that dominate the political process: the government elite, the military elite, and the corporate elite

preconventional morality: the first stage of moral development in Kohlberg's theory, during which behavior is evaluated in terms of whether it will be punished or rewarded

prejudice: biased beliefs or attitudes about individuals based on their membership in a particular group; in the context of race and ethnic relations, biased beliefs about individuals based on their membership in a particular racial or ethnic group

preoperational stage: the second developmental stage in Piaget's theory, during which the child builds on language and reasoning skills and learns to represent the world symbolically

presentation of self: the careful control of one's appearance and behavior in order to convey to others a specific image of one's self

preventive medicine: medicine that establishes conditions that preclude the onset of illness

primary deviation: rule breaking

primary group: a social group, typically small in size, that is characterized by strong emotional attachments among the members and that endures over time

primary labor market: made up of high-paying, high-prestige jobs with extensive benefits

primary sector (of the economy): the segment of the economy made up of activities that extract products directly from the natural environment

8. Some defense lawyers encourage their clients to consider

_____ to avoid jail time.

9. One way to cope with the increasing costs of health care is to encourage

_____.

10. _____ describes ancient Greek and

Roman religions.

■ ■ ■ ■ ■

Learn New Words from General Reading

The best way to expand your vocabulary is to read regularly. Try to find at least 45 minutes each day for reading. Get a morning newspaper that you can read while eating breakfast or between classes. Consider a subscription to one of the weekly newsmagazines: *Time, Newsweek,* or *U.S. News & World Report.* In addition to the week's news, newsmagazines contain interesting cover stories ranging from dinosaurs to artificial intelligence. Look in your library for a magazine related to your hobbies or interests. Your library has hundreds of magazines from which to choose.

| EXERCISE 2-10 | **Newspaper or Magazine Reading** |

Find a newspaper or magazine that you want to read each week. (If you select a monthly magazine, plan to read at least one article each week.) Answer the following questions about the work you have selected.

1. What is the name of the work you have selected?

_____

2. Is the periodical published daily, weekly, or monthly?

_____

3. List the title and author of one article you have read.

_____

4. Briefly state what the article is about.

_____

_____

_____

_____

5. What is one new fact or idea you learned from your reading?

_____

_____

_____

■ ■ ■ ■ ■

In addition to developing the habit of magazine reading, you want to become comfortable reading books. Always get a good start into a new book. When you begin, read for at least 45 minutes without stopping. This way you will have a better idea what is happening in the book when you return to it later.

EXERCISE 2-11	Reading a Book

Select a book from the list that follows this exercise, or one that your instructor approves, and complete the following questions.

1. What is the name of the book you have selected?

_____

2. Who is the author and when was the book published?

_____

3. Based on reading the first 50 pages, explain what the book is about. If it is a novel, include the characters introduced so far and where the story takes place.

_____

_____

_____

_____

_____

_____

_____

_____

4. When you complete the book, be prepared to summarize and evaluate it in a five-minute talk for classmates.

A BRIEF BOOK LIST

Mitch Albom, *Tuesdays with Morrie*   An old man, a young sportscaster, and insights into life's meaning and purpose.

Maya Angelou, *I Know Why the Caged Bird Sings*   A moving autobiography of an African-American girl from Arkansas.

Saul Bellow, *A Theft*   A short, engaging tale of Clara Velde and her lost ring.

Willa Cather, *My Antonia*   The story of an immigrant American farmgirl and of the country she grew up with.

Sandra Cisernos, *The House on Mango Street*   Growing up in a Hispanic family on a street that does not represent the American dream.

Stephen Crane, *The Red Badge of Courage*   Placed in the Civil War, an important comment on growing up—and on war.

William Golding, *Lord of the Flies*   A group of young boys, alone, try to create their own society.

Richard Harris, *The Fatherland*   Romance and intrigue in Europe after World War II—with Germany winning the war.

Ernest Hemingway, *The Old Man and the Sea*   A story of deep-sea fishing and courage.

James Herriot, *All Creatures Great and Small, All Things Wise and Wonderful, Every Living Thing*   Engaging memoirs of an English veterinarian.

Harper Lee, *To Kill a Mockingbird*   A best-selling novel, made into a successful movie, about problems in a small town as seen through the eyes of a young girl.

Bernard Malamud, *The Natural*   A washed-up baseball player makes a comeback.

Mary Mebane, *Mary*   About Mebane's life growing up in rural North Carolina.

George Orwell, *Animal Farm*   Orwell's satiric portrait of a society of animals who seem very much like us.

J. D. Salinger, *Catcher in the Rye*   The experiences of one of literature's most famous teenagers.

Mark Salzman, *The Soloist*   About music, performing, growing up, and knowing oneself.

Bernhard Schlink, *The Reader*   A story of a boy's relationship with an older woman, a woman with a past and a secret.

Jane Smiley, *A Thousand Acres*   The relationships among a father, with his desire for a thousand-acre farm, and his three daughters.

Amy Tan, *The Joy Luck Club*   Life in an Asian-American community in California.

Mark Twain, *Adventures of Huckleberry Finn*   Adventures of a young boy and a runaway slave on the Mississippi River before the Civil War.

Edith Wharton, *Ethan Frome*   The sad tale of stoic Ethan, his sickly wife, and a young cousin who comes to live with them.

E. B. White, *Charlotte's Web*   A wonderful tale of friendship with Wilbur— some pig!

■ ■ ■ ■ ■

GLOBAL COOLING

The following short "box" on global cooling appeared in the *Washington Post* with the longer article, "Frozen in Time," that follows.

Prepare

1. Identify the author and the work. What do you expect the author's purpose to be?

   _____

   _____

2. Preread to identify the subject and make predictions. What do you expect to read about?

   _____

   _____

3. What do you already know about the subject?

_____

_____

4. Raise two questions that you expect the article to answer.

_____

_____

_____

■ ■ ■ ■ ■

1   What was the Ice Age anyway? Let's start at the beginning: About 2 million years ago the Earth's temperatures started getting cooler. In northern and southern latitudes (that is, the top and bottom of the planet) more snow fell each year than melted.

2   When the flakes keep falling for so long, the snow on the bottom turns to ice. The whole frozen sheet is called a glacier.

3   At times during the Pleistocene (pronounced "PLISE-tuh-seen") Epoch, the period of time from 1.6 million years ago to 10,000 years ago, glaciers covered North America south to what is now Wisconsin, and Europe south to modern London. All of Antarctica was locked in ice, so were parts of the Andes and Himalaya mountains.

4   Glaciers creep like icy blobs, advancing and retreating depending on the snowfall and temperature. They generally move one to 10 feet a day, but some glaciers have traveled as fast as 70 feet per day. Glaciers grind along the Earth's

■ Glaciers from the last ice age, which ended 10,000 years ago, reached as far south as Wisconsin.

Source: The Washington Post

surface like a scouring pad, pushing rocks and boulders along for hundreds of miles and leaving grooves underneath.

5   The constant motion of glaciers can create entire valleys that then turn to lakes when the ice finally melts. Glaciers moving from Canada created the Great Lakes.

6   How did people cope with the Ice Age? Many humans in the northern latitudes moved south, following the animals they depended on for food.

7   The last ice age ended only about 10,000 years ago, when the planet warmed, glaciers melted and ocean levels rose. Some scientists think the world's glaciers might only be in a temporary retreat, and we may be in for another ice age someday.

272 words

Comprehension Check

Answer with a, b, c, or d to indicate the phrase that best completes each statement.

_____   1. A glacier is

a. a blob.

b. a scouring pad.

c. a frozen sheet of ice.

d. snow.

_____   2. Glaciers are formed by

a. cold weather.

b. snow falling without melting so that bottom layers turn to ice.

c. melting ice creating lakes.

d. mountains such as the Andes getting higher.

_____   3. The last ice age

a. occurred during the Pleistocene Epoch.

b. ended about 10,000 years ago.

c. ended about 100,000 years ago.

d. both a and b.

_____   4. The last ice age is called the Wisconsin because

a. it missed Wisconsin.

b. it came as far south as Wisconsin.

c. a scientist named Wisconsin named it.

d. it needed to be called something.

_____   5. Glaciers start near

a. the Andes.

b. Wisconsin.

c. the northern and southern latitudes.

d. the Pleistocene Epoch.

_____ 6. Glaciers advance or retreat depending on
      a. snowfall and temperature.
      b. how many lakes they make.
      c. the number of polar bears.
      d. the height of nearby mountains.

_____ 7. The movement of glaciers
      a. can create huge valleys.
      b. created the Great Lakes.
      c. both a and b.
      d. b but not a.

_____ 8. During the last ice age, humans living in Canada
      a. moved south.
      b. lost their food supply and starved.
      c. lived in caves.
      d. liked the cold.

_____ 9. Scientists believe that
      a. ice ages are over.
      b. ice ages are good for us.
      c. another ice age will occur someday.
      d. ice ages are fun.

_____ 10. When the author writes that glaciers "creep like icy blobs," the author is using
      a. sarcasm.
      b. a simile.
      c. irony.
      d. a silly statement.

Expanding Vocabulary

Study the sentences in which the following words occur and use context clues to define each one. The number in parentheses is the number of the paragraph in which the word appears.

1. blobs (4) _____

2. grind (4) _____

3. scouring pad (4) _____

4. depended on (6) _____

5. retreat (7) _____

Additional Exercise

1. Find the latitude for London. (Think about what sources you can use to get this information.)
2. Locate either the Andes or Himalayas mountain range. Describe the location of the one you selected by referring to continents and countries. (Think about what sources you can use to get this information.)

FROZEN IN TIME

Uncovering the 5,300-Year-Old Mysteries of the European Iceman

Elizabeth Kastor

Elizabeth Kastor is a journalist. Her article appeared in the *Washington Post* (2001).

Prepare

1. Identify the author and work. What do you expect the author's purpose to be?

_____

_____

2. Preread to identify the subject and make predictions. What do you expect to read about?

_____

_____

3. What do you already know about the subject?

_____

_____

4. Raise two questions that you expect the article to answer.

_____

_____

_____

■ ■ ■ ■ ■

1   The man had a family and a home, but we don't know anything about them. He had a name, but we don't know that either, so people call him Iceman or Otzi, after the Otztal Alps—the European mountains where he lived.

2   There are many mysteries about Otzi, but we still know more about him than any other person who lived when he did.

3   And we know it all because Otzi had some very bad luck.

4   One day, 5,300 years ago, Otzi wandered into the mountains. He was in his forties. He had recently eaten a meal of Alpine mountain goat and hard crackers. He was a hunter, and wore a backpack filled with his tools—arrows and knives and an unfinished bow.

5   Then, he was attacked. Someone shot an arrow into his back. The arrow sliced deeply into his body and Otzi bled to death.

6   His body came to rest in a trench. Cold winds blew across him. Snow covered him and turned to ice. A glacier slid over the trench just above his head, hiding his body and protecting him and his tools. Slowly, his skin, flesh and organs were mummified within an icy pool. And time passed.

7   In Egypt, the pharoahs built the pyramids.

8   In Greece, men invented democracy.

9   Jesus was born and died.

10 And then, one warm September day in 1991, two German hikers saw a head sticking out of a melting pool of ice. And Otzi's second life began.

11 At first, police thought Otzi was a hiker who had died recently. But scientists tested the body for a chemical called carbon-14, or radiocarbon. (All animals and people have carbon-14 in them. Carbon-14 falls apart slowly, but at a predictable rate. If you test how much carbon-14 is left in something that was once alive, you can tell how old it is.)

12 Scientists were amazed when they learned Otzi's age. The people who lived in Europe 5,000 years ago did not leave much behind to teach us about their lives. Their clothes fell apart long ago, and their bones can only tell so much. But not this time.

13 Along with his body, they found other items:

   • A sewn leather pack, which he probably wore around his waist, holding three small tools made of flint.

   • The wooden frame of his backpack.

   • Bits of his cape made of long grass.

   • Two small birch bark containers holding leaves picked while they were still green (so they wouldn't burn) and a few small lumps of charcoal. He may have carried embers from his last fire so he could easily start a new one.

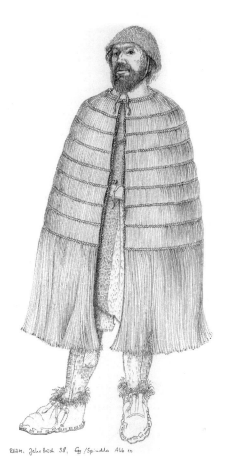

■ **Drawing of Otzi man**

Source: Drawing by Julia Ribbick, Roman-Germanic Central Museum, Mainz, Germany.

RGZM, Jahrbuch 38, Egg/Spindler Abb 10

14   "It's like a snapshot of a man in real life," one scientist said soon after Otzi was found.

15   The scientists studying Otzi are like detectives: They have to use the clues he left behind to figure out as much as they can about him and the world he lived in.

16   Around his body were many pieces of a deerskin coat. Most of the seams were sewn very carefully with animal sinew. Some seams were sewn with cording made from twisted dry grass, and those stitches weren't as neat. Some scientists think the good sewing was done by someone else in Otzi's village, and he repaired holes ripped in his clothes when he was away from home—and he wasn't that good at sewing.

17   You may have heard about Otzi recently. Even though 10 years have passed since he was found, scientists are still discovering new things about him. For 10 years, it wasn't clear how he died. His skin was well preserved, but even so it was shriveled up, and so no one could see the small wound the arrow made as it entered his back.

18   But in July, scientists in Italy announced that they had used a new kind of X-ray to make threedimensional pictures of Otzi's inside. For the first time they saw the arrow lodged in his back.

19   Was Otzi escaping from his enemies into the cold mountains when he was killed? Did a hunter shoot him by accident? Did someone kill him for his herd of animals?

20   After 5,310 years, Otzi has taught us a lot, but some of his secrets remain.

781 words

Comprehension Check

Answer with a, b, c, or d to indicate the phrase that best completes each statement.

_____   1. Otzi was found
      a. in a melting pool of ice.
      b. in the Andes.
      c. by skiers.
      d. by scientists.

_____   2. Otzi died
      a. 5,300 years ago.
      b. 300 years ago.
      c. 10,000 years ago.
      d. in 1991.

_____   3. Otzi's body was.
      a. covered by a glacier.
      b. preserved as if it were a mummy.
      c. a skeleton only.
      d. both a and b.

_____   4. Scientists discovered Otzi's age by
      a. measuring his skull.
      b. testing for the amount of Carbon-14 remaining in his body.
      c. analyzing his clothes.
      d. determining how he died.

_____   5. Otzi has told us a great deal about his time because
      a. his tools and clothes were preserved.
      b. he was a special person of his time.
      c. he was very old.
      d. he had many possessions.

_____   6. Otzi's preserved body was discovered
      a. in 1999.
      b. in 5000 B.C.

c. in 1991.

d. when the Greeks invented democracy.

_____ 7. Otzi was discovered with

a. a leather pack with tools.

b. a cape made of silk.

c. several friends.

d. a gunshot wound.

_____ 8. Otzi also carried lumps of charcoal

a. in green leaves to keep them from burning his things.

b. to more easily start his next fire.

c. to mark his trail.

d. both a and b.

_____ 9. Recently when scientists x-rayed Otzi's body, they learned

a. what he had eaten.

b. that he died from an arrow wound.

c. that he was shot by accident.

d. that he was a hunter.

_____ 10. Scientists think that Otzi's deerskin coat was first sewn by some-one in his village and then repaired by Otzi. Their thinking is a

a. conclusion based on the evidence and their knowledge of early peoples.

b. guess that is as good as any other.

c. fact clearly established by the evidence of the coat.

d. fact drawn from a diary left by Otzi.

Expanding Vocabulary

Study the sentences in which the following words occur and use context clues to define each one. The number in parentheses is the number of the paragraph in which word appears.

1. mummified (6) _____

2. pharaohs (7) _____

3. predictable (11) _____

4. embers (13) _____

5. shriveled (17) _____

Reflection and Discussion

1. What, for you, is the most fascinating part of the discovery of Otzi? Why?
2. When you imagine human living conditions 5,000 years ago, what do you picture?

MAKING CONNECTIONS

WORKSHOP

1. Can you imagine how scientists felt when Otzi was discovered? What words might best describe their responses?
2. Why is it both interesting and important to piece together the history of the earth and human history? List as many answers to the question as you can, either on your own or with your class partner.

"E" CONNECTIONS

Select one of the following topics to learn more about: Mass Extinctions, The Earth's Ice Ages, Early Human History, Dinosaur Extinctions. Be prepared to explain the topic, as simply as possible, to classmates. Be sure to identify all Web-sites used. Conduct your own search or start your search at <refdesk.com>.

WORD POWER 1

Sorting Out Words That Are Often Confused

This chapter and each of the remaining chapters will end with additional vocabulary study. Remember: The greater your vocabulary, the easier reading becomes!

A number of common words sound alike but have different spellings and different meanings. Be sure that you know the differences to avoid errors in both reading and writing. Study the words and their meanings. Then select the correct word to complete each of the sentences below.

---

isle island
aisle passage between rows

bare naked, lacking decoration; to reveal
bear to carry; an animal

brake device for stopping
break reduce to pieces, make unusable

buy purchase
by next to, through use of

capital major city, wealth/assets
capitol government building

cite refer to
sight vision
site a place

coarse rough
course path, part of a meal

fair just, light coloring
fare money for transportation; food

(continued on next page)

(continued from previous page)

forth forward	**hear** sense sound by ear
fourth number four	**here** in this place

1. It's not _____ *(fair/fare)* cried the boy so loudly we could

   _____ *(hear/here)* him across the school yard.

2. After crossing the bridge, we had a clear _____ *(cite/sight/site)* of

   the construction _____ *(cite/sight/site)*.

3. In spite of his _____ *(coarse/course)* hands and faded suit, the farmer

   strode confidently up the _____ *(capital/capitol)* steps.

4. The governor entered the chamber _____ *(by/buy)* a side door and

   walked down the _____ *(aisle/isle)*.

5. Come _____ *(hear/here)* and show me the proper _____

   (coarse/course) to follow!

6. When the shelves are _____ *(bare/bear)* neither rich nor poor can

   _____ *(by/buy)* bread.

7. The wealthy merchant invested a _____ *(forth/fourth)* of his

   _____ *(capital/capitol)* in the purchase of a tropical _____

   (aisle/isle).

8. A popular bumper sticker announces that the driver will _____

   (break/brake) for animals.

9. Not wanting to get a bad grade in the _____ *(coarse/course)*, the stu-

   dent was careful to _____ *(cite/sight/site)* her sources correctly in her

   research paper.

10. I'll have to _____ *(brake/break)* a $20 to purchase a metro _____

    (fair/fare) card.

CHAPTER REVIEW

Complete each of the following statements or answer the questions.

1. One way to guess the meaning of new words is to study their _____

_____.

2. A word's context refers to _____

_____.

3. Three strategies for recognizing the meanings of words in their contexts are:

   a. _____

   b. _____

   c. _____

4. Two strategies for studying vocabulary words are:

   a. _____

   b. _____

5. A *glossary* is _____.

6. Sociologists use the term *power elite* to refer to _____

_____.

7. Most adults build their vocabularies from _____.

Take a Reading Road Trip!

For additional practice with your reading skills, use the Reading Road Trip CD-ROM or visit Reading Road Trip on the Web at <http://www.ablongman.com/readingroadtrip> (password required).

CHAPTER 3

Recognizing Word Parts and Knowing Your Dictionary

LEARNING OBJECTIVES

- ■ To understand how a knowledge of word parts can help you understand new words

- ■ To learn the meanings of some common roots, prefixes, and suffixes

- ■ To learn how to read a dictionary entry

- ■ To learn strategies for pronouncing new words

- ■ To know the kinds of information available in a dictionary

▪ PREPARE TO READ

Read and reflect on the chapter's title and objectives. Glance through the chapter, observing headings to see what is covered. Now answer these questions:

1. What do you expect to learn from this chapter?

_____

_____

2. What do you already know about the chapter's topic?

_____

_____

3. What two or three questions do you want answered from reading this chapter?

_____

_____

_____

_____

In Chapter 2 you learned how to use context clues to make good guesses about a word's meaning. Using context clues lets you keep reading through a passage without having to look up words in a dictionary. But suppose the context alone does not help you with an unfamiliar word. You have another strategy to use before turning to the dictionary. You can study the word's parts.

COMPOUND WORDS

You probably already study the parts of compound words—those made up of two words—to get their meaning. There are many compound words in English, words such as:

over/flow	to flow over the top
sea/shore	land by the sea
sales/person	one who sells merchandise
farm/land	land suitable for farming
good/hearted	kind, generous

EXERCISE 3-1	Workshop on Compound Words

With your partner or in small groups, make compound words using each of the words in the following list. List all the compound words you can make. Briefly define each compound word you make.

sky/_____

over/_____

watch/ _____

back/ _____

news/ _____

▪ ▪ ▪ ▪ ▪

Think of how many words you know that are actually made up of two separate words. Of course compound words are not always spelled as one word. They can be written as two words (ice cream) or hyphenated (mother-in-law). But since we are concerned with "seeing words within words," we have looked only at compound words written as one word. When you come to an unfamiliar word, if you can recognize that it is made up of two smaller words, you may be able to figure out its meaning.

▪ LEARNING FROM WORD PARTS: PREFIXES, ROOTS, AND SUFFIXES

We also make words by combining parts that do not, by themselves, make a word. Or, we can attach a word part to a complete word to make a new word.

Word parts that are placed at the beginning of a word (or word part) are called *prefixes*. Word parts that carry the primary meaning of a word are called *roots*. And word parts that are placed at the end of a word (or word part) are called *suffixes*. Consider the root *mort* (or *mor*). It means "death." If we add a suffix, we can make the word *mortal*. (We are only *mortal* because we will die.) If we add the prefix *im*, meaning "not," we can make the word *immortal*. *Immortal* refers to one who is not mortal.

Prefix	*Root*	*Suffix*
im	mort	al

We can add another suffix and make the noun *immortality*, the state or condition of being immortal. *Immortality* may seem at first glance to be a challenging word, but if we see the parts that make up the word and know their separate meanings, then we can figure out what the longer word means.

Many roots and prefixes come from Latin; others come from Greek. If you can learn to recognize twenty or so roots—and learn the meanings of the most common prefixes and suffixes that can alter those roots—you will build your word power by hundreds of words. The key is to recognize the root, even though it may have more than one spelling, and to understand what the prefix (or suffix) does to alter the root. Look, for example, at the root *vis* (or *vid*) which means "see." This root gives us the word *vision*. Can you find the root in each of the following words and decide on the word's meaning? Divide the word into its parts and then define it. The first has been done for you.

video _vid/eo visual portion of a television show_

visibility _____

revise _____

invisible _____

To define these three words, you need to know the root meaning, but you also need to understand the effect of two suffixes and two prefixes on that root. We will begin with a study of prefixes, but first some important reminders.

Remember:

1. You cannot learn every word part at once; some practice and drilling may be necessary.
2. You are already familiar with many of the word parts on the following lists.
3. Not all words have a prefix or suffix, even though they may begin or end with letters that can make a prefix or suffix. For example, *mis/take* begins with the prefix *mis*, but *missile* does not begin with a prefix.
4. Words can have more than one prefix or root or suffix, as do some of the *vis* words you just studied.
5. Some word parts change spelling when they combine with other word parts, so they may be difficult to recognize at first. You have already seen that *vis* and *vid* are two spellings of the same word part.

Prefixes That Express Time or Place

Here is a list of the most common prefixes that express an idea of time or place. Study the prefixes and their meanings for a few minutes and add your examples to the chart. Then complete the exercise that follows.

Prefix	Meaning	Example	Your Example
circum	around	circumference	_____
de	away, undo	depart	_____
ex	from, out of	export	_____
inter	between	interchange	_____
intro/intra	within, in	intramural	_____
post	after	postgraduate	_____
pre	before	prefix	_____

re	back, again	regain	_____
retro	backward	retroactive	_____
sub	under	submarine	_____
super	above	supernatural	_____
trans	across, over	transatlantic	_____

| EXERCISE 3-2 | **Working with Time and Place Prefixes** |

I. Fill in the blank with the appropriate prefix to make a word that fits the context of the sentence.

1. Jane spends some time each day in quiet _____ spection.

2. The instructor asked students to _____ view their notes for the next quiz.

3. The meeting was _____ poned until Thursday so that all committee members could attend.

4. Grade school teachers need to help students with their _____ personal relationships.

5. As the plane approached the airport, it began to _____ crease its speed, or _____ celerate.

6. It is important to _____ serve our natural resources.

II. Fill in the blanks to complete the statement or answer the question.

7. When Magellan *circumnavigated* the world, what did he do?

_____

8. When the actress puts a *superhuman* effort into her role, has she performed well or poorly? _____

9. When the cowboy *subjugated* the wild horse, he

_____

10. If *gress* means to step, then to *transgress* means to

_____

11. If the vacation *revitalized* the tired executive, how does the executive feel. now?

_____

12. If *spect* means to look at or see, then *retrospect* means

_____

■ ■ ■ ■ ■

Prefixes That Create a Negative or Reversal

Here is a list of some key prefixes that express a negative concept or reverse the meaning of the root. For example, when you add *dis* to the word *agree*, you reverse the meaning; you no longer agree. Similarly, if you are not settled in your new home, then you are *un*settled. Notice the several spellings that have the same meaning as *in*. The spelling of this prefix is affected by the first letter of the root to which it is attached. We say *inactive* but *illicit*. Study the prefixes and their meanings and add your example to the chart. Then complete the exercise that follows.

Prefix	Meaning	Example	Your Example
a	not	asymmetrical	_____
anti	against	anticlimax	_____
contra	against	contraception	_____
dis	apart, not	disagree	_____
in/il/ir/im	not, into	inactive	_____
mis	wrong	misrepresent	_____
non	not	nonfiction	_____
un	not	unsettled	_____

| **EXERCISE 3-3** | **Working with Negative Prefixes** |

Fill in the blank with the appropriate prefix to make a word that fits the context of the sentence.

1. The protestors' signs made clear their _____ war feelings.

2. The players objected to the change of match time as highly _____ regular.

3. Heroes have _____ common abilities.

4. Michael Johnson's running skill is truly _____ typical.

5. The accountant argued that the error was a _____ take.

6. The magician made the rabbit _____ appear.

7. The manager insisted that her decision was _____ reversible.

8. Marie thought that Peter's argument was _____ logical.

9. During the meeting, Tran felt that he had to _____ dict his colleague and present a different explanation of the problem.

10. Ruth enjoyed reading biographies and other _____ fiction works.

■ ■ ■ ■ ■

Additional Prefixes

Here are a few more prefixes you should know. Study them and add your example to the chart. Then complete the exercise that follows.

Prefix	Meaning	Example	Your Example
auto	self	autograph	_____
bi	two, twice	bimonthly	_____
hetero	different	heterogeneous	_____
mono	one, single, alone	monorail	_____

| poly | many | polygraph | _____ |
| semi | half, partial | semidarkness | _____ |

| EXERCISE 3-4 | **More Work with Prefixes** |

Fill in the blanks to answer each of the following questions.

1. If the conference is held *semiannually*, how many times a year is it held?

    _____

2. *Gam* is a root for marriage. Those who practice *polygamy* have what kind of marriage?

    _____

3. A *heterosexual* relationship describes what kind of sexual relationship?

    _____

4. If *lateral* refers to a side, then *bilateral* means

    _____

5. Why are cars called *automobiles?*

    _____

    _____

6. If you talk in a *monotone*, how are you talking?

    _____

■ ■ ■ ■ ■

Suffixes

Suffixes, word parts placed at the end of words, have two functions. Sometimes a suffix changes the word's part of speech and therefore how the word is used in a sentence. For example:

> Martha showed *sympathy* for her brother. (noun)
> Martha has a *sympathetic* feeling for her brother. (adjective)
> Martha spoke *sympathetically* to her brother. (adverb)

You already know that you can turn many adjectives into adverbs by adding the suffix *ly* (angry/angrily; beautiful/beautifully).

Suffixes can also make new words, or alter the meaning of a root. For example, the adjective *kind* becomes a noun referring to the state of being kind when *ness* is added: *kindness*. When *er* is added to the verb *teach*, we have "one who" teaches, a *teacher*. More than one suffix can be added to many words, and some new words are made by adding two suffixes to a root word. The following table organizes suffixes by the way they alter a word. Study the table, add your example, and then work the exercise that follows.

Common Suffixes

Suffix	*Example*	*Your Example*
Suffixes meaning "one who":		
-an	comedian	_____
-ant	communicant	_____
-ee	employee	_____
-eer	pamphleteer	_____
-er	teacher	_____
-ist	tourist	_____
-or	sailor	_____
Suffixes meaning "referring to":		
-al	seasonal	_____
-ship	ownership	_____
-hood	bachelorhood	_____
-ward	backward	_____
Suffixes establishing a condition, doctrine, or quality:		
-able/ible	audible	_____
-ance/ence	excellence	_____
-ic	angelic	_____

-ion/tion	election	_____
-ish	babyish	_____
-ism	realism	_____
-ity	inferiority	_____
-ive	restive	_____
-less	worthless	_____
-ness	meanness	_____
-ous	fabulous	_____
-ty	eternity	_____
-y	cloudy	_____

EXERCISE 3-5 | **Working with Suffixes**

Fill in the blank with an appropriate suffix to make a word that fits in the sentence.

1. When Barbara saw improve _____ in her tennis game, she began to practice harder.

2. Anyone planning to become an engin _____ has many years of schooling ahead.

3. The union lead _____ rallied the factory work _____.

4. The train slowed at the crossing and then lurched for _____.

5. Angela was fam _____ for her gourmet cooking.

6. If you study nineteenth-century literature, you will study romantic _____.

7. In spite of the doctor's efforts, the patient became less and less respons

_____.

8. Margaret threatened to quit unless she was given part owner _____

of the shop.

9. The cruel _____ and vicious _____ of the murders frightened

the community.

10. The committee thought the mayor's solutions were worth _____.

By adding suffixes, make two new words from each of the following. Note: Sometimes you need to delete a letter before adding a suffix.

1. boy _____

2. capital _____

3. operate _____

4. prevent _____

5. form _____

▪ ▪ ▪ ▪ ▪

Roots

Roots are the main parts of words. They may be complete words to which a prefix or suffix is added (*agreement*). Or, they may be word parts that are completed with a prefix or suffix or another root (*biography*). At the beginning of the discussion of word parts, you were introduced to two roots: *mor/mort* and *vis/vid*. Here are eighteen more roots, divided into two groups, for you to study. Study each group and add your example. Then complete each exercise that follows.

Common Roots

Root	Meaning	Example	Your Example
aster/astro	star	astronomy	_____
dict/dic	say, tell	dictate	_____

graph/gram	write	autograph	_____
path	feeling, suffering	pathos	_____
phon/phono	sound	symphony	_____
script/scrib	write	manuscript	_____
sen/sent	feel	sentiment	_____
tact/tang	touch	tactile	_____
terr/terre	land, earth	terrain	_____

EXERCISE 3-6	**Working with Roots**

Fill in the blanks to complete the statement or answer the question.

1. The suffix *-ible* refers to a condition or quality; what does *tangible* mean?

   _____

2. What kind of physics does an *astrophysicist* study?

   _____

3. *Celestial* refers to the sky or heavens. What word can you make that refers to or is "of the land"?

   _____

4. A *dictator* is a ruler with absolute power. Explain how the parts of the word lead to that definition.

   _____

   _____

5. By adding suffixes, make two more words from *sentiment*.

   _____

6. Journalists have been described as "ink-stained scribblers." Explain why the expression is appropriate.

_____

_____

7. What two roots in the list can be put together to make a word?

_____

8. *Logy* means the study of, as in *biology*. What does *pathology* mean?

_____

More Common Roots

Root	Meaning	Example	Your Example
cess/cede	go, move, yield	cessation	_____
cred	belief	credence	_____
dic/duct/duce	lead, take	ductile	_____
mit/miss	send, let go	missile	_____
port	carry	transport	_____
psych	mind	psychoanalysis	_____
spec/spect	look at, watch	spectacle	_____
ven/vent	come	convene	_____
voc/vok	call	vocation	_____

EXERCISE 3-7	More Work with Roots

Fill in the blanks to complete the statement or answer the question.

1. If your story lacks *credibility*, will anyone believe you?

_____

2. The prefix *con* (*com/col*) means "together" or "jointly." If the candidate *concedes* victory to his opponent, which person has won the election?

   _____

3. The word for "study of the mind" is _____.

4. By adding suffixes, make two words from the word *vocal*.

   _____

5. If exercise is *conducive* to weight loss, will exercise help or hinder weight

   loss? _____

6. After overloading her suitcase, Joan found that it was no longer

   _____ able.

7. If you are an observer at an event, you are a

   _____

8. A judge who *commits* you to jail has done what to you?

   _____

9. A *missionary* is one who

   _____

10. When a committee chair *conducts* a meeting, what does she do?

    _____

EXERCISE 3-8	Quiz on Word Parts

Put one line under each prefix and two lines under each suffix in the following words. Then define each word. Do not look back in the chapter. See how much you have learned about word parts. The first one has been completed for you.

1. interpersonal   that which is between people   _____

2. amorality   _____

3. benediction _____

4. microbiology _____

5. monogamy _____

6. autobiography _____

7. mortician _____

8. dispassionate _____

9. inaudible _____

10. nonparticipant _____

■ KNOWING YOUR DICTIONARY

Most of the time we use a dictionary to check the spelling of a word. But dictionaries give us other important information. To illustrate, let's look at the following dictionary entry in Figure 3.1.

Guide Words

The two words at the top of the page, on the same line as the page number, tell you that the first word on page 14 is *aerosol* and the last word is *afford*. Since dictionaries list words in alphabetical order, we know that *affiliate* will be found between *aer-* and *affo-*.

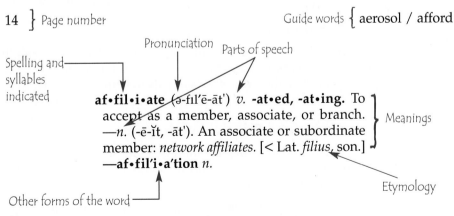

■ **FIGURE 3.1** **Dictionary Entry for *Affiliate***

Entry Word

Each entry word is listed in **bold** type with dots separating the word into its syllables. The syllables show how to divide the word at the end of a line of writing. They also help you see what parts make up the word.

Pronunciation

Immediately after the entry word comes the information needed to pronounce the word. This phonetic spelling of the word, given in parentheses, uses special marks to indicate the word's pronunciation. These marks or symbols are explained in a pronunciation guide in the opening pages of your dictionary. (A shorter version also appears at the bottom of each page of some dictionaries.) We will return to the pronunciation guide shortly.

Parts of Speech

Preceding the meanings listed for each entry word is an abbreviation, in *italic* type, of the word's part of speech. For words that function in more than one part of speech, definitions are grouped by each part of speech. In our example, you can see that *affiliate* is both a verb (*v.*) and a noun (*n.*).

Meanings

The definitions of *affiliate* follow after the part of speech abbreviation. When more than one definition is given, the definitions are numbered and listed (usually) from the most common to the least common meaning. Definitions of some words are specialized; the meaning is special to a particular area or field. Special meanings are indicated by a word (or abbreviation) in italics, such as *Mus.* or *Law.*

Etymology

A word's etymology—its history or origin—concludes most entries. It is placed in square brackets [like this]. Various abbreviations are used; these are listed and explained in the opening pages of your dictionary. We will return to these.

Other Forms of the Word

Some entries conclude with other forms of the word—and their parts of speech. Our example includes the noun *affiliation*, formed by adding the suffix *-ion* to *affiliat*. Because the word *affiliation* is given with the entry word *affiliate*, it is not listed separately as an entry word. Keep this in mind when you are looking up words.

Plurals and Principal Verb Forms

When a noun forms its plural in an irregular way, or when a verb's principal parts are irregular, this information is also included. For example, the entry for *drink* begins this way:

drink (dringk) *v.* **drank** (drangk), **drunk** (drungk), **drinking.**
The irregular past tense (*drank*) and past participle (*drunk*)—and their phonetic spellings—are given, followed by the present participle *drinking.*

■ PRONUNCIATION

The second spelling of each entry word—the phonetic spelling that shows how to pronounce the word—will help you with unfamiliar words. To succeed, study your dictionary's pronunciation key and practice the pronunciation of the various sounds. Figure 3.2 presents *The American Heritage Dictionary*'s pronunciation guide.

This key tells you that there are three sounds represented by the letter "a," plus one more when "a" is followed by an "r." Simple words are used to illustrate each sound. Pronounce *pat, pay, care*, and *father* to hear the different sounds that "a" can have. Now work through the rest of the key, pronouncing each

Symbols	Examples	Symbols	Examples
ă	pat	p	**p**o**p**
ā	pay	r	**r**oar
âr	**c**a**r**e	s	**s**au**c**e
ä	**f**ather	sh	**sh**ip, di**sh**
b	**b**i**b**	t	**t**igh**t**, stopp**ed**
ch	**ch**ur**ch**	th	**th**in
d	**d**ee**d**, mil**l**e**d**	*th*	**th**is
ě	**p**e**t**	ŭ	**c**u**t**
ē	**b**ee	ûr	**ur**ge, t**er**m, f**ir**m
f	**f**i**f**e, **ph**ase, rou**gh**		w**or**d, h**ear**d
g	**g**a**g**	v	**v**al**v**e
h	**h**at	w	**w**ith
hw	**wh**ich	y	**y**es
ĭ	**p**i**t**	z	**z**ebra, **x**ylem
ī	**p**ie, b**y**	zh	vi**s**ion, plea**s**ure
îr	**p**ie**r**		gara**g**e
j	**j**u**dg**e	ə	**a**bout, it**e**m, edibl**e**
k	**k**i**ck**, **c**at, pi**que**		gall**o**p, circ**u**s
l	**l**id, need**le** (nēd'l)	ər	butt**er**
m	**m**u**m**		
n	**n**o, sudde**n** (sŭd'n)	**Foreign**	
ng	thi**ng**		
ŏ	**p**o**t**	œ	*French* f**eu**
ō	**t**oe		*German* sch**ö**n
ô	**c**au**ght**, p**aw**, f**or**,	ü	*French* t**u**
	h**or**rid, h**oar**se*		*German* **ü**ber
oi	n**oi**se	KH	*German* i**ch**
ŏŏ	t**oo**k		*Scottish* lo**ch**
ōō	b**oo**t	N	*French* bo**n**
ou	**ou**t		

Primary stress′ **bi•ol′o•gy** (bī-ŏl′ə-jē)
Secondary stress′ **bi′o•log′i•cal** (bī′ə-lŏj′ĭ-kəl)

■ **FIGURE 3.2**   **Pronunciation Key**

sample word to hear the sounds and to connect those sounds to both the spellings and the symbols used to represent the sounds.

The key also indicates the marks used to show where to put the stress (or emphasis) when pronouncing a word of two or more syllables. Some words have only one stress. As the example shows, we put emphasis on the second syllable of *bi•ol'o•gy*. However, when this noun is made into the adjective *bi'o•log'i•cal*, then the first syllable receives a slight stress and the third syllable gets the primary emphasis. Sometimes, with long unfamiliar words, the problem is figuring out where to put the stress as we pronounce the word.

The Schwa

The symbol that looks like an upside down "e"—ə—is called the schwa. You will find it in the phonetic spelling of many words. The exact sound of the schwa varies somewhat depending on the letters around it, but it is the vowel or vowels that get the least emphasis in the word. Often the schwa sounds like *uh*— the extra sound we make when we hesitate while speaking: "The keys are in the, uh, kitchen, I think."

Pronounce each of the following words:

ə•bord' (aboard)

ēvən (even)

səb•skrīb' (subscribe)

Do you hear the schwa? Or, rather, do you hear how each schwa vowel is barely sounded?

EXERCISE 3-9	**Working with Pronunciation**

Pronounce each of the following words and then write the actual spelling of the word in the space provided. Use the pronunciation key as your guide to sounding out each phonetic spelling. You may want to check your dictionary for the correct spelling of the word you have written.

1. en'trəns _____

2. jōōn'yər _____

3. kûr'təsē _____

4. sir'ē-əl _____

5. pər•fôrm' _____

Pronouncing Unfamiliar Words

In your reading, you will find some words that you have trouble pronouncing. Sometimes, if you can pronounce an unfamiliar word correctly, you may recognize it. That is, you will remember having heard the word before, and you may be able to understand the word's meaning. So, pronouncing the word correctly can be helpful.

To pronounce unfamiliar words, you need to be able to separate each word into its syllables. Each syllable has a separate or distinct sound. Each syllable is composed of at least one of the vowels (*a, e, i, o, u,* and sometimes *y*) and often one or more consonants (any of the rest of the letters of the alphabet). Pronounce each of the following words, listening carefully to hear each separate syllable. How many syllables do you hear in the last two words?

periodical	5 syllables
tenacity	4 syllables
expatriate	_____ syllables?
impressionist	_____ syllables?

The following guidelines for dividing words into syllables will help you with unfamiliar words. There will be some exceptions to these guidelines.

Guidelines for Dividing Words into Syllables

1. Divide a word between two consonants coming together.
   Examples: frus/trate   dan/gle   ner/vous

2. Divide a word between a vowel and a single consonant, unless the consonant is *r*.
   Examples: re/port   a/bort   de/mand   BUT: per/use

3. Divide a word between two vowel sounds coming together.
   Examples: vi/a/ble   fi/as/co   mu/se/um

4. Divide a word between its prefix (word beginning) and root (core part).
   Examples: Prefix Root   Prefix Root
                im / moral   sub / marine

5. Divide a word between its root (core part) and suffix (word ending).
   Examples: Root Suffix   Root Suffix
                final / ly   amaz / ing

EXERCISE 3-10	Using Syllables for Pronunciation

Divide each of the following words into syllables by putting a slash in each appropriate place, using the guidelines above. Then, using the pronunciation key, pronounce each word. Finally, check your pronunciation by looking up each word in your dictionary and writing out its phonetic spelling. The first is done for you.

Syllables   **Phonetic Spelling from Dictionary**

1. e v /o /l u /t i o n   <u>ev′-ə-loo′shən</u>

2. a g g r e g a t e   _____

3. e u p h o r i a   _____

4. n e m e s i s   _____

5. o s c i l l a t e   _____

6. p a r s i m o n i o u s   _____

■ ABBREVIATIONS USED IN DICTIONARY ENTRIES

You have seen two abbreviations in the entry for *affiliate:* the *n.* for noun and the *v.* for verb to indicate the word's parts of speech. Additional abbreviations are used to indicate other parts of speech (for example, *adj.* for adjective), to accompany dates (for example, *d.* for died), and to provide information on a word's origin. *Affiliate* comes from (<) a Latin (Lat.) word. Abbreviations used in a dictionary are listed in the opening pages, along with the pronunciation key. The more abbreviations you understand, the quicker you can obtain needed information.

EXERCISE 3-11	Knowing Dictionary Abbreviations

Write in the meaning for each of the following abbreviations found in most dictionaries. Complete as many as you think you know and then check your work by studying the list of abbreviations in your dictionary. Complete the exercise by using your dictionary.

1. adv.   _____   11. obs.   _____

2. L   _____   12. pl.   _____

3. ON   _____   13. ME   _____

4. dial.   _____   14. Gk.   _____

5. Fr.   _____   15. sing.   _____

6. G.   _____   16. poss.   _____

7. Heb.   _____   17. Skt.   _____

8. Dan.   _____   18. Celt.   _____

9. var.   _____   19. conj.   _____

10. OE   _____   20. +   _____

■ WORKING WITH WORD MEANINGS

Entries for some words are quite long because they have several definitions, or perhaps because they are used in idiomatic expressions as well. (An *idiom* is an expression with a particular meaning that you can't figure out from knowing each word in the expression. For example: *fair and square* means "honest" or "just"; it has nothing to do with square objects.) When you find more than one definition for a word, you will need to think about which meaning fits the sentence in which you have found the word.

If you can recognize the part of speech of the word in the sentence, then you can eliminate all definitions of the word that apply to other parts of speech. Suppose, for example, that you read the following sentence:

▌ Many cooks like to use vanilla extract. ▌

Uncertain of the meaning of the word *extract*, you look it up and find that it can be both a verb and a noun. In the sentence the word is used as a noun, so you need to study only the two possible meanings of the word when it is used as a noun. The two noun meanings are: 1. A literary excerpt. 2. A substance prepared by extracting; essence; concentrate. The second definition is clearly the one that works in the sentence. Vanilla extract is a liquid concentrate extracted from the vanilla bean. The following exercise will give you some practice with the long entry for the word *side*.

EXERCISE 3-12	Word Meanings

Using the dictionary entry for "side," answer the questions that follow.

1. For what parts of speech can the word *side* be used?

   _____

2. Excluding idioms, how many separate definitions are given for the word?

   _____

3. What is the word's etymology?

   _____

   _____

4. Explain, in your own words, the meaning of this sentence: John showed his gentler side.

   _____

   _____

5. Use each of the following idioms in a sentence:

   a. *on the side:* _____

   _____

   b. *side by side:* _____

   _____

side (sīd) *n.* **1.** A surface of an object. esp. a surface joining a top and bottom. **2.** Either of the two surfaces of a flat object, such as a piece of paper. **3.** The left or right half in reference to a vertical axis, as of the body. **4.** The space immediately next to someone or something: *stood at her father's side.* **5.** An area separated from another area by an intervening feature. such as a line or barrier: *on this side of the Atlantic.* **6.** One of two or more opposing individuals. groups. teams. or sets of opinions. **7.** A distinct aspect: *showed his kinder side.* **8.** Line of descent. —*adj.* **1.** Located on a side: *a side door.* **2.** From or to one side: oblique: *a side view.* **3.** Minor: incidental: *a side interest.* **4.** Supplementary: *a side benefit.* —*v.* **sid•ed. sid•ing.** To align oneself in a disagreement: *sided with the liberals.* —*idioms.* **on the side.** In addition to the main portion. occupation. or activity. **side by side.** Next to each other. **this side of.** Informal. Verging on: *just this side of criminal.* [< OE *side.*]

Source: From *The American Heritage Dictionary,* 3rd ed.

6. Explain the meaning of *side* in each of the following sentences:

a. After they were stopped on the one-yard line, the momentum shifted to the other side.

_____

b. Joan's red hair comes from her mother's side of the family.

_____

7. Use *side* in three sentences of your own, one for each part of speech.

a. (*n.*) _____

_____

b. (*adj.*) _____

_____

c. (*v.*) _____

_____

**EXERCISE
3-13**

Finding Information in the Dictionary

Use the dictionary entries on the next page to answer the following questions.

1. Who was Guy Fawkes and what happened to him?

_____

_____

2. What is the origin of the art term *fauvism*?

_____

3. What are two synonyms for the word *feat*?

_____

4. What does FDA stand for?

_____

Faust / featherstitch   **308**

nal *adj.* —**fau′nal•ly** *adv.*

Faust (foust) also **Faus•tus** (fou′stəs, fô′-) *n.* A magician and alchemist in German legend who sells his soul to the devil for power and knowledge. —**Faust′i•an** (fou′stē-ən) *adj.*

fau•vism (fō′vĭz′əm) *n.* An early 20th-cent. movement in painting marked by the use of bold, often distorted forms and vivid colors. [Fr. *fauvisme* < *fauve*, wild animal.] —**fau′vist** *adj.*

faux pas (fō pä′) *n., pl.* **faux pas** (fō päz′). A social blunder. [Fr.]

fa•va bean (fä′və) *n.* See **broad bean**. [Ital. *fava* < Lat. *faba*, broad bean.]

fa•vor (fā′vər) *n.* **1.** A gracious, friendly, or obliging act that is freely granted. **2.a.** Friendly regard; approval or support. **b.** A state of being held in such regard. **3.** Unfair partiality; favoritism. **4.a.** A privilege or concession. **b. favors.** Sexual privileges, esp. as granted by a woman. **5.** A small gift given to each guest at a party. **6.** Advantage; benefit. —*v.* **1.** To oblige. See Syns at **oblige**. **2.** To treat or regard with approval or support. **3.** To be partial to. **4.** To make easier; facilitate. **5.** To be gentle with. **6.** *Regional.* To resemble: *She favors her father.* —*idiom.* **in favor of. 1.** In support of. **2.** To the advantage of. [< Lat.]

fa•vor•a•ble (fā′vər-ə-bəl, fāv′rə-) *adj.* **1.** Advantageous; helpful: *favorable winds.* **2.** Encouraging; propitious: *a favorable diagnosis.* **3.** Manifesting approval: *a favorable report.* **4.** Winning approval; pleasing: *a favorable impression.* **5.** Granting what has been requested. —**fa′vor•a•ble•ness** *n.* —**fa′vor•a•bly** *adv.*

fa•vor•ite (fā′vər-ĭt, fāv′rĭt) *n.* **1.a.** One enjoying special favor or regard. **b.** One trusted or preferred above others, esp. by a superior. **2.** A competitor regarded as most likely to win. [< OItal. *favorito*, p.part. of *favorire*, to favor.] —**fa′vor•ite** *adj.*

favorite son *n.* A man favored for nomination as a presidential candidate by his own state delegates at a national political convention.

fa•vor•it•ism (fā′vər-ĭ-tĭz′əm, fāv′rĭ-) *n.* A display of partiality toward a favored person or group.

Fawkes (fôks), **Guy.** 1570–1606. English Gunpowder Plot conspirator; executed.

fawn¹ (fôn) *v.* **1.** To exhibit affection or attempt to please, as a dog. **2.** To seek favor or attention by obsequiousness. [< OE *fagnian*, rejoice < *fægen*, glad.] —**fawn′er** *n.* —**fawn′ing•ly** *adv.*

Syns: fawn, bootlick, kowtow, slaver, toady, truckle v.

fawn² (fôn) *n.* **1.** A young deer. **2.** *Color.* A grayish yellow brown. [< OFr. *faon*, young animal < Lat. *fētus*, offspring.]

fax (făks) *n.* See **facsimile** 2. —*v.* To transmit (printed matter or an image) by electronic means. [Alteration of FACSIMILE.]

fay (fā) *n.* A fairy or elf. [< OFr. *fae*. See FAIRY.]

faze (fāz) *v.* **fazed, faz•ing.** To disconcert. See Syns at **embarrass**. [< OE *fēsian*, drive away.]

FBI also **F.B.I.** *abbr.* Federal Bureau of Investigation.

FCC *abbr.* Federal Communications Commission.

FDA *abbr.* Food and Drug Administration.

FDIC *abbr.* Federal Deposit Insurance Corporation.

Fe The symbol for the element **iron** 1. [Lat. *ferrum*, iron.]

fe•al•ty (fē′əl-tē) *n., pl.* **-ties. 1.** The fidelity owed by a vassal to his feudal lord. **2.** Faithfulness; allegiance. [< Lat. *fidēlitās*, faithfulness.]

fear (fîr) *n.* **1.a.** A feeling of agitation and anxiety caused by the presence or imminence of danger. **b.** A state marked by this feeling. **2.** A feeling of disquiet or apprehension. **3.** Reverence or awe, as toward a deity. **4.** A reason for dread or apprehension. —*v.* **1.** To be afraid of. **2.** To be apprehensive about. **3.** To be in awe of. **4.** To expect: *I fear you are wrong.* [< OE *fǣr*, danger.] —**fear′er** *n.* —**fear′less** *adj.* —**fear′less•ly** *adv.* —**fear′less•ness** *n.*

fear•ful (fîr′fəl) *adj.* **1.** Causing or capable of causing fear; frightening. **2.** Experiencing fear; frightened. See Syns at **afraid**. **3.** Timid; nervous. **4.** Indicating anxiety or terror. **5.** Feeling dread or awe. **6.** Extreme, as in degree or extent. —**fear′ful•ly** *adv.* —**fear′ful•ness** *n.*

fear•some (fîr′səm) *adj.* **1.** Causing or capable of causing fear. **2.** Fearful; timid. —**fear′some•ly** *adv.* —**fear′some•ness** *n.*

fea•si•ble (fē′zə-bəl) *adj.* **1.** Capable of being accomplished or brought about; possible. **2.** Used successfully; suitable. [< OFr. *faire, fais-,* do.] —**fea′si•bil′i•ty, fea′si•ble•ness** *n.* —**fea′si•bly** *adv.*

feast (fēst) *n.* **1.** A large elaborate meal; banquet. **2.** A religious festival. —*v.* **1.** To entertain or feed sumptuously. **2.** To eat heartily. **3.** To experience something with gratification or delight. —*idiom.* **feast (one's) eyes on.** To be delighted by the sight of. [< Lat. *festum.*] —**feast′er** *n.*

feat (fēt) *n.* A notable act or deed, esp. of courage. [< Lat. *factum.*]

Syns: feat, achievement, exploit, masterstroke n.

feath•er (fĕth′ər) *n.* **1.** One of the light, flat, hollow-shafted growths forming the plumage of birds. **2. feathers.** Plumage. **3.** Character, kind, or nature. —*v.* **1.** To cover, dress, or decorate with or as if with feathers. **2.** To fit (an arrow) with a feather. **3.** To turn (an oar blade) almost horizontal as it is carried back after each stroke. **4.** To alter the pitch of (a propeller) so that the chords of the blades are parallel with the line of flight. —*idioms.* **feather in (one's cap).** An act or deed to one's credit. **feather (one's) nest.** To grow wealthy esp. by abusing a position of trust. **in fine feather.** In excellent form, health, or humor. [< OE *fether.*] —**feath′er•y** *adj.*

feath•er•bed (fĕth′ər-bĕd′) *v.* **-bed•ded, -bed•ding.** To employ more workers than are needed for a job.

feather bed *n.* A mattress stuffed with feathers.

feath•er•brain (fĕth′ər-brān′) *n.* A flighty or empty-headed person. —**feath′er•brained′** *adj.*

feath•er•edge (fĕth′ər-ĕj′) *n.* A thin fragile edge.

feath•er•stitch (fĕth′ər-stĭch′) *n.* An embroidery stitch that produces a decorative

Source: From *The American Heritage Dictionary*, 3rd ed., 1992 (paperback edition).

5. What meaning of *favor* do you find in this sentence: I'm in favor of your running for class president?

_____

_____

6. What is a *fax*? _____

What word does it come from? _____

7. Why are there two entry words for *fawn*? Why not combine all the definitions into one entry, as you find with most words?

_____

_____

8. What is the symbol for the element iron? _____

9. What does the French expression *faux pas* mean?

_____

10. What is the meaning of *feather* in the following sentence: Only two weeks after her operation, she appeared in fine feather?

_____

_____

| **EXERCISE 3-14** | **Workshop on the Dictionary** |

WORKSHOP

Working with your class partner, use a dictionary to answer the following questions about words.

1. a. What is the meaning of the word *zeitgeist*?

_____

_____

   b. From what language does the word come? _____

2. a. What is a *triceratops*? _____

   b. What is the origin of the word?

   _____

3. Explain the meaning of the word *zonked* in the following sentence: Before the end of the party, Jerry was zonked.

   _____

4. Which gets eaten, *zircon* or *ziti*? _____

5. What is the origin of the word *sandwich*?

   _____

6. Who was Phillis Wheatley?

   _____

7. What does *e.g.* stand for? _____

8. Which meaning of the word *what* is used in the sentence:

   What a fool she is? _____

9. What does *SIDS* stand for? _____

10. a. How many syllables does the word *epicurean* have? _____

    b. Write out the word's phonetic spelling and pronounce the word.

    _____

    c. What kind of person is an *epicurean*?

    _____

■ ■ ■ ■ ■

OPEN SEASON: CHILDREN AS PREY

James M. Henslin

A professor of sociology at Southern Illinois University, James Henslin is the author of numerous books and articles on his areas of interest, which include the sociology of ordinary life and the homeless. The following is an excerpt from his textbook *Sociology: A Down-to-Earth Approach* (3rd ed., 1997).

Prepare

1. Identify the author and work. What do you expect the author's purpose to be?

_____

_____

2. Preread to identify the subject and make predictions. What do you expect to read about?

_____

_____

3. What do you already know about the subject?

_____

_____

_____

4. Raise two questions that you expect the article to answer.

_____

_____

_____

_____

■ ■ ■ ■ ■

1   What is childhood like in the poor nations? The answer depends primarily on who your parents are. If you are the son or daughter of rich parents, childhood can be extremely pleasant. If you are born into poverty, but living in a rural area where there is plenty to eat, life can still be good—although there likely will be no books, television, and little education. If you live in a slum, however, life can be horrible—worse even than in the slums of the highly industrialized nations. Let's take a glance at what is happening to children in the slums of Brazil.

2   Not having enough food, this you can take for granted—as well as broken homes, alcoholism, drug abuse, and a high crime rate. From your knowledge of ghettos in the highly industrialized nations, you would expect these things. What

you may not expect, however, are the brutal conditions in which Brazilian slum (*favela*) children live.

3   Sociologist Martha Huggins, who has summarized life in these slums, reports that poverty is so deep that children and adults swarm over garbage dumps to try to find enough decaying food to keep them alive. And you might be surprised to discover that in Brazil the owners of these dumps hire armed guards to keep the poor out—so they can sell the garbage for pig food. And you might be shocked to learn that poor children are systematically killed. Each year, the Brazilian police and death squads murder about 2,000 children. Some associations of shop owners even put hit men on retainer and auction victims off to the lowest bidder! The going rate is half a month's salary—figured at the low Brazilian minimum wage.

4   Life is cheap in the poor nations—but death squads for children? To understand this, we must first note that Brazil has a long history of violence. Brazil has an extremely high rate of poverty, only a tiny middle class, and is controlled by a small group of families who, under a veneer of democracy, make the country's major decisions. Hordes of homeless children, with no schools or jobs, roam the streets. To survive, they wash windshields, shine shoes, beg, and steal. These children, part of the "dangerous classes," as they are known, threaten the status quo.

5   The "respectable" classes see these children as nothing but trouble. They hurt business, for customers feel uncomfortable or intimidated when they see a group of begging children clustered in front of stores. Some shoplift; others dare to sell items in competition with the stores. With no social institutions to care for these children, one solution is to kill them. As Huggins notes, murder sends a clear message—especially if it is accompanied by ritual torture—pulling out the eyes, ripping open the chest, cutting off the genitals, raping the girls, and burning the victim's body.

6   Not all life is bad in the poor nations, but this is about as bad as it gets.

494 words

Comprehension Check

Answer the following with a, b, c, or d to indicate the phrase that best completes each statement.

_____   1. The best statement of Henslin's topic is

a. deer season.

b. problems of poor children in poor nations.

c. problems of poor children in rich nations.

d. farm life in poor nations.

_____   2. In poor countries, poverty causes the most suffering in

a. city slums.

b. the country.

c. the South.

d. in the "respectable" classes.

_____ 3. In Brazil poor children and adults
    a. search for food in dumps.
    b. are sometimes kept out of garbage dumps by guards.
    c. both a and b.
    d. eat in soup kitchens.

_____ 4. In Brazil homeless children
    a. attend school regularly.
    b. beg and steal.
    c. have jobs.
    d. live in orphanages.

_____ 5. The homeless children in Brazil are
    a. regularly killed by death squads.
    b. helped by social programs.
    c. fed in soup kitchens.
    d. sent to orphanages.

_____ 6. The homeless children of Brazil are not only killed but
    a. buried.
    b. tortured.
    c. mourned.
    d. thrown in dumps.

_____ 7. The poor, homeless children are
    a. seen as trouble by businesspeople.
    b. invited to restaurants for food handouts.
    c. encouraged to seek vocational training.
    d. aided by wealthy families.

_____ 8. Sociologist Martha Huggins notes that murdering the children sends "a clear message." That message is that
    a. the children should go away and not cause problems.
    b. the children should go to school.
    c. the children should stop searching for food.
    d. life is easy for poor children who should just stop complaining.

_____ 9. When Henslin writes that the "respectable" classes see the children as trouble, he
    a. feels sorry for the respectable classes who have to put up with the children.
    b. agrees that the children are not respectable.

   c. does not consider people who abuse children to be
      respectable, whatever their income.

   d. admires Brazil's democracy.

_____ 10. The best statement of the main idea in this passage is

   a. life is hard.

   b. poor children have difficult lives.

   c. poor urban children in poor nations suffer terribly.

   d. rural life is better than city life.

Expanding Vocabulary

*Answer with a, b, c, or d to indicate the best definition of the word in **bold** as it was used in this selection. The number in parentheses is the number of the paragraph in which the word appears.*

_____ 1. "your knowledge of **ghettos**" (2)

   a. garbage dumps

   b. sections of a city where, usually, poor
      minorities live

   c. ghosts

   d. salvage areas

_____ 2. "highly **industrialized** nations" (2)

   a. having highly developed industries

   b. highly indulgent

   c. industrious

   d. institutional

_____ 3. "**swarm** over garbage dumps" (3)

   a. swear

   b. sweat

   c. gather and move in large numbers

   d. graze

_____ 4. "find enough **decaying** food" (3)

   a. disgusting

   b. rotting

   c. decadent

   d. rousing

_____ 5. "hit men on **retainer**" (3)

    a. restitution

    b. restrictions

    c. fellowship

    d. fee paid to employee

_____ 6. "**auction** victims off" (3)

    a. audit

    b. sell to, usually, the highest bidder

    c. asylum

    d. slip

_____ 7. "a **veneer** of democracy" (4)

    a. surface appearance

    b. slipshod version

    c. venture

    d. variation

_____ 8. "**Hordes** of homeless children" (4)

    a. holdovers

    b. hoodlums

    c. throngs, crowds

    d. threats

_____ 9. "threaten the **status quo**" (4)

    a. stations

    b. senses

    c. energy level

    d. existing state of affairs

_____ 10. "uncomfortable or **intimidated**" (5)

    a. made fearful

    b. eliminated

    c. inaccessible

    d. formulated

Reflection and Discussion

1. What was your reaction to this selection? Explain how you felt.
2. How do you think the author wants readers to react?

IT'S TIME WE REJECTED THE RACIAL LITMUS TEST

Cecelie Berry

Cecelie Berry has a law degree from Harvard University and is currently a freelance writer. Her articles have been published in both newspapers and magazines. The following "My Turn" article appeared in *Newsweek* on February 7, 2000.

Prepare

1. Identify the author and the work. What do you expect the author's purpose to be?

   _____

   _____

2. Preread to identify the subject and make predictions. What do you expect to read about?

   _____

   _____

3. What do you already know about the subject?

   _____

   _____

4. Raise two questions that you expect the article to answer.

   _____

   _____

   _____

   _____

Vocabulary Alert: Do You Know These Words?

Here are eight words you need to know to read the following article with understanding.

litmus test test that uses a single indicator to reach a decision

swivel exaggerated turns

dogeared having pages with corners turned down

honky disparaging label for a white person used primarily by black persons

a mace heavy medieval war club with a round head with spikes

feign pretend

defied boldly challenged

quicksilver another term for mercury, the silvery-white element used in thermometers

■ ■ ■ ■ ■

1   I recognize the sassy swivel of the head, the rhythmic teeth sucking and finger snapping. My son Spenser has come home from kindergarten talking like he's black. Never mind that he *is* black; somehow his skin color is no longer adequate to express his racial identity. Sometimes, in diverse schools like the one he attends, black children feel pressure to "act" black. My 8-year-old son Sam asks me to tell Spenser not to use "that phony accent" around his friends. "I'll talk to him," I say with a sigh.

2   "Be yourself" seems insufficient at times like this. I know from my experience with integration that it takes a long time to own your identity. In an all-black elementary school in Cleveland, I carried around a dogeared copy of *A Little Princess* and listened to Bach on my transistor radio. Nobody paid attention. When my family moved to Shaker Heights, an affluent suburb known for its successfully integrated schools, I encountered the war over who was authentically black. I had hoped that when I raised my own children there wouldn't be any more litmus tests, that a healthy black identity could come in many styles. But the impulse to pigeonhole each other endures.

3   As I considered what to say to Spenser, I recalled my own struggles over my accent. In seventh grade, I was rehearsing a play after school when a group of black girls passed by. "You talk like a honky," their leader said. "You must think you're white." In the corner of my eye, I could see her bright yellow radio, shaped like a tennis ball, swinging like a mace. A phrase I'd found intriguing flashed through my mind: "The best defense is a good offense." I stepped forward and slapped her hard.

4   I was suspended for that fight, but I felt I deserved a medal. My true reward came later, when I heard two girls talking about me in the hallway. "I heard she's

an oreo," one said. "Don't let her hear you say that," the other replied, " 'cause she'll kick your butt!"

5   I hesitate to tell Spenser to be himself because I know it's not that simple. From integration, I learned that you have to fight for the right to be yourself, and often, your opponents have the same color skin as you. My sons will discover, as I did, that you can feign a black accent, but your loyalty will continue to be tested as long as you allow it.

6   In high school, I enhanced my reputation as an "oreo" by participating in activities that most black students didn't: advanced-placement classes, the school newspaper and the debate team. Mostly, I enjoyed being different. It put me in a unique position to challenge the casually racist assumptions of my liberal classmates. I remember a question posed by my social-studies teacher, "How many of you grew up addressing your black housekeepers by their first names?" Many students raised their hands. "And how many of you addressed white adults that way?" The hands went down. One girl moaned: "That's not racist. Everybody does that."

7   "We never addressed our housekeeper that way," I said. In the silence that followed, I could feel myself being reassessed. I'd challenged my classmate on the fairness of a privilege she had, like many whites, taken completely for granted. I had defied the unspoken understanding of how blacks in white settings are supposed to be: transparent and accommodating.

8   If black students inflicted upon each other a rigid code of "blackness," liberal whites assumed that the blacks in their midst would not dispute their right-mindedness. Being myself, I found, could be lonely. In high school, I grew weary of walking the tightrope between black and white.

9   By college, I was eating regularly at the controversial "black tables" of Harvard's Freshman Union. I talked black, walked black and dated black men. My boyfriend, an Andover graduate, commented on my transformation by saying that I had never been an oreo; I was really a "closet militant." I laughed at the phrase; it had an element of truth. I had learned that people—black or white—tend to demonize what they don't understand and can't control. So I sometimes hid the anger, ambition and self-confidence that provoked their fear. Integration taught me to have two faces: one that can get along with anybody and one that distrusts everybody.

10   I've seen both sides, now. I've "hung" white and I've "hung" black, and been stereotyped by both groups. I choose integration for my children, not out of idealism, but a pragmatic assessment of what it takes to grow up. When it comes to being yourself—and finding out who that person is—you're on your own. Experimentation is a prerequisite, trying on various accents and dress styles, mandatory. Diversity is the best laboratory for building individuality.

11   I am about to explain this to Spenser, when I see him change, like quicksilver, into someone else. Playfully, he stretches his arm out toward my face, turns his gap-toothed smile in the opposite direction and, in a tone as maddening as it is endearing, he says, "Mom, talk to the hand."

857 words

Comprehension Check

Respond to the following statements with either a T (true) or F (false).

		T	F
1.	When Berry was growing up, she called their housekeeper by her first name.	____	____
2.	When Berry was in high school, she was suspended for hitting a girl.	____	____
3.	When Berry was in high school, she acted black by taking advanced courses and working on the school newspaper.	____	____
4.	Berry writes that her 5-year-old son feels that he has to act white, even though he is black.	____	____
5.	When Berry was in college, she talked black, walked black, and dated black.	____	____
6.	Berry felt that she had to hide her self-confidence and ambition because it made others fearful.	____	____
7.	The author believes that young people need to experiment with various identities to find out who they are.	____	____
8.	Berry believes that integration does not work well as a way to finding one's identity.	____	____
9.	Berry is saddened by her son's feeling pressured to prove his black identity.	____	____
10.	The main idea of the essay is that it is time to stop stereotyping people, particularly by race—and within racial groups.	____	____

Expanding Vocabulary

Match each word in the left column with its definition in the right column by placing the correct letter in the space next to each word. When in doubt, read again the sentence in which the word appears in the essay. The number in parentheses tells you what paragraph the word appears in.

_____   diverse (1)   a. small radio

_____   transistor (2)   b. genuinely

_____   affluent (2)   c. one who fights

_____	authentically (2)	d. open to debate
_____	controversial (9)	e. having variety; different
_____	militant (9)	f. practical
_____	demonize (9)	g. requirement
_____	stereotyped (10)	h. wealthy
_____	pragmatic (10)	i. characterized by an oversimplified image
_____	assessment (10)	j. required
_____	prerequisite (10)	k. represent as evil
_____	mandatory (10)	l. evaluation

Reflection and Discussion

1. Has your experience in high school or college been similar to Berry's in any way? Do you think there is a greater acceptance of diversity today? Support your responses.
2. Berry writes that she had to hide her ambition and self-confidence. Should any person have to hide these traits? Why would some people fear these traits in others?

MAKING CONNECTIONS

1. If young people really understood how much some children around the world suffer, would they be kinder to others at their school or in their neighborhood? If you think so, how can this message get out? If you think not, why not?
2. What can young people do to encourage individuality in high school?
3. What can all of us do to help poor children everywhere? On your own or with your class partner, make a list of possible actions.

"E" CONNECTIONS

What programs exist to help children in need around the world? Find several Websites of organizations whose purpose is to help children. Of those you study, which organization seems, to you, to be especially helpful in its activities and approach? Why? There are many groups helping children in various ways. Here are four, each with its own purpose and strategies:

<http://www.children-of-the-Andes.org/>

<http://www.globalvolunteers.org>

<http://www.missingkids.com>

<http://web.mit.edu/mitpsc/programs>

WORD POWER 2
Sorting Out Words That Are Often Confused

Here is a second set of common words that sound alike but have different spellings and different meanings. Study the words and their meanings. Then select the correct word to complete each of the sentences below.

hole opening **whole** complete, entire	**rain** water that falls to earth **reign** rule **rein** to control an animal; to restrain
its possessive form of it **it's** contraction of *it is*	
miner one who works in a mine **minor** one who is under-age	**right** correct; opposite of left **rite** ritual **write** put words on paper

peace absence of fighting;
      harmony
piece part; musical arrangement
	role part played
	roll move by turning over; list
	      of names; small piece of
	      shaped bread

plain simple; not fancy **plane** aircraft; to shave wood	**scene** part of a play; place of action **seen** viewed
principal first; most important; school head **principle** basic truth; moral belief	

1. The _____ *(plain/plane)* truth is,_____*(its/it's)* time for

   _____ *(peace/piece)*.

2. Although still a _____ *(miner/minor)*, the young prince was asked

   to _____ *(rain/reign/rein)*.

3. The actress chose a big _____ *(role/roll)* so that she would be

   _____ *(scene/seen)* a lot throughout the movie.

4. The _____ *(hole/whole)* point of the exercise is to help students

   _____ *(right/rite/write)* more clearly.

5. The _____ *(principal/principle)* read the _____ *(role/roll)* and

   recognized the new students.

6. _____ (Its/It's) important to stick to your _____ (principals/principles).

7. The big _____ (hole/whole) from the collapsed mine was frightening to the _____ (miners/minors).

8. A spring _____ (right/rite/write) in Washington, D.C., is to enjoy the _____ (scene/seen) of blooming cheery trees.

9. The boys shared a _____ (role/roll), each putting butter on a small _____ (peace/piece).

10. The _____ (plain/plane) landed on the runway, _____ (its/it's) tires schreeching.

CHAPTER REVIEW

Complete each of the following statements.

1. A prefix is found at the _____ of a word.

2. A suffix is found at the _____ of a word.

3. Underline the prefixes and circle the suffixes in the following list:

able	il	non	pre	ic
ant	or	ity	bi	eer

4. Make two compound words out of each of the following:

under _____

base _____

foot _____

5. Etymology is a word's _____.

6. Divide the word *degenerate* into its syllables:

   d e g e n e r a t e

7. The dictionary abbreviation OE stands for _____.

8. Muthər is the phonetic spelling of the word _____.

9. Circle each of the following words that would be found on the dictionary page with the following guide words: imply/impressive.

   impress   impose   impulse   important

   immerse   improve   impotent   impoverish

10. The word *inconsequential* to composed of _____ prefix(s), _____

    root(s), and _____ suffix(es).

Take a Reading Road Trip!

For additional practice with your reading skills, use the Reading Road Trip CD-ROM or visit Reading Road Trip on the Web at **<http://www.ablongman.com/readingroadtrip>** (password required).

CHAPTER 4	Separating General and Specific Statements

LEARNING OBJECTIVES

■ To distinguish between general and specific words

■ To recognize levels of specificity or generality

■ To distinguish between general and specific statements

■ To understand how general and specific statements relate in writing

■ To understand long, complex sentences

PREPARE TO READ

Read and reflect on the chapter's title and objectives. Glance through the chapter, observing headings to see what is covered. Now answer these questions:

1. What do you expect to learn from this chapter?

   _____

   _____

2. What do you already know about the chapter's topic?

   _____

   _____

3. What two or three questions do you want answered from reading this chapter?

   _____

   _____

_____

_____

Suppose you came out of a fancy restaurant that provides valet parking. You hand your keys to the attendant and say, "Please bring me my car." Would the attendant be able to get your car? Probably not. Suppose you asked instead for "my VW." Now will you get your car? Possibly, but you wouldn't want to count on it. To identify your car to the attendant, you need to be more *specific*, to ask for your "1999 four-door blue Jetta."

GENERAL AND SPECIFIC STATEMENTS

General statements cover a broad range of subject matter. Specific statements narrow the focus to a smaller range. Specific statements exclude and limit possibilities. General statements are broad enough to cause confusion, raise questions, or allow for more than one way to understand the statement. If there are one hundred cars in the parking garage, and I ask simply for "my car," my statement is too general to guide you to the car I have in mind. If I name the make, model, year, color, and style of my car, I have made a much more specific statement. The following exercises will help you become more alert to general and specific words.

EXERCISE 4-1	Practice in Generalizing

For each group of specific items, write a word or phrase general enough to include the group of items. The first has been completed for you.

1. works of literature _____

    novels

    plays

    poems

    short stories

2. _____

    pens

    chalk

    pencils

    crayons

3. _____

Carter
Reagan
Bush
Clinton

4. _____

chemistry
botany
geology
physics

5. _____

roses
daffodils
pansies
tulips

6. _____

Sports Illustrated
Car and Driver
Glamour
Newsweek

7. _____

Lord of the Rings
Terminator II
A Beautiful Mind
Ice Age

8. _____

sofa
lamp
desk
table

9. _____

coaches
professors
deans
librarians

10. _____

football
baseball
tennis
basketball

| EXERCISE 4-2 | **Workshop on Specifics** |

WORKSHOP

With your class partner, think of three or four specific items that could be included under each of the more general words listed below. The first one has been started for you.

1. novels

The Scarlet Letter _____

Gone with the Wind _____

2. professional athletes

_____

_____

_____

_____

3. trees

_____

_____

_____

_____

4. college departments

_____

_____

_____

_____

5. party snacks

_____

_____

_____

_____

6. tools

_____

_____

_____

_____

7. types of music

_____

_____

_____

_____

8. recent movies

_____

_____

_____

_____

9. math courses

_____

_____

_____

_____

10. models of cars

_____

_____

_____

_____

■ LEVELS OF SPECIFICITY

In Exercise 4-1, what phrase did you use to generalize about the presidents? Did you write "former U.S. presidents"? That's a good answer, but you could be more specific and write "recent U.S. presidents." "Former U.S. presidents" is more general because it includes more items; it covers *all* presidents except the current one. We can also come up with a label that is more general than the one you probably used. We can use the label "former world leaders." The following diagram illustrates the four levels of specificity we have been discussing.

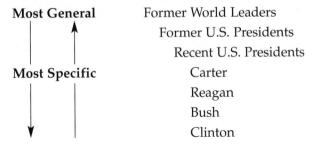

Most General   Former World Leaders

Former U.S. Presidents

Recent U.S. Presidents

Most Specific   Carter

Reagan

Bush

Clinton

Notice that the diagram shows that the four presidents are equally specific, so they are all indented with the same spacing under "Recent U.S. Presidents." We could list only one of the presidents, or more than one, but we indent them all the same to show that they are equally specific or *parallel* words.

Your question now may be, what do the words *general* and *specific* really mean? The answer is that what they mean is always *relative*. That is, a word (or phrase) is general only in relation to a more specific word (or phrase). Let's go back to cars to illustrate the point. We can be more specific by referring to a *VW Jetta*; we can be more general by creating the category *forms of transportation*. We can also be more specific than *cars* but more general than *VW Jetta*, as the following diagram illustrates.

Most General

Forms of transportation (This includes cars but also includes other forms of transportation such as motorcycles or bicycles or boats.)

Cars (This includes all cars, but no other means of transportation.)

German-made cars (This includes all cars made by German companies, but excludes cars made by companies in other countries.)

Volkswagens (This includes all cars made by one German company, but excludes all other German cars, such as BMW or Mercedes.)

Most Specific   VW Jetta (We have finally come to a specific model of car made by Volkswagen. Can you think of an even more specific category than this one?)

Now it is your turn. On the following lines, make a similar diagram, beginning with the same first two categories. You add three new items that have the same level of specificity as the last three in the previous diagram.

Most General   **Forms of transportation** _____

                        Cars _____

                        _____

                        _____

                        _____

Most Specific   _____

The following exercise will give you practice with levels of specificity.

| EXERCISE 4-3 | **Recognizing Levels of Specificity** |

Each item contains four words or phrases. Rearrange them on the lines to the right to put them in order from most general to most specific. Indent the items when you write them to show the two that are equally specific. The first one has been completed for you.

1. newspapers

   forms of communication

   television

   the media

   <u>forms of communication</u>
   <u>the media</u>
   <u>television</u>
   <u>newspapers</u>

2. basketball players

   Michael Jordan

   athletes

   Magic Johnson

3. dogs

   my cat Meffie

   cats

   pets

4. writing instruments

   pens

   #2 pencil

   pencils

5. United Airlines

   airlines

   forms of transportation

   US Air

6. Missouri River _____

   water _____

   river _____

   Colorado River _____

7. boots _____

   shoes _____

   footwear _____

   loafers _____

8. CNN _____

   MTV _____

   Cable TV Stations _____

   TV Stations _____

9. English classes _____

   American Lit. _____

   World Lit. _____

   Literature classes _____

10. Barbie _____

    dolls _____

    Ken _____

    Toys _____

You have been distinguishing between general and specific words and phrases. Words are the building blocks of sentences, and phrases are often used as headings and subheadings in books and articles, especially textbooks. Be sure to observe levels of specificity in the organization of textbook chapters.

◼ RECOGNIZING GENERAL AND SPECIFIC STATEMENTS

Words and phrases are important. But most reading involves working with sentences. Sentences are more—or less—general, just as words are. To see how sentences connect to one another in a passage, you first need to be able to recognize the sentences that are more general and those that are more specific. Remember that general statements, just like general words, *include more*, refer to broader ideas or experiences. Specific statements *exclude*; they cover a subject more narrowly. Consider the following sentences, for example.

> America has had several presidents who were great leaders.
>
> Abraham Lincoln and Franklin D. Roosevelt were great leaders.

Which is the more general statement? The first one—because it does not *specify* particular presidents. If the writer stopped after the first sentence, we would not know which presidents the writer thinks were great leaders. The second sentence is more specific. It mentions two particular presidents who, in the writer's view, were great leaders. It excludes other presidents who might be considered by some to be great leaders.

Here are two more sentences to consider.

> Attending college for the first time can be stressful.
>
> Many new students worry about making friends and doing well in their courses.

Which is the more general sentence? The first is, because it includes more possibilities. We are not told what situations or activities may cause stress, only that new students may experience it. The second sentence mentions two specific situations that make students anxious.

EXERCISE 4-4	General and Specific Sentences

Circle the letter next to the most general sentence in each of the following pairs.

1. a. Many words are created by putting together word parts.

   b. Word parts include prefixes, roots, and suffixes.

2. a. A tomato is a fruit.

   b. A fruit, by definition, is a ripened ovary of a seed-bearing plant.

3. a. For example, you are more likely to quit smoking if you work in a smoke-free office.

   b. The situations you are in can influence your behavior.

4. a. Almost 800 million Indians and about 5 million people elsewhere in the world are Hindus.

   b. Hinduism is the world's third largest religion.

5. a. Probably the greatest factor influencing how long you live is your parents' longevity.

   b. If you are born into a family in which heart disease or cancer is common, you are at greater risk for these life-threatening diseases.

6. a. An African elephant can weigh 15,000 pounds.

   b. The elephant is the largest land animal.

7. a. Children need to be cared for, houses need to be cleaned, and groceries need to be purchased.

   b. Even though more than 50 percent of mothers work outside the home, the work in the home still needs to be done.

8. a. The great thing about a good novel is that you can live more lives than one.

   b. Novels take us back in time, to many different places, and even into the future, all "trips" we may never take in person.

9. a. People who watch a great deal of television are likely to believe that violence occurs in the world more often than it actually does.

   b. Television violence scares people more often than it encourages violence.

10. a. One of the best places to find fossils is the Calvert Cliffs area along the western shore of the Chesapeake Bay.

    b. Many fossils can be found along the coastal plain of Maryland and Virginia.

■ ■ ■ ■ ■

Recognizing Levels of Specificity in Sentences

In long passages you will find sentences ranging through several levels of specificity. Authors do not write one general and then one specific sentence again and again. They move up and down a scale of three or more levels of specificity, with some sentences at the *same level* and others *more general*, or *more specific*. Here is an example.

Most General	Twenty million years ago a warm sea covered the eastern edge of Maryland and Virginia.
More Specific	The sea was home to many kinds of marine life.
Most Specific	Shellfish and corals lived on the sea floor. Sharks and primitive whales and dolphins swam above.

Here we have three levels of specificity in four statements. As you read, be alert to an author's use of levels of specificity so that you can see how the sentences connect to one another. The following exercise will give you practice.

EXERCISE 4-5	Working with Levels of Specificity in Sentences

Place the letters representing each of the sentences on the lines to the right of the sentences in order from most general to most specific. So, if c is the most general sentence, then the letter c goes on the top line, as in the first item, which has been started for you.

1. a. Children need to be cared for, houses need to be cleaned, and groceries need to be purchased.   c
   b. Even though more than 50 percent of mothers work outside the home, the work in the home still needs to be done. _____
   c. Some of the changes in today's workforce create problems for families and communities. _____

2. a. Almost 800 million Indians and about 5 million people elsewhere in the world are Hindus. _____
   b. About 1.2 million Americans are Hindu. _____
   c. Hinduism is the world's third largest religion. _____

3. a. If you add iron-rich foods to your diet, you will soon feel more energetic. _____
   b. Some foods are rich in iron; others are not. _____
   c. Meat, fish, poultry, and legumes are iron-rich foods. _____

4. a. Researchers periodically find bones of a fearsome seabird with spikes lining its bill. _____
   b. In spite of many years of searches, scientists still find surprises at Calvert Cliffs. _____
   c. The seabird would have been six feet tall with a wingspan of 18 feet. _____

5. a. Some educators argue that there is a new college crisis. _____
   b. Students are selecting schools based solely on what they can afford. _____
   c. The new crisis is an economic one. _____

6. a. Studies show that students who mark up their textbooks get better grades. _____
   b. Active reading produces the best results. _____
   c. Students who annotate their texts do better than those who only highlight. _____

7. a. The early Greeks thought the ideal life included excellence in both mental and physical activities. _____

b. The dramatist Sophocles was also a general, a diplomat, and a priest. _____

c. The complete person would be equally active as athlete, philosopher, poet, or judge. _____

8. a. When American children graduate from high school, they will have spent twice as much time watching TV as attending school. _____

b. In an average family's home, the TV set is on 11 hours a day. _____

c. U.S. citizens of all ages watch astoundingly large amounts of television. _____

9. a. In 1992 there were almost 2 million violent crimes. _____

b. The U.S. crime rate is many times higher than that of other industrialized countries. _____

c. The United States is a violent nation. _____

10. a. The power of the dramatist Sophocles lies in his compassion for his characters. _____

b. An example is his treatment of Oedipus in his play *Oedipus Rex*. _____

c. He makes Oedipus a good-hearted, although headstrong, young man. _____

SEEING CONNECTIONS BETWEEN SENTENCES IN WRITING

Sometimes writers want to express ideas—general statements. To make sure that readers understand those general statements, or to convince readers of those statements, writers illustrate and support their general ideas. To follow a writer's development of ideas, you need to separate the general from the specific. Then see how the specific sentences explain or support the general sentences. Here is an excerpt from a textbook on mass media:

Begins with a general statement: Early magazines helped create nationalism.

(1)
The first successful magazines in the United States, in the 1820s,...contributed to a sense of nationhood at a time when an American culture, distinctive from its European heritage, had not yet emerged. (2) The American people had their magazines in common. (3) The *Saturday Evening Post*, founded in

More specific: Americans had magazines in common.

Returns to general idea of nationalism, connecting the stories and national identity.

1821, carried fiction by Edgar Allan Poe, Nathaniel Hawthorne and Harriet Beecher Stowe to readers who could not afford books. (4) Their short stories and serialized novels . . . helped Americans establish a national identity.

Most specific.

John Vivian, *The Media of Mass Communication*, 3rd ed.

| **EXERCISE 4-6** | **Finding Specific Statements That Give Support** |

WORKSHOP

For each of the sentences below, write three sentences that give support. You may want to work on this exercise with your class partner.

1. *General statement:* Attending college for the first time can be stressful.
   Specific statements

   a. _____

   _____

   b. _____

   _____

   c. _____

   _____

2. *General statement:* Some situations you may be in can influence your behavior in negative ways.
   Specific statements

   a. _____

   _____

   b. _____

   _____

   c. _____

   _____

3. *General statement:* Our modern lifestyle damages the planet in many ways.
   Specific statements

   a. _____

   _____

   b. _____

   _____

   c. _____

   _____

4. *General statement:* Recent movies are filled with violence of one sort or another.
   Specific statements

   a. _____

   _____

   b. _____

   _____

   c. _____

   _____

5. *General statement:* Active readers use several strategies.
   Specific statements

   a. _____

   _____

   b. _____

   _____

   c. _____

   _____

UNDERSTANDING COMPLICATED SENTENCES

The sentences you have been working with have been relatively short. In your college study, you will find longer and more complicated sentences. Complicated sentences often combine general and specific information. To understand them, you need to find the key parts and ask yourself questions to understand how the rest adds to those key parts. To "figure out" complicated sentences, try these steps.

1. Find the main idea of each sentence by finding the subject, the verb, and the rest of the predicate. Every sentence is about someone or something—the sentence's subject. The verb tells us what the subject does/did or something about the subject's nature (is/were) or mood (thinks/feels). The rest of the parts add more details about the subject. Study the following sentences.*

Subject   Verb
a. With 850 species of birds, Costa Rica accounts for one-tenth of the world's bird population.

Subject
b. Birds (that have almost disappeared from other areas of the world, such as the endangered scarlet macaw and resplendent quetzal,) still can be seen in Costa Rica with relative ease.

c. This Central American country prides itself on its conservation and eco-tourism efforts, making it one of the best places on earth to see vast numbers of birds in their natural habitats.

Notice that the subject of the first sentence is not at the very beginning of the sentence. What does the opening phrase tell us about Costa Rica? What does Costa Rica have?

2. If necessary, to find the subject or the verb, begin by marking off less important parts of the sentence. The subject of the second sentence is "birds." Can you find the verb in the second sentence? Words that modify, or give more information about, the subject—birds—have been marked off to help you. Put two lines under the verb. Put parentheses around the less important parts of sentence three and then find and mark its subject and verb.

3. Now study the modifying words or phrases to see how they add to or qualify the information in the main parts of the sentence. You cannot ignore the rest of the sentence because you will find important information there. Look at all the words in sentence two that come between its subject and verb. What birds is this sentence about? What two kinds of birds are given as examples? Are these birds easy to see in Costa Rica?

4. Put the sentence into your own words—and into several sentences if necessary. The best way to check your understanding is to state the ideas in your

*These sentences have been adapted from an advertisement section in the March 2002 issue of *Natural History* magazine.

Keep track of the subject as you read on.

own words, using more than one sentence for long, complicated sentences. When you can say the ideas to yourself, in your own words, you are reviewing right away to be sure that you understand what you have read. Here, to practice, write what you have learned. The first sentence has been done; you do sentences (b) and (c).

a. Costa Rica has 850 types of birds. One-tenth of the birds of the world live in Costa Rica.

b. _____

_____

_____

_____

c. _____

_____

_____

_____

| EXERCISE 4-7 | **Understanding Complicated Sentences** |

*Read the clusters of sentences below and answer the questions about them.**

1. Birds are essentially reptiles specialized for flight. Their bodies contain air sacs, and their bones are hollow.

   a. Underline each sentence's subject with one line and each sentence's verb with two lines.

   b. What animals are birds like? _____

   c. How do birds differ from reptiles?

   _____

   d. Whose "bodies" is the second sentence about? _____

_____

*These sentences are taken from Curtis and Barnes, *An Invitation to Biology* (Worth, 1985) and from "A Forgotten Naturalist" (*Natural History*, May 1996).

e. Turn the two sentences into three sentences. Put the most general statement first and indent to show levels of specificity and any parallel statements.

_____

_____

_____

_____

2. The largest known dinosaur, *Brachiosaurus*, was 25 meters in length and weighed, it is estimated, almost 50 metric tons, far larger than any land animal that has succeeded it.

a. Put one line under the subject and two lines under the verb. (Hint: There are two main verbs in this sentence.)

b. Who was the largest dinosaur?_____

c. What two specifics do you learn about the largest dinosaur?

_____

d. What else do you learn about the largest dinosaur?

_____

e. On the following lines, write the four pieces of information in the sentence to show levels of specificity and any parallel statements.

_____

_____

_____

_____

3. When Titian Ramsay Peale died at the age of 85, he left behind an extraordinary body of work—journals, specimens, artifacts, memorabilia, paintings, and drawings based on travels of exploration—that documents natural history in America and abroad in the first half of the 19th century.

a. Put one line under the subject and two lines under the verb.

b. Who died? _____

c. At what age? _____

d. Who is the subject of the sentence? _____

e. What did the subject do? That is, what is the main idea of the sentence?

_____

_____

f. The subject's work grew out of what activities?

_____

g. When did the subject live?

_____

■ ■ ■ ■ ■

IN THE RAIN FOREST

Michael Scott

Michael Scott studied botany and then worked briefly for the World Wide Fund for Nature. He now concentrates on writing and lecturing about nature, and on working for conservation. The following excerpt is from *Ecology*, published in 1995.

Prepare

1. Identify the author and work. What do you expect the author's purpose to be?

_____

_____

2. Preread to identify the subject and make predictions. What do you expect to read about?

_____

_____

3. What do you already know about the subject?

_____

_____

_____

4. Raise two questions that you expect the article to answer.

_____

_____

_____

▪ ▪ ▪ ▪ ▪

1   In 1832, the great naturalist Charles Darwin was one of the first Europeans to explore the jungle of Brazil. He wrote in his journal, "Delight is a weak term to express the feelings of a naturalist who for the first time has wandered by himself in the Brazilian forest," and added that "nothing but the reality can give any idea how wonderful, how magnificent the scene is."

2   Jungles are known more correctly as tropical rain forests (they are often not as dense and tangled as the name "jungle" suggests). As Darwin had seen, they are incredibly rich in wildlife. For example, the rain forests of South America are home to 30,000 species of flowering plant, and an estimated 30 million species of insect live in the world's rain forests. Altogether, although rain forests cover less than 7 percent of the world's land surface, they hold at least half the world's species of plant and animal.

3   Much of this life lives high in the trees, hidden from anyone walking on the dark, damp forest floor. In fact, the forest is like an apartment building, with many different plants and animals living on each level. This multi-story existence of life partly explains the richness of the forest, but the real key is the climate.

Rain and Cloud

4   The name "tropical rain forest" perfectly sums up the weather that creates the forest. All rain forests lie close to the equator, where days are uniformly 12 hours long and the climate is warm throughout the year. Typically, the average temperature will only range between 73°F and 87°F throughout the year.

5   The warmth of the land heats the air above, causing it to rise and shed its moisture as rain. Most rain forests, therefore, have at least 98 inches of rainfall a year, and some have twice that amount.

6   This wet, warm world with plentiful sunlight is perfect for plant growth, so dense forest flourishes. The trees grow and flower throughout the year and have evergreen leaves.

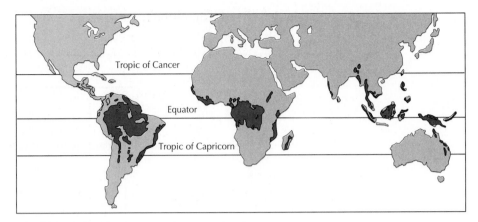

■ FIGURE 4.1

Most rain forests are found within the band of the Tropics, where the climate is constantly mild and there are long hours of sunshine.

7   The trees themselves also affect the climate. They gather water from the soil and pass it out through their leaves through the process of transpiration. This further moistens the air, so that clouds form and hang over the treetops like smoke. This blanket of cloud protects the forest from the baking daytime heat and the night-time chill of nearby desert regions, keeping temperatures within the perfect range for plant growth.

8   Rain forests slightly farther away from the equator remain just as warm, but they have a dry season of three months or more when little rain falls. Many trees shed their leaves during this dry season, and grow new leaves when the wet sea-son, or monsoon, begins—hence, the name "monsoon forest" for these areas.

9   Another type of rain forest grows on tropical mountains. It is often called "cloud forest" because clouds constantly hang over the trees, like fog.

Jungle Giants

10   The warmth, sunlight, and moisture allow trees of many varieties to flourish in the rain forest. Most are between 130 and 164 feet tall, and their leafy branches interlock to form a continuous, high-level expanse of green, called the canopy. A few taller trees, up to 196 feet tall, tower above the canopy. They are called emergents, because they emerge above the surrounding sea of green. Often there are shorter trees in the gaps beneath the canopy, creating leafy layers below.

11   All these trees rely for their survival on tiny organisms in the ground. The soil in rain forests is often surprisingly poor in nutrients. However, the mild, damp con-ditions are perfect for a variety of insects, bacteria, and fungi that live as decom-posers. These rapidly break down all the dead plant and animal material that falls to the forest floor, releasing nutrients and minerals in a form that is soon absorbed by the dense network of tree rootlets spreading through the soil. The decomposers work so well in the rain forest that a leaf will disappear completely within six weeks, compared with a year for a leaf in a European oakwood.

The Struggle for Life

12   The rain forest is the ideal environment for the growth of many different trees. As many as 200 species can be found in an area of rain forest the size of a football field. The result is fierce competition for living space.

13   This struggle is mainly confined to the first months of a tree's growth. Tree seedlings generally cannot grow in the shade of the forest floor, because there is not enough light for photosynthesis. However, when a canopy tree dies and falls to the ground, the sunlit gap in the forest floor is soon invaded by tree seedlings.

14   Some forest trees produce fruits and seeds in huge numbers. These fruits and seeds can lie on the forest floor for several years before germinating when a tree falls and sunlight reaches them. Other species produce a few large fruits with plenty of stored food to allow their seedlings to establish themselves quickly.

15   Most rain forest trees rely on animals to eat their fruits and spread their seeds. Some fruits are dropped by the animals, spreading the seeds. Others are eaten, and the seeds pass undamaged through the animal's digestive system and are passed out in its droppings....

In the Canopy

16   Most rain forest animals, however, live in the bustling world of the canopy. There flowers, fruits, and leaves provide abundant food throughout the year and the branches form a convenient, high-level walkway.

17   The fruit eaters include a wide variety of monkeys, squirrels, fruit bats, and birds. The strong beaks of parrots and macaws allow them to crack open hard nuts....

18   At any time in the rain forest some trees will have fruit or be in flower, but they will often be far apart. Animals that rely on flowers or fruit for food, therefore, need to move widely in search of a meal. This is not a problem for birds or bats that can fly, but for monkeys it means they must be very swift and agile to move through the branches. To help, some South American monkeys have a prehensile (grasping) tail, which acts like an extra arm or leg and speeds up their movement.

19   Some squirrels and lizards move between trees in another way. They have a flap of skin between their legs that allows them to glide down from high up in one tree to the trunk of a neighboring tree, saving a long climb to ground level. Some snakes can move in the same way by flattening their body and spreading their rib cage to help them glide.

20   All the apes—gibbons, chimpanzees, orangutans, and gorillas—live in the rain forest, eating leaves and fruits. Large adult male orangutans and gorillas can become so large and heavy that trees will not support their weight. They have to live on the ground, moving between clearings where there is plenty for them to eat.

21   Leaf eaters in general do not need to move far in search of food and can afford to be slow-moving, like the sloth. Similarly, many insects spend their young or larval stage grazing on a single tree. Only when they hatch into adults do they fly off to find other trees on which to lay their eggs, ensuring an abundant supply of leafy food for their young....

Forest Hunters

22 The largest predators live on the forest floor, hunting pigs, antelope, and deer. Jaguars, tigers, and smaller cats such as the ocelot are typical of these forest-floor hunters. Other cats, such as the margay and clouded leopard, are skilled climbers, well able to catch monkeys, squirrels, and birds high in the trees.

23 In the canopy, snakes lie in wait, hidden by their camouflage, to grab any animal that strays too close. Hawks and eagles fly over the canopy, ready to snatch their prey from the branches.

24 All these rain forest animals lead complex, interlocking lives, but all depend ultimately on the climate, which supports the rich plant growth. However, all of their lives are threatened by the destruction of the rain forest by humans. Unless this greed and thoughtlessness can be controlled, most of the rain forest will be destroyed within 10 to 15 years, and what Charles Darwin called the "sublime grandeur" of the rain forest will be lost forever.

1308 words

Comprehension Check

Answer the following with a, b, c, or d to indicate the phrase that best completes the statement.

_____ 1. Tropical rain forests have
  a. no rain.
  b. a lot of rain.
  c. snow.
  d. a little rain.

_____ 2. Tropical rain forests have
  a. more plants than in all the rest of the world.
  b. fewer animals than in all the rest of the world.
  c. at least half of the world's plants and animals.
  d. at least 80 percent of the world's plants and animals.

_____ 3. One reason for the many plants and animals is that they live
  a. on many levels of the rain forest.
  b. throughout the large areas of the rain forest.
  c. in conditions that are too crowded.
  d. happily together.

_____ 4. Trees contribute to the damp climate by
  a. creating rain clouds.
  b. passing water out of their leaves.
  c. not using much water.
  d. not growing very tall.

_____ 5. Rain forest temperatures keep

  a. varying from very warm to chilly.

  b. consistently cool.

  c. beastly hot.

  d. consistently warm.

_____ 6. Emergents are

  a. very tall trees that rise above the forest canopy.

  b. new trees trying to grow.

  c. squirrel-like animals that live in the trees.

  d. vines that cling to the trees.

_____ 7. Most rain forest animals live

  a. outside the forest and come in only to eat.

  b. on the forest floor where they eat decomposed leaves.

  c. on walkways throughout the forest built by humans.

  d. in the canopy where they eat flowers, fruits, and leaves.

_____ 8. Some rain forest animals

  a. must be agile to reach all the fruit.

  b. live on the forest floor and eat other animals.

  c. never eat.

  d. both a and b.

_____ 9. Human greed and thoughtlessness may

  a. destroy the rain forests in 100 years.

  b. destroy the rain forests in 10 to 15 years.

  c. destroy the predators in the rain forest.

  d. destroy the hawks and eagles that fly over the canopy.

_____ 10. The best statement of the passage's main idea is

  a. Charles Darwin traveled to the rain forests.

  b. many large trees form a canopy in the rain forest.

  c. the complex, interconnected life of the rain forest relies on the particular climate of those areas.

  d. the grandeur of the rain forests may be destroyed.

Expanding Vocabulary

Answer the following with a, b, c, or d to indicate the best definition of the word in **bold** _as it was used in the selection. The number in parentheses is the number of the paragraph in which the word appears._

_____ 1. "**naturalist** Charles Darwin" (1)

    a. natural resource

    b. nationalist

    c. one with knowledge of natural history

    d. one not altered, natural

_____ 2. "**tangled** as the name 'jungle' suggests" (2)

    a. intertwined, snarled

    b. tangible

    c. angled

    d. targeted

_____ 3. "they are **incredibly** rich" (2)

    a. incrementally

    b. artistically

    c. amazingly

    d. incurably

_____ 4. "30 million **species** of insect" (2)

    a. specific

    b. narrowest grouping of organisms

    c. swath

    d. swarm

_____ 5. "so **dense** forest flourishes" (6)

    a. tidy

    b. fragile

    c. decomposed

    d. thick

_____ 6. "so dense forest **flourishes**" (6)

    a. thrives

    b. flows

    c. flurries

    d. thrashes

_____ 7. "is soon **invaded** by tree seedlings" (13)

    a. invalidated

    b. invented

    c. inventoried

    d. intruded

_____ 8. "for several years before **germinating**" (14)

    a. gesturing

    b. gravitating

    c. beginning to gravel

    d. beginning to grow

_____ 9. "The largest **predators**" (22)

    a. premiums

    b. those who predominate

    c. those who eat other animals

    d. packages

_____ 10. "hidden by their **camouflage**" (23)

    a. native dress

    b. camp

    c. canopy

    d. natural disguise

Analyzing General and Specific Statements

1. Reread the second, third, and fourth sentences of paragraph 2. Organize some of the statements into three levels of specificity, with one level having parallel items. The first has been started for you.

    The rain forests are incredibly rich in wildlife.

    _____

    _____

    _____

2. Reread the first two sentences of paragraph 26. Organize the statements into three levels of specificity, with several parallel items at one level. (Hint: Make the first sentence into two statements.)

    _____

    _____

    _____

    _____

_____

_____

MAKING CONNECTIONS

1. Have you ever seen a tropical rain forest? If so, how did your response compare to Darwin's? If not, would you like to? Why or why not?

2. Scott uses an interesting comparison between the rain forest and an apartment building. Try to visualize the world he has described. Then, either sketch the scene you are visualizing or write a paragraph describing the sounds you would hear standing in the rain forest.

3. Are you aware of rain forest destruction? Why should we be concerned about this problem?

 ## "E" CONNECTIONS

Scott's article contains a map showing the location of rain forests. Find a specific country that contains a rain forest. Learn some key facts about that country, including the size of the rain forest and if it is being preserved or destroyed. Create your own search. The following site has good, basic introductions to countries:

<http://www.atlapedia.com>

WORD POWER 3

Sorting Out Words That Are Often Confused

Here is a third set of common words that sound alike but have different spellings and different meanings. Study the words and their meanings. Then select the correct word to complete each of the sentences below.

stationary not moving	**waist** midsection of body
stationery writing paper	**waste** trash; to use carelessly
their possessive of *they*	**weather** climatic condition
there in that place	**whether** if
they're contraction of *they are*	
	which one of a group
through finished; by way of	**witch** female sorcerer
threw past tense of *to throw*	
	who's contraction of *who is*
	whose possessive of who
to toward	
too also; excessively	**your** possessive of *you*
two the number after one	**you're** contraction of *you are*

1. _____ (Whose/Who's) going _____ (to/too/two) the movies?

2. So, _____ (your/you're) going _____ (to/too/two).

3. _____ (Their/There/They're) going _____ (to/too/two).

4. But, first _____ (their/there/they're) driving _____ (through/threw) the McDonald's.

5. A _____ (which/witch) _____ (through/threw) her potions into a pot and brewed the mix for a _____ (weak/week).

6. Are you _____ (through/threw) using my _____ (stationary/stationery)? I have some letters to write _____ (which/witch) must get mailed today.

7. _____ (Whose/Who's) car is in the driveway? _____ (Their/There/They're) lights are still on.

8. The twins were cute, but the _____ (to/too/two) were not _____ (stationary/stationery) for a minute.

9. If you _____ (waist/waste) _____ (your/you're) time, you won't get _____ (through/threw) with the work.

10. My _____ (waist/waste) is getting thick, but I'm _____ (to/too/two) _____ (weak/week) to stay on a diet.

CHAPTER REVIEW

Complete each of the following statements.

1. The terms *general* and *specific* are always_____.

2. Textbook chapter headings and subheadings reveal the chapter's organization of material into levels

_____.

3. On the lines to the right, indicate the order from most general to most specific of the following statements.

   a. Alcohol gets into the cells of the frontal lobe. _____

   b. Alcohol affects the brain in serious ways.   _____

   c. There the alcohol interferes with reasoning   _____
      and judgment.

4. To read complicated sentences, begin by finding the

   _____.

5. Write a general statement that is supported by the following specific statements.
   a. Alcohol first affects reasoning and judgment.
   b. More alcohol impairs speech and vision.
   c. Eventually alcohol affects the brain's control of movement.

   General statement: _____

   _____

Take a Reading Road Trip!

For additional practice with your reading skills, use the Reading Road Trip CD-ROM or visit Reading Road Trip on the Web at <http://www.ablongman.com/readingroadtrip> (password required).

CHAPTER 5

Moving from Topic to Main Idea

LEARNING OBJECTIVES

■ To identify a paragraph's topic

■ To understand the main idea in paragraphs

■ To separate main ideas from details

PREPARE TO READ

Read and reflect on the chapter's title and objectives stated above. Glance through the chapter, observing headings to see what is covered. Now answer these questions:

1. What do you expect to learn from this chapter?

   _____

   _____

2. What do you already know about the chapter's topic?

   _____

   _____

3. What two or three questions do you want answered from reading this chapter?

   _____

   _____

   _____

   _____

Have you ever tried to tell a joke, but your listener didn't laugh? The listener just "didn't get it." How frustrating. A joke makes a point. If we don't laugh, we have not understood the joke. (Unless it's a very bad joke!) What makes this Hagar the Horrible cartoon funny? What point or idea does the cartoon make? What key words are basic to make the joke? Briefly explain the joke in the space below the cartoon.

HAGAR THE HORRIBLE   DIK BROWNE

Source: Reprinted with special permission of King Features Syndicate

_____

_____

_____

_____

_____

To understand what we read, we need to "get the point." Details lose some of their value if we don't see the point they illustrate or support. Some readers are good at getting the general idea but have trouble remembering details. Others are good at the details, but sometimes have trouble expressing the point or main idea of the passage. If you are better at details than at the general point, then you need to make a conscious effort to work on getting the point—the main idea.

IDENTIFYING A PARAGRAPH'S TOPIC

One good way to understand the main idea of a paragraph is to start by deciding on the paragraph's *topic. A paragraph's topic is the subject being discussed.* When identifying a paragraph's topic, try to make it general enough to cover all the discussion in the paragraph. But don't make it so general that the topic label could fit many paragraphs. Remember your work in Chapter 4 on *levels of speci-*

ficity. The topic needs to be at the right level of specificity to cover the paragraph. Let's look at this paragraph.

> In the United States alone, tens of millions of workers are engaged in marketing-related jobs. They include people employed in the retailing, wholesaling, transportation, warehousing, and communications industries and those involved with marketing jobs for manufacturing, financial and other services, agricultural, mining, and other industries. About 20 million people work in retailing, 6 million in wholesaling, and 4 million in transportation.
>
> Evans and Berman, *Marketing*, 6th ed.

What is this paragraph about? The first sentence tells us that it is about people who work in marketing-related jobs. All marketing-related workers? No; only those in the United States. So, can we say that the topic is the number of jobs in retail in the United States? No, because the details tell us that "marketing-related" also includes those who work in wholesale and those who transport the goods and services. Now, is the paragraph just about the *number* of people in the United States in these jobs? Notice how many *types* of jobs are listed, as well as numbers. The writers want us to understand the types of jobs that should be included in marketing, not just the numbers of people in those jobs. The paragraph's topic: *The number and types of marketing jobs in the United States.*

Here is another paragraph to study.

> The mass media are expensive to set up and operate. The equipment and facilities require major investment. Meeting the payroll requires a bankroll. Print media must buy paper by the ton. Broadcasters have gigantic electricity bills to pump their messages through the ether.
>
> John Vivian, *The Media of Mass Communication*, 3rd ed.

Here are three possible topic statements. First, put the letters *a*, *b*, and *c* on the lines to the right to show the order from most general statement to most specific. Then circle the phrase that best states the paragraph's topic.

a. the mass media   _____

b. the costs of broadcasting   _____

c. the expenses of the mass media   _____

How did you rank them? The first (a) is the most general, and (b) is the most specific—radio and TV broadcasting are only two of the mass media. The best choice of a topic statement is (c).

 Note: The word *media* is plural. We say "the mass media *are*." The singular form of the word is *medium*. TV is one medium; newspapers are another medium.

As you work the exercises that follow, keep in mind these guidelines for topic statements.

Guidelines for Topics

1. The topic is the subject of the paragraph.
2. You can find the topic by answering the question, "What or who is this paragraph about?"
3. The topic statement should be general enough to cover all the details in the paragraph.
4. The topic statement should be specific enough to exclude other paragraphs on related topics.

EXERCISE 5-1 | **Selecting the Best Topic Statement**

After reading each paragraph, circle the letter of the best topic statement. Then briefly explain why you rejected the other two possibilities.

1. Global warming will change climate in several ways. Summer in the Northeast will be hotter and more humid. Sea levels will rise, and there may be more hurricanes, affecting homes and beaches on the Atlantic coast. Warmer temperatures in the West and Southwest will result in more snow melting in the winter and early spring and more drought in the summer.

   a. the evils of global warming
   b. the warmer temperatures from global warming
   c. some of the consequences of global warming

   Reason: _____

   _____

2. When high school students are faced with a state or national test over which even their teacher has no control, rivalries often evaporate. The class unites to slay the big, mean, three-hour-long dragon. The teacher's grades become both less intimidating and more likely to be accepted as useful information about what must be done to improve.

   Jay Mathews, "Grade Expectations"

   a. teachers and students working together to slay dragons
   b. teachers and students can work together so students test well
   c. how grades can intimidate

Reason: _____

_____

3. South Africa's cape buffalo are in the same "family" as our cattle. You might think they would be easygoing grass eaters—but you would be wrong. The cape buffalo, moving in large herds, stick close together and will quickly turn on lions—or humans—who threaten them. The buffalo will charge attacking lions again and again until the lions retreat.

a. cape buffalo

b. attacking lions and the South African buffalo

c. group defenses among the cape buffalo

Reason: _____

_____

4. Wanting each new release to make lots of money, Hollywood studios spend lots of time and money preparing their previews. The previews—called trailers—can be carefully put together to make a movie seem more, or less, packed with trills or violence or romance. One concern is to give a good sense of the movie's story without giving away too much of the plot. The trailers are usually tested on focus groups to be sure that they have just the right appeal.

a. making successful trailers

b. Hollywood movie previews

c. how to make movies sell

Reason: _____

_____

5. Costa Rica is small in size (about as big as West Virginia) but big in unusual plants and animals. Oddly shaped and brightly colored plants fill the rain forest, and tropical flowers add beauty to resorts and homes. Costa Rica has more butterflies than in Africa, and plenty of scarlet macaws, squawking green parrots, sea turtles and tree frogs, chattering monkeys, anteaters, bats, and prowling jaguars. Costa Rica's plants and animals are a feast for both eyes and ears.

a. the bright colors of animals in Costa Rica

b. the many butterflies in Costa Rica

c. the amazing variety of animal and plant life in Costa Rica

Reason: _____

_____

6. Among the most important awards given each year are the Nobel Prizes. These awards were established a century ago by Alfred Nobel. Born in 1833 in Sweden, Nobel was a great inventor. He held 355 patents for his inventions and became very wealthy from his invention of dynamite. He was "international" in spirit. He could read in six languages; he wrote dramas and poetry; he traveled the world over. The Nobel Prizes are a good reflection of the great mind and wide interests of the man who founded them.

   a. a biography of Alfred Nobel

   b. the brilliant life of the founder of the Nobel Prizes

   c. the inventor of dynamite

   Reason: _____

   _____

7. Just as the mass media help to shape our ideas of gender and relationships between men and women, so they also influence our ideas of the elderly. Like females, the elderly are underrepresented on television, in advertisements, and in the most popular magazines. Their omission implies a lack of social value. The covert message is that the elderly are of little consequence and can be safely ignored.

   James M. Henslin, *Sociology*, 2nd ed.

   a. treatment of the elderly by the mass media

   b. the mass media

   c. underrepresentation of the elderly on television

   Reason: _____

   _____

8. Minoan Crete must have seemed a fairyland to travelers in 1500 B.C. Magnificent palaces, luxurious villas, and bustling towns sprinkled the mountainous countryside. From its harbors mighty fleets set sail for the far frontiers of the world it knew—Egypt, the Near East, and Greece—laden with timber, pottery, and agricultural goods. Across the Aegean and eastern Mediterranean seas the sailing ships coursed, and they returned to Crete bearing treasures of gold, ivory, and precious stones.

   National Geographic Society, *Mysteries of the Ancient World*, 1979

   a. Crete in Minoan times

   b. the riches of Minoan Crete

   c. Minoan ships

Reason: _____

_____

9. A logical error in a program is called a **bug.** The term was coined in 1947 by Grace Hopper when she and her colleagues, after hours of careful study, discovered that the cause of the Mark II computer's failure was a moth that had apparently flown into the machine and short-circuited two wires. Ever since that day, the process of removing errors from the code has been called **debugging.**

William S. Davis, *Computers and Information Systems: An Introduction*

a. why computer-program errors are called bugs

b. Grace Hopper's discovery of bugs

c. the Mark II computer failure

Reason: _____

_____

10. It may be difficult for some of us—particularly those who may have heard or seen him only in his later years—to realize what a great instrumentalist and important American musician Louis Armstrong was. His influence is everywhere. Anyone, anywhere in the world, in any musical idiom, who writes for trumpet is inevitably influenced by what Louis Armstrong and his progeny have shown can be done with the instrument—not only in terms of extending its range, but also in the variety of mutes, half-valve effects, and the like, that have expanded its timbral potential. All of our jazz, real and popularized, is different because of him, and our popular singers of all kinds are deeply in his debt.

Joseph Machlis, *The Enjoyment of Music*

a. jazz in the United States

b. Louis Armstrong

c. Louis Armstrong's influence on music

Reason: _____

_____

EXERCISE 5-2	**Stating the Topic**

Write a topic statement for each of the paragraphs below. Follow the guidelines given previously for identifying and stating a paragraph's topic.

1. Almost all living things, ourselves included, ultimately run on sunshine. Animals get their energy eating plants or other animals that ate plants. Green plants get their energy straight from the sun, using photosynthesis to change the sun's energy into chemical energy. So, we are all "cruising" on sunlight.

   Adapted from Curt Suplee, *Everyday Science Explained*

   Topic: _____

2. The mining frontier contributed to the development of American life. In addition to adding the mined gold and silver to the country's financial wealth, it provided jobs for the miners. It also encouraged people to move to what is now Nevada, Montana, Idaho, and Colorado. And, because the miners needed services, many merchants, and teamsters, and blacksmiths, and farmers were given work for each of the mineral "rushes." The supply centers these people created grew into cities surrounded by farms and the mineral fields.

   Adapted from Robert G. Athearn, *Winning the West*, vol. 9, *American Heritage Illustrated History of the United States*

   Topic: _____

3. It is one of the most beautiful spots in the United States, and yet it's almost entirely under water. The Tortugas Ecological Reserve is a stunning coral reef filled with magnificent structures of living coral and multicolored marine life. Its 100 square miles comprise a protected area that lies hidden from normal view, largely invisible to sailors on ships and not obvious from the air. But with mask, fins, and snorkel, it is possible to peer below the water surface and see a whole new world of indescribable grandeur.

   David H. Levy, "A Hidden, Vanishing World"

   Topic: _____

4. Researchers have found a way to reduce the amount of begging for new toys by young children. It's so simple, actually. Just turn off the TV. The researchers calculated that the average 9-year-old sees about 40,000 TV ads a year and about half of those are for toys. In a study of two groups of children, they found that the group that watched much less television begged for new toys far less often than the other group—and less than they had before they watched much less TV.

   Topic: _____

5. Some people are not happy with the role of computers in both business and industry. They see computers as stealing jobs from workers. Have computers reduced available jobs? Many kinds of unskilled jobs are now performed by computers. But computers have also created new jobs. These range from data

entry to computer engineering. Computers have not so much eliminated jobs as changed the types of jobs available today.

Topic: _____

6. "I'll take a fresh cup of water, please." Well, not really. Unless an icy comet brings us some new water, we just keep recycling what we already have. Water molecules keep busy: evaporating into the atmosphere, coming back as rain, and running from streams to rivers to the oceans. Still, it's all basically the same water.

Topic: _____

7. It was in the North that Sojourner Truth gained fame and prominence. At a time when oratory was a fine art, though illiterate, she was one of the best and most famous anti-slavery speakers of her day.... With her deep bass voice, her uncanny wit and the eloquence of her speeches, she held her audiences spellbound. She wore across her chest a satin banner bearing the slogan, "Proclaim liberty throughout the land unto all the inhabitants thereof." Often lashing out in her speeches against the evils of slavery, she shamed many people who were apathetic and passive toward the institution of slavery.

George F. Jackson, *Black Women Makers of History: A Portrait*

Topic: _____

8. In close, rewarding, intimate relationships, partners or friends meet each other's needs. They disclose feelings, share confidences, and discuss practical concerns, helping each other and providing reassurance. They serve as major sources of social support and reinforce our feelings that we are important and serve a purpose in life.

Donatelle and Davis, *Access to Health*, 4th ed.

Topic: _____

9. The Amish are bound by many communal ties, including language (a dialect of German known as Pennsylvania Dutch), a distinctive style of plain dress that has remained unchanged for almost three hundred years, and church-sponsored schools. Nearly all Amish marry, and divorce is forbidden. The family is a vital ingredient in Amish life; all major events take place in the home, including weddings and worship services, even births and funerals. Most Amish children attend church schools only until the age of 13.

James M. Henslin, *Sociology*, 2nd ed.

Topic: _____

10. The baboon must cope with a wide range of behavioral interactions during its lifetime. The relationship between mother and infant, among individuals in a friendship or play group, among males in a dominance hierarchy or among those individuals that cooperate to defend their dominance rank, between the male and female in a consort pair—all produce a complex social environment.

Robert E. Ricklefs, *Ecology*, 3rd ed.

Topic: _____

IDENTIFYING MAIN IDEAS

Identifying a paragraph's topic is a good first step to understanding the point of the paragraph—but it is not exactly the same. The *topic* answers the question: What or who is the paragraph about? The **main idea** answers the question: What does the writer say about the topic? Or, what does the writer want me to understand about the topic?

Distinguishing Between Topic and Main Idea

To see the difference between topic and main idea, consider these four specifics: baseball, football, basketball, and volleyball. What is my topic? *Team sports*. Now, what main idea could I make about this topic? There are many possibilities. One might be:

> Team sports are best for youngsters because they learn cooperation and working as part of a group.

How does this main idea differ from the topic? The topic refers to a broad category. The main idea makes a point. It asserts something about the topic. That's why main ideas need to be stated in full sentences, not a word or phrase. Read and identify the topic in the following paragraph.

Another Secret Weapon: Good Manners

Good manners are back, and for a good reason. As the world becomes increasingly competitive, the gold goes to the team that shows off an extra bit of polish. The person who makes a good impression will be the one who gets the job, wins the promotion, or clinches the deal. Manners and professionalism must become second nature to anyone who wants to achieve and maintain a competitive edge.

Nichels, McHugh, and McHugh, *Understanding Business*, 5th ed.

Topic: _____

Did you chose "good manners" as the paragraph's topic? That's a good start, but you could be more precise. How about "good manners in business"? Now, what is the paragraph's main idea? What do the writers *say* about the role of good manners in business? Each sentence stresses the *importance* of good manners for business success. The writers clearly have an attitude toward their topic that they emphasize throughout. We can state the paragraph's main idea this way:

Good manners and professional behavior are essential for success in today's business world.

Writers often help readers separate topic and main idea. In many textbooks and magazine articles, writers use headings and subheadings. These make good topic statements. When writers identify the topic for you, you can focus on stating the main idea.

Writers also frequently state a paragraph's main idea in one sentence known as the *topic sentence.* (*Note:* Even though it is called a "topic" sentence, it actually states the main idea. Do not be confused by these similar terms.) Here are guidelines for identifying main ideas.

Guidelines for Identifying Main Ideas

1. **Use headings.** Headings announce the section's topic. They are usually in **bold** or *italic* type. Identifying the topic is the first step to recognizing the main idea.

2. **Ask questions.** If there are no headings, ask yourself: "What or who is this paragraph about?" to decide on the topic. Then ask, "What does the writer assert—or want me to understand—about this topic?"

3. **List specifics.** If you are having trouble generalizing, make a list of the paragraph's specifics. Then ask, "What do these specifics have in common?"

4. **Read for general statements.** The main idea is a more general statement than the specifics that support it. Underline the most general statements and then ask, "Which statement best represents the main point of the paragraph?"

5. **State the main idea as a complete sentence.** A word or phrase can state a topic, but only a complete sentence can make a point about the topic.

EXERCISE 5-3	Distinguishing among Topics, Specific Statements, and Main Ideas

For each group of statements, identify the topic, the main idea, and the more specific statement. The first one has been completed for you.

1.

topic   **Composition and Structure of Ceramics**

specific   Silicate ceramics, which include the traditional pots, dishes, and bricks, are made from aluminosilicate clay minerals.

main idea   Ceramics employ a wide variety of chemical compounds, and useful ceramic bodies are nearly always mixtures of several compounds.

   Oxtoby, Nachibrieb, and Freeman, *Chemistry: Science of Change*

2.

_____   U.S. producers lost market share to foreign producers and have used price incentives (and quality) to win it back.

_____   The auto industry is in a fierce international battle to capture and hold market share.

_____   *Achieving greater market share.*

   Nickels, McHugh, and McHugh, *Understanding Business*, 5th ed.

3.

_____   **COST-BASED PRICING**

_____   They develop elaborate cost accounting systems to measure production costs (including materials, labor, and overhead), add in some margin of profit, and come up with a price.

_____   Producers often use cost as a primary basis for setting price.

   Nickels, McHugh, and McHugh, *Understanding Business*, 5th ed.

4.

_____   **The Mass Media: Source of Powerful Symbols**

_____   Like females, the elderly are underrepresented on television, in advertisements, and in the most popular magazines.

_____   Just as the mass media help to shape our ideas of gender and relationships between men and women, so they also influence our ideas of the elderly.

   James M. Henslin, *Sociology*, 2nd ed.

5.

_____ If you wish to feel greater calmness, behave in a calm way.

_____ **Act Calm to Feel Calm**

_____ Evidence suggests that you can bring on certain emotions by behaving as if you were feeling those emotions.

Beebe and Beebe, *Public Speaking: An Audience-Centered Approach*

6.

_____ Keeping financial accounts, both for the household and the landed estate, alone required considerable financial knowledge.

_____ Role of aristocratic women in medieval society

_____ Aristocratic women had numerous opportunities for playing important roles.

Jackson J. Spielvogel, *Western Civilization*, 2nd ed., Vol. 1

7.

_____ Regular aerobic exercise is beneficial for people of all ages.

_____ Even preschoolers have been shown to receive cardiovascular benefits from planned exercise.

_____ **Exercise: Keeping Fit Is Healthy**

Wood and Wood, *The World of Psychology*, 2nd ed.

8.

_____ **Stress Management**

_____ We balance rest, relaxation, exercise, nutrition, work, school, family, finances, and social activities.

_____ Stress management consists primarily of finding balance in our lives.

Donatelle and Davis, *Access to Health*, 4th ed.

9.

_____ Developing mature relationships means being comfortable with and open to persons different from yourself.

_____ **Mature Relationships and Cultural Diversity**

_____ You need to respond to individuals in their own right, not as members of some group.

10.

_____ The role of the atmosphere

_____ The atmosphere acts like a warming blanket, preventing heat from escaping into space.

_____ The atmosphere plays an important role for all life on Earth.

Michael Scott, *Ecology*

■ ■ ■ ■ ■

Locating the Main Idea in Paragraphs

When you look for the most general statement in a paragraph, you are looking for its topic sentence. **Remember: A paragraph's topic sentence is the paragraph's main idea statement.** See if you can identify the topic sentence—the main idea—in the following paragraph. Underline the paragraph's topic sentence.

> Most experts agree that shifting away from automobiles as the primary source of transportation is the only way to reduce air pollution significantly. Many cities have taken steps in this direction by setting high parking fees, imposing bans on city driving, and establishing high road-usage tolls. Community governments should be encouraged to provide convenient, inexpensive, and easily accessible public transportation for citizens.
>
> Donatelle and Davis, *Access to Health*, 4th ed.

Did you underline the first sentence? It announces the topic (a shift from cars as the primary source of transportation) and asserts that experts believe this is the only way to reduce air pollution. The next two sentences are more specific. The first sentence is the paragraph's main idea and therefore its topic sentence.

Here is another paragraph to study. Read and then underline the topic sentence, or that part of a sentence that states the main idea.

> When we are at the highest level of consciousness, we are fully absorbed, and our thoughts are fixed on the details of our concentration, such as studying, taking an exam, learning a new skill, and so on. But at such times we are less conscious of other potentially competing stimuli, both external (the noise around us) and internal (whether we are hungry). Athletes at full concentration during a game may be oblivious to pains signaling potentially serious injuries.
>
> Wood and Wood, *The World of Psychology*, 2nd ed.

Did you underline the first sentence of this paragraph? All of the first sentence? The first part of the first sentence is the paragraph's main idea, but the examples (studying, taking an exam, learning a new skill) should not be included. Keep in mind that a paragraph's main idea may be stated in part of a sentence that also includes specific details.

Placement of the Topic Sentence

Topic sentence at the beginning. You have found, in the two paragraphs on the previous page, that the topic sentence is the first sentence. The most frequent placement (slightly more than 50 percent) of a topic sentence is as a paragraph's first sentence. To give a visual representation of this pattern, we can use the following diagram:

topic sentence (main idea)
specific detail
specific detail
specific detail

Topic sentence at the end. Another placement of the topic sentence is at the end of a paragraph. In this pattern, the topic sentence "sums up" the paragraph. Read the following paragraph and then underline the topic sentence.

> To meet their expenses, the mass media sell their product in two ways. Either they derive their income from selling a product directly to mass audiences, as do the movie, record and book industries, or they derive their income from advertisers who pay for the access to mass audiences that the media provide, as do newspapers, magazines, radio and television. In short, the mass media operate in a capitalistic environment, and, with few exceptions, they are in business to make money.
>
> John Vivian, *The Media of Mass Communication*, 3rd ed.

Did you underline the first or the last sentence in the paragraph? Although the first sentence sounds like a generalization that could be a topic sentence, the last sentence is more general. Note also the signal words "in short" that announce a summary statement: The media are in business to make money. We can represent paragraphs with topic sentences at the end with this diagram:

specific detail
specific detail
specific detail
topic sentence (main idea)

Topic sentence in the middle. Occasionally you will find the topic sentence in the middle of a paragraph. Often, with this placement, the writer begins with a transition from the previous paragraph or with specifics to catch the reader's attention. The writer then states the main idea and follows the topic sentence with more specifics. Read the following paragraph and then underline the topic sentence.

> The average American preschooler watches more than twenty-seven hours of television per week. This might not be bad if these young children understood what they were watching. But they don't. Up through ages three and four, most children are unable to distinguish fact from fantasy on TV, and remain unable to do so despite adult coaching. In the minds of young children, television is a source of entirely factual information regarding how the world works. There are no limits to their credulity. To cite one example, an Indiana school board had to issue an advisory to young children that, no, there is no such thing as Teenage Mutant Ninja Turtles. Children had been crawling down storm drains looking for them.
>
> Brandon Centerwall, "Television and Violent Crime"

This paragraph begins with a startling statistic. It then moves to the even more distressing fact that these children do not know what they are watching. The author then restates the idea positively: Children believe that what they see on TV is a picture of the real world. The writer concludes with a specific example. Which sentence is the topic sentence? Sentence 5. We can illustrate this structure with the following diagram:

specific detail
topic sentence (main idea)
specific detail

Topic sentence at the beginning and end. Finally, in some paragraphs the topic sentence appears both at the beginning and at the end. Sometimes the restatement at the end extends or enlarges on the first statement of the main idea. When you aren't sure if the first or the last sentence is the topic sentence, look at them closely to see if they are making essentially the same point. You may have a paragraph with the topic sentence at both the beginning and the end. Read the following paragraph and underline the topic sentence.

> Media-depicted violence scares far more people than it inspires to violence, and this, according to George Gerbner, a leading researcher on screen violence, leads some people to believe the world is more dangerous than it really is. Gerbner calculates that 1 in 10 television characters is involved in violence in any given week. In real life, the chances are only about 1 in 100 per *year*. People who watch a lot of television, Gerbner found, see their own chances of being involved in violence nearer the distorted television level than their local crime statistics or even their own experience would sug-

gest. It seems that television violence leads people to think they are in far greater real-life jeopardy than they really are.

John Vivian, *The Media of Mass Communication*, 3rd ed.

Which sentence did you underline? The first? The last? Both? The first sentence is a much longer statement of the idea because it includes a reference to researcher George Gerbner, but it and the last sentence make the same point. The author introduces the idea, presents specifics from Gerbner's research, and then restates Gerbner's point, agreeing that the evidence supports Gerbner's idea. We can illustrate this structure with our last diagram:

| topic sentence (main idea) |
| specific detail |
| specific detail |
| topic sentence (main idea) |

The following paragraphs will give you practice in identifying the paragraph's topic, identifying the paragraph's main idea, and locating the paragraph's topic sentence. Before you begin, you may want to review the guidelines for identifying main ideas. Here is a brief review of key terms.

1. The **topic** is the paragraph's subject. It is what the paragraph is about. The topic is usually stated in a phrase.
2. The **main idea** is what the writer wants to say about the topic. The main idea makes an assertion and so needs to be stated as a complete sentence.
3. The **topic sentence** is the sentence in a paragraph that states the paragraph's main idea. It is the most general sentence in the paragraph. It may appear anywhere in the paragraph but is often found at the beginning or at the end.
4. Some paragraphs have no stated topic sentence, so readers must infer the main idea. (More about this in Chapter 11.)

| EXERCISE 5-4 | **Identifying the Topic and Locating the Topic Sentence** |

After reading each paragraph, circle the letter next to the word or phrase that best states the paragraph's topic. Then underline the paragraph's topic sentence. The first one has been started for you.

1. Most of us pass through two stages in our attitudes toward statistical conclusions. At first we tend to accept them, and the interpretations placed on

them, uncritically. In discussion or argument, we wilt the first time somebody quotes statistics, or even asserts that he has seen some. But then we are misled so often by skillful talkers and writers who deceive us with correct facts that we come to distrust statistics entirely, and assert that "statistics can prove anything"—implying, of course, that statistics can prove nothing.

Wallis and Roberts, Statistics: A New Approach

Topic:

(a.) attitudes toward statistical conclusions

b. misleading statistics

2. It is hard to stretch a small vocabulary to make it do all the things that intelligent people require of words. It's like trying to plan a series of menus from the limited resources of a poverty-stricken, war-torn country compared to planning such a series in a prosperous, stable country. Words are one of our chief means of adjusting to all the situations of life. The better control we have over words, the more successful our adjustment is likely to be.

Bergen Evans, The Word-a-Day Vocabulary Builder

Topic:

a. control over words

b. the importance of a good vocabulary

3. Harry Truman lived seventy years of his life in Jackson County, Missouri. Think of that. He didn't come to Washington until he was fifty years old. Then he was in Washington as a senator and as Vice President and President for another twenty years. And *then* he went back to Jackson County after he left the White House for another twenty years. So it stands to reason that if you want to understand Harry Truman you'd better know a good deal about Jackson County, Missouri, and you'd better know a good deal about the people there who mattered to him, not just when he was growing up, but during his whole life.

David McCullough, "The Unexpected Harry Truman"

Topic:

a. Harry Truman's years in Washington

b. the influence of Jackson County, Missouri, on Truman

4. By the Louisiana Purchase of 1803, the United States acquired the remote reaches between the Mississippi and the Rockies, but little could be done at once to develop that territory.... Although settlement of the Western plains was delayed, the region we call the Midwest was rapidly populated between 1815 and the 1840s. Migration into this region had important

influences upon the nation as a whole. It provided a growing market for Eastern manufactures and encouraged the rising industrial areas to develop all possible means of transportation to and from the West. Both influences were accelerated when settlers moved into the treeless plains, where they required outside help to get fencing, lumber, furniture, and hardware. Once the farmer moved to where he could market his crops for cash, his dependence upon manufactures grew fast.

Robert G. Athearn, *The Frontier*, Vol. 6, *American Heritage Illustrated History of the United States*

Topic:

a. influence of Midwest settlement on manufacturing and transportation

b. settling the treeless plains

5. Galileo was the first European to make systematic observations of the heavens by means of a telescope, thereby inaugurating a new age in astronomy. He had heard of a Flemish lens grinder who had created a "spyglass" that magnified objects seen at a distance and soon constructed his own after reading about it. Instead of peering at terrestrial objects, Galileo turned his telescope to the skies and made a remarkable series of discoveries: mountains and craters on the moon, four moons revolving around Jupiter, the phases of Venus, and sunspots.

Jackson J. Spielvogel, *Western Civilization*, 2nd ed., Vol. 1

Topic:

a. Galileo's observations of the heavens

b. the impact of Galileo's use of a telescope

6. World population continues to increase. However, in some countries the rate of increase is much greater than in others. Bangladesh, for example, now has 115 million people but will have 250 million by 2025. Mexico, with a current population of 85 million, will have 150 million by 2025. These and other rapid increases in mostly poor countries are likely to result in damage to the environment, famines, and social unrest. Continued rapid population increases in poor countries are a ticking time bomb for the entire world.

Topic:

a. population increases in Bangladesh and Mexico

b. the effects of population increases on the world

7. What does a young polar bear have to cope with the first summer it is on its own? It must find food for itself in spite of its small size and limited experience. And it really needs a lot of food, not just for the moment but also

to build up a layer of blubber to use during lean times. It also faces competition from older bears who may steal the seals it manages to catch. And, it must remember a great deal about the land and coastlines and even prevailing winds. It is no wonder that the stage between being a cub with its mother and becoming a grown bear is the most difficult and dangerous period for the polar bear.

Topic:

a. the dangers facing a young polar bear

b. a young polar bear's search for food

8. The idea that the earliest Native Americans walked across a land bridge between Siberia and Alaska and then, as the glaciers receded, continued through North America south to, finally, Chile has been questioned. New evidence of human settlements in southern Peru and southern Chile predate the receding of the glaciers about 11,500 years ago. How did these people get to South America? The new thinking of scientists is that they must have been capable of making some kind of boat and also traveled on water, down the coast, drawn south by the warmer weather.

Adapted from William Booth, "Early Migrants
May Have Come by Land and Sea"

Topic:

a. how the first human populations traveled to and throughout the Americas

b. how human populations traveled on land to populate the Americas

9. From as early as 1739, foreign-language newspapers provided immigrants with news from home. German-language newspapers were among the first to appear. They dominated the ethnic-press field until World War I, but newspapers written in French, Welsh, Italian, Norwegian, Swedish, Spanish, Danish, Dutch, Bohemian, Polish, Portuguese, and Chinese all appeared during the nineteenth century.

Folkerts and Lacy, *The Media in Your Life*, 2nd ed.

Topic:

a. German-language newspapers in nineteenth century

b. Foreign-language newspapers in the United States

10. [Radio] networks provided programs at lower cost than it would have cost individual stations to produce them, which meant higher profits. From an advertiser's perspective, networks simultaneously connected homes throughout the United States. A company could reach millions of people with the same message at the same time. A modern mass medium had arrived.

Folkerts and Lacy, *The Media in Your Life*, 2nd ed.

Topic:

a. economics of network programs

b. development of radio as a mass medium

<table>
<tr><td>EXERCISE
5-5</td><td>Stating the Topic, Finding Details, and Identifying
the Topic Sentence</td></tr>
</table>

After reading each paragraph, state the paragraph's topic, list one specific detail, and then underline the paragraph's topic sentence. The first one has been started for you.

1. Even though many who "rushed" to California did not make big fortunes, the California Gold Rush had an important effect on the development of the country. In 1848, San Francisco grew from a village of 800 to more than 20,000 inhabitants. The total population of California increased from 15,000 in 1848 to 250,000 in 1852. The most important effect of the Gold Rush can be found in the number of new settlers in California.

   Robert G. Athearn, *Winning the West,* vol. 9, American Heritage
   Illustrated History of the United States

   Topic: _effect of the Gold Rush on California_

   Specific detail: _____

   _____

2. Today, most of the books that shape our culture are adapted to other media, which expands their influence. Magazine serialization put Henry Kissinger's memoirs in more hands than did the publisher of the book. More people have seen Carl Sagan on television than have read his books. Stephen King thrillers sell spectacularly, especially in paperback, but more people see the movie renditions. Books have a trickle-down effect through other media, their impact being felt even by those who cannot or do not read them. Although people are more in touch with other mass media day to day, books are the heart of creating American culture and passing it on to new generations.

   John Vivian, *The Media of Mass Communication,* 3rd ed.

   Topic: _____

   Specific detail: _____

   _____

3. Although many of the world's volcanoes erupt violently, there are others that erupt quietly. Two of these are Mauna Loa and Kilauea on the island of Hawaii. Mauna Loa, which reaches up some 30,000 feet from the floor of the Pacific, is the tallest mountain in the world and still growing. Every

few years an eruption adds more lava to it. When these volcanoes erupt, there is no explosion. Instead, long fissures, or cracks, open up. Fountains of liquid lava spurt into the air, and lava flows slowly from the fissures.

Patricia Lauber, *This Restless Earth*

Topic: _____

Specific detail: _____

_____

4. Exercise is good for us; we all know that. But recent studies are showing just how good. Apparently, getting active has an impact on such bad habits as smoking and junk-food eating. Studies show that people who start an exercise program have a higher rate of quitting smoking. They also are more likely to eat better, to choose such foods as fruits and vegetables instead of potato chips.

Topic: _____

Specific detail: _____

_____

5. In many areas of work that once belonged almost entirely to men, women have made significant inroads. For example, many women today are successful doctors and lawyers. However, women lag behind in the academic world. In the most prestigious universities, especially in the sciences, there are still few women. Additionally, the few female professors are often discriminated against in pay, office space, research grants, and promotion.

Topic: _____

Specific detail: _____

_____

6. Even if you have bought one of the newest and best equipped PCs, you do not own a supercomputer. Supercomputers are both faster and more powerful than even the best PC at your local computer store. One of the best-known names in supercomputers is Seymour Cray. His supercomputers are used by government, research institutions, and even the movie industry to crunch large numbers, to predict the weather, or to "animate" a movie.

Topic: _____

Specific detail: _____

_____

7. Leopards are the most intelligent of the cats and the finest feline athletes by far. Their superbly proportioned bodies excel at running, jumping, tree-climbing, and swimming. Pound for pound, they are remarkably strong: a 120-pound leopard has been known to haul a large giraffe calf up a tree. I have seen a leopard leap at least nine feet vertically and a good twenty-five feet or more horizontally. It would be easy to take the view that no other carnivore has reached such heights of evolutionary adaptation.

P. Jay Fetner, *The African Safari*

Topic: _____

Specific detail: _____

_____

8. Sexual harassment in the workplace is unpleasant, but there are specific steps you can take to deal with the problem. First, speak to the person harassing you. Say, specifically, that you do not like the dirty jokes or the excessive compliments or the constant touching. If the person continues, keep a record. Write down the details of time and place and what happened. Then speak to your supervisor. If your complaint is not taken seriously, find out from your human resource department what grievance procedures are available to you.

Topic: _____

Specific detail: _____

_____

9. It is interesting to consider the animals that appear in the animated film *Ice Age*. The lead "characters" in the movie—a sloth, a saber-toothed tiger, and a woolly mammoth—are presented correctly, but the rhinos in the movie should have been shown with shaggy fur. Some animals, such as horses, bison, and reindeer, lived during the Ice Age but were not included in the film. So, we can conclude that the movie correctly represents some—but not all—animals from the Ice Age period.

Topic: _____

Specific detail: _____

_____

10. Fujiyama, a volcano which is the highest mountain in Japan, . . . is associated with the national symbol of the rising sun. The shrine of the goddess

Sengen-Sama at the top is visited by many pilgrims, who venerate the rising sun. The Shinto religion holds many natural features sacred, including mountains.

Richard Cavendish, ed. *Mythology: An Illustrated Encyclopedia*

Topic: _____

Specific detail: _____

_____

■ ■ ■ ■ ■

TV LAND VERSUS REAL LIFE

Jean Folkerts and Stephen Lacy

Both authors teach in mass communication programs at their colleges, Jean Folkerts at George Washington University, and Stephen Lacy at Michigan State University. This selection is a boxed insert in their textbook, *The Media in Your Life: An Introduction to Mass Communication* (2nd ed., 2001).

Prepare

1. Identify the author and work. What do you expect the author's purpose to be?

   _____

   _____

2. Preread to identify the subject and make predictions. What do you expect to read about?

   _____

   _____

3. What do you already know about the subject?

   _____

   _____

   _____

4. Raise two questions that you expect the article to answer.

_____

_____

_____

■ ■ ■ ■ ■

1   In a research project called "Distorted Viewing: TV's Reflection of Life," _USA Today_ staffers found that "any similarity between life as depicted on television and as lived in the United States appears to be coincidental." Some of their observations include the following:

2   • _Gender is misrepresented._ Women make up only 37 percent of television characters, yet women make up more than half of the population (51 percent). Male characters dominate television shows (63 percent), although they account for less than half the population (49 percent).

3   • _Age is misrepresented._ Children, teens, and older people make up only 18 percent of television characters but represent 43 percent of U.S. society. Young adults and middle-age adults are vastly overrepresented, making up 82 percent of TV-land population but only 57 percent of the U.S. population.

4   • _Race/ethnicity is misrepresented._ Native Americans, Asians, and Hispanics are shown as only 3.4 percent of TV characters, but they make up 13 percent of U.S. society. African Americans represent 13 percent of TV characters, which is only 1 percent more than reality. Whites comprise 84 percent of TV characters, whereas 76 percent of the real-life population is white.

5   • _Physical differences are misrepresented._ Characters are rarely handicapped (1 percent compared to 17 percent in society), overweight (10 percent compared to 68 percent in society), or wear glasses (14 percent compared to 38 percent in society).

6   • _Violence is misrepresented._ TV violence—assaults and killings—appears more often in "TV Time" than in society in "real time." Of the 94 non-news programs watched, 48 showed 276 acts of violence.

7   These distortions are consistent with decades of content research that show television programming is not representative of reality. These misrepresentations of society cause serious concerns among scholars and critics of media. Research has demonstrated that people who lack experience with other social groups or with traumatic events such as crime base their opinions about society on television. In the absence of direct experience, we tend to draw on the next best thing. It is no wonder that some people are unnecessarily afraid of crime and many people do not understand the personal experiences of people from other ethnic and racial groups.

Source: "Distorted Viewing: TV's Reflection of Life,"
The Detroit News, July 22, 1993, p. 3E.
358 words

Comprehension Check

Answer with a, b, c, or d to indicate the phrase that best completes each statement.

_____ 1. The best statement of the passage's topic is
   a. distortion.
   b. television.
   c. television's representation of reality.
   d. gender misrepresentation.

_____ 2. The information in the passage is based on
   a. a research project by the authors.
   b. a research project by *USA Today* staff members.
   c. decades of research.
   d. the personal views of the authors.

_____ 3. The study revealed that gender is misrepresented because
   a. female characters dominate TV shows.
   b. females make up 51 percent of the population.
   c. males make up 49 percent of the population but 63 percent of TV characters.
   d. males dominate the population.

_____ 4. Age is misrepresented on television because
   a. young adults and middle-aged adults make up 82 percent of TV characters.
   b. older people make up 18 percent of TV characters.
   c. young adults and middle-aged adults make up 18 percent of TV characters.
   d. teens make up 82 percent of TV characters.

_____ 5. Race is distorted on TV because
   a. Native Americans make up 13 percent of TV characters.
   b. Asians are never shown on TV.
   c. Whites make up 84 percent of TV characters but only 76 percent of the real population.
   d. Hispanics are counted with Asians.

_____ 6. Few TV characters
   a. are thin.
   b. wear glasses.
   c. are young.
   d. are physically fit.

_____ 7. Violence on TV

    a. occurs more than in real life.

    b. occurs less than in real life.

    c. usually includes only minor fights.

    d. is counted only when the violence is murder.

_____ 8. TV's distortions of society

    a. should not concern us.

    b. are a problem because some people use TV as a guide to reality.

    c. bother only scholars but no one else.

    d. provide interesting variations on reality.

_____ 9. Studies show that

    a. TV viewers tend to think that crime is more widespread than it actually is.

    b. TV viewers have correct views of other ethnic groups.

    c. TV viewers have more accurate views of other racial groups.

    d. TV viewers have learned much about the real world.

_____ 10. The best statement of the passage's main idea is

    a. television and society.

    b. television shows us how the world really is.

    c. TV distorts reality in a number of significant ways.

    d. TV exaggerates crime in society.

Expanding Vocabulary

*Answer with a, b, c, or d to indicate the best definition of the word in **bold** as it was used in the selection. The number in parentheses is the number of the paragraph in which the word appears.*

_____ 1. "TV Land **versus** Real Life" (title)

    a. verso

    b. in contrast with

    c. veritable

    d. in calculation with

_____ 2. "called '**Distorted** Viewing'" (1)

    a. misleading account of

    b. meandering approach to

    c. miscellaneous

    d. divine

_____ 3. "TV's **Reflection** of Life" (1)

    a. relaxation

    b. mirroring

    c. monitoring

    d. reformation

_____ 4. "life as **depicted** on television" (1)

    a. deposited

    b. denied

    c. shown

    d. strewn

_____ 5. "appears to be **coincidental**" (1)

    a. accidental

    b. collaborated

    c. attained

    d. concocted

_____ 6. "**Gender** is misrepresented" (2)

    a. genetics

    b. gentility

    c. sex-based categories

    d. sensuality

_____ 7. "Gender is **misrepresented**" (2)

    a. misnamed

    b. fantastic

    c. falsely presented

    d. misplaced

_____ 8. "Whites **comprise** 84 percent" (4)

    a. make up

    b. compete with

    c. manipulate

    d. cancel

_____ 9. "Research has **demonstrated**" (7)

    a. dismissed

    b. clearly shown

    c. compromised

    d. demonized

_____ 10. "or with **traumatic** events" (7)
      a. trendy
      b. tranquil
      c. long-lasting emotional shock
      d. short-term aid

Analysis of Ideas and Details

1. The main idea in paragraph 2 is

    _____

2. One detail from paragraph 7 is

    _____

Reflection and Discussion

1. Are you surprised by the _USA Today_ study results? Why or why not?
2. What TV distortion is the most serious, in your view? Why?

■ ■ ■ ■ ■

"AMERICAN FAMILY": UNREALITY TV

Ruben Navarrette, Jr.

Ruben Navarrette is a journalist from Dallas, Texas. His column appeared in the _Washington Post_ on February 22, 2002.

Prepare

1. Identify the author and work. What do you expect the author's purpose to be?

    _____

    _____

2. Preread to identify the subject and make predictions. What do you expect to read about?

_____

_____

3. What do you already know about the subject?

_____

_____

_____

4. Raise two questions that you expect the article to answer.

_____

_____

_____

Vocabulary Alert: Do You Know These Words?

Here are seven words you need to know to read the following essay with understanding.

caricatures exaggerated representations for comic or stereotyping effects

stereotypes conventional, oversimplified images of a group

episode incident

clichés trite, overused expressions

salsa a spicy sauce

INS Immigration and Naturalization Service

la migra INS officers

■ ■ ■ ■ ■

1   DALLAS—Latinos in the United States are rightly hungry for more television shows that reflect their experiences, but that doesn't mean they have to swallow caricatures and stereotypes.

2   PBS's "American Family" is the first Latino-driven dramatic series on a major network in the 50-year history of broadcast television. The show's pilot episode—which was filmed two years ago while the series was under consideration by CBS—looked like quality television. The series' creator, Gregory Nava, won

praise from critics for telling the story of a Mexican American family in East Los Angeles.

3   The one concern, as I noted in an earlier column, was the cultural clichés that came across like too much salsa on the taco. Now, after seeing more episodes, one discovers that there is not much quality. And no taco. Just more salsa.

4   The plot laid it on thick: the shouting patriarch, the Mexican kids painting murals, the overuse of "Spanglish" (a blend of Spanish and English), etc. But it was a later episode that contained something really tough to stomach—the obligatory raid by the INS.

5   Watching Mexican field workers scamper through lettuce fields with *la migra* chasing them, Mexican Americans everywhere wondered: "We waited 50 years for this?"

6   Americans of Mexican descent can lay claim to a complexity that is rarely captured on film. When those folks in the entertainment industry continually portray Mexicans who live in the United States as gardeners or gang members, activists can blame it on ignorance. But what do you call it when Latino producers make the same mistake by portraying Mexican Americans as foreigners or farm workers?

7   Perhaps this depiction comes from some misguided notion of romanticism, much the way those in the middle class look back at their immigrant roots and glorify what it was like for their ancestors to arrive as strangers on U.S. shores.

8   There is nothing wrong with that. Every ethnic group is allowed its share of nostalgia for whatever images linger in the rearview mirror.

9   But where are the television shows that offer new generations of Mexican Americans a glimpse down the road?

10   Our grandfather was an immigrant farm worker. Okay, we got that. But our sister with the poor Spanish and the blue contacts—the one who spends her days at the mall—could grow up to be the first Latina on the U.S. Supreme Court.

11   Where in the prime-time television lineup is that story?

12   Not on CBS, where a new series about the high court—"First Monday"—is at least demographically accurate. The fictitious court, like the real one, has no Latinos in the brethren. The only Latino in the cast is a brash law clerk who can salsa. Naturally.

13   Generations of hard work, sacrifice and perseverance by a people who put their trust in a remarkable country that can change a family's destiny have produced untold numbers of Mexican American surgeons and judges and Rhodes scholars who, strangely enough, might go their whole lives without being involved in an INS raid.

14   It was the feeling that the creators of "American Family" had missed this reality that inspired my father's telephone call the other night. One episode was only half over when he switched the channel in disgust. He lamented the fact, after all the effort it took for Mexican Americans to leave behind dusty grape fields for something better, that the best television could do was draw a picture of where they had been—when what mattered was where they had arrived.

15   Apparently, that was also the view of a class full of Mexican American journalism students at a University of Texas campus. Their professor, who had assigned

the students the task of critiquing the series, told me that some of them called it "cheesy and unrealistic." He said that one class discussion centered around the character—played by Esai Morales—who, having spent time in prison and fathering a child out of wedlock, seems to have pulled his life together. Would I consider him a good role model?

16   Not particularly, I would say. But if it is role models that young people want, may I suggest they turn off the television. They can then take a good look at the people responsible for getting them to a point in the mainstream where hard-luck lives can be dismissed as "unrealistic"—their parents.

703 words

Comprehension Check

Answer with a, b, c, or d to indicate the phrase that best completes each statement.

_____ 1. The best statement of the essay's topic is
   a. Latinos in the United States.
   b. caricatures.
   c. treatment of Latinos on TV.
   d. families on TV.

_____ 2. The TV show "American Family" is
   a. the first TV dramatic series about Latinos.
   b. on CBS.
   c. about Gregory Nava.
   d. about the First Family.

_____ 3. The TV show's pilot episode
   a. had no salsa.
   b. was trashed by critics.
   c. avoided cultural clichés.
   d. won initial praise from critics.

_____ 4. The current series on PBS
   a. has tacos.
   b. contains cultural clichés and stereotypes.
   c. gives a realistic view of Hispanics.
   d. contains no Spanish.

_____ 5. Problems with the series include
   a. not enough "Spanglish."
   b. an INS raid.

c. no nostalgia.

d. too many Hispanics.

_____ 6. The author is distressed that Latino producers

    a. are the only ones portraying Mexicans realistically.

    b. portray Mexican Americans as foreigners or farmworkers.

    c. portray Mexican Americans only as lawyers.

    d. are making the lives of their characters too complex.

_____ 7. The author wonders if part of the explanation is

    a. a desire of this ethnic group to look back at its past.

    b. a rejection of nostalgia.

    c. ignorance on the part of Latino producers.

    d. bad acting.

_____ 8. The author thinks that "American Family"

    a. should be about the Supreme Court.

    b. fails to show the stories of the many successful Mexican Americans.

    c. should be about Hispanics shopping at the mall.

    d. fails to show the immigrant farmworker.

_____ 9. The author wants

    a. TV shows to portray Mexican Americans who are poor and struggling.

    b. young Latinos to find role models in their parents.

    c. young Latinos to see more movies.

    d. more Mexican American journalism students.

_____ 10. The best statement of the essay's main idea is

    a. "American Family" is a realistic portrayal of Mexican Americans.

    b. "American Family" is not a realistic portrayal of Mexican Americans.

    c. Mexicans should be on the Supreme Court.

    d. young people should not watch TV.

Expanding Vocabulary

*Answer with a, b, c, or d to indicate the best definition of the word in **bold** as it was used in the selection. The number in parentheses is the number of the paragraph in which the word appears.*

_____ 1. "the shouting **patriarch**" (4)
    a. male president
    b. male ruler of family or clan
    c. female governor
    d. female head of family

_____ 2. "kids painting **murals**" (4)
    a. mumbo jumbo
    b. muddles
    c. painting applied directly to a wall
    d. painting using charcoal

_____ 3. "the **obligatory** raid by the INS" (4)
    a. compulsory, expected
    b. obstinate
    c. oblivious
    d. compassionate

_____ 4. "This **depiction** comes" (7)
    a. duplicity
    b. regulation
    c. dependency
    d. representation

_____ 5. "notion of **romanticism**" (7)
    a. view that stresses strict representation of reality
    b. view that stresses emotion and imagination
    c. emphasis on government of the Romans
    d. emphasis on art of the Romans

_____ 6. "Every **ethnic** group" (8)
    a. group sharing neighborhood
    b. group sharing language, religion, and cultural heritage
    c. ethical
    d. essential

_____ 7. "its share of **nostalgia**" (8)
    a. cynicism
    b. eagerness for the future
    c. longing for the past
    d. romanticism

_____ 8. "at least **demographically** accurate" (12)

    a. democratically

    b. demonstratively

    c. statistics about TV shows

    d. statistics about human populations

_____ 9. "work, sacrifice, and **perseverance**" (13)

    a. commitment to pursuing a goal

    b. commitment to penalizing mistakes

    c. persuasion

    d. perspective

_____ 10. "**critiquing** the series" (15)

    a. crimping

    b. regulating

    c. reviewing

    d. confusing

Analysis of Ideas and Details

1. What is the main idea in paragraph 6?

_____

2. List two details from paragraph 6.

_____

Reflection and Discussion

1. Have you see any episodes of "American Family"? If so, did you find it realistic or unrealistic? If not, do you think you would watch it after having read Navarette's essay? Why or why not?

2. Are you someone who tends to romanticize the past? Why or why not?

MAKING CONNECTIONS

Plan a brief study of TV characters with your class partner. Agree on 10 TV shows to watch. Make them a mix of comedies and dramas, of one-half hour and hour-long shows, and on different channels. Divide the list between you and each watch 5 of the shows. Make a list of all the characters on the shows you watch and indicate, for each one, age, gender, and race or ethnicity. Note if any have apparent disabilities. List the jobs of the characters. (Do the white males, in general, have the best jobs?) Combine your information and see how your study compares to the information in these articles. How accurately does television mirror the world we live in?

"E" CONNECTIONS

Studies show that TV programs are filled with stereotypes. What about advertising? Conduct an online search to learn about stereotyping in print or TV ads. Search with keywords such as "advertising and stereotyping." One useful site to visit is:

<http://www.media-awareness.ca.>

WORD POWER 4

Sorting Out Acronyms and Abbreviations

We use many "shorthand" labels today, labels for organizations, for concepts, for diseases. Some of these labels are abbreviations formed by putting together the initial letters of the multiple-word label. These abbreviations are pronounced by saying each letter. Other labels are acronyms, words formed from using the initial letter of each word in the multiple-word label. The resulting "word" is pronounced as a word.

For each of the abbreviations/acronyms listed below, first write out the full name and then indicate if you pronounce each letter or if you pronounce the letters as a word. The first has been completed for you.

1. ASAP means _as soon as possible_

   It is pronounced _letter by letter_

2. NAFTA means _____

   It is pronounced _____

3. CAT scan means _____

   It is pronounced _____

4. URL means _____

   It is pronounced _____

5. FBI means _____

   It is pronounced _____

6. RSVP means _____

   It is pronounced _____

7. OSHA means _____

   It is pronounced _____

8. UN means _____

   It is pronounced _____

9. RBI means _____

   It is pronounced _____

10. INS means _____

   It is pronounced _____

11. PC means _____

   It is pronounced _____

CHAPTER REVIEW

Complete each of the following statements.

1. The _____ is the subject of the passage.

2. The _____ is what the writer asserts about the subject.

3. When a paragraph's main idea is stated, that sentence is called the

_____.

4. A paragraph's topic sentence can be found in several places, including at the

_____ or at the _____ of the paragraph.

5. Read the following paragraph, write the paragraph's topic, and then under-line the topic sentence.

> The atmosphere is still another thing that makes the earth a planet of life. We could not live without the atmosphere. It is the air we breathe: the source of oxygen for animal life and of carbon dioxide for plant life. It is the source of rain. It is the blanket that traps part of the day's heat from the sun and keeps it from escaping at night. It is the shield that protects us from the sun's ultraviolet radiation and other dangerous rays.
>
> Patricia Lauber, *This Restless Earth*

Topic: _____

Take a Reading Road Trip!

For additional practice with your reading skills, use the Reading Road Trip CD-ROM or visit Reading Road Trip on the Web at **<http://www.ablongman.com/readingroadtrip>** (password required).

LEARNING OBJECTIVES

■ To recognize main ideas in longer passages

■ To distinguish among levels of details

■ To recognize implied main ideas

■ To learn from longer passages by writing summaries

PREPARE TO READ

Read and reflect on the chapter's title and objectives stated above. Glance through the chapter, observing headings to see what is covered. Now answer these questions:

1. What do you expect to learn from this chapter?

_____

_____

2. What do you already know about the chapter's topic?

_____

_____

3. What two or three questions do you want answered from reading this chapter?

_____

_____

_____

_____

READING LONGER PASSAGES

In Chapters 4 and 5 you have studied main ideas primarily in paragraphs. Although you will rarely read just one paragraph, paragraphs are the building blocks of longer works, so understanding their structure is essential. Now let's apply what you have learned to longer passages.

Identifying Main Ideas in Longer Passages

Most articles and textbook sections develop one main idea. To observe this, read the following section from a speech textbook. Annotate as you read, focusing on finding each paragraph's main idea.

Know How You React to Stress

(1) . . . nervousness affects different people in different ways. (2) Perhaps you feel that your hands or knees shake uncontrollably as you speak in public. (3) The people sitting next to you may not ever experience those symptoms of nervousness, but they may have difficulty breathing comfortably and feel that their voices are shaky or quivery. (4) Whatever your individual responses to stress, don't wait until you are delivering a public speech to discover them.

(1) Knowing your reactions to stressful situations helps you in two ways. (2) First, this knowledge lets you predict and cope with these physical conditions. (3) Your dry mouth or sweaty palms will not surprise you; instead, you will recognize them as signs that your body is performing well under pressure. (4) Second, since you are anticipating these physical conditions, you will be better able to mask them from the audience. (5) How do you do this? (6) Try these techniques.

(1) If you know that your hands shake when you are nervous, don't hold a sheet of paper during the speech; the shaking paper will only amplify the movement of your hands and will telegraph this sign of nervousness to your audience. (2) If your voice is likely to be thin and quivery as you begin speaking, take several deep, slow breaths before you begin to speak. (3) If you get tense before speaking, try some muscle relaxation techniques:

Tense your hands, arms, and shoulders, and then slowly relax them. (4) If you get flustered before speaking, make sure you arrive on time or even a little early—never late. (5) If looking at an audience intimidates you, talk to audience members before class, and when you speak, look for friendly faces in the audience.

Grice and Skinner, *Mastering Public Speaking*, 2nd ed.

Now, look back over paragraph 1. Although sentence 1 is the most general, the paragraph's main idea is stated in sentence 4. Sentence 1 serves as an introduction. Sentences 2 and 3 contain specific examples. And then the key point is made in sentence 4: *Know how you show stress before you make a speech.*

Here are questions for you to answer about paragraph 2.

1. What sentence contains the main idea in paragraph 2?

   _____

2. What words connect to the main idea statement and give the paragraph its structure?

   _____

Finally, what about paragraph 3? It contains a list of techniques for hiding nervousness. The idea that controls all of these specifics really comes at the end of paragraph 2.

What, then, is the main idea of the entire section? If we take the section heading and add a second thought, we will have a good main idea statement:

> Know how you react to stress so that you can hide your nervousness from your audience.

Distinguishing Among Details

Some paragraphs are made up of a main idea (the topic sentence) and several statements at the same level of specificity that support the main idea. Other paragraphs contain three levels of specificity: a main idea, one or more *major details*, and one or more *minor details*, statements that are even more specific than the major details. Paragraph 2 of the preceding passage shows this pattern:

Main Idea: Knowing your reactions to stressful situations helps you in two ways.

Major Detail: First, this knowledge lets you predict and cope with these physical conditions.

Minor Detail: Your dry mouth and sweaty palms will not surprise you....

When paragraphs become parts of longer passages, we will usually find either three or (probably) four levels of specificity. When paragraph 2, which we used previously, becomes part of its longer passage, we have this pattern of levels of details:

Main Idea: Know how you react to stress so that you can hide your nervousness from your audience.	**(main idea of passage)**
Major Detail: Knowing your reactions to stressful situations helps you in two ways.	**(main idea of paragraph)**
Minor Detail: First, this knowledge lets you predict and cope with these physical conditions.	**(major detail of paragraph)**
Second Minor Detail: Your dry mouth and sweaty palms will not surprise you….	**(minor detail of paragraph)**

As you read, try to focus mostly on the passage's main ideas and major details. Minor details are quite interesting, but you want to be sure to understand the big ideas in the passage. *Exception: Some textbook sections contain many details that are important.* Often minor details in textbooks need to be learned. On the other hand, as you can see from the passage on stress in public speaking, there are details that illustrate the ways in which we get nervous. Those lowest-level minor details would not have to be learned for a test.

EXERCISE 6-1	**Distinguishing Among Details**

After reading each paragraph, underline the topic sentence and then list one major detail and one minor detail.

1. The white-out is another familiar deceptive phenomenon. It commonly occurs under an overcast sky or in a fog bank, where light traveling in one direction at a certain angle has the same flux, or strength, as light traveling at any angle in any other direction. There are no shadows. Space has no depth. There is no horizon. On foot you stumble about in missed-stairstep fashion. On a fast-moving snow machine your heart nearly stops when the bottom of the world disappears.

   Barry Lopez, *Arctic Dreams*

   Major detail: _____

   Minor detail: _____

2. A survey conducted among personnel executives by the Bureau of National Affairs concluded that the interview was the single most important factor in landing a job and that most applicants were rejected because they didn't promote themselves well during the interview. They frequently preface their

description of an experience with, "Well, I only ..." or "That wasn't a major part of my job." By such a deprecating phrase, they devalue their experience.

John P. Aigner, "Putting Your Job Interview into Rehearsal"

Major detail: _____

Minor detail: _____

3. In truth, there is no rational argument for guns in this society. This is no longer a frontier nation in which people hunt their own food. It is a crowded, overwhelmingly urban country in which letting people have access to guns is a continuing disaster. Those who want guns—whether for target shooting, hunting, or potting rattlesnakes (get a hoe)—should be subject to the same restrictions placed on gun owners in England—a nation in which liberty has survived nicely without an armed populace.

Molly Ivins, "Ban the Things. Ban Them All."

Major detail: _____

Minor detail: _____

4. Compared to Americans, the British are extremely class conscious. Like Americans the British recognize class distinctions on the basis of the type of car a person drives, or the stores that person patronizes. But the most striking characteristics of the British class system are language and education. Differences in speech have a powerful impact on British life. Accent almost always betrays class, and as soon as someone speaks, the listener is aware of that person's class—and treats him or her accordingly.

James M. Henslin, *Sociology*, 3rd ed.

Major detail: _____

Minor detail: _____

5. What used to be called "fringe" benefits for employers aren't "fringe" anymore. These benefits include paid vacations, paid sick leave, health plans, and pension plans. In 1929 such benefits made up 1.7 percent of payrolls. By 1995 these benefits made up 32.5 percent of payrolls. U.S. companies now average about $13,000 a year per employee in the costs for these benefits.

adapted from Nichels, McHugh, and McHugh,
Understanding Business, 5th ed.

Major detail: _____

Minor detail: _____

6. According to a *Time* magazine article (March 18, 2002), several studies have found a disturbing change in recent movies: more smoking. Stanton Glantz, a professor of medicine at the University of California, San Francisco, found that the 20 films making the most money in 2000 showed 50 percent more times that a character smoked than in the 20 top films of 1960. Another study, by the American Lung Association, found that 61 percent of the smoking in movies in 2001 occurred in G, PG, and PG-13 movies, movies watched by children and teens.

Major detail: _____

Minor detail: _____

7. In spite of this country's belief in free expression, the censorship, or attempts at censorship, of books remains a troubling issue. Censorship can range from keeping books out of libraries to pressuring teachers not to assign them to their classes. *Catcher in the Rye* and *Huckleberry Finn* are frequently targeted. Even the very popular Harry Potter books have been targeted for removal from libraries on the argument that they contain too much of the "occult."

Major detail: _____

Minor detail: _____

8. Some social scientists recently studied the effect of one's general appearance on how soon a person is helped at a store. One week they sent a woman shopping, badly dressed with no makeup and her hair pulled back. Another week they sent the same woman to the store in a skirt, hose, makeup, and a nice hairstyle. When the woman looked nice, she was always waited on more quickly. The conclusion: appearance matters; if you want to be treated nicely, look nice.

Major detail: _____

Minor detail: _____

9. If you are like many travelers to Scotland, you will probably drive through the Highlands, particularly around the area known as the Great Glen. In this area is the famous Loch Ness. Loch Ness has more water than any other Scottish Loch, with a depth of more than 800 feet. And, it has its own monster—according to popular legend. Because of the lake's depth, it creates a warm spot in this generally cool area. This may lead to mirages—imagined images—on the lake. Fact or mirage, the Loch Ness monster is good for the tourist business.

Major detail: _____

Minor detail: _____

10. The theory of plate tectonics tells us that the Earth's land masses rest on plates that shift. About 225 million years ago, Pangaea, the "supercontinent," began to break up. It first divided into two large land masses and then slowly took the shape we find today. About 135 million years ago, during the Jurassic Period, North America and Europe were still very close together. South America and Africa were also very close, and Australia was much closer to Africa than it is today.

Major detail: _____

Minor detail: _____

■ RECOGNIZING UNSTATED OR IMPLIED MAIN IDEAS

You have learned that paragraphs have topic sentences that state the paragraph's main idea. You know that these topic sentences often but not always come at the beginning of the paragraph. You have also learned to pay attention to essay titles and to section headings as clues to a passage's topic. These are good guides to reading—most of the time. Sometimes, though, you will read paragraphs—and longer passages, too—that do not state a main idea. When you find a paragraph that does not seem to include a topic sentence, keep these points in mind:

- The details in the paragraph are not accidental. They have been selected to develop and lead to a main idea.
- We, the readers, must infer or "figure out" the point—the main idea—that the details support.
- Inferring does not mean guessing. It means drawing a conclusion from evidence. The author wants us to understand the main idea that the details add up to.
- Asking readers to state the main idea for themselves is a way for authors to involve us more actively in the reading process. This is a good thing, so we should not be upset.

What is the best way to figure out the main idea when it is unstated? Let's read and then work with the following paragraph to answer that question.

1. Read

Some cyberslackers operate their own private online businesses during office hours. Others can hardly wait to get to work so they can play games; many spend most of their "working" hours battling virtual enemies. (One computer programmer even became a national champion playing Star-craft at work.) Some spend a good part of their "working" hours down-loading pornography. Xerox fired 40 employees for mixing their pornographic pleasure with business.

James M. Henslin, *Sociology*, 5th ed.

2. Ask questions to decide on the paragraph's topic

As you read, keep asking yourself: What is this passage about? For the para-graph you just read, here are three possible topics:

a. pornography and job loss

b. using the computer at work

c. using the office computer for nonwork activities

Which statement best states the paragraph's topic? The first possible topic statement is too narrow. It refers only to one interesting detail in the paragraph. It is not general enough to "cover" the entire paragraph. What about topic b? It seems broad enough.

3. Reflect some more on the meaning of the details in the paragraph

Let's reflect some more on the details in the paragraph and on the term *cyberslackers*. A cyberslacker is someone who is using his or her com-puter at work to do something *other than* work. And, the examples given are of workers who are playing games or doing personal business on the computer. So, topic b. above, while broad enough, is not accurate as a topic statement for the paragraph. The best statement of the paragraph's topic is c.

4. Think some more about the topic and the paragraph's details and "feel-ing" to decide on the main idea

What does the writer want us to understand about the topic? There is more than one way to state a main idea, but we do want to capture the idea that cyberslackers are not doing what they are supposed to be doing at the office. We might state the main idea this way: *The computer has led some office work-ers to use their computers to play games or engage in personal rather than company business.* This is a good beginning; we have the idea that workers are using the computer for something other than office business.

5. Make sure to write a complete sentence that *asserts* something about the details

Remember that you need a complete sentence to express an idea. Remem-ber also that the main idea should include the author's attitude about the issue, if one is implied in the language and details. Let's revise our main idea statement to include the author's attitude: *The computer has led some office workers to abuse company time, using their computers to play games or engage in personal rather than company business.*

EXERCISE 6-2	Steps in Deciding on a Paragraph's Main Idea

Practice the steps outlined above with the following paragraph to determine the paragraph's implied main idea.

1. **Read**

   When land within tropical rain forests is cleared, animals die. In the 1990s, scientists estimated that one species per hour was being wiped out because of the rate at which tropical forests were being cleared. In addition, destroying these tropical forests causes soil erosion, flooding, loss of soil quality, and therefore loss of productivity from the land. Further, carbon dioxide increases in the atmosphere because there are fewer trees to absorb it and because the usual way to clear the forest is by burning the trees down.

2. **Ask questions to decide on the paragraph's topic**

   List 3 possible statements of the paragraph's topic.

   _____

   _____

   _____

   _____

3. **Reflect some more on the meaning of the details in the paragraph**

   Think about your possible topic statements to decide on the best one. Do you have a topic statement about rain forests? If so, think again. The details are about tropical rain forests, but what do the details have in common?

   Topic statement: _____

   _____

4. **Think some more to decide on the paragraph's main idea**

   What are we to learn from these details? Does the clearing of rain forests seem like a good idea?

   Main idea: _____

   _____

   _____

5. Check to be sure that your main-idea statement is a complete sentence that makes an assertion about the topic. If necessary, revise.

Revised main idea (if necessary): _____

_____

_____

EXERCISE 6-3	Identifying the Main Idea When It Is Unstated

For each paragraph, go through the process you have just practiced to decide on the paragraph's main idea. For each paragraph list key details, write a topic statement, and then write the paragraph's main idea.

1. A recent study by the National Science Foundation examines the preparation of young women to enter science fields. They report that high school girls are taking advanced math and science classes at almost the same rate—or percentage—as boys. Also, their success rate in these courses is about the same as the boys'. The proportion of women getting Ph.D.s in science fields increased from 26 percent in 1985 to 31 percent in 1995. Still, we need to remember that two-thirds of the doctoral degrees in the sciences are awarded to men, and women are still a very small minority of the students getting undergraduate degrees in engineering and computer science.

    Details: _____

    _____

    _____

    _____

    Topic: _____

    Main idea: _____

    _____

2. In an intriguing study Joy, Kimball, and Zabrack (1986) compared three Canadian towns, one of which did not receive television transmission until 1974. The researchers tested the children before the introduction of television and two years after. The children in the town that had received tele-

vision two years earlier showed a substantial increase in aggressiveness that was not observed among the youngsters in the other two towns. They also exhibited a sharp increase in sex-role stereotyping (Kimball, 1986).

Anne-Marie Ambert, Families in the New Millennium

Details: _____

_____

_____

_____

Topic: _____

Main idea: _____

_____

3. Dan Marino, a veteran quarterback for the Miami Dolphins who currently holds most of the National Football League's records for his position, is an example of an athlete who consistently has performed at an extremely high level but is considered unsuccessful by some of the media because he has not been able to win a Super Bowl. Similarly, Frank Solich, head coach of the University of Nebraska football team, has been heavily criticized for not living up to the previous success of coach Tom Osborne, who won three national championships in 4 years. Many followers of college football actually deemed Solich unsuccessful in his first season with the Cornhuskers, despite their finishing with a 9-4 win-loss record.

Silva and Stevens, Psychological Foundations of Sport

Details: _____

_____

_____

_____

Topic: _____

Main idea: _____

_____

4. *USA Today* uses short, easily digested articles and snappy visuals. It has few home subscribers, making most of its sales from racks, especially those in airports. It provides discounted copies in large numbers to quality hotels to provide to their guests each day. In less than 10 years after its beginning in 1981, *USA Today*'s circulation was 1.6 million daily. By 2000 it was selling 2.1 million daily, beating the sales of the *Wall Street Journal.*

Adapted from John Vivian's *The Media of Mass Communications,* 6th ed.

Details: _____

_____

_____

_____

Topic: _____

Main idea: _____

_____

5. In a survey of almost 2,000 doctors in San Francisco who treated AIDS patients, slightly more than half said they had granted the request of at least one patient for assistance in dying. A survey of doctors in the state of Washington published last year in *The Journal of the American Medical Association* found that 1 in 4 said they had received a request for suicide assistance, and that a fourth of the patients who asked for help were given prescriptions for lethal drugs. In a study of cancer doctors in Michigan, nearly 1 in 5 said they had participated in assisted suicide.

David E. Rosenbaum, "Americans Want a Right to Die. Or So They Think"

Details: _____

_____

_____

_____

Topic: _____

Main idea: _____

_____

6. Baseball produces not just athletic contests but an infinity of statistics, which all true fans love to quote endlessly. Crowds at football and basketball games chant, "we're number one!" while the Dow Jones index measures daily our economic health and well-being…. Millions of pocket calculators are sold every year. The list could go on to include the body count of Vietnam and the numbers of nuclear warheads and intercontinental ballistic missiles cited as the measure of national security.

William Lutz, *Doublespeak*

Details: _____

_____

_____

_____

Topic: _____

Main idea: _____

_____

7. Computers make no distinctions based on race, class, gender, or age. Unfortunately, not all people in these categories are "plugged in" to today's computerized world. Many older people are uncomfortable with computers. Students at expensive private schools take computers for granted and probably have their own PCs at home. Students in poor inner-city and rural schools are lucky to have a turn on the schools' few outdated models. Poor households do not have computers.

Details: _____

_____

_____

_____

Topic: _____

Main idea: _____

_____

8. Nails go in crooked; glue dries and cracks; buttons pull off; zippers get stuck! How could anyone keep things orderly in the past? Today we can staple pages together or use a paper clip. Scotch tape is much less messy than glue. Then, thanks to the aerospace industry, we have Velcro to hold all kinds of things together from diapers to food on trays on the space ships. And for the office, let's not forget the handy Post-it in many sizes, shapes, and colors, one just right for your note.

Details: _____

_____

_____

_____

Topic: _____

Main idea: _____

_____

9. Should you visit Norway? In the summer you can watch sunsets at 10:30 P.M.—and sunrises at 3:00 A.M. You can see snow-covered mountains from a boat on a clear mountain fjord—a glacier-formed lake. There are numerous sea birds nesting along the coasts. Hikes in the woods near Oslo will reveal eagles, puffins, and many other species of birds, in addition to wildlife and unusual plants and flowers.

Details: _____

_____

_____

_____

Topic: _____

Main idea: _____

_____

10. The corner of the office where I work has no windows. The climate is what they call controlled. I can be there all day without knowing if it's hot or cold outside. I commute in a machine on pavement, following the directions

of red and green lights. My work is determined by a clock that remains the same through all tides, moons and seasons.

Ellen Goodman, "Content to Be in My Place"

Details: _____

_____

_____

_____

Topic: _____

Main idea: _____

_____

■ THE SUMMARY

One good way to review longer passages is to write a summary. A summary helps you prepare for class discussion and makes a useful record for future study. Also, instructors frequently assign summaries because they are good measures of how well you have understood a writer's main ideas. A *summary* is a *brief* restatement of the main ideas of a work. Make a summary shorter than the original by including only the main ideas and major details. To make the summary *your* writing, restate the main ideas in your own words. Make each summary a fair and accurate restatement of the original work.

Read the following passage and then the first summary that follows. Decide if the summary is appropriately condensed, clear, and accurate.

Social and Economic Structures in Ancient Egypt

Egyptian society had a simple structure in the Old and Middle Kingdoms;* basically, it was organized along hierarchical lines with the god-king at the top. The king was surrounded by an upper class of nobles and priests who participated in the elaborate rituals of life that surrounded the pharaoh. This ruling class ran the government and managed its own landed estates, which provided much of its wealth.

Below the upper classes were merchants and artisans. Within Egypt, merchants engaged in an active trade up and down the Nile as well as in town and village markets. Barter was the primary means by which goods were exchanged. Some merchants also engaged in international trade; they were sent by the king to Crete and Syria where they obtained wood and other

*[2700–1567 B.C.]

products. Expeditions traveled into Nubia for ivory and down the Red Sea to Punt for incense and spices. Egyptian artisans displayed unusually high standards of craftsmanship and physical beauty, while producing an incredible variety of goods: stone dishes; beautifully painted boxes made of clay; wooden furniture, especially of Lebanon cedar; gold, silver, and copper tools and containers; paper and rope made of papyrus; and linen clothes.

By far, the largest number of people in Egypt simply worked the land. In theory, the king owned all the land, but granted out portions of it to his subjects. Large sections were in the possession of nobles and the temple complexes. Moreover, although free farmers who owned their own land had once existed, by the end of the Old Kingdom, this group had disappeared. Most of the lower classes were serfs or common people bound to the land who cultivated the estates. They paid taxes in the form of crops to the king, nobles, and priests, lived in small villages or towns, and provided military service and labor for building projects.

Jackson J. Spielvogel, Western Civilization, 2nd ed., Vol. 1

Summary 1

Ancient Egyptian society had a simple structure. The king was at the top along with nobles and priests. They managed the government and their estates—which produced much wealth. The next group down the social structure were merchants and artisans. Merchants traded along the Nile. Some were international traders with countries such as Crete and Syria where they bought wood. The artisans made many beautiful things such as dishes, furniture, tools, paper, and linen clothes. Most people were in the lowest group who worked the land. They were bound to the land and had to pay the wealthy owners taxes in crops. They also lived in villages and served in the military.

We can agree that the writer of this summary has read and understood the passage. But, the summary contains some details that should be removed (that merchants bought wood), and it needs some ideas added for clarity. For example, since the Egyptian king was considered a god, he really is above the upper class; this is an important distinction. Also, some major details can be grouped into one sentence to shorten the summary. Carefully compare the two versions.

Summary 2

Ancient Egypt had a simple hierarchial social structure. The king, considered a god, was at the top, followed by wealthy nobles and priests who managed both the government and their estates. The next social class included merchants and artisans. Merchants traded along the Nile and with nearby countries. Artisans were highly skilled and also produced a great variety of goods from tools to clothes. The largest group were lowly farm laborers living in small villages and bound to the land they farmed. They were also in the military and worked on large building projects.

The second version is a clearer restatement of the original and relies less on the wording of the original. From these summaries we can set some guidelines for summary writing.

Guidelines for Summary

1. Write in your own words, except for key terms that need to be included.
2. Begin with the topic or thesis and then add supporting ideas.
3. Do not include your opinion. Be careful that your word choice does not misrepresent the meaning of the original.
4. Do not include minor details. *Do* include important definitions when appropriate.
5. Combine several ideas into one sentence as a way to condense the original.

EXERCISE 6-4 | Summary

Read the following passage, "Selling Coca-Cola in Japan," from Understanding Business *(Nichels, McHugh, and McHugh, 5th ed.). Then write a brief summary of the passage, keeping your focus on main ideas. Do not write more than five sentences.*

■ ■ ■ ■ ■

1   Coca-Cola and Pepsi are major competitors throughout the world as well as in the United States. When it comes to Japan, however, Coke is the clear winner. Why? The sale of soft drinks in Japan began on military bases after WWII. However, the rapid growth stage didn't begin until 1957 when a Japanese businessperson bought a license to manufacture Coke in Japan.

2   What made Coke a success in Japan over time was its willingness to partner with local businesspeople. Rather than simply being a multinational firm, Coke was successful in becoming a multilocal firm. That is, it found partners in various cities and worked closely with them to develop sales in those areas.

3   As many U.S. firms have found, it wasn't easy to break into the Japanese market. For one thing, Coke wanted to sell directly to retailers. That simply was not—and *is* not—the tradition in Japan. The tradition is to sell through a whole series of middlemen that control the distribution.

4   When trying to sell in a different country, it is fundamentally important to adapt as much as possible to the local culture. Coca-Cola did that by setting up in-house social clubs like those in other Japanese firms. It also helped employees buy homes with low-interest loans. Every effort was made to adjust to the tastes of the local people, including the creation of a 50 percent juice drink.

5   Relationship marketing is especially important in Japan, where negotiations take time, and patience is truly a virtue. Consensus building is the norm, and that requires more time than U.S. firms are used to investing. Nonetheless, the payoff can be extraordinary. For example, Coke has approximately 1,000,000 dealers and 700,000 vending machines in Japan as a result of its patience and care in establishing local relationships.

6   Pepsi, on the other hand, remains a minor competitor due to its failure to invest the time necessary to establish local partners and relationships. Consequently, Pepsi's market penetration in Japan continues to be hindered and shallow.

Your Summary:

_____

_____

_____

_____

_____

_____

_____

_____

_____

_____

_____

_____

■ ■ ■ ■ ■

THE PYRAMIDS

Jackson J. Spielvogel

Professor Spielvogel teaches at The Pennsylvania State University. A winner of three university-wide teaching awards, Spielvogel is the author of many articles and the book *Hitler and Nazi Germany* (1987/91) in addition to his two-volume textbook, *Western Civilization*. The following excerpt comes from Volume I of the second edition of *Western Civilization* (1994).

Prepare

1. Identify the author and work. What do you expect the author's purpose to be?

   _____

   _____

2. Preread to identify the subject and make predictions. What do you expect to read about?

   _____

   _____

3. What do you already know about the subject?

   _____

   _____

   _____

4. Raise two questions that you expect the article to answer.

   _____

   _____

   _____

■ The Sphinx
and one of the
pyramids at
Giza, Egypt

■ ■ ■ ■ ■

1   One of the great achievements of Egyptian civilization, the building of the pyramids, occurred in the time of the Old Kingdom. Pyramids were not built in isolation but as part of a larger complex dedicated to the dead, in effect, a city of the dead. The area included a large pyramid for the king's burial, smaller pyramids for his family, and mastabas, rectangular structures with flat roofs as tombs for the pharaoh's noble officials. In order to hold services for the dead, a mortuary temple was built at the eastern base of the pyramid. From this temple, a causeway led to a valley chapel about a quarter of a mile away near the river bank. This causeway served as a processional avenue for the spirits of the dead. The tombs were well prepared for their residents. The rooms were furnished and stocked with numerous supplies, including chairs, boats, chests, weapons, games, dishes, and a variety of food. The Egyptians believed that the physical body had an etheric counterpart or vital force, which they called the *ka*. If the physical body was properly preserved (hence mummification) and the tomb furnished with all the various objects of regular life, the *ka* could return and continue its life despite the death of the physical body. The pyramid was not only the king's tomb, it was also an important symbol of royal power. It could be seen for miles away as a visible reminder of the glory and might of the ruler who was a living god on earth.

2   The first pyramid was built in the third dynasty during the reign of King Djoser. The architect Imhotep, a priest of Heliopolis, the center dedicated to the sun cult, was responsible for the step pyramid at Saqqara. Beginning with Djoser, wives and immediate families of the kings were buried in pyramids, nobles and officials in mastabas.

3   The first real pyramid, in which each side was filled in to make an even surface, was constructed in the fourth dynasty around 2600 B.C. by King Snefru who built three pyramids. But the largest and most magnificent of all was built under Snefru's son Khufu. Constructed at Giza around 2540 B.C., the famous Great Pyramid covers thirteen acres, measures 756 feet at each side of its base, and stands 481 feet high. Its four sides are almost precisely oriented to the four points of the compass.

4   The building of the Great Pyramid was an enormous construction project that used limestone blocks as well as granite from Upper Egypt. The Greek historian Herodotus . . . reported the tradition that it took 100,000 Egyptians twenty years to build the great pyramid. But Herodotus wrote two thousand years after the event, and considerable controversy and speculation still surround the construction of the Great Pyramid, especially in view of the precision with which it was built. The interior included a grand gallery to the burial chamber, which was built of granite with a lidless sarcophagus for the pharaoh's body. The Great Pyramid still stands as a visible symbol of the power of Egyptian kings and the spiritual conviction that underlay Egyptian society. No pyramid built later ever matched its size or splendor.

527 words

Comprehension Check

Answer the following with a, b, c, or d to indicate the phrase that best completes each statement.

_____   1. The best statement of the passage's topic is
     a. the pyramids.
     b. the size of the pyramids.
     c. the significance of the pyramids.
     d. the tombs of kings.

_____   2. The best statement of the passage's main idea is
     a. the pyramids were tombs for kings and those close to them.
     b. the pyramids are a great achievement that tell us much about the early Egyptians.
     c. the Great Pyramid was a big construction project.
     d. the early Egyptians believed in a kind of afterlife.

_____   3. The pyramids were built as a
     a. city for kings.
     b. symbol of royal power.
     c. palace.
     d. shopping mall.

_____ 4. Egyptians believed
   a. that a dead person's vital force can continue, if provided for.
   b. that the physical body never dies.
   c. in no gods.
   d. that only this world matters.

_____ 5. The Great Pyramid was built
   a. in Greece about 756 B.C.
   b. at Heliopolis about 200 A.D.
   c. at Giza about 2500 B.C.
   d. by Herodotus.

_____ 6. The Sphinx was built at
   a. Saqqara.
   b. Heliopolis.
   c. Giza after the pyramids were destroyed.
   d. Giza near the pyramids.

_____ 7. The Great Pyramid was built of
   a. granite and limestone.
   b. adobe.
   c. red brick.
   d. wood.

_____ 8. The Great Pyramid was constructed
   a. on three acres.
   b. of three sides.
   c. with its four sides almost perfectly oriented to the four compass points.
   d. With five sides in a pentagon shape.

_____ 9. The construction of the Great Pyramid
   a. still causes controversy and speculation by scholars.
   b. took 100,000 people 20 years to build.
   c. was faulty, leading to its collapse.
   d. was not anything special.

_____ 10. The Greek historian Herodotus
   a. helped build the Great Pyramid.
   b. was only one of many who have been amazed by the pyramids.
   c. had no interest in pyramids.
   d. Was buried in one of the pyramids.

Expanding Vocabulary

Answer the following with a, b, c, or d to indicate the best definition of the word in **bold** *as it was used in the selection. The number in parentheses is the number of the paragraph in which the word appears.*

_____ 1. "a larger complex **dedicated** to the dead" (1)
   a. derived
   b. set apart for special use
   c. set down for future record
   d. descended

_____ 2. "a **mortuary** temple was built" (1)
   a. place where dead bodies are kept before burial
   b. place for mortals to worship
   c. moonstruck
   d. monumental

_____ 3. "physical body had an **etheric** counterpart" (1)
   a. ethereal
   b. ethical
   c. eternity
   d. airy or spiritual, nonmaterial

_____ 4. "in the third **dynasty**" (2)
   a. dynamic
   b. succession of rulers from the same family
   c. decade of a country's history
   d. durance

_____ 5. "was an **enormous** construction project" (4)
   a. gigantic
   b. gracious
   c. exaggerated
   d. engineered

_____ 6. "considerable **controversy** and speculation" (4)
   a. contribution
   b. contrivance
   c. dispute
   d. displeasure

_____ 7. "considerable controversy and **speculation**" (4)

    a. spectacle

    b. reflection

    c. specification

    d. reformation

_____ 8. "the **precision** with which it was built" (4)

    a. precipitous

    b. practicality

    c. exactness

    d. eventfulness

_____ 9. "a lidless **sarcophagus**" (4)

    a. satellite

    b. sardine box

    c. stone monument

    d. stone coffin

_____ 10. "the spiritual **conviction**" (4)

    a. conveyance

    b. conversion

    c. strong belief

    d. betrayal

Analysis of Main Ideas

1. What is the main idea in paragraph 4? _____

_____

2. Write a summary of the passage. Include the main idea and only major details. Use your own words and write no more than _five_ sentences.

_____

_____

_____

_____

_____

_____

_____

_____

_____

_____

For Reflection and Discussion

1. What is the most interesting new fact you learned about the Egyptian pyramids?
2. Why is this fact interesting/important to you?

■ ■ ■ ■ ■

CARAL: THE FRONTIERS OF SOCIETY
K. Kris Hirst

Archaeologist Hirst is a project archaeologist at Louis Berger Associates, co-owner of a publishing assistance firm, and past editor of the *Journal of the Iowa Archeological Society*. The following article comes from her archaeology web-site <http://archaeology.about.com>, as accessed April 25, 2002.

Prepare

1. Identify the author and work. What do you expect the author's purpose to be?

_____

_____

2. Preread to identify the subject and make predictions. What do you expect to read about?

_____

_____

3. What do you already know about the subject?

_____

_____

_____

4. Raise two questions that you expect the article to answer.

_____

_____

_____

■ ■ ■ ■ ■

1   Earlier this year, a site located on the Pacific coast of Peru which had been known for over a hundred years made headlines all over the world. The reason the site of Caral and the cluster of eighteen similarly dated sites located in the Supe Valley are so important is that together they represent the earliest known urban settlement in the Americas—nearly 4600 years before the present. By contrast, the Inca state rose during the 15th century AD; the Nazca Empire about 0 AD; Teotihuacan first flowered ca. 200 BC; Monte Albán about 500 BC; Chavín society 1000 BC; Olmec society 1200 BC. The culture represented by the Supe Valley sites dates as early as 2600 BC, when Khufu was building the pyramids at Giza.

2   Caral is a 200 acre site located on a dry terrace, fourteen miles inland from the coastline. It has a central public area with six large platform mounds arranged around a huge plaza. The largest of the mounds is 60 feet high and measures 450 × 500 feet at the base. All of these mounds were built within one or two building periods, which suggests a high level of planning, generally associated with state level societies. The public architecture has stairs, rooms, and courtyards; and three sunken plazas suggest society-wide religion. Of the 18 other sites near Caral, ten are more than 60 acres in size; all of them have similar public architecture. Crops included squash, beans, and cotton, grown in the dry desert climate with the assistance of a intricate irrigation system.

3   Excavations at Caral have been undertaken by Jonathan Haas from Chicago's Field Museum, Ruth Shady Solis of the Anthropology Museum at the Universidad Nacional Mayor de San Marcos and the Field Museum, and Winifred Creamer, Northern Illinois University and the Field. It was featured in a *Science* article in April 2001, after a long and careful investigation into the radiocarbon dates from the site. With dates like these, you have to be sure.

4   The interesting thing about Caral and the rest of the Supe Valley sites is that it illustrates the problems archaeologists have dealing with so-called "urban settlements" and "state societies." Building monumental architecture such as pyramids and irrigation canals and cities takes planning, pretty sophisticated planning, in fact. When archaeologists first stumbled across the cities of our ancient pasts, we began developing our theories of why states rise. One of the most prevalent theories was

that it takes a combination of factors to create the political climate that creates public works; and that usually means full scale agriculture, craft specialization, a writing system, ceramic production, social stratification, even metallurgy.

5   But the Supe Valley sites, and other early urban settlements such as Catalhoyuk in Turkey [6300–5500 BC], apparently arose without all of these elements. Although we can't know the political structure of the people who built Caral, we know that they did not have ceramics or metallurgy or writing. This is gonna be interesting.

494 words

Comprehension Check

Answer with a, b, c, or d to indicate the phrase that best completes each statement.

_____ 1. Caral refers to

    a. the pyramids at Giza.

    b. Khufu.

    c. a site in the Supe Valley.

    d. the Inca culture.

_____ 2. The Supe Valley site is in

    a. Mexico.

    b. Peru.

    c. Egypt.

    d. Monte Albán.

_____ 3. The Caral site

    a. is the earliest known "city" in the Americas.

    b. contains only private architecture.

    c. is a 15th-century city.

    d. is located in Brazil.

_____ 4. The best statement of the passage's topic is

    a. the frontiers.

    b. the pyramids.

    c. architecture and society.

    d. Supe Valley archaeological sites.

_____ 5. The Caral site has been dated by

    a. radiocarbon.

    b. finding records at the site.

    c. comparing architecture to other sites.

    d. the residents' skills in metallurgy.

_____ 6. The Supe Valley sites were built

    a. after the pyramids were built.

    b. as early as 2600 B.C.

    c. before the pyramids were built.

    d. as early as 1600 A.D.

_____ 7. The architecture of the Caral sites

    a. suggests no concept of community.

    b. suggests a societywide religion.

    c. is quite primitive.

    d. is small in scale.

_____ 8. Archaeologists hold the theory that

    a. public works usually appear along with writing and metallurgy.

    b. public works are not important to their study of societies.

    c. public works usually require a sophisticated society.

    d. both a and c.

_____ 9. Archaeologists are interested in and confused by Caral because

    a. it is so old.

    b. the Caral people apparently did not have writing and metallurgy.

    c. they know the political structure of Caral.

    d. the Caral people did not build monumental architecture.

_____ 10. When the author writes, "This is gonna be interesting," she implies that

    a. archaeologists are eager to learn more about the Caral site.

    b. archaeologists are happy to have learned all they need to know about the Caral site.

    c. archaeologists like to party.

    d. the Caral peoples may return and give them more information about the culture.

Expanding Vocabulary

Answer the following with a, b, c, or d to indicate the best definition of the word in **bold** _as it was used in the selection. The number in parentheses is the number of the paragraph in which the word appears._

_____ 1. "**intricate** irrigation system" (2)
   a. complex
   b. intrusive
   c. inviting
   d. commanding

_____ 2. "intricate **irrigation** system" (2)
   a. system for supplying irritants
   b. system for supplying water
   c. irreproachable
   d. irritable

_____ 3. "**Excavations** at Caral" (3)
   a. expenditures
   b. extravagances
   c. unearthing
   d. unnerving

_____ 4. "the **radiocarbon** dates" (3)
   a. use of carbon 14 for dating
   b. use of carbon in radios
   c. radioactive
   d. radiology

_____ 5. "Building **monumental** architecture" (4)
   a. makeshift
   b. masculine
   c. impressively large and significant
   d. unusually simple and plain

_____ 6. "most **prevalent** theories" (4)
   a. preventative
   b. widely held
   c. wildly illogical
   d. primitive

_____ 7. "craft **specialization**" (4)
   a. specifics
   b. specification
   c. division into areas of expertise
   d. division by places found

_____ 8. "**ceramic** production" (4)

     a. fired metals

     b. ceremonial

     c. fired clay

     d. centralized

_____ 9. "social **stratification**" (4)

     a. stratosphere

     b. stratagem

     c. separate levels

     d. strain

_____ 10. "even **metallurgy**" (4)

     a. science of creating useful objects from metals

     b. science of dealing with the weather

     c. metamorphosis

     d. methodology

_____ 11. "This is **gonna** be" (5)

     a. a goner

     b. goggle

     c. going to

     d. gotcha

Analysis of Ideas and Details

1. Why does the author provide the details in paragraph 3? What does she want to accomplish?

2. In paragraph 2, Hirst lists specific crops grown at Caral. What is the idea that these details illustrate and support?

3. Hirst states that the discovery of this new site is important because it is so old. She implies a second reason for the site's importance. What is the implied reason?

_____

_____

MAKING CONNECTIONS

1. Nonspecialists can often go on archaeological "digs." Would you like to do this? Why or why not?

WORKSHOP

2. Archaeologists have uncovered and given us information about many societies that have disappeared. What kinds of knowledge and training would be helpful to archaeologists? On your own, or with your class partner, make a list of courses or areas of study that you think archaeologists would need.

WORKSHOP

3. We continue to build monuments today. What are some of the reasons we build monuments? What do they tell others about our society? On your own, or with your class partner, reflect on these questions. List as many reasons as you can for building monuments.

"E" CONNECTIONS

Learn more about the Pyramids of Egypt or about other monoliths, large stones having significance. Select one site of monoliths that interests you and be able to describe it to classmates. You may want to begin your search at this useful introductory site:

<http://www.crystalinks.com/monolith.html>.

WORD POWER 5

Sorting Out Acronyms and Abbreviations

Here is a second set of acronyms and abbreviations, "shorthand" labels that we use for organizations, for concepts, for diseases, and more. Some of these labels are abbreviations formed by putting together the initial letters of the multiple-word label. These abbreviations are pronounced by saying each letter. Other labels, acronyms, words formed from using the initial letter of each word in the multiple-word label. The resulting "word" is pronounced as a word.

For each of the abbreviations/acronyms listed below, first write out the full name and then indicate if you pronounce each letter or if you pronounce the letters as a word. The first has been completed for you.

1. IRS means _Internal Revenue Service_____

   It is pronounced _letter by letter_____

2. UFO means _____

   It is pronounced _____

3. NATO means _____

   It is pronounced _____

4. IQ means _____

   It is pronounced _____

5. EPA means _____

   It is pronounced _____

6. PBS means _____

   It is pronounced _____

7. Ph.D. means _____

   It is pronounced _____

8. HUD means _____

   It is pronounced _____

9. EKG means _____

   It is pronounced _____

10. MPH means _____

   It is pronounced _____

11. OPEC means _____

   It is pronounced _____

CHAPTER REVIEW

1. When a paragraph is part of a longer passage, its main idea becomes a

   _____

2. Complete the possible pattern of main idea and details for a longer passage:

   _____

   _____

   _____

   _____

3. A summary is a brief _____

   _____

4. To write a good summary, leave out _____

   and _____.

5. When reading a paragraph with an implied main idea, think carefully about

   the paragraph's _____ to determine the main idea.

Take a Reading Road Trip!

For additional practice with your reading skills, use the Reading Road Trip CD-ROM or visit Reading Road Trip on the Web at <http://www.ablongman.com/readingroadtrip> (password required).

CHAPTER 7

Recognizing Patterns and the Use of Signal Words

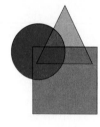

LEARNING OBJECTIVES

■ To understand the primary structures or patterns authors use to give order to their writing

■ Specifically, to recognize the patterns of listing/addition, examples, and comparison/contrast

■ To recognize the words that signal each pattern or structure

■ To annotate each pattern as you read

■ PREPARE TO READ

Read and reflect on the chapter's title and objectives. Glance through the chapter, observing headings to see what is covered. Now answer these questions:

1. What do you expect to learn from this chapter?

_____

_____

2. What do you already know about the chapter's topic?

_____

_____

3. What two or three questions do you want answered from reading this chapter?

_____

_____

In the last two chapters you learned to distinguish between a work's main idea and the details that explain and support the main idea. The pattern of main idea plus details is the primary structure of good writing.

Writers also use other structures, though, that you want to recognize when you read. Why? You can use your knowledge of patterns or structures to improve reading. Identifying a work's structure helps readers understand the writer's purpose and remember the writer's ideas. We remember better when we see how the "pieces" fit together and give meaning to the entire work.

We also read better when we can predict what's coming next. Recognizing a work's structure or strategy lets us anticipate what's coming and where, in general, the work is headed. For example, when we read that World War II was similar to World War I, we can predict a comparison structure as the best pattern to achieve the writer's purpose.

Recognizing patterns is so important to good reading that this text gives three chapters to explanation and practice for you. As you study, keep three points in mind:

■ Most writers reveal their patterns by using words or phrases called *signal words* or *transition words*. The signal words usually used to develop each pattern will be listed; learn to recognize them.

■ Recognizing a structure is a means to an end—better comprehension—not an end in itself. So in the exercises you will need to do more than name the strategy used. You will also need to show that you have understood the passage.

■ Writers often combine patterns. You will need to think about the most important pattern as the best guide to the writer's purpose.

■ LISTING/ADDITION

One of the most frequently used patterns to explain a subject is the list. Sometimes items are presented in an actual list: indented and preceded by a numeral (1, 2, 3, etc.) or by bullets (•, •, •, etc.). You have seen such lists in this text. Lists are also presented within paragraphs, usually in one of three ways:

1. All of the items are listed in the first sentence and then each is discussed, one at a time, in the following sentences.

2. One item at a time is discussed, with each new item introduced with a signal word such as *second, in addition,* or *also*.

3. An opening sentence announces the number of items to be discussed and then each one is explained in turn.

Usually, a list tells us that all the items are equally important. Sometimes the author signals that the last item in the list is the most important. If we read: "Finally, and most important, salespeople must remember . . . ," then we know that the last item is more significant than the others.* When you are studying lists in a textbook, you probably need to learn all of the items.

Signal Words for Listing/Addition

Here are the most common signal words to develop lists.

also	first	last	next
and	furthermore	likewise	second
another	in addition	moreover	third
finally			

Basic Structure for Listing/Addition

The simple listing pattern has this shape.

How to Annotate Listings

Begin by underlining each paragraph's topic sentence. When the list pattern is used, then each item in the list is a major detail to be noted. Circle signal words and use numbers in the margin to indicate each item in the list. Here is an example:

① Basically, human beings have affected the environment in three ways. The (first) factor is the natural growth of the human species. . . . The (second) element ② is the human appetite for natural materials. Coupled with increased population, this need for natural resources has reached a critical point where the depletion of certain goods is a distinct possibility. The (third) element is the ③ rapid development of technology, which generally has resulted in advances in the standard of living, but often at the cost of the natural environment.

Curran and Renzetti, *Social Problems*, 3rd ed.

---

*This variation of the listing pattern is usually called *addition*. As you can see, the two patterns are quite similar. The signal words are also much the same.

Notice that this paragraph announces the number of items in the opening sentence: There are *three* ways we have affected the environment. The first sentence is the topic sentence, so it has been underlined. The key words for each item have been underlined, the signal words circled, and the items numbered in the margin.

EXERCISE 7-1	**Recognizing and Annotating Listing/Addition**

Read and annotate each of the following passages. Then complete the exercise that follows each passage.

I. Ordinary "exercisers," not just "athletes," need to take advantage of the benefits of stretching. Stretching will make you more flexible. Relaxation is another benefit of stretching. Slowly stretch each part of your body and feel the tension go away. A third benefit of stretching is the relief of muscle cramps you may get from fatigue or spending a lot of time in one position. Finally, stretching after exercise will help prevent soreness.

   1. What is the paragraph's topic sentence? Underline it.

   2. Briefly state each of the items listed in the paragraph.

   _____

   _____

   _____

   _____

   3. List the signal words you find in the paragraph.

   _____

II. A number of risks for cardiovascular disease cannot be controlled by the individual. First, there is age. Those over 65 increase their risk of heart disease. Heredity is also a significant factor that can't be changed. If you are related to someone who had heart disease before the age of 65, you are also at risk. Another important factor is race. African-American males have a greater risk of cardiovascular disease because they more frequently have hypertension, a major cause of heart disease. Finally, there is gender. Men have a greater risk of heart disease than women.

   1. What is the paragraph's topic sentence? Underline it.

2. Briefly state each of the items listed in the paragraph.

_____

_____

_____

3. List the signal words you find in the paragraph.

_____

III. What are the qualities you need to be successful starting your own business? First, you need to be a self-starter because there won't be a "boss" to tell you to get up and get to work. Since new businesses take a lot of time, you also need to be healthy and have lots of energy. You need to be ambitious and competitive, too. You also need to be willing to take risks, to try something without being too upset if the plan fails. But, perhaps most important, you need to think creatively about the business, to see some new ways of doing things. Your venture is not likely to succeed if you simply copy what other businesses are already doing.

1. What is the essay's main idea?

_____

_____

2. Briefly state each of the items listed in the paragraph.

_____

_____

_____

_____

3. List the signal words you find in the paragraph.

_____

IV. Companies who want to start a new ad campaign need to decide on their advertising objectives. One kind of objective is referred to as name recognition. Many types of ads are designed to get buyers simply to recognize their brand name. Another typical ad objective is to provide information about a product. Perhaps the product is coming out in a new version, or the company sees a new use for the product. A third choice is the ad that promotes an image. These ads seek to sell indirectly, for example, by creating "Marlboro Country" or using cartoon characters. Finally, there is the approach of adding value to the product, of suggesting, in a perfume ad, for example, that if you wear that perfume you will catch a gorgeous man similar to the one in the ad.

1. What is the paragraph's topic sentence? Underline it.

2. Briefly state each of the items listed in the paragraph.

   _____

   _____

   _____

3. List the signal words you find in the paragraph.

   _____

V. A nutritious diet has five characteristics. One is **adequacy:** the foods provide enough of each essential nutrient, fiber, and energy. Another is **balance:** the choices do not overemphasize one nutrient or food type at the expense of another. The third is **calorie control:** the foods provide the amount of energy you need to maintain appropriate weight—not more, not less. The fourth is **moderation:** the foods do not provide excess fat, salt, sugar, or other constituents. The fifth is **variety:** the foods chosen differ from one day to the next.

   Sizer and Whitney, *Nutrition: Concepts and Controversies*, 6th ed.

1. What is the paragraph's main idea?

   _____

   _____

2. Briefly state each of the items listed.

_____

_____

_____

_____

_____

_____

3. List the signal words and describe any visual signals used in the paragraph.

_____

_____

EXAMPLES

Because most writers use at least some examples, we may forget that it is a specific strategy. Still we need to think about providing examples as a choice writers can make to develop their ideas.

The simplest pattern using examples is to follow an idea with one example. The idea may be stated in one or in several sentences. Then the example is given, and it, too, may be in one or in several sentences. This pattern differs from listing because listing requires at least two items of equal importance. By contrast, writers don't need more than one example—although they may give several. Also, the example illustrates an idea, so it is not as important as the idea. Here is an example:

Main Idea

Exs: Limited/LB
Macy's location
Navy exs. &
200—new
locations

The aging U.S. population, geographic population shifts, and the saturation of many prime markets have resulted in various innovative retailing strategies. For example, Limited, Inc., which began by appealing to young, fashion-conscious women, now operates Lane Bryant for larger-sized women. Macy's has stores in Florida and California, to reduce the emphasis on its Northeast base. Nontraditional locations, which have been underserved, are being used—Baskin-Robbins has outlets in U.S. Navy exchanges and Wendy's has an outlet in the Columbus, Ohio, Zoo.

Evans and Berman, *Marketing*, 6th ed.

Writers can, of course, give as many examples as they wish to develop an idea. Sometimes examples are minor details; your primary concern should be to follow the development of ideas in the passage. Other times examples can be very important and need to be learned.

Signal Words for Examples

Here are the most common signal words used to introduce examples. (Remember that in many cases, no signal words are used. Examples are simply presented without labeling.)

for example	that is	e.g.	for instance	to illustrate	such as

Basic Structure for Examples

The pattern of development by example has this basic shape.

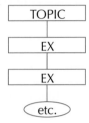

How to Annotate Examples

Begin by underlining each paragraph's topic sentence—if one is stated. Circle signal words and write "ex" in the margin next to each example given. Here is an example:

Main Idea <u>Population mobility offers openings for highly advertised international, national, or regional brands; retail chains and franchises; and major credit cards—among others.</u> Their names are well known when consumers relocate and these names represent an assurance of quality. (For example,) Crest toothpaste, Heineken beer, British Airways, Honda, McDonald's, and Visa are recognized and successful worldwide, as well as throughout the United States. Macy's department stores do good business in Florida and California because a number of Northeasterners who were loyal customers have relocated there.

Exs.

Evans and Berman, *Marketing*, 6th ed.

Note that the main idea is developed in the first two sentences and then the examples are grouped in sentences three and four.

EXERCISE 7-2	**Recognizing and Annotating Examples**

Read and annotate each of the following passages. Then complete the exercise that follows each passage.

I. Fictional television characters can capture the imagination of the public. Perry Mason did wonders for the reputation of the law profession. Mary Tyler Moore's role as a television news writer showed that women could succeed in male-dominated industries. Roles played by Alan Alda were the countermacho models for the bright, gentle man of the 1970s.

John Vivian, *The Media of Mass Communication*

1. What is the paragraph's topic sentence? Underline it.

2. How many examples are given? _____

3. List any signal words you find in the paragraph.

_____

II. Each new technology, then, both destroys old jobs and creates new ones. Some of these jobs, as with the gasoline stations required by automobiles, are readily visible. Others are less evident. The technology that went into airplanes, for example, not only spawned pilots, mechanics, and reservation clerks, but also stimulated global tourism. To put this in a nutshell: Most of us work at jobs that did not even exist a hundred years ago.

James M. Henslin, *Sociology: A Down-to-Earth Approach*, 5th ed.

1. What is the paragraph's topic sentence? Underline it.

2. How many examples are given? _____

3. List any signal words you find in the paragraph.

_____

III. Freedom of speech does not mean that you can say (or write) anything you want about anybody. If you are not careful, you can be sued for libel. To illustrate, there is the famous case of a former Miss Wyoming suing *Penthouse* magazine for a damaging article about her. She won her case. Sometimes the "libeled" person does not win. For instance, when some Texas ranchers sued Oprah Winfrey for, they said, hurting beef prices after she did a piece on mad cow disease, the ranchers lost.

1. What is the paragraph's main idea? Underline it.

2. How many examples are given? _____

3. List any signal words you find in the paragraph.

_____

IV. During the 1970s, punk rock also emerged as a reaction to the commercial success of rock. Groups such as the Sex Pistols and the Ramones played angry, nihilistic music that projected little hope for the future. A somewhat milder form of rebellion against traditional rock came in the form of new wave groups such as the Talking Heads.

Folkerts and Lacy, *The Media in Your Life: An Introduction to Mass Communication*, 2nd ed.

1. What is the paragraph's topic sentence? Underline it.

2. How many examples are given? _____

3. List any signal words you find in the paragraph.

_____

V. Basically, the bandwagon appeal gets us to support an action or an opinion merely because it is popular—because "everyone else is doing it." Advertising relies heavily on the bandwagon appeal ("join the Pepsi people") but so do politicians ("Thousands of people have already shown their support by sending in a donation in the enclosed envelope. Won't you become one of us and work together to build a great America?").

Donna Woolfolk Cross, "Politics: The Art of Bamboozling"

1. What is the paragraph's topic sentence? Underline it.

2. How many examples are given? _____

3. List any signal words you find in the paragraph.

_____

COMPARISON AND CONTRAST

When we compare, we look at similarities between two items; when we contrast, we look at differences. These strategies are widely used because they help make sense of many topics. We can compare or contrast two schools, two books, two jobs, two study methods.

Some writers discuss both similarities and differences. More typically, writers focus on either similarities or differences, not both. In fact, the writer's point may be that in spite of apparent similarities, the two items are really quite different. Or, in spite of apparent differences, they are really quite similar.

Signal Words for Comparison and Contrast

Signal words have two roles in the comparison or contrast pattern. Some words or phrases announce the use of the structure: "Comparing . . . views" or "The difference between . . ." announce the strategy that will be used. Other signal words indicate shifts between the two items. Here are some of the most common.

both	however	likewise
but	in contrast	on the other hand
different	in the same way	similarly
unlike		

Basic Structure for Comparison or Contrast

The comparison/contrast structure has one pattern if both similarities and differences are given, another pattern if only comparison or only contrast is used. The following two models show the structure with contrast as the writer's point. What if the writer wanted to compare instead of contrast? "Similarities" and "differences" in the first model would be reversed for comparison. The differences would be briefly mentioned, and the similarities would be compared one by one. The list in the second model would be showing points of similarity for comparison.

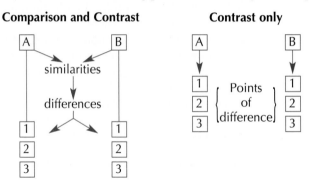

How to Annotate Comparison or Contrast

When you recognize a comparison or contrast pattern, begin by locating the two items being compared or contrasted. Either underline them twice or circle them. Then note the specific points of similarity or difference, or both. Underline key words for each point of similarity (or difference) and number each one in the margin. Here is an example.

Contrast

When the American wants to be alone he goes into a room and shuts the ① door—he depends on architectural features for screening. For an American to refuse to talk to someone is the ultimate form of rejection and a sure sign ② of great displeasure. The English on the other hand, lacking rooms of their own since childhood, never developed the practice of using space as a refuge from others. They have in effect internalized a set of barriers, which they erect ① and which others are supposed to recognize. Therefore, the more the Englishman shuts himself off when he is with an American the more likely the American is to break in to assure himself that all is well.   ③

Edward T. Hall, *The Hidden Dimension*

We can summarize the points of difference in this paragraph thus:

Item A (American)	Item B (Englishman)
shuts door to be alone	uses a set of barriers (nonverbal messages)
uses silence as rejection	uses silence to be alone
sees silence as a problem	sees silence as signal to be alone

EXERCISE 7-3	Recognizing and Annotating Comparison and Contrast

Read and annotate each of the following selections and complete the exercise that follows each selection.

I. A comparison between reading and viewing may be made in respect to the pace of each experience…. The pace of reading, clearly, depends entirely upon the reader. He may read as slowly or as rapidly as he can or wishes to read. If he does not understand something, he may stop and reread it, or go in search of elucidation [clarity] before continuing. The reader can accelerate [speed up] his pace when the material is easy or less than interesting, and slow down when it is difficult or enthralling. If what he reads is moving, he can put down the book for a few moments and cope with his emotions without fear of losing anything.

The pace of the television experience cannot be controlled by the viewer; only its beginning and end are within his control as he clicks the knob on and off. He cannot slow down a delightful program or speed up a dreary one. He cannot "turn back" if a word or phrase is not understood. The program moves inexorably [relentlessly] forward, and what is lost or misunderstood remains so. Nor can the television viewer readily transform the material he receives into a form that might suit his particular emotional needs, as he invariably does with material he reads. The images move too quickly.

Marie Winn, *The Plug-In Drug*

1. What are the two items being contrasted?

_____

2. List the several points of difference.

_____

_____

_____

3. List the signal words that are used.

_____

II.   E-mail may have its advantages in the business world, but it can never match actual letters as the most heartfelt form of communication, especially between parents and their children. While e-mail glows impersonally on a screen, letters come to us wrapped up like small gifts we can hold in our hands, read, re-read and save for later. Yes, e-mail can be printed out. But only as a lifeless facsimile, each copy as tediously similar as the next. Every letter, by contrast, is distinct, original and rich with detail. There is the individuality of the penmanship, whether it flows easily from line to line or scrawls somewhat aimlessly across the page. Even with typed letters, the living hand makes itself known through the signature, as well as any handwritten corrections or additions…. [T]he unique personality of the sender shines through.

Andrew Carroll, "Letter to the Editor," *Washington Post*

1. What two items are being contrasted?

_____

2. List the points of difference.

_____

_____

_____

3. List the signal words that are used.

_____

III. Why should high-achieving American students, but not Asian students, pay a price in terms of psychological distress? The researchers found that Asian teenagers typically enjoy support and encouragement for their academic achievement from family and peers alike. In contrast, high-achieving teenagers in the United States are torn between studying harder to excel academically and pursuing nonacademic social interests. Such interests may be strongly encouraged by their peers and often by parents who want their children to be "well-rounded."

Wood and Wood, The World of Psychology

1. What two items are being contrasted?

_____

_____

2. List the points of difference.

_____

_____

_____

3. List any signal words that are used.

_____

IV. Marshall McLuhan is famous for his contrast of the mass media. McLuhan argued that books, magazines, newspapers, and movies are "hot media," whereas television and, usually, radio are "cool media." Hot media require thinking; cool media require much less intellectual effort. The hot media involve us deeply—if we are to get anything from the experience. By contrast we often have the radio on "in the background" while we do other things, and television also does not demand our full attention. Hot media invite us to use our imaginations; the cool media do not require us to be imaginative.

1. What are the two items being contrasted?

_____

_____

2. Which media fit under Item A and which fit under Item B?

Item A	Item B
_____	_____
_____	_____
_____	_____

3. What are the points of difference?

_____

_____

_____

4. List any signal words that are used.

_____

_____

V.   To explain why some countries are rich and others are poor, economists often look at the factors of production: land, labor, capital, entrepreneurship, and knowledge. Many poor countries have enough land and laborers, and some rich countries have little land or limited numbers of workers. What are the critical differences? Rich countries have entrepreneurs, people willing to take a chance to start a new business. Poor countries often lack entrepreneurs. Entrepreneurs in rich countries probably can get capital more easily than would-be businesspeople in poorer countries. Rich countries have better educational systems and better ways to access knowledge. Most poor countries have workers with limited knowledge and are not as technologically up-to-date to make access to information easy.

1. What two items are being contrasted?

_____

_____

2. List the several points of difference.

_____

_____

_____

_____

3. List any signal words that are used?

_____

_____

EXERCISE 7-4	Distinguishing Among Various Structures

Read, annotate, and then answer the questions that follow each of the paragraphs. Part of your task is to identify the structure/pattern used.

I. Unlike the amusements and games of the colonial years, sport became highly organized and serious business in the 1800s. It was during this time that many of America's more popular sports developed into their present form. Such imported sports as horse racing, boxing lacrosse, handball, cricket, baseball, archery, track and field athletics, soccer, golf, tennis, squash, football, bowling, and rowing all developed into highly organized activities. Other organized sports, notably basketball and volleyball, originated in the United States.

J. Richard Polidoro, *Sport and Physical Activity in the Modern World*

1. What is the paragraph's topic sentence? Underline it.

2. What structure or strategy is used? _____

3. List three points from the paragraph in a pattern that reveals the paragraph's structure. (The first has been done for you.)

   Horse racing became organized in the United States in the 1800s.

   _____

   _____

4. What signals are used?

   _____

   _____

II. In spite of global businesses and communications, there are still differences between cultures, particularly Japanese and American cultures. Japanese culture is very homogeneous whereas American culture is quite diverse. In Japan the group is more important than the individual, but, by contrast, U.S. culture stresses the individual more than the group. The Japanese rely on unspoken agreement so their language is more subtle and ambiguous. In contrast, Americans want to get the facts spelled out and prefer language that is specific and clear.

1. What is the paragraph's topic sentence? Underline it.

2. What structure or strategy is used? _____

3. List three points from the paragraph in a pattern that reveals the paragraph's structure.

_____

_____

_____

4. What signals are used? _____

_____

III. Elementary schools are quite different from only twenty years ago. In the past, teachers used the blackboard or posters as teaching tools. Today, although the blackboard is still used, teachers may turn to the overhead projector or PowerPoint computer presentations. In the past, teachers often had to prepare their own teaching materials. Today, the materials come in kits along with the lesson plans. In addition, yesterday's students learned with books, papers, and pencils. Today's students also do some of their learning by computer.

1. What structure or strategy is used in this paragraph?

_____

2. State the paragraph's main idea in a way that reveals the paragraph's structure.

_____

3. What signals are used?

_____

IV. Some readers have trouble "getting hooked" on classics. It's true that classics are often difficult to read. But following these steps will help you read them with pleasure. First, read about the author and the author's time. Were there any special circumstances in which the work was produced? Next, be sure to know what kind of work you are reading—a novel, a biography, a history. Then, read in big chunks. When the language is difficult or there are many characters to get straight, you will have a better sense of what's going on if you really get into each section you read. Finally, look forward to each reading; you are reading a work that many people before you have read and loved.

1. What structure or strategy is used in this paragraph?

_____

2. What is the paragraph's topic?

_____

3. List three major details in a way that reveals the paragraph's structure.

_____

_____

_____

4. What signals are used?_____

_____

V. Although most people know about the mass extinction that killed the dinosaurs, few know that the Earth has actually had four mass extinctions. The oldest occurred 425 million years ago. The second killed many species 365 million years ago, at the end of the Devonian period. The third extinction, 225 million years ago, resulted in the loss of 95 percent of all species. The last mass extinction, 65 million years ago, wiped out the dinosaurs. However, small mammals survived and developed into the many mammal species we know today.

1. What is the paragraph's main idea?

_____

2. What structure or strategy is used in this paragraph?

_____

3. List three major details in a way that reveals the paragraph's structure.

_____

_____

_____

4. What signals are used?

_____

VI. During the Cretaceous Period (about 160 million to 65 million years ago) in North America, you would have found some familiar growing plants, for example, ferns, palm trees, and redwoods—and you would have been surprised by the mix of animals. At that time you would have found many birds, including giant flying pterosaurs. In the sea, you would have seen an interesting mix, for example, sharks and turtles along with giant marine lizards and fishlike ichthyosaurs. On land there were insects and small, furry mammals, but also the dinosaurs. Although some dinosaurs were already extinct, others still roamed North America, for instance duck-bills, triceratops, and the famous tyrannosaurus rex.

1. What is the paragraph's topic sentence? Underline it.

2. What structure or strategy is used? _____

3. List three points from the paragraph in a pattern that reveals the paragraph's structure.

_____

_____

_____

_____

4. What signals are used? _____

_____

VII. Although the long-running game show *Jeopardy* and the new game show *The Missing Link* have differences, they are ultimately much alike. Both have more than one contestant playing at a time (*Jeopardy* with three, *The Missing Link* starting with six and ending with two). On both shows the player with the most right answers usually makes the most money and wins. Although the rules for competing are somewhat different, on both shows the idea is to do better than your opponents and take home the money, and on both shows only the winner gets a money prize.

1. What is the paragraph's topic sentence? Underline it.

2. What structure or strategy is used? _____

3. List three points from the paragraph in a pattern that reveals the paragraph's structure.

_____

_____

_____

_____

4. What signals are used? _____

_____

VIII. A study of the DNA of African elephants has shown that there are actually two species of African elephants, not one. One species lives in the savanna, the other in Africa's rain forest. Savanna elephants have large, floppy ears whereas the rain-forest elephants have smaller, more rounded ears. The savanna elephants have long, curving tusks, but the rain-forest species have straighter, thinner tusks. Scientists now believe that the two species separated about 2.6 million years ago.

1. What structure or strategy is used in this paragraph?

_____

2. List three points from the paragraph in a way that reveals the paragraph's structure.

_____

_____

_____

_____

3. What signals are used? _____

_____

IX. Some changes in the ways we provide services today may increase quality without necessarily improving productivity. For example, increasing the number of computers on campus may improve education but probably does not increase instructor productivity. In another illustration, advanced computer technology in hospitals (e.g., CAT scans and MRI machines) probably improves the quality of patient care. The technology just doesn't necessarily mean that doctors have time to see more patients.

1. What is the paragraph's topic sentence? Underline it.

2. What structure or strategy is used in this paragraph?

_____

3. List two major and two minor details from the paragraph.

Major details: _____

Minor details: _____

4. What signals are used? _____

_____

X.   Most retail companies have their own advertising departments, for several reasons. First, retailers can save money by doing their own advertising instead of contracting out to an advertising agency. Second, retailers often receive advertising materials either free or at a reduced cost from manufacturers and trade associations. Third, retailers operate on a shorter timetable. They often need to put together an advertising campaign in a few days whereas an agency may take weeks or months to complete a project.

Adapted from Wells, Burnett, and Moriarty, *Advertising:*
Principles and Practice, 3rd ed.

1. What is the paragraph's main idea?

_____

2. What structure or strategy is used in this paragraph?

_____

3. List three ideas from the paragraph in a way that reveals the paragraph's structure.

_____

_____

_____

4. What signals are used? _____

_____

■ ■ ■ ■ ■

LEARNING TO ACT LIKE A PROFESSIONAL

William G. Nickels, Jim McHugh, and Susan McHugh

Dr. Nickels is an associate professor of business at the University of Maryland and the author of several marketing textbooks. Mr. McHugh teaches at St. Louis Community College and does business consulting in St. Louis. Susan McHugh has advanced degrees in education and is an adult-learning-theory specialist. This selection comes from the fifth edition of their textbook *Understanding Business*.

Prepare

1. Identify the authors and work. What do you expect the authors' purpose to be?

   _____

   _____

2. Preread to identify the subject and make predictions. What do you expect to read about?

   _____

   _____

3. What do you already know about the subject?

   _____

   _____

4. Raise two questions that you expect the selection to answer.

   _____

   _____

   _____

   _____

■ ■ ■ ■ ■

1   You can learn a lot about good and bad manners from watching professional sports. During the 1997 basketball playoff series, for example, Michael Jordan of the Chicago Bulls showed that true professionals accept responsibility for the team and never give up. Whenever the game was on the line, the team turned to Michael for the important shot, and, more often than not, he made it.

2   You can probably think of contrasting examples of sports stars who have earned a bad reputation by not acting professionally (e.g., spitting, swearing, criticizing teammates in front of others, and so on). People in professional sports are fined if they are late to meetings or refuse to follow the rules established by the team and coach. Business professionals also must follow set rules; many of these rules are not formally written anywhere, but every sucessful businessperson learns them through experience.

3   You can begin the habits now that will make for great success when you start your career. Those habits include the following:

1. *Making a good first impression.* "You have seven seconds to make an impression. People see your clothes before you even open your mouth. And make no mistake, everything you say following those first few moments will be weighed by how you look," says image consultant Aleysha Proctor. You don't get a second chance to make a good first impression. Skip the fads and invest in high-quality, classic clothes. Remember, "high-quality" is not necessarily the same as "expensive." Take a clue as to what is appropriate at any specific company by studying the people there who are most successful. What do they wear? How do they act?

2. *Focusing on good grooming.* Be aware of your appearance and its impact on those around you. Consistency is essential. You can't project a good image by dressing up a few times a week and then show up looking like you're getting ready to mow a lawn. Wear appropriate, clean clothing and accessories. It is not appropriate, for example, for men to wear hats inside of buildings. It is also not appropriate, usually, to wear wrinkled shirts or to have shirttails hanging out of your pants.

3. *Being on time.* When you don't come to class or to work on time, you're sending a message to your teacher or boss. You're saying, "My time is more important than your time. I have more important things to do than be here." In addition to the lack of respect tardiness shows to your teacher or boss, it rudely disrupts the work of your colleagues. Promptness may not be a priority in some circles, but in the workplace promptness is essential. But being punctual doesn't always mean just being on time. Executive recruiter Juan Menefee recalls a time he arrived at 7:40 A.M. for an 8:00 A.M. meeting only to discover he was the last one there. "You have to look around, pay attention to the corporate culture and corporate clock," says Menefee. To develop good work habits and get good grades, it is important to get to class on time and not leave early.

4. *Practicing considerate behavior.* Considerate behavior includes listening when others are talking, and not reading the newspaper or eating in class. Don't

interrupt others when they are speaking. Wait for your turn to present your views in classroom discussions. Of course, eliminate all words of profanity from your vocabulary. Use appropriate body language by sitting up attentively and not slouching. Sitting up has the added bonus of helping you stay awake! Professors and managers get a favorable impression from those who look and act alert. That may help your grades in school and your advancement at work.

5. *Being prepared.* A businessperson would never show up for a meeting without reading the materials assigned for that meeting and being prepared to discuss the topics of the day. To become a professional, one must practice acting like a professional. For students, that means reading assigned materials before class, asking questions and responding to questions in class, and discussing the material with fellow students.

4   From the minute you enter your first job interview until the day you retire people will notice whether you follow the proper business etiquette. Just as traffic laws enable people to drive more safely, business etiquette allows people to conduct business with the appropriate amount of dignity. How you talk, how you eat, and how you dress all create an impression on others.

734 words

Comprehension Check

Answer with a, b, c, or d to indicate the phrase that best completes each statement.

_____ 1. The best statement of the passage's topic is
  a. professional sports.
  b. corporate cultures.
  c. learning to act professionally.
  d. Michael Jordan.

_____ 2. The authors begin with a discussion of professional sports stars
  a. to make a comparison with business and student behavior.
  b. because that is their topic.
  c. to object to spitting and swearing in the classroom.
  d. to entertain readers.

_____ 3. The authors observe that businesspeople
  a. are different from sports professionals.
  b. are given a written set of rules to follow.
  c. can do whatever they want.
  d. have unwritten rules to follow to be successful.

_____ 4. The authors believe that business rules are
   a. habits that students should also develop.
   b. too demanding.
   c. best learned after one starts working.
   d. not relevant to students.

_____ 5. You can make a good first impression by
   a. dressing in quality, classic clothes.
   b. dressing in the latest fashions.
   c. dressing in a laid-back style.
   d. not worrying about clothes.

_____ 6. A good first impression
   a. affects how people will see you from that time on.
   b. is not important because no one will remember.
   c. is based on how you speak, not how you look.
   d. is based on how you look, not what you say.

_____ 7. Good grooming includes
   a. dressing in appropriate, clean clothes consistently.
   b. wearing shirttails out.
   c. wearing hats indoors.
   d. wearing clean clothes when you have time to do laundry.

_____ 8. Being punctual
   a. means that you can then leave class or a meeting early.
   b. shows that you respect others and their work.
   c. means that you come in on time, regardless of how early others may come.
   d. is important for some jobs but not for class.

_____ 9. Appropriate classroom behavior includes
   a. napping when you are tired.
   b. using profanity when you feel like it.
   c. sitting up straight and listening when others are talking.
   d. talking when students are making a presentation.

_____ 10. Students can develop good habits for the workplace by
   a. planning to learn after they finish college.
   b. reading a good business text.
   c. practicing acting like a professional in their classes.
   d. doing what feels right.

Expanding Vocabulary

*Answer with a, b, c, or d to indicate the best definition of the word in **bold** as it was used in the passage. The number in parentheses is the number of the paragraph in which the word appears.*

_____ 1. "a good first **impression**" (3)
   a. feeling/image created from reading
   b. feeling/image created by an experience
   c. feeling/image created by attending class
   d. imposture

_____ 2. "says image **consultant**" (3)
   a. one who conjures
   b. one who creates an image
   c. one who works as a cook
   d. one who works as an advisor

_____ 3. "Focusing on good **grooming**" (3)
   a. make neat and trim
   b. make gracious
   c. grub
   d. grooving

_____ 4. "clothing and **accessories**" (3)
   a. accommodations
   b. additional items such as jewelry
   c. academics
   d. accolades

_____ 5. "may not be a **priority**" (3)
   a. problem
   b. prize
   c. of little importance
   d. of great importance

_____ 6. "being **punctual**" (3)
   a. on time
   b. private
   c. pure
   d. tireless

_____ 7. "Executive **recruiter** Juan" (3)

    a. recorder

    b. reconciler

    c. one who fires people

    d. one who seeks people for work

_____ 8. "all words of **profanity**" (3)

    a. obscene/irreverent language

    b. proficiency

    c. power

    d. careless language

_____ 9. "proper business **etiquette**" (3)

    a. exercises

    b. accepted behavior and manners

    c. engineering

    d. essentials

_____ 10. "appropriate amount of **dignity**" (4)

    a. behavior unacceptable in class

    b. dominance

    c. difficulty

    d. behavior worthy of respect

Analysis of Context and Strategies

1. What is the main idea of paragraph 3?

    _____

    _____

2. What is the primary structure or strategy used by the authors?

    _____

Reflection and Discussion

1. How many of the habits listed by the authors do you practice regularly? If the answer is fewer than all of them, do you think that you will practice additional ones? Why or why not?

2. Are there any habits listed here that you don't think are important for class or business? If yes, which ones and why?

■ ■ ■ ■ ■

DO WOMEN LEAD DIFFERENTLY THAN MEN?

Claire M. Renzetti and Daniel J. Curran

Claire Renzetti is Chair of the sociology department at St. Joseph's University and Daniel Curran is a professor of sociology and Executive Vice President of St. Joseph's University. This husband-and-wife team has published many books and articles, including *Living Sociology* (2nd ed., 2000), from which the following selection is taken.

Prepare

1. Identify the authors and work. What do you expect the authors' purpose to be?

_____

_____

2. Preread to identify the subject and make predictions. What do you expect to read about?

_____

_____

3. What do you already know about the subject?

_____

_____

4. Raise two questions that you expect the selection to answer.

_____

_____

_____

_____

Vocabulary Alert: Do You Know These Words?

Here are five words you need to know to read the following selection with understanding.

collaborative working together, cooperating

participatory strategy in which people are able to share in something

unilateral involving only one side, or one person

inclusiveness a strategy of involving many or most in an activity

stereotypes conventional, oversimplified concepts/images

■ ■ ■ ■ ■

1 Do women lead differently than men? Researchers who study female and male leaders have discovered remarkable similarities: Both women and men enjoy being leaders and holding positions of influence. Both appear equally able to direct and organize the activities of groups, and their subordinates judge female and male leaders as equally effective (Eagly & Johnson, 1990; but see also Valian, 1998).

2 Nevertheless, research also reveals significant differences between female and male leaders. One area of difference is the reasons women and men give for seeking leadership positions. Women are more likely than men to seek a leadership position because of a desire to help others. In contrast, men more often cite high personal achievement motivation as their primary reason for aspiring to a leadership position (Bridges, 1989).

3 A second area of difference is the way women and men lead. Women leaders typically use collaborative, participatory communication in exercising leadership, whereas men lead with more directive, unilateral communication (Eagly & Karau, 1991). This doesn't mean that women are better or worse leaders than men. Assertiveness and directness are valued traits in leaders, but so are inclusiveness and collaboration. In fact, studies show that the most effective leaders are those who recognize when a situation calls for unilateral decision making and when it is best to foster team building (Cann & Siegfried, 1990).

4 Besides observed differences between female and male leaders, there is also the question of how their subordinates or followers judge them. In our society, there are prevalent stereotypes about how women and men are supposed to behave. Women are expected to be supportive, caring, and cooperative; men are expected to be assertive and to take charge of situations. Research indicates that when the behavior of female and male leaders conforms to these stereotypes, they are judged effective regardless of sex. But when a female leader violates the gender stereotype by being highly assertive or directive, she is evaluated negatively by subordinates, jeopardizing her effectiveness (Basow, 1990; Butler & Geis, 1990; Eagly et al., 1995; Valian, 1998; Yoder et al., 1998). Interestingly, the violation of gender stereotypes by a male leader does not produce the same negative impact on his effectiveness rating. Instead, researchers report that supportiveness and a collaborative style by both female and male leaders tend to raise morale and enhance

productivity (Eagly et al., 1995; Helgesen, 1990). Perhaps as findings such as these accumulate, we may see women's style of leadership becoming the norm in government and business.

405 words

Comprehension Check

Answer the following with a, b, c, or d to indicate the phrase that best completes each statement.

_____ 1. The primary structure or strategy used by the authors is
   a. examples.
   b. listing.
   c. comparison/contrast.
   d. cause/effect.

_____ 2. As their primary reason for wanting to lead, men cite
   a. personal achievement.
   b. wanting to help others.
   c. not wanting a woman to get the position.
   d. wanting to please their parents.

_____ 3. As their primary reason for wanting to lead, women cite
   a. personal achievement.
   b. wanting to help others.
   c. not wanting a man to get the position.
   d. wanting to please their parents.

_____ 4. Men typically lead by using
   a. unilateral decision making.
   b. directness.
   c. assertiveness.
   d. all of the above.

_____ 5. Women typically lead by
   a. fostering team building and collaboration.
   b. using directness.
   c. yelling at others.
   d. making most of the decisions.

_____ 6. Stereotypes about women include that they should be
   a. emotional.
   b. supportive and caring.

     c. take charge types.

     d. as tough as men.

_____ 7. Subordinates judge male and female leaders as equally effective when

     a. women behave like men.

     b. men behave like boys.

     c. women and men behave according to stereotypes.

     d. women and men ignore stereotypes.

_____ 8. Men are judged as effective leaders when they

     a. adhere to male stereotypes.

     b. use a collaborative and supportive style.

     c. yell at others.

     d. do either a or b.

_____ 9. The authors suggest that

     a. men's leadership style is the best.

     b. women should not strive to be leaders.

     c. women's leadership style should be adopted by men.

     d. an assertive style should be the norm.

_____ 10. The best statement of the selection's main idea is

     a. men are better leaders than women.

     b. women are better leaders than men.

     c. men and women have different leadership styles and are judged as equally effective but also by gender stereotypes.

     d. men and women are equally effective as leaders.

Expanding Vocabulary

Answer the following with a, b, c, or d to indicate the best definition of the word in **bold** *as it was used in the selection. The number in parentheses is the number of the paragraph in which the word appears.*

_____ 1. "**aspiring** to a leadership position" (2)

     a. assailing

     b. associating

     c. desiring

     d. opposing

_____ 2. "use **collaborative** . . . communication" (3)

     a. working together

     b. cold-blooded

     c. exclusive

     d. imbalanced

_____ 3. "more directive, **unilateral** communication" (3)

     a. in unison

     b. one-sided

     c. united

     d. collaborative

_____ 4. "best to **foster** team building" (3)

     a. encourage

     b. formulate

     c. give up

     d. fight

_____ 5. "there are **prevalent** stereotypes" (4)

     a. previous

     b. profane

     c. wavering

     d. widely occurring

_____ 6. "prevalent **stereotypes**" (4)

     a. conventional images

     b. unconventional ideas

     c. sound systems

     d. typical music

_____ 7. "female leader **violates** the gender stereotype" (4)

     a. views

     b. destroys

     c. brings about

     d. disregards

_____ 8. "**jeopardizing** her effectiveness" (4)

     a. enhancing

     b. jet propelling

     c. exposing to germs

     d. exposing to loss

_____ 9. "tend to raise **morale**" (4)

     a. morality

     b. group confidence and spirit

    c. manners

    d. group combativeness

_____ 10. "**enhance** productivity" (4)

    a. disregard

    b. destroy

    c. improve

    d. impoverish

Reflection and Discussion

1. Do you picture male and female leaders according to the gender stereotypes described here? If so, are you prepared to rethink the usefulness of those stereotypes? Why or why not?

2. Would you prefer a male or female boss? If you have a preference, how do you explain it? If you do not have a preference, how do you explain that?

MAKING CONNECTIONS

1. What, for you, is the most important idea about the workplace that you have learned from these two selections? Why did you choose that idea?

2. Nickels, McHugh, and McHugh are primarily giving advice about behavior in the workplace. Renzetti and Curran are reporting on both behavior (by gender) and perceptions of that behavior. What advice do the first group of authors give that connects to issues of perceptions raised by the second group of authors? What have you learned from these readings about the role of image? Brainstorm with your class partner to find some answers to these questions.

"E" CONNECTIONS

What is the etiquette for e-mails? We've created a new word, *netiquette,* to refer to online communication. Find some guidelines for business/professional/student e-mailing. You may want to check your own school's Website to see if it has posted netiquette for students, faculty, and staff. If not, conduct an online search for some general guidelines. Here is one site to visit:

    <http://www.bspage.com/Inetiq/Netiq.html>.

WORD POWER 6

Sorting Out Words That Are Often Confused

In this set of common words we have words that are *not* pronounced the same. In addition they are spelled differently and have different meanings. What do they have in common? The pairs are often confused. Study the words and their meanings. Then select the correct word to complete each of the sentences below.

accept to receive	**choose** to select
except other than; only; exclude	**chose** past tense of *choose*
advice recommendation	**clothes** wearing apparel
advise to recommend	**cloths** pieces of fabrics
affect to influence	**conscience** following one's sense
effect result *(noun);* bring into existence *(verb)*	**conscious** awareness; awake of right behavior
allusion indirect reference	**dessert** sweet course of a meal
illusion misleading image; incorrect idea	**desert** to abandon; dry sandy area
breath air taken in	**device** plan; a machine
breathe to take air in and out	**devise** to plan; to invent

1. Walking in a _____ *(dessert/desert)* is difficult; it is hard to

   _____ *(breath/breathe)* in the hot sun.

2. Ben Franklin believed that one's sleep is _____ *(affected/effected)* by

   a good or bad _____ *(conscience/conscious).*

3. Sometimes youngsters do not _____ *(choose/chose)* to listen to their

   parents' good _____ *(advice/advise).*

4. Poems often contain an _____ *(allusion/illusion)* to Greek mythol-

   ogy, a _____ *(device/devise)* for suggesting much in a few words.

5. Mary _____ *(choose/chose)* the chocolate cake for _____

   (desert/dessert).

6. I _____ *(advice/advise)* you not to _____ *(accept/except)* rides

   from strangers.

7. Better stop running and catch your _____ *(breath/breathe);* I want you

   to be _____ *(conscience/conscious)* at the end of our workout.

8. Scotland's Loch Ness monster is probably an _____ *(allusion/illusion),* not a real creature.

9. Boris tried to _____ *(device/devise)* a strategy for beating Art at chess, but his strategy did not have the _____ *(affect/effect)* he wanted.

10. _____ *(Accept/Except)* for polishing the windows, use the clean _____ *(clothes/cloths)* at the top of the pile.

CHAPTER REVIEW

1. *Signal words* are words that

_____ .

2. In textbooks, a typical strategy for signaling listing is

_____ .

3. When annotating a passage that organizes by comparison/contrast, you want to be sure to indicate _____ .

4. It's good to remember that writers who provide examples do not always use

_____ to indicate the strategy they are using.

5. The primary purpose of recognizing a writer's structures or strategies is to improve

_____ .

Take a Reading Road Trip!

For additional practice with your reading skills, use the Reading Road Trip CD-ROM or visit Reading Road Trip on the Web at <http://www.ablongman.com/readingroadtrip> (password required).

CHAPTER 8

Recognizing More Patterns and Signal Words

LEARNING OBJECTIVES

- To understand the primary structures or patterns authors use to give order to their writing

- Specifically, to recognize the patterns of ordering (time sequence and process), definition, and statement with clarification

- To recognize the words that signal each pattern or structure

- To annotate each pattern as you read

PREPARE TO READ

Read and reflect on the chapter's title and objectives. Glance through the chapter, observing headings to see what is covered. Now answer these questions.

1. What do you expect to learn from this chapter?

   _____

   _____

2. What do you already know about the chapter's topic?

   _____

   _____

3. What two or three questions do you want answered from reading this chapter?

   _____

   _____

In Chapter 7 we began our study of the structures or strategies—the patterns—that writers use to give order to their writing and to reinforce their purpose in writing. As indicated in Chapter 7, recognizing a writer's primary pattern is important to reading comprehension.

In this chapter, you will study the structure and accompanying signal words of three more patterns: ordering, which includes both time sequence and process; definition; and statement with clarification. Remember, as you study these three structures, to keep these basic points in mind:

- Writers often reveal their patterns by using signal words, transition and connecting words that are appropriate for the specific pattern in use.

- Recognizing the pattern in use is a means to improved reading comprehension, so exercises will always require that you show you understand the passage.

- Since writers often combine patterns, you want to look for the most important pattern as your guide to the writer's purpose.

ORDERING: TIME SEQUENCE AND PROCESS

The ordering of information in time sequence is familiar to us from stories. Chronological or time order is also found in histories and biographies and in explanations of how to do something (change a tire) or how a process is accomplished (how water is distilled). You will find the use of time sequence or the explanation of a process in most textbooks, from history and psychology (how the brain functions) to biology and geology (how rocks are formed).

Signal Words

Here are the most common signal words for time sequence and process.

after	first	next	then
before	following	now	until
during	later	procedure	when
finally	cycle	second	
process	last	step	

Basic Structure for Time Sequence and Process

In time sequence or process, the items relate to one another, not just to the topic being discussed. They relate in chronological order, and sometimes, with process, in a causal order as well. That is, the first step leads to the second step; the second step could not take place without the first step happening. We can illustrate the pattern this way.

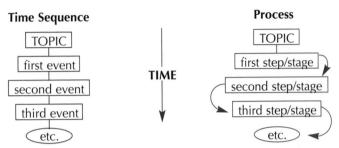

How to Annotate the Pattern of Time Sequence and Process

When reading time sequence or process, annotate to make the stages or steps clear. Underline each topic sentence and the key words in each stage or step. Circle signal words to highlight the time sequence. Indicate steps in a process by numbering. Here is an example:

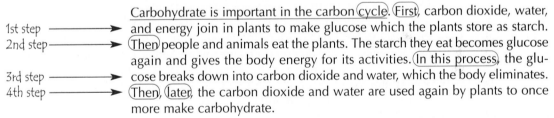

1st step
2nd step

3rd step
4th step

Carbohydrate is important in the carbon cycle. First, carbon dioxide, water, and energy join in plants to make glucose which the plants store as starch. Then people and animals eat the plants. The starch they eat becomes glucose again and gives the body energy for its activities. In this process, the glucose breaks down into carbon dioxide and water, which the body eliminates. Then, later, the carbon dioxide and water are used again by plants to once more make carbohydrate.

Adapted from Sizer and Whitney, *Nutrition: Concepts and Controversies*, 6th ed.

EXERCISE 8-1 | **Recognizing the Use of Ordering: Time Sequence and Process**

Read and annotate each of the following selections. Then complete the exercise that follows each selection.

1. German forces seized the offensive in the west and invaded neutral Belgium at the beginning of August 1914. The Belgians resisted stubbornly but unsuccessfully. Belgian forts were systematically captured, and the capital of Brussels fell under the German advance on 20 August. After the fall

of Belgium, German military might swept into northern France with the intention of defeating the French in six weeks.

Kishlansky, Geary, and O'Brien, *Civilization in the West,* 4th ed.

1. What is the paragraph's topic? _____

_____

2. List three major details in a way that reveals the paragraph's structure.

_____

_____

_____

_____

3. List the signal words that are used. _____

_____

II. To feel your pulse, use two fingers to press gently but firmly on the artery. Do not use your thumb; it also has a pulse and will cause you to miscount. If you can't feel your pulse, you may be pressing too lightly or too hard. Pressing too hard on an artery squeezes it shut so that you can no longer feel any pulsing. Try different pressures while sitting quietly until you can feel and count your pulse easily. Then practice taking it while you move around the room. If you have a lot of trouble counting your pulse, place your hand over your heart and count beats.

Bishop and Aldana, *Step Up to Wellness*

1. What is the paragraph's topic? State it to indicate the use of ordering.

_____

2. Briefly list the steps in the process.

_____

_____

_____

_____

3. List the signal words that are used. _____

_____

III. During the time earth and the other planets were being formed, the release of energy from radioactive materials kept their interiors very hot. When earth was still so hot that it was mostly liquid, the heavier materials collected in a dense core whose diameter is about half that of the planet. As soon as the supply of stellar dust, stones, and larger rocks was exhausted, the planet ceased to grow. As earth's surface cooled, an outer crust, a skin as thin by comparison as the skin of an apple, was formed.

Curtis and Barnes, *An Invitation to Biology,* 4th ed.

1. What is the paragraph's topic? _____

_____

2. State briefly the steps in the process.

_____

_____

_____

3. List the signal words that are used. _____

_____

IV. Between 1347 and 1352, from one-half to one-third of Europe's population died from a virulent combination of bubonic, septicemic, and pneumonic plagues known to history as the Black Death. The disease, carried by the fleas of infected rats, traveled the caravan routes from central Asia. It arrived in Messina, Sicily, aboard a merchant vessel in October 1347. From there the Black Death spread up the boot of Italy and then into southern France, England, and Spain. By 1349 it had reached northern Germany, Portugal, and Ireland. The following year the Low Countries, Scotland, Scandinavia, and Russia fell victim.

Kishlansky, Geary, and O'Brien, *Civilization in the West,* 4th ed.

1. What is the paragraph's topic? _____

_____

2. State three details from the paragraph in a way that reveals its structure.

_____

_____

_____

_____

3. List the signal words that are used. _____

_____

V. The costs of selecting and training a new person on the job are significant, so companies want to be sure to do a good job in their selecting and
hiring process. A typical selection process involves several steps. First, you
need complete application forms or a detailed résumé. Then, if the person looks promising, someone from Human Resources usually will conduct
the first interview—which may be by phone. Next comes the interview with
the new hire's supervisor, and perhaps the supervisor's boss as well. For
some types of jobs, applicants who have done well in their interviews will
be given a test to judge the skills for which they will be hired. Finally, for
the candidate who has been tentatively selected for the job, Human
Resources will check references and the candidate's work and school
records to verify information on the application.

1. What is the paragraph's topic? _____

_____

2. Briefly state the steps in the process.

_____

_____

_____

_____

3. List the signal words that are used. _____

_____

DEFINITION

Defining terms and concepts is an important part of writing. Writers devote many paragraphs or even an entire article to defining controversial terms. Textbooks are filled with definitions, because learning about a new subject includes understanding the terms and concepts of that field of study.

A direct definition consists of placing the term in a category and then distinguishing it from other, similar items in that category. For example:

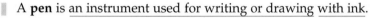

A **pen** is an instrument used for writing or drawing with ink.

term to be defined   category into which pen is placed   distinguishing characteristic

Other items in the category include pencils and chalk. The pen differs because it contains ink. The definition is developed by providing characteristics of the item.

Signal Words and Other Strategies for Definition

In textbooks, the most obvious signal of a definition is that the word is in **bold** or *italic* type. The signal is a visual one. Some brief definitions are placed in parentheses ( ) or set off with dashes —. Also look for the use of "that is" and "or" to introduce a definition:

Diction, that is, the writer's choice of language, . . .
Fossils, or the remains of prehistoric life, . . .

Basic Structure for Definition

The definition strategy can be organized in several ways. When defining complex or debatable terms or concepts, writers often give examples, or contrast the term with others that are similar but not exactly the same, or even give a brief history of the term. You will usually find some, if not all, of the elements illustrated below, but not necessarily in the order shown.

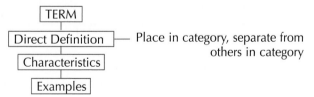

How to Annotate Definitions

If a direct definition is given, underline it. Note characteristics or examples if they are given. If the term is not highlighted in the text, then underline it twice or circle it, remembering to be consistent in your choice of markings. Here is a chemistry text's definition of *matter*.

characteristic

exs.

matter-def.

> The entire universe consists of matter and energy. Every day we come into contact with countless kinds of matter. Air, food, water, rocks, soil, glass, and this book are all different types of matter. Broadly defined, <u>matter is *anything that has mass and occupies space.*</u>
>
> Hein and Arena, *Foundations of College Chemistry*, 5th ed.

Observe that the direct definition follows the characteristics and examples. Also note that while the term *matter* is not highlighted, the word appears in each of the four sentences.

EXERCISE 8-2	**Recognizing and Annotating Definitions**

Read and annotate each of the following selections. Then complete the exercise that follows each selection.

I. **Cultural Lag.** Obgurn coined the term **cultural lag** to describe the situation in which some elements of a culture adapt to an invention or discovery more rapidly than others. Technology, he suggested, usually changes first, followed by culture. The nine-month school year is an example. In the nineteenth century, the school year matched the technology of the time, which required that children work with their parents at the critical times of planting and harvesting. Current technology has eliminated the need for the school year to be so short, but the cultural form has lagged severely behind technology.

James M. Henslin, *Sociology*, 2nd ed.

1. Define the term *cultural lag* in your own words. _____

_____

2. List the strategies used in this definition.

_____

_____

3. What signals are used to indicate that a definition is being given?

_____

_____

II. **Sexual Harassment. Sexual harassment** refers to inappropriate actions of a sexual nature. The law defines two categories of sexual harassment: (1) unwelcome advances and requests for sexual favors that affect promotions and raises, and (2) a "hostile" work environment in which an employee feels hassled or degraded because of unwelcome flirting, lewd comments, or obscene jokes. The courts have ruled that allowing sexually oriented materials like pinup calendars and pornographic magazines at the workplace can create a hostile atmosphere that interferes with an employee's ability to do the job.

Boone and Kurtz, Contemporary Business, 1997 ed.

1. Define *sexual harassment* in your own words. _____

_____

2. List the strategies used in this definition.

_____

_____

3. What signals are used to indicate that a definition is being given?

_____

_____

III. **Scale.** The level of detail and the amount of area covered on a map depend on its scale. The scale of a map is the same concept as the scale of a model car or boat: **Scale** is the relation of a feature's size on a map to its actual size on Earth's surface. For example, if 1 inch of roadway on a map is actually 24,000 inches on the ground, the map scale is 1:24,000.

James M. Rubenstein, An Introduction to Human Geography, 5th ed.

1. Define the term *scale* in your own words. _____

_____

2. List the strategies used to define the term.

_____

_____

3. What signals are used to indicate that a definition is being given?

_____

_____

IV. **Leader.** All groups, no matter what their size, have leaders, although they may not hold formal positions in the group. A **leader** is someone who influences the behaviors, opinions, or attitudes of others. Some people are leaders because of their personalities, but leadership involves much more than this.

James M. Henslin, *Sociology: A Down-to-Earth Approach*, 5th ed.

1. Define *leader* in your own words. _____

_____

2. List the strategies used in this definition.

_____

_____

3. What signals are used to indicate that a definition is being given?

_____

_____

V. **Frustration.** When people are hindered from meeting their goals, they often feel frustrated. **Frustration** is an emotional state that is said to occur when any goal—work, family, or personal—is thwarted or blocked. When people feel that they cannot achieve a goal (often due to situations beyond their control), they may experience frustration and stress. When you are unable to obtain a summer job because of a lack of experience, it can cause feelings of stress; when a grandparent becomes ill, you may feel helpless, and this causes stress.

Lefton and Valvatne, *Mastering Psychology*, 4th ed.

1. Define *frustration* in your own words. _____

_____

2. List the strategies used in this definition.

_____

_____

3. Which strategy is most effective in explaining the term, in your view?

_____

4. What signals are used to indicate that a definition is being given?

_____

_____

◼ STATEMENT WITH CLARIFICATION

This strategy is similar to using examples to develop the main idea in a paragraph or longer passage. But instead of giving examples to illustrate the main idea, the writer explains the main idea, adding further ideas and details but not specific examples. In other words, the major and minor details of the passage work together to explain, add to, and clarify the main idea. The details that clarify may be an important part of what needs to be learned in a textbook selection.

Signal Words for Statement with Clarification

Signal words for this strategy are often those that show a connection between statements, such as "thus" or "in other words." But often no signals are used; readers have to see the connections between sentences in the way the ideas relate. Here are the most common signal words for statement with clarification.

also	in fact	of course	too
clearly	in other words	that is	
evidently	obviously	thus	

Basic Structure for Statement with Clarification

This structure is the hardest to illustrate because it is the most subtle of the patterns. In fact, you could argue that it is not a "pattern" at all. However, it is a common strategy. A complex main idea needs to be commented on further to explain it to readers. We can illustrate the strategy this way:

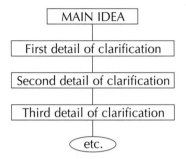

How to Annotate Statement with Clarification

Read the entire paragraph or passage carefully and then underline the main idea. Remember that the passage may contain major details that are rather general statements. The main idea will be the most general statement. Circle any signal words that show connections between statements. Write "detail" or "support" or "clarify" in the margin next to each new point that helps to explain the main idea. Here is an example.

main idea >

individuals choose a party

|

party becomes a coalition of groups

|

that holds together though campaigns

<u>Because there are only two major parties, pragmatic citizens who are interested in politics or public policy are mainly attracted to one or the other standard, creating natural majorities or near-majorities for party office holders to command.</u> The party creates a community of interest that bonds disparate groups over time into a **coalition**. This continuing mutual interest eliminates the necessity of creating a new coalition for every campaign or every issue.

O'Connor and Sabato, *American Government: Continuity and Change*, 2002 ed.

EXERCISE 8-3 | **Recognizing the Use of Statement with Clarification**

Read, annotate, and then complete the exercise for each of the following passages.

1. The most listened-for item in morning newscasts is the weather forecast. People want to know how to prepare for the day. The quality of their lives is at stake. Not carrying an umbrella to work if rain is expected can mean getting wet on the way home, perhaps catching pneumonia, at worst dying. There used to be a joke that the most important thing the mass media did was to tell us whether a tornado was coming or whether the Russians were coming.

John Vivian, *The Media of Mass Communications*, 6th ed.

1. What is the paragraph's topic sentence? Underline it.

2. Briefly state, in your own words, the key points to be learned from the paragraph.

_____

_____

_____

_____

3. List any signal words used. _____

II.   The majority of people—about 90% of the world's population—are right-handed. Left-handedness occurs more often in males than in females. People who are left-handed are generally also left-footed, and to a less extent left-eyed and left-eared as well. There is a difference in the motor control provided by the two hemispheres of the brain. Thus, in a person whose left hand is dominant, the right hemisphere is providing superior motor control for that hand.

Wood and Wood, *The World of Psychology,* 4th ed.

1. What is the paragraph's topic? _____

2. Briefly state, in your own words, the key points to be learned from the paragraph.

_____

_____

_____

_____

3. List any signal words used. _____

III.   The first comprehensive study of the dinosaurs that lived on earth millions of years ago was presented by Sir Richard Owen. In 1842, Owen delivered his "Report on British Fossil Reptiles" to the eleventh meeting of the British Association for the Advancement of Science. In the report, he not only introduced the term "dinosaur" to the English language, he introduced the notion of the "terrible lizard" itself, distinguishing it from all other reptiles past and present.

Steve Fiffer, *Tyrannosaurus Sue: The Extraordinary Saga of the Largest, Most Fought over T. Rex Ever Found*

1. What is the paragraph's topic sentence? Underline it.

2. Briefly state, in your own words, the key points to be learned from the passage.

   _____

   _____

   _____

   _____

3. List any signal words used. _____

IV. It's important to be able to laugh and to get others to laugh at jokes and funny stories, but it is also important to be able to laugh at ourselves. When we can laugh at our mistakes or when we embarrassed ourselves in some silly way, we demonstrate emotional balance and well-being. Laughing at ourselves is a way of saying that we realize that we are not perfect or that we can handle a bad situation. In other words, when we can "laugh it off," we accept that we are not the most important person in the universe or that what has happened is not "the end of the world" for us. Laughing at ourselves is, clearly, a good habit to develop.

1. What is the paragraph's main idea?

   _____

   _____

2. Briefly state, in your own words, the key points to be learned from the passage.

   _____

   _____

   _____

   _____

3. List any signal words used. _____

V. When a group is small, its members are informal, but as the group grows, they lose their sense of intimacy and grow more formal. No longer can the members assume that the others are "insiders" in sympathy with what they say. Now they must take a "larger audience" into consideration, and instead of merely "talking," they begin to "address" the group. As their speech becomes more formal, their body language stiffens, too.

James M. Henslin, *Sociology: A Down-to-Earth Approach*, 5th ed.

1. What is the paragraph's topic sentence? Underline it.

2. Briefly state, in your own words, the key points to be learned from the passage.

_____

_____

_____

_____

3. List any signal words used. _____

EXERCISE 8-4	Distinguishing Among Various Structures

Read, annotate, and then answer the questions that follow each of the paragraphs. Part of your task is to identify the structure/pattern used.

I. What is a classic? A **classic** is a book that has been read and valued by many, many people. Although we use the expression "contemporary classic," most classics have continued to appeal to readers over a fairly long period of time. The plays of the Greek writer Sophocles are over a thousand years old; Shakespeare's plays are over four hundred years old. Arthur Miller's *Death of a Salesman* is a good example of a contemporary classic. Classics are enjoyed because they help us understand human life and experience. They remind us that certain truths endure over time.

1. What structure or strategy is used in this paragraph?

_____

2. What techniques are used to develop the strategy?

_____

3. What signals are used?

_____

II.   The first written messages were simply pictures relating familiar objects in some meaningful way—pictographs. Yet there were no images for much that was important to human life. What, for instance, was the image for sorrow or bravery? So from pictographs humans developed ideograms to represent more abstract ideas. An eye flowing with tears could represent sorrow, and a man with the head of a lion might be bravery.

The next leap occurred when the figures became independent of things or ideas and came to stand for spoken sounds. Written figures were free to lose all resemblance to actual objects. Some societies developed syllabic systems of writing in which several hundred signs corresponded to several hundred spoken sounds. Others discovered the much simpler alphabetic system, in which a handful of signs represented the basic sounds the human voice can make.

Don Lago, "Symbols of Humankind"

1. What structure or strategy is used in this paragraph?

_____

2. Briefly state, in your own words, the main points in a way that reveals the pattern of the paragraph.

_____

_____

_____

_____

3. List the signal words that are used. _____

_____

III. **Potential energy** is stored energy, or energy an object possesses due to its relative position. For example, a ball located 20 ft above the ground has more potential energy than when located 10 ft above the ground and will bounce higher when allowed to fall. Water backed up behind a dam represents potential energy that can be converted into...electrical or mechanical energy. Gasoline is a source of chemical potential energy.

Hein and Arena, *Foundations of College Chemistry*, 5th ed.

1. What is the paragraph's topic sentence?

   _____

2. What structure or strategy is used in this paragraph?

   _____

3. What techniques are used to develop the strategy?

   _____

4. What signals are used?

   _____

IV. To really learn a language, you also need to learn the perceptions about life and the world that are embedded (a fundamental part of) in that language. In other words, language both reflects cultural experiences and shapes those experiences. Language both describes the world and defines the world for children learning that language. It is because language is such an important shaper of our experience and definer of our culture that people who do not share the same language have difficulties. In short, language is the basis of culture.

1. What is the paragraph's topic sentence? Underline it.

2. What structure or strategy is used? _____

3. Briefly state, in your own words, the key ideas in the paragraph.

   _____

   _____

   _____

4. List any signal words that are used.

   _____

V. Some readers have trouble "getting hooked" on classics. It's true that classics are often hard to read. But following these steps will help you read them with pleasure. First, read about the author and the author's time. Were there any special circumstances in which the classic was produced? Next, be sure to know what kind of work you are reading—a novel, a biography, a poem. Then, read in "big chunks." You will have a better sense of what is going on in a difficult work if you really get into each chapter or section. Finally, look forward to each reading; you are reading a work that many people before you have read and loved.

1. What structure or strategy is used in this paragraph?

   _____

2. What is the paragraph's topic?

   _____

3. List three major details in a way that reveals the paragraph's structure.

   _____

   _____

   _____

   _____

4. List any signal words that are used.

   _____

VI. Philip II (1180–1223) greatly expanded the holdings of his father and developed an administration system to run his French kingdom. But, perhaps most importantly, he established Paris as the central city in France. In 1183 Philip built the first permanent Paris market, Les Halles, which continued to be the primary market for the city until the 1960s. Before leaving for a crusade in 1192, he ordered a new city wall that enclosed land both on the left and right banks of the Seine River. The protection from the city walls allowed the University on the Left Bank to grow quickly. Philip also built a new fort just outside the city wall, the Louvre, which would become the new palace of French kings. When he returned from his crusade, victorious, in 1214, Parisians partied for a week.

Adapted from Kishlansky, Geary, and O'Brien,
Civilization in the West, 4th ed.

1. What is the paragraph's topic sentence? Underline it.

2. What structure or strategy has been used? _____

3. Briefly state, in your own words, the main points in a way that reveals the pattern of the paragraph.

_____

_____

_____

_____

4. List the signal words that are used.

_____

VII. **Stereotypes** are fixed, overly simple (and often wrong) ideas, usually about traits, attitudes, and behaviors attributed to groups of people. Often, stereotypes are negative. People hold stereotyped ideas about Native Americans, Catholics, women, and mountain folk; the stereotypes can lead to prejudice.

Lester A. Lefton, *Psychology*, 5th ed.

1. What is the paragraph's topic sentence? Underline it.

2. What structure or strategy is used in this paragraph?

_____

3. What techniques are used to develop the paragraph's strategy?

_____

_____

4. What signals are used? _____

VIII. Because their authority is based only on their personal ability to attract followers, charismatic leaders pose a threat to the established political system. They lead followers according to personal inclination, not according to the paths of tradition or the regulations of law. Accordingly, they can inspire followers to disregard—or even to overthrow—traditional and rational-legal authorities. This means that charismatic leaders pose a threat to the established order. Consequently, traditional and rational-legal authorities are often quick to oppose charismatic figures.

James M. Henslin, *Sociology: A Down-to-Earth Approach*, 5th ed.

1. What is the paragraph's topic?

   _____

2. What structure or strategy is used in this paragraph?

   _____

3. Briefly state, in your own words, the main points in a way that reveals the strategy of the paragraph.

   _____

   _____

   _____

   _____

4. List the signal words that are used.

   _____

IX. All human societies began as hunting and gathering groups. Then, about ten to twelve thousand years ago, some groups discovered that they could tame animals (pastoral society) and other learned to grow plants, using hand tools. The next revolution in human society occurred about five to six thousand years ago with the invention of the plow. This new agricultural society created cities and the elements of culture. In the 1700s another revolution changed society; the Industrial Revolution was based on the development of the steam engine—and hence machinery—to do some of the work. Finally, in the twentieth century, we entered the postindustrial society, often referred to as the Information Age, and based on the microchip. Each revolution, making for great changes in the way people lived, came about because of a major technological development.

1. What is the paragraph's topic sentence? Underline it.

2. What structure or strategy is used in the paragraph?

   _____

3. Briefly state, in your own words, the main points in a way that reveals the pattern of the paragraph.

_____

_____

_____

_____

4. List the signal words that are used.

_____

X. Water is different from most other substances. Most molecules, when they get colder, become denser and thus sink. But water, when it gets colder, actually expands. When it freezes at 32°F, it is much less dense, and therefore lighter, than other liquids—or unfrozen water—and so it rises to the top rather than sinking. This characteristic of water allows ponds to freeze over in the winter without freezing all the way to the bottom and then evaporating to nothing in the spring. Instead, the ice forms on top of the pond, forming a protective shield for the water below so that it does not freeze.

1. What is the paragraph's topic sentence? Underline it.

2. What structure or strategy is used in the paragraph?

_____

3. State briefly, in your own words, the main points that reveals the pattern of the paragraph.

_____

_____

_____

_____

4. List any signal words that are used.

_____

▪ ▪ ▪ ▪ ▪

MAKING SPORTS FUN

Martin G. Miller

Dr. Miller is a sociologist at Iowa State University and a youth softball and volleyball coach. The following passage comes from his essay "Sport Is Too Important to Be Just a Game!" The essay is one chapter in the textbook *Applying Sociology*, by William Du Bois and R. Dean Wright.

Prepare

1. Identify the author and the work. What do you expect the author's purpose to be?

   _____

   _____

2. Preread to identify the subject and make predictions. What do you expect to read about?

   _____

   _____

3. What do you already know about the subject?

   _____

   _____

   _____

4. Raise two questions that you expect the article to answer.

   _____

   _____

   _____

   _____

■ ■ ■ ■ ■

1   We all agree on the importance of fun in sport, but we seldom take the time to reflect on its meaning. If we know what fun means, then we have a better chance of establishing it in our programs and teams. We will be better able to meet the needs of our athletes. So here is my shot at the meaning of *fun*.

2   Having fun is participating in meaningful activities, being with people who don't yell and who offer encouragement. Fun is using a ball, bat, glove, stick, or racquet as often as possible. It is serving an ace, hitting a softball, shooting hoops, pitching balls, kicking goals, splashing water, playing games, being with friends, eating pizza.

3   Fun is not being yelled at. It is not being on a team that fights and argues. Fun is not enduring long boring practices, coaches who talk too much and don't listen, or sitting on the bench too long. Fun is play, venturing out, trying new things.

4   Fun is being understood; having a coach who cares about the team and who knows the game and how to execute skills; having shared team experiences; learning new sports skills. Fun is not having a coach who does not understand what it is like to be a child, or not having a team that has no spirit or unity, or missing out on learning the technical aspects of the game. Fun is having a coach who knows the game and teaches it in a way that makes you feel free to try and learn new things.

5   Creating a climate of fun means that the youngsters will practice and play harder and take a personal interest in their team, in each other, and in their own learning. It can make a big difference in how young athletes play—as a team or simply as a group of individuals—if all the players truly enjoy the sports experience created for them.

6   If fun isn't evident with your team, then it's time to rethink and change coaching styles and program goals. A guiding coaching principle should be: *No matter what, keep it fun!*

354 words

Comprehension Check

Respond to the following statements with either a T (true) or F (false).

	T	F
1. The author's purpose in this passage is to define fun as a guide for coaches of young people playing sports.	____	____
2. Sports are not fun if young athletes are yelled at.	____	____
3. Fun is eating pizza after long, boring practices.	____	____
4. Fun is getting to play often, not just sitting on the bench.	____	____
5. Young athletes have fun when they are free from learning technical skills of the game.	____	____

6. Youngsters can have fun on a team even though their coach doesn't know much about the game and doesn't listen to their questions.   ____ ____

7. When youngsters are having fun they will practice and play harder.   ____ ____

8. Fun means feeling free to try new things.   ____ ____

9. Children can have fun and learn at the same time.   ____ ____

10. Coaches should not have to worry about making the sport fun for youngsters.   ____ ____

Expanding Vocabulary

Read each word in its sentence in the passage and use context clues to help you understand its meaning. Then write a brief definition or synonym for each word. The numbers in parentheses tell you what paragraph the word appears in.

1. establishing (1) _____

2. participating (2) _____

3. encouragement (2) _____

4. enduring (3) _____

5. venturing (3) _____

6. execute (4) _____

7. technical (4) _____

8. evident (6) _____

Reflection and Discussion

1. Did you play a sport as a youngster? If so, did you have fun? Did your coach help to make it fun? Were any parents yelling at their children? Reflect on your experiences in relation to Martin's definition of fun in sports.

2. Martin includes learning skills and feeling free to try new things as part of the fun of sport. Do you agree that learning can be fun? Why or why not? What conditions help to make learning fun?

HERMAN CAIN OF GODFATHER'S PIZZA

William G. Nickels, Jim McHugh, and Susan McHugh

Dr. Nickels is an associate professor of business at the University of Maryland. Jim McHugh teaches at St. Louis Community College and does business consulting. Susan McHugh is an adult learning theory specialist. This article comes from their textbook, *Understanding Business,* 5th edition.

Prepare

1. Identify the authors and work. What do you expect the authors' purpose to be?

   _____

   _____

2. Preread to identify the subject and make predictions. What do you expect to read about?

   _____

   _____

3. What do you already know about the subject?

   _____

   _____

4. Raise two questions that you expect the selection to answer.

   _____

   _____

   _____

   _____

■ ■ ■ ■ ■

1   Luther and Lenora Cain left farm life to find more opportunity in the business world. Luther found a job as a porter and Lenora as a maid. In fact, to earn enough to rear a family, Luther took on three jobs, including one as a chauffeur at Coca-Cola. Soon he became the chauffeur and personal valet to the president of Coca-Cola.

2   Herman Cain is Luther and Lenora's son. He learned from his parents that hard work and dedication pay off in the long run. He finished high school second in his class and attended Morehouse College, working after school and summers to help pay his tuition. His father had saved enough money to buy a grocery store, and Herman worked in that store for a while. Inspired by Dr. Martin Luther King, Cain went on to get a master's degree at Purdue University and landed a job at Coca-Cola as an analyst. Four years later, he and his supervisor moved to Pillsbury, where in another five years he was vice president for corporate systems and services. His goal was to become president of a firm.

3   The president of Pillsbury told Cain that he would most likely reach his goal by rising up through the ranks at Burger King, a division of the company. But that meant starting from the bottom, flipping hamburgers and giving up his company car and nice office! Cain hoped it was the right thing to do and, as it turned out, it was. He completed the usual two-year training program in nine months and was named Burger King's vice president of the Philadelphia region, in charge of 450 units. It had been a slow-growing region, but Cain turned it into the company's best one for growth, sales, and profit.

4   Cain was so successful at Burger King that he became the president of Pillsbury's Godfather's Pizza. Having reached his goal, Cain began his work as president by streamlining operations. Unprofitable units were closed, and others were made more efficient. Eventually Cain and a partner bought Godfather's from Pillsbury for $50 million. Since then, the value of the company has doubled.

5   Cain says that service is the driving force behind his business. His number one rule is, "The customer is always right." He also says that if you love what you are doing, you will be successful. Following that philosophy, Cain became the first black president of the National Restaurant Association.

6   Now Cain is working hard to support his community. He supports an outreach program for troubled teens and gives speeches about what it takes to be a success. Many young people think the fast-food industry offers only dead-end jobs. Herman Cain doesn't see it that way. He sees such jobs as a chance to eventually run something—to own something. He sees opportunity.

466 words

Comprehension Check

Answer the following with a, b, c, or d to indicate the phrase that best completes each statement.

_____   1. The authors begin by describing Herman Cain's parents to show that

a. his father worked for Coca-Cola.

b. his parents set an example of hard work and seeking opportunity.

c. his parents set a bad example that Cain overcame.

d. he was lucky to have parents with jobs.

_____ 2. Herman Cain

a. earned a master's degree.

b. finished high school only.

c. attended college but did not finish.

d. went from high school to Burger King.

_____ 3. After working for Coca-Cola, Cain worked for

a. Godfather's Pizza.

b. Burger King.

c. Pillsbury and became president.

d. Pillsbury and became vice president.

_____ 4. Because Cain wanted to be president of a company, he

a. stayed at Pillsbury.

b. went to work in a Burger King.

c. delivered pizzas.

d. opened a grocery store.

_____ 5. After finishing the training course with Burger King, Cain became

a. president of Burger King.

b. president of Coca-Cola.

c. a vice president of Burger King in Philadelphia.

d. a vice president of Burger King in Chicago.

_____ 6. Because of his success at Burger King, Cain

a. retired early.

b. became the president of Godfather's Pizza.

c. became the president of Burger King.

d. went back to his father's store.

_____ 7. To improve Godfather's Pizza, Cain

a. changed the recipe.

b. fired people he did not like.

c. closed unprofitable units and streamlined others.

d. opened many more units.

_____ 8. After Cain and a partner bought Godfather's Pizza,

a. Cain retired and let his partner run the company.

b. the company's value decreased.

c. the company's value doubled.

d. Cain was unhappy.

_____ 9. Cain believes that

    a. service is very important.

    b. if you love what you do, you will be successful.

    c. you should support your community.

    d. all of the above.

_____ 10. The authors have used Cain's story to show that

    a. Pillsbury owns Burger King and Godfather's Pizza.

    b. some people are lucky and get ahead.

    c. you need to see and take opportunities and work hard to get ahead.

    d. heads of big companies don't care about others.

Expanding Vocabulary

Match each word in the left column with its definition in the right column by placing the correct letter in the space next to each word. When in doubt, read again the sentence in which the word appears. The numbers in parentheses tell you what paragraph the word appears in.

_____ 1. porter (1)   a. a man's personal male servant

_____ 2. chauffeur (1)   b. fee for instruction

_____ 3. valet (1)   c. not making money

_____ 4. dedication (2)   d. stimulated to action

_____ 5. tuition (2)   e. occurring at some time in the future

_____ 6. Inspired (2)   f. person employed to carry bags or do general tasks

_____ 7. streamlining (4)   g. commitment of oneself to a course of action

_____ 8. Unprofitable (4)   h. one hired to drive a car

_____ 9. Eventually (4)   i. system of values, principles

_____ 10. philosophy (5)   j. improving efficiency by simplifying

Reflection and Discussion

1. Do you see flipping burgers as a job with opportunity? Does Cain's story affect your thinking in any way?

2. What did Cain have going for him in addition to hard work and a goal?

3. Why would the authors choose to include Cain's story in a business textbook?

MAKING CONNECTIONS

1. With your class partner or on your own, make a list of ways that you, as a student, can make classroom learning more fun.

2. With your class partner or on your own, make a list of specific actions that you think would make Americans, as a society, happier.

"E" CONNECTIONS

Many of us have a favorite sports figure. Conduct a search of your library's electronic databases for a detailed biography of your favorite sports figure. See if you can get beyond "stats" to learn how the person started his or her successful career. You will need a detailed biography or a newspaper or magazine article. Try Proquest or Expanded Academic ASAP or a biographical dictionary.

WORD POWER 7

Sorting Out Words That Are Often Confused

This is the second set of common words that are *not* pronounced the same. In addition they are spelled differently and have different meanings. What do they have in common? The pairs are often confused. Study the words and their meanings. Then select the correct word to complete each of the sentences below.

elicit to draw out **illicit** illegal	**moral** distinguishing right from wrong **morale** attitude of person or group
envelop to surround **envelope** container for papers	**personal** private **personnel** employees
human Homo sapiens **humane** compassionate	**presence** state of being, or person who is present **presents** gifts
later after a time **latter** second one of two	**sense** perception, understanding **since** from then until now; ago
loose not tightly fastened **lose** to misplace	**than** in comparison with; besides **then** at that time; next

1. The _____ *(loose/lose)* behavior of the gang may not have been

_____ *(elicit/illicit)*, but it certainly wasn't _____

(moral/morale).

2. Sometimes in Germany the fog _____ (envelops/envelopes) an area, and _____ (than/then) the autobahn must be closed.

3. Of the two teens, the _____ (later/latter) one seems to lack good _____ (sense/since).

4. The _____ (presence/presents) of the candidate _____ (elicited/illicited) cheers and applause.

5. The CEO gathered her _____ (personal/personnel) for a meeting; _____ (than/then) she gave a fiery speech.

6. In the face of terrorism, it is sometimes hard to maintain one's _____ (moral/morale); it is only _____ (human/humane) to get discouraged.

7. The birthday boy gathered all his _____ (presence/presents), not wanting to _____ (loose/lose) any of them.

8. Those who oppose the death penalty argue that it is not _____ (human/humane); as a nation we should be better _____ (than/then) the criminal.

9. These views _____ (elicit/illicit) strong reactions and the counterargument that the criminal has removed him- or herself from the _____ (human/humane) race.

10. _____ (sense/since) the issue was _____ (personal/personnel), the candidate would not discuss it.

CHAPTER REVIEW

1. Two strategies that organize by chronology are _____ and

   _____.

2. "Cycle," "until," and "step" are signal words often found with the strat-

   egy of _____.

3. In textbooks, the most common signal for definitions is the use of

   _____ or _____ type.

4. Two good ways to develop a definition are giving _____ and

   _____.

5. "In other words" and "in fact" are signal words often found with the

   strategy of _____.

Take a Reading Road Trip!

For additional practice with your reading skills, use the Reading Road Trip CD-ROM
or visit Reading Road Trip on the Web at **<http://www.ablongman.com/readingroadtrip>**
(password required).

CHAPTER 9

Recognizing More Patterns and the Use of Mixed Patterns

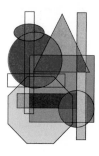

LEARNING OBJECTIVES

■ To understand the primary structures or patterns authors use to give order to their writing

■ Specifically, to recognize the patterns of cause/effect and problem/solution and to recognize mixed patterns

■ To recognize the words that signal each pattern or structure

■ To annotate each pattern as you read

PREPARE TO READ

Read and reflect on the chapter's title and objectives. Glance through the chapter, observing headings to see what is covered. Now answer these questions:

1. What do you expect to learn from this chapter?

   _____

   _____

2. What do you already know about the chapter's topic?

   _____

   _____

3. What two or three questions do you want answered from reading this chapter?

   _____

   _____

In Chapter 7 we began our study of the structures or strategies—the patterns—that writers use to give order to their writing and to reinforce their purpose in writing. As indicated in Chapters 7 and 8, recognizing a writer's primary pattern is important to reading comprehension.

In this chapter, you will study the structure and accompanying signal words of two more patterns: cause and effect and problem/solution. In addition, this chapter contains a summary chart of basic structures or patterns and a discussion of the use of mixed patterns. As you study these last two patterns, keep in mind that your goal is improved reading comprehension. Also remember that not all writers use common signal words; readers have to determine the pattern from the relationship of ideas. Finally, writers often combine patterns, in which case you want to look for the most important pattern as your guide to the writer's purpose.

CAUSE AND EFFECT

The cause/effect pattern is an important tool for writers explaining why something happened (Why did the Roman Empire collapse?), what is causing a current problem (Why is there a greater fear of violence?), and what might happen in the future (Will lowering taxes improve the economy?). Writers can focus on cause or effect, but they are really writing about both. If I describe the effects of smoking on health, I am also explaining the cause of those health problems.

Signal Words for Cause and Effect

The best signals of the cause/effect structure are the words *cause* and *effect*. You will often find them in titles, section headings, and opening sentences. "Why" questions also announce that causes will be examined. The following words are also found in cause/effect writing.

as a result	due to	impact on
because	follows	therefore
changes	hence	thus
consequently		

Basic Structure for Cause and Effect

Cause/effect structures can take several forms. First, a writer can explain how one cause produces one effect:

Cause   **Effect**
Dissolve zinc in sulfuric acid ⟶ zinc sulfate forms

In many cases, one cause produces several effects:

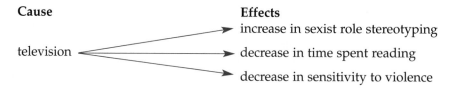

Cause

television

Effects

increase in sexist role stereotyping

decrease in time spent reading

decrease in sensitivity to violence

In addition, several causes may work together to produce one effect:

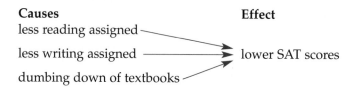

Causes

less reading assigned

less writing assigned

dumbing down of textbooks

Effect

lower SAT scores

Finally, several causes may produce several effects:

Causes

improved reading skills

improved study skills

Effect

better grades

more pleasure from school

Remember that in a complicated world we rarely find one simple cause producing one simple effect.

How to Annotate Cause and Effect

When you recognize that a writer is discussing causes and effects, be sure to understand which is the cause and which the effect. Then, note all the causes, or all the effects, that are given. Underline the topic sentence and the key words that state the cause(s) or effect(s). If there are several, then use numbers in the margin to note each one. Here is an example.

Effects

①

②

③

Pleistocene (Ice-Age) glaciers . . . had <u>other, sometimes profound, effects upon the landscape</u>. For example, as the ice advanced and retreated, animals and plants were forced to migrate. This led to stresses that some organisms could not tolerate. Hence, a number of <u>different plants and animals became extinct</u>. Furthermore, <u>many present-day stream courses bear little resemblance to their preglacial routes</u>. The Missouri River once flowed northward toward Hudson Bay, while the Mississippi River followed a path through central Illinois. . . . <u>Other rivers that today carry only a trickle of water but nevertheless occupy broad channels</u> are testimony to the fact that they once carried torrents of glacial meltwater.

Tarbuck and Lutgens, *The Earth: An Introduction to Physical Geology*, 4th ed.

| EXERCISE 9-1 | Recognizing and Annotating the Use of Cause and Effect |

Read and annotate each of the following selections and complete the exercise that follows each selection.

I. Once upon a time, many species of giant animals lived in both Australia and North America. These included mastodons, woolly mammoths, and saber-toothed tigers in North America up to 13,000 years ago. In Australia, around 50,000 years ago, one could find giant kangaroos and wombats. What led to the disappearance of all these giant vertebrates? Some scientists have blamed climate change or a virus, but new studies show that the arrival of humans was the cause of extinction on both continents. Within one to four thousand years after people arrived, the giant animals were all extinct. Early humans apparently became good hunters of the giant animals.

1. State the topic of the paragraph so that a cause/effect pattern is shown.

_____

2. Briefly list the specific effect(s) that took place.

_____

_____

_____

3. List the signal words that are used.

_____

II. In most cities in the United States, the rate of violent crime has dropped. Yet many Americans still say they are fearful. How can we explain this? Sociologists suggest that a major cause is television. The more hours of TV watched, the more fearful people are, according to several studies. There is so much violence on TV—in movies, cop shows, even the news—and viewers assume that the real world is similar to what they see on television.

1. State the topic so that a cause/effect pattern is shown.

_____

2. Briefly list the specific effect(s).

_____

_____

_____

3. List the signal words that are used.

_____

III. Whatever the cause or causes of mass extinctions, their effects on the course of evolution are clear. When entire groups of plants or animals die out, new opportunities are available to other plants or animals that survive. The survivors then diversify and make use of the newly available living space and find new solutions to their problems of survival and development.

Adapted from Curtis and Barnes, *An Invitation to Biology,* 4th ed.

1. State the topic so that a cause-effect pattern is shown.

_____

2. Briefly list the specific effect(s).

_____

_____

_____

3. List the signal words that are used.

_____

IV. Aggression in sports has several significant consequences. The effects on the target of the aggression include anger, intimidation, and possibly injury. The athlete committing the aggression may be penalized, and the focus on being aggressive rather than playing the game may lead to a bad performance. Also, spectators are learning that aggression seems to pay off. Finally, the sport's image with the public is hurt. Athletes need to learn that aggression has serious effects for the players and the game.

1. State the topic so that a cause/effect pattern is shown.

_____

2. Briefly list the specific effect(s).

_____

_____

_____

3. List the signal words that are used.

_____

V. **Alcohol's Effects on the Brain.** When alcohol flows to the brain, it first sedates the frontal lobe, the reasoning part. As the alcohol molecules diffuse into the cells of this lobe, they interfere with reasoning and judgment. With continued drinking, the speech and vision centers of the brain become sedated, and the area that governs reasoning becomes more incapacitated. Still more drinking affects the cells of the brain responsible for large-muscle control; at this point people under the influence stagger or weave when they try to walk. Finally the conscious brain becomes completely subdued, and the person passes out.

Sizer and Whitney, *Nutrition: Concepts and Controversies*, 6th ed.

1. State the topic of the paragraph so that a cause/effect pattern is indicated.

_____

2. Briefly list the specific effects.

_____

_____

_____

3. List the signal words that are used.

_____

PROBLEM/SOLUTION

Another structure to look for—both in textbooks and in arguments—is the problem/solution pattern. This pattern usually has either two or three parts, depending on the problem and the writer's approach to it.

Signal Words

Often the words *problem* and *solution* appear. Other signal words include:

answers	crisis	issue(s)

Basic Structure for Problem/Solution

First, the writer needs to introduce the problem: poverty or violence on TV, for example. If the problem is well known, writers will not give much space to introducing the problem. However, if the problem is new or not properly understood (in the view of the writer), then several paragraphs may be given to explaining the problem.

If there are three parts to this structure, the second part is devoted to examining the cause or causes of the problem. If the writer's solution rests on removing the cause, then the writer must explain the cause first. (Hunger is caused by poverty. If you want to find solutions to hunger, you will need to find solutions to poverty.) If the causes are unknown or no longer relevant to solving the problem, then there is no section on cause.

The third part (or second part if there is no discussion of cause) presents the writer's solution or solutions. One solution may be presented, or several, depending on the problem and on the writer's view of the issue. You will often find the problem/solution pattern extending over several paragraphs since both problems and their solutions of usually complicated.

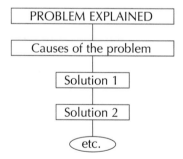

How to Annotate Problem/Solution

When you recognize that a problem is being explored and solutions offered, begin by finding the best, most complete statement of the problem. Sometimes the problem will be explained in more than one sentence. Underline the sentence or sentences that best state the problem. Next, look for a cause or causes to be presented. If they are there, label and number, if more than one. Finally, locate and label the solution, or each solution if more than one is given. Here is an example:

Problem: Singles face problems purchasing, storing, and preparing food. It doesn't matter if you are a college student or senior citizen, if you buy and cook for one, you have a particular challenge. Here are some suggestions for deal-
Solutions: ing with this problem.[1] Select bags of salad greens rather than a head of lettuce and a big bag of carrots.[2] Buy small containers of food even though they are more expensive—it's also expensive to throw away uneaten food. [3] Buy milk in pint sizes; if the large store doesn't stock them, try a deli.[4] Divide larger portions of food into one-size servings and freeze them that way.[5] Put bread, or bagels after you've sliced them, in the freezer and take out just what you need for each meal.[6] Cook for two or four and store the leftovers in single-serving portions in the freezer.

EXERCISE 9-2	**Recognizing and Annotating Problem/Solution Patterns**

Read and annotate each of the following selections and complete the exercise that follows each selection.

I.   The research shows—and teachers will tell you—that more girls than boys like to read and manage to complete required books. Since developing good readings skills is important, we need to find ways to get boys to read more. The key is motivation—but that is also the problem: How do we get boys to be more motivated to read? One strategy that seems to make a difference is the male teacher who emphasizes reading. If the solution here is providing a role model—a male who values reading—then clearly another solution is for dads to read and to show that they value reading and want their sons to read. Another solution is to find books that boys are likely to find interesting. In other words, stress *Harry Potter* rather than *Little House on the Prairie*.

1. State the problem discussed in this paragraph.

_____

_____

2. List the solutions offered.

_____

_____

_____

      3. List the signal words that are used.

_____

II.   Parents are wise to be concerned about highly aggressive children. There are some approaches parents can take to ease this problem. They should not encourage or reward aggression. They should try to avoid physical punishment (a form of aggression) and instead give the child a "time out" for aggressive behavior. Parents can also reinforce nonaggressive behavior in their children while teaching children responsibility for their actions.

      1. State the problem discussed in this paragraph.

_____

_____

      2. List the solutions offered.

_____

_____

_____

      3. List any signal words that are used.

_____

III. In the last 20 years about 800,000 elephants have been killed by people who wish to sell their ivory tusks. This in itself is a problem, but the problem becomes more serious when we consider that it is the older elephants, those with the largest tusks, that are most desired by poachers. But studies have shown that the older elephants are the wisest ones. They have more sense to get their group to bunch protectively when they hear an unfamiliar contact call from another elephant. Also, elephant families with the oldest leaders produce more babies within the group. So, the problem for elephant survival increases if poachers are not stopped from killing the oldest family leaders. Wardens in game preserves need to take special care to protect large elephant families with the oldest leaders, perhaps by regularly tracking their movements within the game preserve.

1. State the problem discussed in this paragraph.

_____

_____

2. List the solutions offered.

_____

_____

_____

3. List the signal words used.

_____

IV. Some doctors are calling it an epidemic. Obesity in American children has tripled in the last 20 years. Kelly Brownell and David Ludwig write that "the average child sees 10,000 food advertisements per year, 95 percent of them for fast food, soft drinks, candy and sugared cereals." The food industry, in other words, is spending an enormous amount of money to encourage children to eat food that is high in calories, sugar, and fat, and low in nutrition. How do we deal with this problem? We need to end all food ads aimed at children. We need to remove all vending machines containing soft drinks and snacks from schools. We need to get the food industry to cooperate in these moves, or we need to make it happen by law.

1. State the problem discussed in this paragraph.

_____

_____

2. List the solutions offered.

_____

_____

_____

3. List the signal words that are used.

_____

V.   Rudeness seems to be everywhere these days, from aggressive driving on the highway to loud and tasteless behavior in public places such as restaurants to pushing ahead in lines at the store or bank. What can each one of us do to try to make our community lives more pleasant, less dominated by rudeness? One solution may be to "kill them with kindness." Sometimes if we are especially nice to someone who is behaving badly, the rude person will become embarrassed by his or her behavior and stop being so unpleasant. Of course, we can always set a good example as well. Finally, sometimes we may have to speak up, to say to the person, "You are rude; now just stop."

1. State the problem discussed in this paragraph.

_____

_____

2. List the solutions offered.

_____

_____

_____

3. List the signal words that are used.

_____

| EXERCISE 9-3 | **Distinguishing Among Various Structures** |

Read, annotate, and then answer the questions that follow each of the paragraphs. Part of your task is to identify the structure/pattern used.

I.   Exercise is good for you. It has many positive effects. Aerobic exercise, such as walking, jogging, or swimming, helps to reduce depression and stress. Whenever possible, exercise outdoors because studies have shown that sunlight can reduce depression. Having a fit and toned body can increase self-confidence, and exercise has been shown to help reduce the major risk factors for heart failure: high blood pressure, high cholesterol, and obesity. And, the better shape you are in the more easily you will recover from accident or illness. So, seek the benefits of exercise on a regular basis.

1. What structure or pattern is used in this paragraph?

_____

2. List three major details in the paragraph in a way that reveals the paragraph's pattern.

_____

_____

_____

3. List any signal words used.

_____

II. Most skin cancers, if caught early, are not life threatening; however, malignant melanomas, which spread quickly, are much more dangerous. You have a 1 in 120 chance of developing a melanoma, so this is a problem you want to avoid. How can you best avoid all types of skin cancers, including the problem melanomas? First, be sure to use sun screen when you are outside. Apply it 30 minutes before you go outside and reapply if you are in the sun for several hours. Second, keep covered up, including wearing a hat. Several severe sunburns increase your risk of skin cancer, so be sure to avoid burning. Finally, avoid outdoor activities during the midday hours when the sun is the strongest in the summer months. Exercise early in the morning or after three in the afternoon.

1. What structure or pattern is used in this paragraph?

_____

2. List three major details from the paragraph in a way that reveals the paragraph's pattern.

_____

_____

_____

3. List any signal words used.

_____

III. Cities offer solutions to the problems of education and jobs and opportunity, but cities also create problems. Humans need more than a job to provide for basic needs; they also need a sense of community, of belonging. Successful—that is happy—city dwellers find that community in several ways. Shopping at the same stores, especially small stores in your neighborhood, leads to getting to know the clerks and to recognize others who shop there. Neighborhood restaurants and bars provide an even greater opportunity for a sense of belonging. Professional sports teams also provide a sense of community, so much so that many people who have moved elsewhere continue to be loyal fans of the teams in the cities where they grew up.

1. What structure or pattern is used in this paragraph?

_____

2. List three major details from the paragraph in a way that reveals the paragraph's pattern.

_____

_____

_____

_____

3. List any signal words used.

_____

IV. A recent study has shown that high school students attending Catholic schools pull ahead of public school students by a full grade in math and verbal skills. Why? The researchers argue that the major cause is higher educational standards. They teach more and demand more of their students, and the students deliver. Another cause may be greater involvement by parents who, with the teachers, expect and reward learning.

1. What structure or pattern is used in this paragraph?

_____

2. List three major details from the paragraph in a way that reveals the paragraph's pattern.

_____

_____

_____

_____

3. List any signal words used.

_____

V. What leads some people to join groups that have a strong racist agenda—groups such as the Ku Klux Klan or neo-Nazis? Studies have given us a profile, although we need to understand that the causes of individual behavior are always a complex mix. Still, we can say that the leaders of such groups see the world as clearly divided into racial and ethnic groups and that group identity is each person's primary identity. Also, the leaders tend to see life as a battle, a constant struggle among these groups. So, if you don't want to be destroyed, you must destroy the other group. Followers joining racist groups tend to be poor, poorly educated, or underemployed—that is, not successful. The group offers a "home," a community and a commitment to a cause that offers meaning in lives that are missing any sense of belonging.

1. What structure or pattern is used in this paragraph?

_____

2. List three major details in the paragraph in a way that reveals the paragraph's pattern.

_____

_____

_____

3. List any signal words used.

_____

■ ■ ■ ■ ■

SUMMARY LIST OF PATTERNS
WITH KEY SIGNAL WORDS

Pattern or Strategy	Key Signal Words
Cause/effect: The reasons for an event or situation; the consequences of an action or condition.	as a result, because, changes, due to, consequently, follows, hence, impact on, therefore, thus
Classification: Explanation of how ideas, events, or items fit into categories, e.g., organizing a society by income levels, or by age groups or educational level	category, rank, group, types, parts
Comparison/contrast: Discussion of similarities or differences of two items or events or ideas.	both, compared with, different, however, in contrast, in the same way, likewise, on the other hand, similarly
Definition: Explanation of the meaning of a word, concept, or term.	means, that is, is, or; use of **bold** or *italic* type
Examples: Use of specifics to illustrate and clarify a statement.	for example, for instance, that is, e.g., to illustrate
Listing/Addition: The simple presentation of information, one item at a time.	also, and, another, finally, first furthermore, in addition, last, likewise, moreover, next, second, third
Location/spatial order: Explaining the physical placement of items, particularly as they relate to other items in space.	above, adjacent to, below, beyond inside, nearby, next to, opposite, within, without
Ordering: Chronology and Process: Explaining by using time sequence, emphasizing the order in which something took place or must be followed.	after, before, finally, first, following, last, later, next, now, second, then, thereupon, until, when
Statement with Clarification: Explanation of a fact or idea with further discussion, including restating or expanding upon the idea.	also, clearly, evidently, in fact, in other words, obviously, of course, that is, thus, too

◼ MIXED PATTERNS

The longer the essay or textbook section, the more likely you are to find a mix of several patterns. As you read, try to recognize the *primary* structure. This will help you recognize what the passage is about. For example, if you observe a list but don't see that it is a list of *effects*, you will miss the writer's analysis of cause and effect. As you read and annotate the following example, try to recognize all of the strategies used but also decide which one is the primary strategy.

> There are three types of technology. The first is **primitive technology**, natural items that people have adapted for their use such as spears, clubs, and animal skins. Both hunting and gathering societies and pastoral horticultural societies are based on primitive technology. Most technology of agricultural societies is also primitive, for it centers on harnessing animals to do work. The second type, **industrial technology**, corresponds roughly to industrial society. It uses machines powered by fuels instead of natural forces such as winds and rivers. The third type, **postindustrial technology**, centers on information, transportation, and communications. At the core of postindustrial technology is the microchip.
>
> James M. Henslin, *Sociology*, 2nd ed.

The opening sentence announces the topic (types of technology) and signals the use of a list (three types). But is listing the paragraph's primary purpose? Notice the use of **bold** type, often a visual signal of definition. Isn't the author's purpose to define the three kinds of technology? You could also argue that a contrast structure is suggested because the writer distinguishes among the three terms.

Let a recognition of the primary structure guide your understanding of the main ideas of the passage, for comprehension is your purpose in reading. The following passages will give you more practice.

EXERCISE 9-4	Recognizing and Learning from Mixed Patterns

Read, annotate, and then answer the questions that follow the selection.

TYPES OF VOLCANIC MOUNTAINS

Volcanic mountains have three main shapes. The shape of the mountain is determined by the shape of the vent and the kind of material that pours out of it.

Some mountains are built chiefly by liquid lava that pours out of long fissures in the sides of the volcano. The lava flows pile up, forming a broad, gently sloping mountain. Such a mountain is called a **shield volcano**, because it is shaped like a shield laid flat on the ground. The Hawaiian volcanoes, which are the largest

■ Popocatepetl
Volcano, Parque
National, Mexico

on earth, are shield volcanoes. There are shield volcanoes in northeastern California and in parts of Oregon. There are many small shield volcanoes in Iceland.

An explosive eruption may pile up a big hill of cinder and ash around the vent. The hill is shaped like a cone with the point cut off and so is called a **cinder cone**. The top of the cone forms a bowl-shaped dent called a crater. The crater takes shape because the explosions tend to blow away material from the vent. While the cone itself is being built of cinder and ash, lava may flow out at its base. Some cinder cones occur alone. Others are found on the sides of bigger volcanoes. Particutin is one of hundreds of cinder cones in the state of Michoacán, Mexico. The western United States has many cinder cones, among them Sunset Crater in Arizona and Mount Pisgah in southern California.

The third type of volcano is built both of lava flows and of cinder and ash. It is called a **composite volcano**. (The name means that it is made of various materials.) A composite volcano develops because more than one kind of eruption occurs. For example, a volcano may start by erupting like a shield volcano, with flows of liquid lava. The next time it erupts, it may erupt like a cinder cone, laying down layers of cinder and ash. Its third eruption may consist of lava flows. Most of the world's famous and beautiful volcanoes are composite volcanoes. Among them are Mounts Hood, Rainier, and Shasta in the United States and Mount Fuji in Japan.

Patricia Lauber, *This Restless Earth*

1. What strategies does the author use?

2. Which strategy connects to the author's primary purpose in writing?

_____

3. What signals are used?

_____

4. Explain, in your own words, how each volcano is formed or how it gets its name.

_____

_____

_____

_____

_____

■ ■ ■ ■ ■

CYBERSLACKERS AND CYBERSLEUTHS: SURFING AT WORK

James M. Henslin

A professor of sociology at Southern Illinois University, James Henslin is the author of many books and articles on the sociology of ordinary life and the homeless. The following selection is from his textbook *Sociology: A Down-to-Earth Approach* (5th edition).

Prepare

1. Identify the author and work. What do you expect the author's purpose to be?

_____

_____

2. Preread to identify the subject and make predictions. What do you expect to read about?

_____

_____

3. What do you already know about the subject?

_____

_____

_____

4. Raise two questions that you expect the article to answer.

_____

_____

_____

_____

◼ ◼ ◼ ◼ ◼

1   Few people work constantly at their jobs. Most of us take breaks and, at least once in a while, goof off. We meet fellow workers at the water cooler, and we talk in the hallway. Much of this interaction is good for the company, for it bonds us to fellow workers and ties us to our jobs.

2   Part of our workday may even cross over into our personal lives. Some of us make personal calls from the office. Bosses know that we need to check in with our child's preschool or make arrangements for a baby-sitter; they expect such calls. Some even wink as we call a friend to chat, make arrangements to have our car worked on, or set up a date. And most bosses make personal calls of their own from time to time. It's the abuse of this policy that bothers them, and they're likely to fire anyone who hangs on the phone all day for personal reasons.

3   Now comes *cyberslacking,* using computers at work for personal purposes. With almost every office equipped with at least one computer, cyberslacking was bound to emerge. Perhaps most workers fritter away some of their workday online. Some play games, others shop online, and many send personal e-mail. Some Web sites even protect cyberslackers: They feature a panic button to be used in case the boss pokes her head in your office. You just click the button and a phony spreadsheet pops onto your screen while typing sounds emerge from your speakers.

4   Some cyberslackers operate their own private online businesses during office hours. Others can hardly wait to get to work so they can play games; many spend most of their "working" hours battling virtual enemies. (One computer programmer even became a national champion playing Starcraft at work.) Some spend a good part of their "working" hours downloading pornography. Xerox fired 40 employees for mixing their pornographic pleasure with business (Naughton 1999).

5   To combat cyberslacking, a new specialty, the cybersleuth, has emerged. Using specialized software, cybersleuths examine everything employees have read online, everything they've written, and every Internet site they've visited. What some of us don't know (and what some of us forget) is that delete does not mean delete. Although we hit the delete button, our computers still contain a permanent record of what appears to be erased. Without knowing it, we have left behind a hidden diary of our computer activities. Just a few clicks on the cybersleuth software and this "deleted" information becomes visible, our personal diary exposed for anyone who wants to read it.

417 words

Comprehension Check

Answer the following with a, b, c, or d to indicate the phrase that best completes each statement.

_____   1. The best statement of the selection's topic is
    a. cyberslackers.
    b. computers.
    c. personal use of computers at work.
    d. tracking sites employees visit.

_____   2. The author says that
    a. few people work all the time while at their jobs.
    b. spending some time chatting with colleagues is good for the organization.
    c. most people work all the time while at their jobs.
    d. both a and b.

_____   3. On the job,
    a. bosses never make personal calls.
    b. bosses will fire workers who are on the phone a lot.
    c. bosses do not care if workers make many calls.
    d. bosses would not think of watching how workers spend their time.

_____ 4. The new problem in the office today is
   a. cyberslacking.
   b. using the phone for personal calls.
   c. chatting with fellow workers.
   d. coming to work late.

_____ 5. Cyberslackers
   a. play games.
   b. shop online.
   c. send personal e-mails.
   d. all of the above.

_____ 6. Some cyberslackers have been
   a. fired for downloading pornography.
   b. promoted for becoming computer-game experts.
   c. applauded by bosses for using their computer
      for something.
   d. wasting their personal time shopping online.

_____ 7. A new solution to the problem of cyberslacking is
   a. cybersleuths.
   b. taking away the computer.
   c. fake spreadsheets that give the impression of work.
   d. firing.

_____ 8. Cybersleuths
   a. spend too much time on the phone.
   b. note all Internet sites visited by workers.
   c. can't see workers' deleted e-mails.
   d. are members of the FBI.

_____ 9. Henslin suggests or implies that
   a. workers who "surf" will be discovered.
   b. cyberslackers are not good workers and deserve firing.
   c. when workers create problems, bosses will
      seek solutions.
   d. all of the above.

_____ 10. Henslin's primary strategy is
   a. cause/effect.
   b. problem/solution.
   c. listing.
   d. definition.

Expanding Vocabulary

Match each word in the left column with its definition in the right column by placing the correct letter in the space next to each word. When in doubt, read again the sentence in which the word appears. The numbers in parentheses tell you what paragraph the word appears in.

_____	1. Surfing (title)	a. mutual involvement
_____	2. goof off (1)	b. carelessly or casually toss away
_____	3. interaction (1)	c. "enemies" in Internet games
_____	4. fritter away (3)	d. material designed to arouse sexual passion
_____	5. phony (3)	e. uncovered, revealed
_____	6. virtual enemies (4)	f. visiting a variety of Internet sites
_____	7. pornography (4)	g. not real
_____	8. exposed (5)	h. waste time

Reflection and Discussion

1. Have you spent time at work "not working"? How much time spent not working is okay?
2. If you were the boss, would you hire a cybersleuth to check on employees? Why or why not?

■ ■ ■ ■ ■

WHY I QUIT THE COMPANY

Tomoyuki Iwashita

After graduating from college, Iwashita worked for a well-known Japanese company until he quit to become a journalist. His essay was originally published in May 1992 in *The New Internationalist*.

Prepare

1. Identify the author and work. What do you expect the author's purpose to be?

_____

_____

2. Preread to identify the subject and make predictions. What do you expect to read about?

_____

_____

3. What do you already know about the subject?

_____

_____

_____

4. Raise two questions that you expect the article to answer.

_____

_____

_____

_____

Vocabulary Alert: Do You Know These Words?

Here are five words you need to know to read the following article with understanding.

yuppie young, affluent, usually urban professional

brainwashing forceful indoctrination into a set of beliefs

status quo existing state of affairs

fetters something that restricts or restrains one

opt out choose not to

■ ■ ■ ■ ■

1   When I tell people that I quit working for the company after only a year, most of them think I'm crazy. They can't understand why I would want to give up a prestigious and secure job. But I think I'd have been crazy to stay, and I'll try to explain why.

2   I started working for the company immediately after graduating from university. It's a big, well-known trading company with about 6,000 employees all over the world. There's a lot of competition to get into this and other similar companies, which promise young people a wealthy and successful future. I was set on course to be a Japanese "yuppie."

3   I'd been used to living independently as a student, looking after myself and organizing my own schedule. As soon as I started working all that changed. I was

given a room in the company dormitory, which is like a fancy hotel, with a twenty-four-hour hot bath service and all meals laid on. Most single company employees live in a dormitory like this, and many married employees live in company apartments. The dorm system is actually a great help because living in Tokyo costs more than young people earn—but I found it stifling.

4   My life rapidly became reduced to a shuttle between the dorm and the office. The working day is officially eight hours, but you can never leave the office on time. I used to work from nine in the morning until eight or nine at night, and often until midnight. Drinking with colleagues after work is part of the job; you can't say no. The company building contained cafeterias, shops, a bank, a post office, a doctor's office, a barber's…. I never needed to leave the building. Working, drinking, sleeping, and standing on a horribly crowded commuter train for an hour and a half each way: This was my life. I spent all my time with the same colleagues; when I wasn't involved in entertaining clients on the weekend, I was expected to play golf with my colleagues. I soon lost sight of the world outside the company.

5   This isolation is part of the brainwashing process. A personnel manager said: "We want excellent students who are active, clever, and tough. Three months is enough to train them to be devoted businessmen." I would hear my colleagues saying: "I'm not making any profit for the company, so I'm not contributing." Very few employees claim all the overtime pay due to them. Keeping an employee costs the company 50 million yen ($400,000) a year, or so the company claims. Many employees put the company's profits before their own mental and physical well-being.

6   Overtiredness and overwork leave you little energy to analyze or criticize your situation. There are shops full of "health drinks," cocktails of caffeine and other drugs, which will keep you going even when you're exhausted. *Karoshi* (death from overwork) is increasingly common and is always being discussed in the newspapers. I myself collapsed from working too hard. My boss told me: "You should control your health; it's your own fault if you get sick." There is no paid sick leave; I used up half of my fourteen days' annual leave because of sickness.

7   We had a labor union, but it seemed to have an odd relationship with the management. A couple of times a year I was told to go home at five o'clock. The union representatives were coming around to investigate working hours; everyone knew in advance. If it was "discovered" that we were all working overtime in excess of fifty hours a month our boss might have had some problem being promoted; and our prospects would have been affected. So we all pretended to work normal hours that day.

8   The company also controls its employees' private lives. Many company employees under thirty are single. They are expected to devote all their time to the company and become good workers; they don't have time to find a girlfriend. The company offers scholarships to the most promising young employees to enable them to study abroad for a year or two. But unmarried people who are on these courses are not allowed to get married until they have completed the course! Married employees who are sent to train abroad have to leave their families in Japan for the first year.

9   In fact, the quality of married life is often determined by the husband's work. Men who have just gotten married try to go home early for a while, but soon have to revert to the norm of late-night work. They have little time to spend with

their wives and even on the weekend are expected to play golf with colleagues. Fathers cannot find time to communicate with their children and child rearing is largely left to mothers. Married men posted abroad will often leave their family behind in Japan; they fear that their children will fall behind in the fiercely competitive Japanese education system.

10 Why do people put up with this? They believe this to be a normal working life or just cannot see an alternative. Many think that such personal sacrifices are necessary to keep Japan economically successful. Perhaps, saddest of all, Japan's education and socialization processes do not equip people with the intellectual and spiritual resources to question and challenge the status quo. They stamp out even the desire for a different kind of life.

11 However, there are some signs that things are changing. Although many new employees in my company were quickly brainwashed, many others, like myself, complained about life in the company and seriously considered leaving. But most of them were already in fetters—of debt. Pleased with themselves for getting into the company and anticipating a life of executive luxury, these new employees throw their money around. Every night they are out drinking. They buy smart clothes and take a taxi back to the dormitory after the last train has gone. They start borrowing money from the bank and soon they have a debt growing like a snowball rolling down a slope. The banks demand no security for loans; it's enough to be working for a well-known company. Some borrow as much as a year's salary in the first few months. They can't leave the company while they have such debts to pay off.

12 I was one of the few people in my intake of employees who didn't get into debt. I left the company dormitory after three months to share an apartment with a friend. I left the company exactly one year after I entered it. It took me a while to find a new job, but I'm working as a journalist now. My life is still busy, but it's a lot better than it was, I'm lucky because nearly all big Japanese companies are like the one I worked for, and conditions in many small companies are even worse.

13 It's not easy to opt out of a life-style that is generally considered to be prestigious and desirable, but more and more young people in Japan are thinking about doing it. You have to give up a lot of superficially attractive material benefits in order to preserve the quality of your life and your sanity. I don't think I was crazy to leave the company. I think I would have gone crazy if I'd stayed.

716 words

Comprehension Check

Answer the following with a, b, c, or d to indicate the phrase that best completes each statement.

_____ 1. The author

        a. became a journalist right after college.

        b. joined a large company right after college.

    c. joined the navy.

    d. went crazy.

_____ 2. When the author joined the company, he lived

    a. with his parents.

    b. independently.

    c. in a company dormitory.

    d. with his girlfriend.

_____ 3. The author's life with the company involved

    a. working long days.

    b. drinking with colleagues.

    c. commuting three hours a day.

    d. all of the above.

_____ 4. The author asserts that the demanding, isolating company lifestyle is

    a. easy to cope with.

    b. busy but fun.

    c. part of the company's brainwashing strategy.

    d. part of the company's desire to take care of its employees.

_____ 5. The demands of Japanese companies

    a. lead many to collapse from overwork.

    b. are quite acceptable.

    c. provide meaning for workers.

    d. were fun for the author.

_____ 6. The author sees overwork and fatigue as

    a. making young workers more committed to the company.

    b. causing young workers to lack energy to analyze their situation.

    c. a way to toughen up young workers.

    d. worth it because the workers have so much fun together.

_____ 7. Japanese companies' policies

    a. are accepted by all young workers.

    b. have negative effects on family life.

    c. should be admired by Americans.

    d. will never change.

_____ 8. The author explains that

    a. it is good to work hard.

    b. many workers cannot get out because they are in debt to the company.

    c. the company does not lend money to workers.

    d. the company does not separate married couples.

_____ 9. The author implies that you

    a. need to make the right decisions for your life.

    b. need to do what society expects of you.

    c. need a prestigious job.

    d. are better off without a wife.

_____ 10. The author's primary strategy is

    a. definition.

    b. cause/effect.

    c. comparison/contrast.

    d. examples.

Expanding Vocabulary

Answer with a, b, c, or d to indicate the best definition of the word in **bold** as it was used in the selection. The number in parentheses is the number of the paragraph in which the word appears.

_____ 1. " a **prestigious** . . . job" (1)

    a. pressured

    b. prominent

    c. passing

    d. potential

_____ 2. "found it **stifling**" (3)

    a. stimulating

    b. sticky

    c. suffocating

    d. straightforward

_____ 3. "a **shuttle** between the dorm" (4)

    a. regular travel between two points

    b. rapid transit

    c. short range

    d. shoot out

_____ 4. "Drinking with **colleagues**" (4)

    a. clients

    b. collectors

    c. college students

    d. coworkers

_____ 5. "This **isolation** is part of" (5)

    a. set apart from others

    b. issue

    c. island

    d. seasoning

_____ 6. "energy to . . . **criticize** your situation" (6)

    a. evaluate

    b. alleviate

    c. calculate

    d. concentrate

_____ 7. "to **investigate** working hours" (7)

    a. examine systematically

    b. invade

    c. introduce

    d. expose

_____ 8. "**prospects** would have been affected" (7)

    a. purposes

    b. propositions

    c. chances of success

    d. calculations

_____ 9. "**revert** to the norm" (9)

    a. retreat

    b. replicate

    c. retrench

    d. return

_____ 10. "**superficially** attractive material benefits" (13)

    a. tantalizingly

    b. trivially

    c. superlatively

    d. spectacularly

Reflection and Discussion

1. What is the most surprising detail for you in this essay? Explain why.

2. Would you stay in a demanding but status job that was making you sick? Why or why not?

MAKING CONNECTIONS

1. How important is socializing with coworkers? Should they be required to—encouraged to—discouraged from—partying and playing together? Should the socializing, if there is any, take place only during office hours and at the office? Explain your views.

2. With your class partner or on your own, make a list of some important ways that the workplace has changed in the last 15 years. Then, make another list of ways that you think it may change in the next 20–50 years.

WORKSHOP

"E" CONNECTIONS

Today there are many workplace "privacy" issues. Some include monitoring an employee's computer use, monitoring phone calls employees make, and even videotaping their movements to note, for example, when they take breaks. Learn more about one of the many privacy issues. Be prepared to discuss your findings with classmates. You will find articles in your library's electronic databases. (Try Proquest, SIRS, or Expanded Academic ASAP.) Or, conduct an Internet search. You may want to begin by visiting the American Civil Liberties Union site at:

<http://www.aclu.org>.

WORD POWER 8

Knowing Common Foreign-Language Words

Many English words have their origin in another language, but these words have been made into English words. Some words, though, retain their foreign language spelling and pronunciation while used by English speakers. Often these words are shown to be foreign terms by the use of italics, for example, *ad hominem*. You will want to be able to recognize these words in your reading and spell and pronounce them correctly.

Look up each of the following words in your dictionary. Spend some time practicing the word's pronunciation. Then write each word's definition in the space below.

1. status quo

_____

_____

2. *faux pas*

_____

_____

_____

3. barrio

_____

_____

_____

4. *non sequitur*

_____

_____

_____

5. zeitgeist

_____

_____

_____

II. *Select the correct word for each of the sentences that follow.*

1. Conservatives want to maintain the _____ (barrio/status quo).

2. The candidate's argument was flawed by a _____ (*non sequitur*/zeitgeist).

3. A _____ (zeitgeist/*faux pas*) or two and you will be rejected by polite society!

4. Many Hispanic-Americans are eager to move out of the _____ (barrio/status quo).

5. The study of history is more than learning names and dates; you should also understand the _____ (*faux pas*/zeitgeist) of each time and place.

CHAPTER REVIEW

1. When reading about cause and effect, you want to be sure to recognize and label each _____.

2. A problem/solution strategy may or may not include a discussion of _____.

3. Remember that one cause may have one or _____ effects.

4. When you recognize that a writer is using more than one strategy, you should try to determine the writer's _____ strategy.

5. Signal words you may find in a problem/solution strategy, other than *problem* and *solution*, include _____ and _____.

Take a Reading Road Trip!

For additional practice with your reading skills, use the Reading Road Trip CD-ROM or visit Reading Road Trip on the Web at <**http://www.ablongman.com/readingroadtrip**> (password required).

<table>
<tr><td>CHAPTER 10</td><td>Understanding Tone and Drawing Inferences</td></tr>
</table>

LEARNING OBJECTIVES

■ To draw sound inferences

■ To recognize connotation and figurative language

■ To understand tone as a guide to a writer's attitude

■ To state main ideas that are implied

PREPARE TO READ

Read and reflect on the chapter's title and objectives. Glance through the chapter, observing headings to see what is covered. Now answer these questions:

1. What do you expect to learn from this chapter?

_____

_____

2. What do you already know about the chapter's topic?

_____

_____

3. What two or three questions do you want answered from reading this chapter?

_____

_____

_____

_____

Drawing inferences is an essential part of interacting with the world around us. It is also an essential part of the reading process. The cartoon in Figure 10.1 will get you started thinking about the process of drawing inferences. Study the cartoon and then answer the following questions.

1. Who are the men in the cartoon? _____

2. Where are they? _____

   How do you know the answer to this question?

   _____

   _____

3. What has just happened?

   _____

   _____

"I'll get it!"

■ FIGURE **10.1** **Laugh Parade, by Bunny Hoest and John Reiner**

Source: © 1999. Reprinted courtesy of Bunny Hoest and *Parade*.

4. Why does one of the men say "I'll get it!"?

_____

_____

5. Which of these questions are you answering with facts?

_____

Which ones are you answering based on conclusions you are drawing from the details in the cartoon?

_____

WHAT ARE INFERENCES?

When you look at the cartoon, you see men playing baseball, and you can see that one of them has just hit the ball over the wall. So, your answer to question 3 is a fact, a specific detail that we can see in the cartoon. Your answers to the other questions, though, are inferences. An **inference** is a conclusion based on evidence. An inference is an assumption about something that is *unknown* based on something that is *known*. Nowhere in the cartoon are the words *prison* or *prisoners*. You have inferred this condition based on the details in the drawing. How many details did you list in answer to question 2? If you did not observe the barbed wire around the wall, the watch tower, and the numbers on the prisoner's shirt, you would not be able to draw the inference that this game is being played in prison.

Drawing Inferences from Life Experiences

Every day you draw inferences about the people and the situations around you. You decide how people are feeling based on their actions and body language in a particular situation. (Remember that 90 percent of communication is *nonverbal*. Often behavior is a better clue to how someone is feeling than what the person actually tells you.) Use the following exercise to increase your awareness of the inferences you regularly draw.

| **EXERCISE 10-1** | **Workshop on Drawing Inferences from Life Situations** |

With your class partner or in small groups, answer the questions following each situation.

1. Walking down the street, you pass a young boy peering down a grate. One pocket of his pants is pulled out; it has a hole in it. As he leans over the grate, his lower lip begins to tremble.

a. What has happened?

_____

_____

b. How does the boy feel?

_____

2. As you jog the bike path along the river, you pass a man carrying a metal case and a long pole. He is whistling.

a. What is the man about to do? _____

b. Is he looking forward to the activity? _____

3. You move into the left lane to pass a truck. Suddenly a car is on your rear bumper, with lights flashing and horn sounding. As you move quickly around the truck and back into the right lane, the driver of the car behind you goes by, yelling and gesturing in your direction.

a. What did the driver want to do? _____

b. What is his attitude toward you? _____

c. What can you infer about the driver's emotions?

_____

_____

4. You overhear the following dialogue at work.

Barry, stopping by Joan's desk, says, "Let's have lunch today."
Joan, "I'm sorry. I'm too busy to stop for lunch today."
Barry, "This is the second day this week that I've suggested lunch and you have been too busy."
Joan, "I'm sorry, Barry. This McGarvey project is driving me crazy."
Barry, "You just don't want to have lunch with me."

a. What can you infer about Barry's feelings?

_____

b. What inference has Barry made?

_____

c. If Joan really is busy but wants to keep Barry as a lunch partner, what should she say after Barry's last remark?

_____

_____

■ DRAWING INFERENCES FROM READING

We also need to draw inferences to construct meaning out of the words on the page. We construct meaning from both what those words say and what they suggest or imply. Sometimes we need to "fill in" information or ideas that are suggested but not stated outright. Other times we need to draw a conclusion from the specifics that have been presented, to infer a main idea that has been implied but not directly stated. Always, as active readers, we need to work with the author to understand what we are reading.

The Role of Knowledge

How well we read is also connected to the knowledge we bring to the reading. Writers assume their readers have certain information. Those lacking the assumed knowledge may have trouble drawing appropriate inferences from their reading. For example, think back to the previous exercise. If you have never seen a fishing pole or tackle box, you will not know what the man is about to do in the second situation. You will be puzzled, or perhaps not take much notice of the man, because the details of the situation do not offer you any clues on which to draw an inference. See what inferences you can draw in the following exercise.

EXERCISE 10-2	Recognizing the Role of Knowledge in Drawing Inferences

Read each of the brief selections and then answer the questions that follow.

1. In addition to saying no to drugs, teenagers today need to spit in Joe Camel's eye.

   a. What does the writer actually want teens to do?

   _____

   _____

b. To answer (a), what information do you need to have, or what do you need to infer from the statement?

_____

_____

2. Pete Townshend of The Who has severely damaged hearing and, in addition, is plagued by tinnitus, an annoying condition in which there is a continuous ringing in the ears.

Wood and Wood, *The World of Psychology*, 2nd ed.

a. How did Pete Townshend damage his hearing?

_____

b. To answer (a), what information do you need to have, or what do you need to infer from the statement?

_____

_____

c. From the reference to Townshend, what point do you infer the authors want to make?

_____

_____

3. The skeleton of an elephant lies out in the grasses near a baobab tree and a scattering of black volcanic stones. The thick-trunked, gnarled baobab gesticulates with its branches, as if trying to summon help. There are no tusks lying among the bones, of course; ivory vanishes quickly in East Africa.

Lance Morrow, "Africa," *Time*

a. From the passage, what do you infer about the elephant's probable cause of death?

_____

b. To understand the last statement, what do you need to know—or infer—about ivory?

_____

_____

     c. How does the author want readers to feel about the elephant's death?

_____

_____

4. In the Royal Free Hospital was my mother, Sister McVeagh. He married his nurse which, as they both said often enough (though in different tones of voice), was just as well. That was 1919.

                        Doris Lessing, "My Father" (a biographical essay)

     a. Why was it "just as well" that Lessing's father married her mother? What are readers to infer from this passage?

_____

_____

     b. What do you infer to be her father's tone of voice?

_____

     c. What do you infer to be her mother's tone of voice? (Consider the time period when reflecting on her tone.)

_____

5. Susan Smith came to national fame as a distraught mother, a self-described victim of carjacking and kidnapping. When it all unraveled, and she was taken to court for arraignment, many people lined the streets shouting epithets at her. One woman said it all: "We believed you!" It was strikingly easy to play upon the fear of the stranger.

                        Ellen Goodman, "Stranger-Danger"

     a. What did Susan Smith *say* had happened to her?

_____

     b. Why was she taken to court? What actually happened?

_____

_____

     c. Did you answer (b) from inference or knowledge of the Susan Smith case?

_____

d. Were you unable to answer (b) because of lack of information?

_____

e. Do you think the author expects readers to have knowledge of Susan Smith or to infer from the passage?

_____

On what is your answer based?

_____

_____

▪ CONNOTATION

Connotation is one strategy writers use to develop implied ideas. A word's *connotation* is what the word suggests, what we associate the word with. For example, the words *house* and *home* both refer to a structure in which people live. These words have a similar denotation. But the word *home* suggests or is associated with ideas and feelings of family and security and comfort. So, the word *home* has a strong positive connotation. By contrast, the word *house* does not carry any "emotional baggage." Many words do not have connotations, but those that do often carry powerful associations. Studying a writer's use of emotionally charged words is an important way to understand a writer's attitude toward his or her subject.

Because we are familiar with the connotations of many common words, we may read "right over" key words without being aware of the writer's choice of language to direct our attitudes and affect our feelings. As you read, try to be especially sensitive to a writer's choice of words.

| EXERCISE 10-3 | **Becoming Alert to Connotation** |

I. For each of the following pairs of words, check the one that has the more positive connotation. The first has been done for you.

1. ✓ quiet   _____ withdrawn
2. _____ miserly   _____ economical
3. _____ stubborn   _____ persistent
4. _____ naive   _____ trusting
5. _____ child   _____ brat

6. _____ hard   _____ brittle
7. _____ laid back   _____ lazy
8. _____ female parent _____ mom
9. _____ pushy   _____ assertive
10. _____ neat   _____ neat freak

II. Select one of the two words provided to complete each of the following sentences. Briefly explain why you did not select the other word.

1. Some events in my brother's life have been quite _____. (amazing/bizarre)

   _____

2. Madonna has become _____ for her sexual openness. (notorious/famous)

   _____

3. Mary buys her clothes at sales because she is _____. (smart/cheap)

   _____

4. Tony's plan to buy out his chief competition showed a _____ business sense. (shrewd/cunning)

   _____

5. Helena studies hard all the time; she must be a _____. (nerd/serious student)

   _____

6. Unfortunately, Javier has to have dinner with one of his _____ (coworkers/friends) tonight.

   _____

7. Horror movies can cause viewers, especially children, to have _____ (nightmares/dreams).

   _____

8. The teams took the field, looking over their _____ (opponents/enemies).

_____

9. Art _____ (questioned/challenged) his boss's guidelines for setting up the new program.

_____

10. Anticipating their trip to the zoo, the children became quite _____ (excited/hysterical).

_____

◢ FIGURATIVE LANGUAGE

Sometimes the most effective way to express an idea and create a feeling is to take ordinary words but put them together in ways that do not make sense *literally*. When you read an expression that seems to make no sense, you may be reading a *figure of speech*. Figurative language isn't found only in poetry; it is actually quite common. For example, we say we are on pins and needles over a test grade and complain about the rat race. Now these examples are called *clichés*, because they are worn out from overuse. Understanding figurative language can be difficult at first because the figures of speech are new. The first step to understanding is to recognize that the language is figurative and not take the statement literally. Momma's son in Figure 10.2 below has some trouble with figurative language. Look at the cartoon and then answer the following questions.

1. Why has Momma's son been fired?

_____

MOMMA MELL LAZARUS

■ FIGURE 10.2 **Momma, by Mell Lazarus**

Source: Reprinted by permission of Mell Lazarus and Creators Syndicate.

2. Why is he confused by the boss's statement?

_____

_____

Metaphors

A *metaphor* is a comparison of two things that are not alike but seem alike in some significant way. The boss in the comic strip has used a metaphor to describe his problem with the young man. The young man is not *really* a rotten apple; he is *like* a rotten apple.

There are several ways to express a metaphor, and some of these ways have their own names, but they all fit the basic definition. Here are the most common.

Simile: A leader is like a mirror.

Think of the expression as having two terms, one literal and one figurative, as if it were an equation: X (leader) = Y (mirror). (Because a leader is a person, not an object with a reflective surface, the expression is figurative, not literal.) In a simile the "equals" sign is spelled out with "like" or "as."

Metaphor: A leader mirrors the desires of his or her followers.

This metaphor makes the same point as the simile does; it just doesn't spell out the comparison with "like." In some metaphors, only one of the terms is stated. The other part of the comparison is implied.

Metaphor (figurative term implied): A leader reflects the desires of his or her followers.

Even though the term "mirror" is not stated, the *idea* of a mirror is there in the word "reflects."

Personification: The daffodils tossed their heads in sprightly dance.

Personification is a metaphor in which the Y term is always a person. When an idea, animal, or object is personified, it is given human qualities. In the example above, the daffodils are compared to humans who can toss their heads and dance. Actually, the daffodils are being blown by the wind but appear to the poet to be dancing.

To respond to metaphors, follow these steps:

1. Recognize that you are reading a metaphor.

2. Recognize the two terms being compared. Know what is the X and what is the Y of the comparison.

3. Reflect on the point of the comparison and the emotional impact of the comparison. How are we to take the metaphor? (Would you want to be called a "rotten apple"?)

EXERCISE 10-4	Understanding Metaphors

I. Read the following passage and then answer the questions below.

About a mile farther, on a road I had never travelled, we came to an orchard of starved appletrees writhing over a hillside among outcroppings of slate that nuzzled up through the snow like animals pushing out their noses to breathe. Beyond the orchard lay a field or two, their boundaries lost under drifts.

Edith Wharton, *Ethan Frome*

1. What metaphor is used to describe the orchard of apple trees?

   _____

2. What *type* of metaphor has Wharton used? _____

3. What metaphor is used to describe the outcroppings of slate?

   _____

4. What *type* of metaphor has Wharton used? _____

5. How do Wharton's metaphors make us feel? What do they add to the passage?

   _____

II. Read the following poem by Langston Hughes and then answer the questions that follow.

Dreams
Hold fast to dreams
For if dreams die
Life is a broken-winged bird
That cannot fly.

Hold fast to dreams   5
For when dreams go
Life is a barren field
Frozen with snow.

1. Explain the metaphor in lines 3 and 4. What is being compared? What point is made?

   _____

   _____

2. Explain the metaphor in lines 7 and 8. What is being compared? What point is made?

_____

_____

3. Is it good or bad if dreams die? _____

4. What is the idea of the poem? What does the poet want us to understand about dreams?

_____

_____

■ ■ ■ ■ ■

Irony

Irony is a difference between what we expect to happen and what actually happens, or what a writer says and what the writer means. In narratives (stories, plays, narrative poems), the characters and action may lead us to expect events to end in a particular way. Sometimes the author surprises us with events that are quite different from what we expected. This is irony of situation.

Verbal irony occurs when writers write the opposite of what they mean. Somewhere in the context of the work are clues to help us understand the use of irony. We also use verbal irony in speech. For example, if you see a friend dashing into an early class with clothes that don't match and hair uncombed, you might say, "You're looking great this morning." Of course you—and your friend—understand that you are really commenting on how awful she looks.

Metaphors and irony are two effective figures of speech. Using them, a writer can play with words or move us with a powerful picture or lead us to reflect on the surprises in life.

| EXERCISE 10-5 | **Understanding Figures of Speech** |

Read and reflect on the following passage and then answer the questions that follow.

We set out for the gallows. Two warders marched on either side of the prisoner, with their rifles at the slope; two others marched close against him, gripping him by arm and shoulder, as though at once pushing and supporting him. The rest of us, magistrates and the like, followed behind. Suddenly, when we had gone ten yards, the procession stopped short without any order or warning. A dreadful thing had happened—a dog, come goodness knows whence [from where], had appeared in the yard. It came bounding among us with a loud volley of barks and leapt round us wagging its whole body wild with glee at finding so many human beings together. It was a large wooly dog, half Airedale, half pariah [social outcast]. For a moment it pranced around us, and then, before anyone could stop it, it had made a dash for the prisoner, and jumping up tried to lick his face. Everybody stood aghast, too taken aback even to grab the dog.

George Orwell, "A Hanging"

1. What is about to take place? _____

2. Is the narrator a part of the scene or not? _____

   How do you know?

   _____

3. Why is it important that the dog is half pariah?

   _____

4. Why does the narrator say that the dog's appearance was "a dreadful thing"? Why was everybody "aghast"?

   _____

   _____

   _____

5. What type of figurative language does Orwell use in this passage? (Hint: Is the dog's appearance in this particular scene unexpected and out of place?)

   _____

   _____

6. What does the passage comment on? What does Orwell want us to understand about hangings?

   _____

   _____

▬ TONE AND THE WRITER'S ATTITUDE

Words and sentence patterns are every writer's basic tools. When writers choose connotative language, or figures of speech, or sentences that are long and formal, they are selecting specific strategies to express their views. The *voice* we hear expressing these views is the *tone* of the passage. We need to "listen" for a writer's tone as a guide to the writer's attitude.

As always, recognizing the use of a strategy—irony, for example—can help us get a sense of the writer's tone. And tone helps us recognize the writer's attitude toward his or her subject. Recognizing tone is especially important if the main idea of a passage is implied rather than stated. Remember that one can express the same point of view using different strategies and creating different tones.

| EXERCISE 10-6 | **Workshop on Tone and Attitude** |

WORKSHOP

With your class partner or on your own, study each of the following paragraphs on the topic of war. Answer the questions that follow to practice recognizing tone, strategies, and attitude.

I. Surely you can't be serious! War is never an answer! It is always so destructive. Not only are many killed, but the lives of those who survive are also destroyed forever as they suffer from the loss of loved ones, the disruption of ordinary life, the splintering of families. War is never an answer to world problems!

1. How would you describe the tone of this passage? _____

_____

2. What strategies (word choice, sentence patterns, etc.) help to create the tone?

_____

3. What is the writer's attitude toward war? _____

II. Why do humans continue to turn to war as a solution to conflicts? When we use violence, we toss away the advances that we call civilization. We suggest that we cannot really rise above the more limited choices of other animals.

1. How would you describe the tone of this passage? _____

_____

2. What strategies (word choice, sentence patterns, etc.) help to create the tone?

_____

3. What is the writer's attitude toward war? _____

III. Hey, why not go to war? Let's not be sissies. War is part of our great human tradition, after all. Oh yes, war does get a bit messy at times, but then nothing's perfect! We send our best young people to shoot at them. We drop a few bombs; they drop some on us, and when the dust settles we have a winner—right? Oh yes, war is good.

1. How would you describe the tone of this passage? _____

_____

2. What strategies help to create tone? _____

_____

3. What is the writer's attitude toward war? _____

| EXERCISE 10-7 | Analyzing Strategies and Understanding Attitude |

Read and answer the questions for each of the following passages.

I.   The city energizes the people who live there. The noises wake them and urge them to get going. There is excitement "pounding the pavement" with all the others forming that energetic force of workers heading for offices. The tall buildings, the honking of taxis, the dense crowds, the opportunities to fulfill ambitions: All add to the thrill of living in the city.

1. What is the writer's subject? _____

2. What is the writer's position on the subject?

_____

3. What particular words help you understand the writer's attitude?

_____

4. What is the writer's tone—angry, excited, somber, something else?

_____

II. How can you even think about restricting smoking on your flights to Europe and Asia? Don't you know how long those flights are? What do you think smokers are going to do all those hours without a cigarette? Whether you like it or not, smoking is an addiction; we *have* to have a cigarette—and we will, damn it! What are you going to do about it? Throw us out of the plane?

1. What is the writer's subject? _____

2. What is the writer's position on the subject?

   _____

3. What particular words help you understand the writer's attitude?

   _____

4. What is the writer's tone—angry, excited, sad, something else?

   _____

5. Is the writer's approach a persuasive one? Why or why not?

   _____

   _____

III. Modern technology has isolated us from one another. Television restricts games and conversation. In many homes there are several TVs, so the family no longer even watches the same show. Children play electronic games by themselves rather than playing with each other. Teenagers plug in their Walkmans and tune out the rest of the world.

1. What is the writer's subject? _____

2. What is the writer's position on the subject?

   _____

3. What is the writer's tone—angry, thoughtful, excited, something else?

   _____

4. Is the writer's approach a persuasive one? Why or why not?

   _____

   _____

IV. In a nation of 40 million handguns—where anyone who wants one can get one—it's time to face a chilling fact. We're way past the point where registration, licensing, safety training, waiting periods, or mandatory sentencing are going to have much effect. Each of these measures may save some lives or help catch a few criminals, but none—by itself or taken together—will stop the vast majority of handgun suicides or murders. A "controlled" handgun kills just as effectively as an "uncontrolled" one.

Josh Sugarmann, "The NRA Is Right, but We Still Need to Ban Handguns"

1. What is the writer's subject? _____

2. What is the writer's position on the subject?

   _____

3. What words are important in expressing the writer's attitude?

   _____

4. Does the writer's position seem reasonable to you? _____

   _____

5. Is your answer to question 4 influenced by the writer or by your strongly held opinions?

   _____

V. Let me start this discussion by pointing out that I am not anti-gun. I'm pro-knife. Consider the merits of the knife. In the first place, you have to catch up with someone to stab him. A general substitution of knives for guns would promote physical fitness. We'd turn into a whole nation of great runners. Plus, knives don't ricochet. And people are seldom killed while cleaning their knives.

Molly Ivins, "Ban the Things. Ban Them All"

1. What is the writer's topic? _____

2. What is the writer's position on the subject? _____

   _____

3. What words and what strategy are important in expressing the writer's attitude?

   _____

   _____

4. What is the tone of the passage? _____

◼ UNDERSTANDING IMPLIED MAIN IDEAS AND DRAWING APPROPRIATE INFERENCES

Let's review: An *inference* is a conclusion based on *evidence*. It is not an idea we make up rather than doing the hard word of studying the evidence. It is not *our* idea on the subject instead of the author's. Paying attention to the details, recognizing a writer's strategies, and understanding the tone of a passage all work together to help us draw sound inferences and understand implied main ideas. We can review by applying these points to the following paragraph.

> When a colonial housewife went to the village well to draw water for her family, she saw friends, gathered gossip, shared the laughs and laments of her neighbors. When her great-great-granddaughter was blessed with running water, and no longer had to go to the well, this made life easier, but also less interesting. Electricity, mail delivery and the telephone removed more reasons for leaving the house. And now the climax of it all is Television.
>
> Boorstin, "Television: More Deeply Than We Suspect,
> It Has Changed All of Us"

Boorstin's paragraph contains specific details but no stated main idea. What idea should we infer from the details and the word choice? Here are three choices. Circle the one you think is best.

1. Modern conveniences developed over time.
2. Television is a great modern technological achievement.
3. Some technological advances, especially television, separate us from others.

Which one did you circle? If you focus on the paragraph's list of conveniences, you might choose the first statement. But it does not "cover" or take account of the paragraph's discussion of the colonial housewife's lifestyle. If you focus on the word *climax* in the last sentence, you might choose the second inference. But it seems to contradict Boorstin's idea that modern life results in less mingling with neighbors and is "less interesting." You may think that TV is a great achievement, but Boorstin does not seem to agree with that view. The best inference is the third choice, the statement that stresses modern isolation.

What are the characteristics of appropriate inferences?

- They cover all the details in the passage.
- They do not contradict any of the details in the passage.
- They explain the writer's ideas, not the reader's, on the topic.
- They take into account the tone of the passage that helps to suggest the writer's attitude toward the subject.

The following box summarizes the steps for deciding on implied main ideas that were established in Chapter 6. Review these guidelines and use them as you work the rest of the exercises in this chapter.

> ## Guidelines for Recognizing Implied Ideas
>
> 1. Read actively. Pay attention to details.
> 2. Ask questions to decide on the passage's topic.
> 3. Reflect on the meaning of the details in the passage.
> 4. Observe the writer's strategies for creating tone and identify the tone of the passage.
> 5. Decide on the implied idea, making sure to state it as a complete sentence that makes an assertion about the topic.

EXERCISE 10-8

Identifying the Best Main-Idea Statement

After reading each paragraph, circle the best main-idea statement.

1. A student of botany and geology, John Muir traveled through much of the Midwest and Plains states on foot. He also traveled through Nevada, Utah, and the Northwest to study forests and glaciers. After discovering many glaciers in the Sierra Mountains, Muir explored Alaska, where he also discovered glaciers, one of which was named after him. Throughout his travels he wrote and published his observations, and he called for forest conservation and establishing national parks. He helped with the campaign to create Yosemite National Park and later camped there with then President Theodore Roosevelt. Roosevelt set aside public lands as forest preserves and named a redwood forest in California after Muir shortly before Muir's death in 1908.

Adapted from *American Heritage History of the United States*

a. Muir explored the United States and discovered many glaciers.

b. Muir was an important geologist and conservationist who contributed to the development of our national parks.

2. The Nile was responsible for creating an area several miles wide on both banks of the river that was fertile and capable of producing abundant harvests. . . . The river . . . was seen as life enhancing, not life threatening. Although a system of organized irrigation was still necessary, the small villages along the Nile could make the effort. . . . In addition to providing food, it [the Nile] promoted easy transportation and encouraged communication.

Jackson J. Spielvogel, *Western Civilization*, 2nd ed., Vol. 1

a. The Nile River was central to the development of Egyptian civilization.

b. The Nile was a means of transportation from one part of Egypt to another.

3. Young males and females are equally likely to try alcohol, tobacco or illegal drugs. But males, particularly young men 18 to 21 years old, do so more often and in larger quantities.

   a. There are some gender differences among young people in behavior that threatens health.

   b. Young men are more foolish than young women.

4. H. M. Skeels and H. B. Dye . . . placed thirteen infants whose mental retardation was so obvious that no one wanted to adopt them, in Glenwood State School, an institution for the mentally retarded. Each infant, then about 19 months old, was assigned to a separate ward of women ranging in mental age from 5 to 12 and in chronological age from 18 to 50. The women were pleased with this arrangement. . . . The researchers left a control group of twelve infants, also retarded but higher in intelligence, at the orphanage, where they received the usual care. Two and a half years later, Skeels and Dye tested all the children's intelligence. Their findings were startling: Those assigned to the retarded women had gained an average of twenty-eight IQ points while those who remained in the orphanage had lost thirty points.

   James M. Henslin, *Sociology*, 2nd ed.

   a. Orphanages should be done away with.

   b. Intelligence is at least partly learned through stimulating social interaction.

5. In 1982, scientists in Antarctica discovered that the ozone layer above them was getting thinner. The cause is a buildup in the atmosphere of chemicals called chlorofluorocarbons (CFCs). These are used in aerosol spray cans, foam plastics, refrigerators, and air-conditioning systems. When these products are dumped, the CFCs slowly rise into the atmosphere, and, in the Antarctic winter, they go through complex chemical reactions that destroy the ozone.

   Michael Scott, *Ecology*

   a. Discarded products containing CFCs are causing serious damage to the ozone layer in the atmosphere above Antarctica.

   b. CFC's are found in many modern products.

| EXERCISE 10-9 | Recognizing Topics and Inferring Main Ideas |

After reading each paragraph, circle the best statement of the paragraph's topic. Briefly explain your choice. Then write a main-idea statement for the paragraph.

1. Elephant babies are eagerly accepted not only by the members of their own groups but by all other elephants as well, including strange bulls—a phenomenon almost unique in animal behavior. There are many well-documented

stories about unrelated bulls rescuing young calves in swamps, for example, and under all manner of other circumstances. Moreover, orphans are readily adopted by new families, even for nursing. Unrelated or only distantly related herds will intermingle and mix freely at waterholes, the adults greeting one another with quiet dignity and the youngsters frolicking together.

P. Jay Fetner, The African Safari

Topics:
   a. acceptance of baby elephants
   b. social nature of elephants

Explain your choice: _____

_____

_____

Main idea: _____

_____

2.   As far back as 500 B.C., when the Nok culture flourished in Nigeria, furnaces were being used to smelt iron. The Nigerian state of Benin exchanged ambassadors with Portugal in 1486. At that time Timbuktu in Mali was a major trading center of international fame. The splendors of the Songhai Empire, which stretched from Mali to Kano, Nigeria, in the fifteenth and sixteenth centuries, were compared by early travelers with those of contemporary Europe.... Iron-Age Africans started building stone structures in the area we call Zimbabwe as early as A.D. 1100, and sixteenth-century Portuguese maritime traders found that some West African textiles were superior to anything then being made in Europe.

David Lamb, The Africans

Topics:
   a. African buildings
   b. early cultures in Africa

Explain your choice: _____

_____

_____

Main idea: _____

_____

3. The Black Death of the mid-fourteenth century . . . ravaged Europe, wiping out 25 to 50 percent of the population and causing economic, social, political, and cultural upheaval. A Sienese chronicler wrote that "father abandoned child, wife husband, one brother another, for the plague seemed to strike through breath and sight. And so they died. And no one could be found to bury the dead, for money or friendship."

Jackson J. Spielvogel, *Western Civilization*, 2nd ed., vol. 1

Topics:
   a. the Black Death in the fourteenth century
   b. the devastation of the Black Death

Explain your choice: _____

_____

_____

Main idea: _____

_____

4. In the past ten years, Miami's population grew only 3.4 percent, but its Spanish-speaking population grew 15 percent, making the city 62 percent Hispanic. Throughout the United States, 83 percent of residents speak English at home, but only 25 percent of Miami residents do so.

Topics:
   a. Hispanic growth in Miami
   b. Hispanic growth in the United States

Explain your choice: _____

_____

_____

Main idea: _____

_____

5. In real sports, winners are determined by an objective measure: by number of points won or the greatest distance or the fastest speed. Winners in ice skating are selected by the opinions of judges. When skiers charge down the mountain, their clothes do not matter, only their speed. In a real sport, style points, a subjective judgment, do not count.

Topics:
  a. difference between real sports and ice skating
  b. skiing and ice skating

Explain your choice: _____

_____

_____

Main idea: _____

_____

6.   Obesity in children has tripled in the past 20 years. A staggering 50 percent of adolescents in some minority populations are overweight. There is an epidemic of type 2 (formerly "adult onset") diabetes in children. Heart attacks may become a disease of young adults.

Brownell and Ludwig, "Fighting Obesity and the Food Industry"

Topics:
  a. obesity in children
  b. increasing obesity in children

Explain your choice: _____

_____

_____

Main idea: _____

_____

7.   Within the next five years—for the first time—there will be more people living in cities than in rural areas throughout the world, and most population growth will occur in teaming cities in Asia, Africa, and South America. . . . Cities generate close to 80 percent of all carbon dioxide . . . and account for 75 percent of industrial wood use. Throughout the world atmospheric pollution affects more than 1.1 billion people, mostly in cities. An additional 2.5 billion are at risk from high levels of indoor air pollution.

Eric Planin, "Around the Globe, Cities Have Growing Pains"

Topics:
  a. growth of cities
  b. problems of city growth

Explain your choice: _____

_____

_____

Main idea: _____

_____

8.   The answering machine talks to us, and for us, somewhere above the din of the TV; the Walkman preserves a public silence but ensures that we need never—in the bathtub, on a mountaintop, even at our desks—be without the clangor of the world. White noise becomes the aural equivalent of the clash of images, the nonstop blast of fragments that increasingly agitates our minds.

Pico Iyer, "The Eloquent Sounds of Silence"

Topics:
  a. modern technology
  b. the constant sounds of modern times

Explain your choice: _____

_____

_____

Main idea: _____

_____

9.   When I was about 12, I heaved a cinder block over my neighbor's fence and nearly killed her. I didn't know she was there. When I was about the same age, I started a small fire in a nearby field that spread until it threatened some nearby houses. I didn't mean to do it. When I was even younger, I climbed on top of a toolshed, threw a brick in the general direction of my sister and sent her, bleeding profusely and crying so that I can still hear her, to the hospital. I didn't mean to do that, either.

Richard Cohen, "Kids Who Kill Are Still Kids"

Topics:
   a. a youngster throwing things
   b. the trouble children can cause

Explain your choice: _____

_____

_____

Main idea: _____

_____

10. The popular *Triceratops* has lost weight! Paleontologists now describe this dinosaur as slimmer and more upright. The old lumbering *Brontosaurus* has both a new look and a new name. Now named *Apatosaurus,* this dinosaur has a longer face, and it did not need to sit in water but could move easily on land. The Jurassic meat-eater *Allosaurus* also needs to be made slimmer and more agile. Juveniles were probably swift runners.

Topics:
   a. changes in dinosaur characteristics
   b. dinosaurs

Explain your choice: _____

_____

_____

Main idea: _____

_____

■ DRAWING INFERENCES AND UNDERSTANDING IMPLIED MAIN IDEAS IN LONGER PASSAGES

The tasks of drawing inferences and understanding implied main ideas are much the same for longer passages as for sentences or paragraphs. The only difference is that you have to keep working for a longer time. If you stop concentrating too soon, you may miss important details. So, review the characteristics of appropriate inferences, study the guidelines for recognizing implied main ideas, and commit to active reading through the entire passage.

| EXERCISE 10-10 | Recognizing Implied Meanings in Longer Passages |

Read and annotate each passage. After reading a passage, complete the exercise that follows.

I.   Exactly what are they teaching in our schools these days? . . . A new national survey suggests that, on average, college graduates today know fewer selected basic facts about government and politics than college graduates did in 1947.

   Likewise, today's high school grads appear to know less about government and politics than their educational equals of five decades ago.

   For example, a Gallup survey in 1947 found that 77 percent of all Americans surveyed who had graduated from high school but not gone on to college knew which party controlled the U.S. House of Representatives.

   Today, barely half—54 percent—of all high school graduates know that the Republicans control the House. . . . [in 1996]

   Political knowledge also has slipped among college graduates: 90 percent knew which party controlled the House in 1947, compared to 80 percent in the latest survey.

   Richard Morin, "Dumbing Down Democracy"

1. What is the passage's topic?

_____

2. What is implied in the opening question?

_____

_____

3. What are we to infer about the cause or causes for the decline in knowledge about government and politics?

_____

_____

4. What is the author's attitude toward the decline in knowledge?

_____

II.

■ Amelia
Earhart

1   Amelia Earhart was the first woman of flight—with an array of first's unmatched in the world. Her daring flights in the 1920s and 1930s captured the imagination of the American public and signaled that women could participate fully in pioneering this new frontier.

2   As a child, Amelia Earhart liked to ride horseback and a miniature homemade roller coaster. After high school, she tried nursing and premedical studies before she first flew—with barnstormer[1] Frank Hawks in Glendale, California, in 1920. Two years later she was flying her own Kinner Canary in California air shows.

3   Amelia Earhart was working in a settlement house in Boston and flying in her free time when publisher George Putnam chose her to fly as a passenger on a transatlantic flight a year after Lindberg's historic crossing. Wilmer Stultz piloted the Fokker trimotor from Newfoundland to Wales; Amelia Earhart kept the flight log. She was the first woman to cross the Atlantic by air, and suddenly she was famous. New York gave "Lady Lindy" a ticker-tape parade. In 1931 Miss Earhart married George Putnam—with an agreement that she have complete freedom to travel. Putnam managed her affairs.

4   On May 21–22, 1932, Amelia Earhart flew solo from Newfoundland to Ireland. In a Lockheed monoplane she flew the 2026 miles in 14 hours, 56 minutes, much of it through storms and fog—the first woman to fly the Atlantic alone. She was smothered with honors—among others, the cross of the French Legion of Honor and the U.S. Distinguished Flying Cross. Other first's followed:

---

[1]One who tours as a stunt pilot.

two transcontinental records and the first non-stop flight from Mexico City to New York.

5   In 1937 a round-the-world flight (another first) was planned, to test long-range performance of crew and aircraft. After an unsuccessful attempt, on June 1st Amelia Earhart and navigator Fred Noonan left Miami, Florida, flying east on an equatorial route that took them across the Atlantic Ocean, Africa, and the Indian Ocean. At Lae, New Guinea, on July 2, they took off to fly 2570 miles to Howland Island, a spot in the Pacific scarcely longer than its runway. They never reached it. Hours after they were due, the Coast Guard cutter *Itaska*, near Howland, received their last voice messages: ". . . gas is running low . . ." and "We are on a line of position. . . ." Sea and air searches found nothing.

6   For years rumors persisted that Miss Earhart had been on an espionage mission and might have been captured by the Japanese. But the facts—including recent (1992) discoveries of possible plane parts in the Howland area—strongly suggest that the plane simply missed Howland and crashed into the sea.

7   Amelia Earhart had a passion for flying—she even wrote verse about it—but she was also deeply committed to the cause of feminism: both as a woman and a flyer, she was a pioneer. She once confided to her husband that, for her, the ideal way to die would be swiftly to go down with her plane.

Vincent Wilson, Jr., The Book of Distinguished American Women

1. State the article's topic:

    _____

2. Circle the best main-idea statement:
   a. Amelia Earhart made history in the 1920s and 1930s.
   b. Amelia Earhart was a pioneer for women and in the history of flight.

3. Briefly explain your selection of a main idea.

    _____

    _____

4. What main idea are we to infer from reading paragraph 2?

    _____

    _____

5. Why was Earhart called "Lady Lindy" in paragraph 3?

    _____

6. Why does the author conclude with Earhart's statement to her husband? What are we to infer from the conclusion?

_____

_____

■ ■ ■ ■ ■

EARLY AUTUMN

Langston Hughes

Langston Hughes was a journalist, fiction writer, and poet, the author of more than sixty books. Known as "the bard of Harlem," Hughes became an important public figure and voice for black writers. "Early Autumn" comes from his short fiction collection *Something in Common* (1963).

Prepare

1. Identify the author and work. What do you expect the author's purpose to be?

_____

2. Preread to identify the subject and make predictions. What do you expect to read about?

_____

■ ■ ■ ■ ■

1   When Bill was very young, they had been in love. Many nights they had spent walking, talking together. Then something not very important had come between them, and they didn't speak. Impulsively, she had married a man she thought she loved. Bill went away, bitter about women.

2   Yesterday, walking across Washington Square, she saw him for the first time in years.

3   "Bill Walker," she said.

4   He stopped. At first he did not recognize her, to him she looked so old.

5   "Mary! Where did you come from?"

6   Unconsciously, she lifted her face as though wanting a kiss, but he held out his hand. She took it.

7   "I live in New York now," she said.

8   "Oh"—smiling politely. Then a little frown came quickly between his eyes.

9   "Always wondered what happened to you, Bill."

10   "I'm a lawyer. Nice firm, way downtown."

11   "Married yet?"

12   "Sure. Two kids."

13   "Oh," she said.

14   A great many people went past them through the park. People they didn't know. It was late afternoon. Nearly sunset. Cold.

15   "And your husband?" he asked her.

16   "We have three children. I work in the bursar's office at Columbia."

17   "You're looking very . . ." (he wanted to say *old*) ". . . well," he said.

18   She understood. Under the trees in Washington Square, she found herself desperately reaching back into the past. She had been older than he then in Ohio. Now she was not young at all. Bill was still young.

19   "We live on Central Park West," she said. "Come and see us sometime."

20   "Sure," he replied. "You and your husband must have dinner with my family some night. Any night. Lucille and I'd love to have you."

21   The leaves fell slowly from the trees in the Square. Fell without wind. Autumn dusk. She felt a little sick.

22   "We'd love it," she answered.

23   "You ought to see my kids." He grinned.

24   Suddenly the lights came on up the whole length of Fifth Avenue, chains of misty brilliance in the blue air.

25   "There's my bus," she said. He held out his hand, "Good-by."

26   "When . . ." she wanted to say, but the bus was ready to pull off. The lights on the avenue blurred, twinkled, blurred. And she was afraid to open her mouth as she entered the bus. Afraid it would be impossible to utter a word.

27   Suddenly she shrieked very loudly, "Good-by!" But the bus door had closed.

28   The bus started. People came between them outside, people crossing the street, people they didn't know. Space and people. She lost sight of Bill. Then she remembered she had forgotten to give him her address—or to ask him for his—or tell him that her youngest boy was named Bill, too.

402 words

Comprehension Check

For items 1–4, fill in the blank with the word or phrase that best completes each sentence. For items 5–7 select either T (true) or F (false).

1. When Mary and Bill were young, they were _____.

2. Both characters now live in _____; both are

   _____ and have _____.

3. Bill thinks that Mary looks _____.

4. Mary gets on her bus without getting Bill's _____.

	T	F
5. Mary is upset when she gets on the bus.	____	____
6. Bill is upset when he parts from Mary.	____	____
7. Mary still loves Bill.	____	____

Drawing Inferences

1. What is Bill's reaction to seeing Mary?

   _____

   What specific details support your inference?

   _____

   _____

2. What can we infer from Mary's response to the question: "And your husband?"

   _____

3. What is happening to Mary when the "lights . . . blurred, twinkled, blurred"?

   _____

4. Why did the author call the story "Early Autumn"? (Look at the details of the scene—the time of year, the time of day, the activity around Mary and Bill.)

   _____

   _____

5. Briefly state the story's theme.

   _____

   _____

   _____

NEAT PEOPLE vs. SLOPPY PEOPLE

Suzanne Britt

Suzanne Britt graduated from Salem Academy, has a master's degree in English, and currently teaches at Meredith College in North Carolina. She is the author of several books and many poems and articles. The following article is from *Show and Tell,* a collection of her essays.

Prepare

1. Identify the author and the work. What do you expect the author's purpose to be?

_____

_____

2. Preread to identify the subject and make predictions. What do you expect to read about?

_____

_____

3. What do you already know about the subject?

_____

_____

4. Raise two questions that you expect the article to answer.

_____

_____

_____

Vocabulary Alert: Do You Know These Words?

Here are four words you need to know to read the following selection with understanding. The number in parentheses is the number of the paragraph in which the word appears.

rectitude (2): moral uprightness

stupendous (2): amazingly large or great

métier (3): one's specialty

rasslin' (7): southern pronunciation of "wrestling"

■ ■ ■ ■ ■

1   I've finally figured out the difference between neat people and sloppy people. The distinction is, as always, moral. Neat people are lazier and meaner than sloppy people.

2   Sloppy people, you see, are not really sloppy. Their sloppiness is merely the unfortunate consequence of their extreme moral rectitude. Sloppy people carry in their mind's eye a heavenly vision, a precise plan, that is so stupendous, so perfect, it can't be achieved in this world or the next.

3   Sloppy people live in Never-Never Land. Someday is their métier. Someday they are planning to alphabetize all their books and set up home catalogs. Someday they will go through their wardrobes and mark certain items for tentative mending and certain items for passing on to relatives of similar shape and size. Someday sloppy people will make family scrapbooks into which they will put newspaper clippings, postcards, locks of hair, and the dried corsage from their senior prom. Someday they will file everything on the surface of their desks, including the cash receipts from coffee purchases at the snack shop. Someday they will sit down and read all the back issues of *The New Yorker*.

4   For all these noble reasons and more, sloppy people never get neat. They aim too high and wide. They save everything, planning someday to file, order, and straighten out the world. But while these ambitious plans take clearer and clearer shape in their heads, the books spill from the shelves onto the floor, the clothes pile up in the hamper and closet, the family mementos accumulate in every drawer, the surface of the desk is buried under mounds of paper and the unread magazines threaten to reach the ceiling.

5   Sloppy people can't bear to part with anything. They give loving attention to every detail. When sloppy people say they're going to tackle the surface of the desk, they really mean it. Not a paper will go unturned; not a rubber band will go unboxed. Four hours or two weeks into the excavation, the desk looks exactly the same, primarily because the sloppy person is meticulously creating new piles of papers with new headings and scrupulously stopping to read all the old book catalogs before he throws them away. A neat person would just bulldoze the desk.

6   Neat people are bums and clods at heart. They have cavalier attitudes toward possessions, including family heirlooms. Everything is just another dustcatcher to them. If anything collects dust, it's got to go and that's that. Neat people will toy with the idea of throwing the children out of the house just to cut down on the clutter.

7   Neat people don't care about process. They like results. What they want to do is get the whole thing over with so they can sit down and watch the rasslin' on TV. Neat people operate on two unvarying principles: Never handle any item twice, and throw everything away.

8   The only thing messy in a neat person's house is the trash can. The minute something comes to a neat person's hand, he will look at it, try to decide if it has immediate use and, finding none, throw it in the trash.

9   Neat people are especially vicious with mail. They never go through their mail unless they are standing directly over a trash can. If the trash can is beside the mailbox, even better. All ads, catalogs, pleas for charitable contributions, church bulletins and money-saving coupons go straight into the trash can without being opened. All letters from home, postcards from Europe, bills and paychecks are opened, immediately responded to, then dropped in the trash can. Neat people keep their receipts only for tax purposes. That's it. No sentimental salvaging of birthday cards or the last letter a dying relative ever wrote. Into the trash it goes.

10   Neat people place neatness above everything, even economics. They are incredibly wasteful. Neat people throw away several toys every time they walk through the den. I knew a neat person once who threw away a perfectly good dish drainer because it had mold on it. The drainer was too much trouble to wash. And neat people sell their furniture when they move. They will sell a La-Z-Boy recliner while you are reclining in it.

11   Neat people are no good to borrow from. Neat people buy everything in expensive little single portions. They get their flour and sugar in two-pound bags. They wouldn't consider clipping a coupon, saving a leftover, reusing plastic nondairy whipped cream containers or rinsing off tin foil and draping it over the unmoldy dish drainer. You can never borrow a neat person's newspaper to see what's playing at the movies. Neat people have the paper all wadded up and in the trash by 7:05 A.M.

12   Neat people cut a clean swath through the organic as well as the inorganic world. People, animals, and things are all one to them. They are so insensitive. After they've finished with the pantry, the medicine cabinet, and the attic, they will throw out the red geranium (too many leaves), sell the dog (too many fleas), and send the children off to boarding school (too many scuffmarks on the hardwood floors).

840 words

Comprehension Check

Answer with a, b, c, or d to indicate the phrase that best completes each statement.

_____ 1. The best statement of the essay's topic is

    a. the land of sloppy people.

    b. the morality of neatness.

    c. the differences between neat and sloppy people.

    d. what's good about sloppy people.

_____   2. The best statement of the essay's main idea is

     a. sloppy people ignore the real world.

     b. sloppy people are not really sloppy.

     c. neat people are compulsive.

     d. sloppy people are superior to neat people.

_____   3. Sloppy people aren't really sloppy; they just

     a. have too perfect a plan.

     b. can't bear to part with anything.

     c. both (a) and (b).

     d. neither a nor b.

_____   4. Neat people are bums because they

     a. care more about results than process.

     b. pile papers up on their desks.

     c. borrow from their neighbors.

     d. are very energetic.

_____   5. Neat people believe in

     a. keeping everything on their desks.

     b. never handling anything twice.

     c. getting rid of their children.

     d. getting rid of the trash can.

_____   6. Neat people

     a. keep sentimental cards.

     b. read old book catalogs before throwing them away.

     c. throw away tax receipts.

     d. read their mail standing by the trash can.

_____   7. You can't borrow a newspaper from neat people because

     a. they have read and trashed it by 7:05 A.M.

     b. they are too cheap to buy a paper.

     c. they stack old papers in a disorderly fashion.

     d. they need to reread each paper.

_____   8. When Britt writes that neat people "will sell a La-Z-Boy recliner while you are reclining in it," she is

     a. warning you not to sit in a recliner.

     b. emphasizing how mean neat people are.

     c. exaggerating to make a point in an amusing way.

     d. writing precisely what she means.

_____ 9. The primary writing strategy in this essay is

    a. contrast.

    b. listing.

    c. example.

    d. cause/effect.

_____ 10. The tone of this essay is

    a. angry.

    b. amusing.

    c. serious.

    d. mean.

Expanding Vocabulary

Match each word in the left column with its definition in the right column by placing the correct letter in the space next to each word. When in doubt, read again the sentence in which the word appears. The numbers in parentheses tell you what paragraph the word appears in.

_____ 1. ambitious (4)	a. carefully, precisely	
_____ 2. mementos (4)	b. move or clear away with heavy equipment	
_____ 3. excavation (5)	c. savage, dangerous	
_____ 4. meticulously (5)	d. saving from loss	
_____ 5. scrupulously (5)	e. a hole created by digging	
_____ 6. bulldoze (5)	f. path left from mowing	
_____ 7. cavalier (6)	g. marks on floor made by scraping one's shoes	
_____ 8. vicious (9)	h. reminders of the past, keepsakes	
_____ 9. salvaging (9)	i. compressed into a ball	
_____ 10. wadded up (11)	j. conscientiously, painstakingly	
_____ 11. swath (12)	k. full of ambition	
_____ 12. scuffmarks (12)	l. carefree, possibly disdainful	

For Reflection and Discussion

1. Are you a neat or a sloppy person? If you are a neat person, have you felt a bit superior to sloppy people? Has Britt given you another way to look at these two kinds of people?

2. How would you argue for the superiority of neat people over sloppy people?

MAKING CONNECTIONS

WORKSHOP

1. How well do you know yourself? Are there ways in which others might see you differently than you see yourself? (For example, do you see yourself as a neat person, but you know that family members see you as sloppy?) Reflect on these questions and be ready to discuss your thoughts.

2. What are some things we could do to know ourselves better? On your own or with your class partner develop a list of possible strategies for knowing yourself better.

"E" CONNECTIONS

One way to know yourself better is to use the Myers/Briggs personality grid. There is a "test" you can take that is then "scored" to reveal each person's personality profile. At some colleges, students can arrange to take this test and have a counselor "score" it and discuss the results with the student. You can learn more about Myers/Briggs online and see if you are interested in following through on this approach to learning about yourself. One useful site to explore is:

<www.teamtechnology.co.uk/ad.html>.

WORD POWER 9

Knowing Common Foreign Language Words

Many English words have their origin in another language, but these words have been made into English words. Some words, though, retain their foreign language spelling and pronunciation while used by English speakers. Often these words are shown to be foreign terms by the use of italics, for example, *ad hominem*. You will want to be able to recognize these words in your reading and spell and pronounce them correctly.

I. Look up each of the following words in your dictionary. Spend some time practicing the word's pronunciation. Then write each word's definition in the space below.

1. *Homo sapiens* _____

_____

_____

2. *coup d'état* _____

_____

_____

3. *ad hominem* _____

_____

_____

4. aficionado _____

_____

_____

5. genre _____

_____

_____

II. Select the correct word for each of the sentences that follow.

1. In modern times, most of the _____ (*coup d'états*; aficionados) have occurred in Central and South America.

2. One all-too-common fallacy in arguments is called the _____ (*ad hominem*; genre) fallacy.

3. Marcel particularly liked to teach _____ (genre/aficionado) courses such as modern drama and the Russian novel.

4. It seems that sometimes humans like to forget that the biological classification system includes _____ (genres/*Homo sapiens*).

5. Many South Americans and Europeans are great soccer _____ (aficionados/*Homo sapiens*).

CHAPTER REVIEW

Complete each of the following statements.

1. An *inference* is _____

_____.

2. We draw inferences from both _____

and _____.

3. To draw some inferences, we need to "fill in" from our _____

_____.

4. A *metaphor* compares two _____

_____.

5. *Irony* turns on or "works" based on _____

_____.

Take a Reading Road Trip!

For additional practice with your reading skills, use the Reading Road Trip CD-ROM or visit Reading Road Trip on the Web at **<http://www.ablongman.com/readingroadtrip>** (password required).

CHAPTER 11

Understanding Graphics and Separating Fact and Opinion

LEARNING OBJECTIVES

- To know the purposes of graphics or visuals
- To acquire guidelines for reading graphics
- To understand the information in diagrams, tables, graphs, and charts
- To distinguish between fact and opinion

PREPARE TO READ

Read and reflect on the chapter's title and objectives. Glance through the chapter, observing headings, to see what is covered. Now answer these questions.

1. What do you expect to learn from this chapter?

_____

_____

2. What do you already know about the chapter's topic?

_____

_____

3. What two or three questions do you want answered from reading this chapter?

_____

_____

_____

_____

A picture, as the saying goes, is worth a thousand words. Many graphics (or visuals) appear in textbooks and in other books and magazines. *Graphics* include pictures, diagrams, maps, tables, charts, and graphs. Even though they are used to aid the reader, many readers ignore them. This is a mistake. Graphics have three important uses:

- They are aids to learning. They help clarify material that may be difficult to follow in the text alone. They help us *see* relationships.
- They provide information that may be referred to only briefly in the text.
- They add interest, often dramatically so.

Perhaps you have skipped over graphics in the past because you were uncertain how to "read" them. This chapter provides guidelines for reading plus practice.

In addition, this chapter explores differences between fact and opinion. We think of tables and charts as presenting facts, but sometimes graphics are presented in a way that slants the facts. Readers must always be alert to opinions that are pretending to be facts.

◢ HOW TO READ GRAPHICS

Graphics present a good bit of information in less space than would be needed for an explanation in words only. But words are also part of graphics. First, you will find a reference in the text to every kind of visual except, usually, photographs. Second, there is writing connected to the graphic itself—above, below, and even within the visual representation. The first step to reading graphics is to turn to the graphic when it is referred to in the text, or to examine photographs as they appear. As you study the following steps to reading graphics, continue to refer to Table 11.1 as your example.

1. **Locate the particular graphic referred to in the text.** Tables are always labeled Tables; other graphics are labeled Figures, except for photographs, which are usually not labeled. In books containing many visuals, tables and figures will be numbered, usually by chapter (11) and then by the order in which they appear in the chapter (11.1).

2. **Read the title or heading of the graphic.** What is the topic of the graphic? What specific information is provided? The topic of Table 11.1 is "Civilian Employees of the Federal Government." The table is limited in two important ways: (1) It covers the years from 1816 to 1991 and (2) it includes numbers for *civilian* employees only. (What group of government employees is not included

in these numbers? _____)

TABLE 11.1   Civilian Employees of the Federal Government, 1816–1991

Year	Total Number of Employees	Number Employed in the Washington, D.C. Area
1816	4,837	535
1821	6,914	603
1831	11,491	666
1841	18,038	1,014
1851	26,274	1,533
1861	36,672	2,199
1871	51,020	6,222
1881	100,020	13,124
1891	157,442	20,834
1901	239,476	20,044
1911	395,905	39,782
1921	561,142	82,416
1931	609,746	76,303
1941	1,437,682	190,588
1951	2,482,666	265,980
1961	2,435,804	246,266
1971	2,874,166	322,969
1981	2,858,742	350,516
1991	3,108,899	374,187

Source: United States Bureau of the Census, *Historical Statistics of the United States, Colonial Times to 1970,* Part 2; pp. 1102–03; U.S. Office of Personnel Management, *Federal Civilian Workforce Statistics: Employment and Trends as of July 1989*; idem, *Employment and Trends as of January 1992.*
From Everett C. Ladd, *The American Polity,* 5th ed.

3. **Read any notes, description, and the source of information, material that appears at the bottom of the graphic.** In Table 11.1 the information has been compiled from two sources. Many textbooks contain diagrams and charts prepared just for that textbook. Photographs will have a brief description under them, perhaps followed by the name of the photographer or organization owning the original image.

4. **Read the headings for tables and graphs, the legend for maps.** Each column in a table will be labeled to show what it represents. (For example, from Table 11.1: "Year" and "Total number of employees.") A graph will label what is being shown on the vertical line and what is being shown on the horizontal

line. A map's legend gives you the scale of the map or what the colors or shadings represent. You cannot draw accurate conclusions from a graphic until you understand exactly what information you have been given. In Table 11.1 we are given the total number of employees and the number of those employees who work in the D.C. area, for each year covered.

5. **Study the information.** Look at the numbers or drawings. Make comparisons. Observe trends or patterns. You might be surprised by the total number of federal employees in 1991—over 3 million. You might be equally surprised by the number who work in D.C., between 350 and 400 thousand.

6. **Draw conclusions.** Think about the information in several ways. First, what does the author want to accomplish by including the graphic? Second, what is your reaction to the information provided? What can we conclude from Table 11.1? You might want to reflect, for example, on the fact that in 1931, while the number of federal employees increased, the number working in Washington decreased. How might your knowledge of the time help you explain these numbers? Also, what do you think about such a small percentage of employees actually working in D.C.? What are some types of federal employees who work in other parts of the country?

_____

_____

Graphics provide information, raise questions, explain processes, make us think. Use this information in your studies. Let's look more closely at each type of graphic.

■ PICTURES AND PHOTOGRAPHS

Many printed materials today include photographs. They support the author's discussion and add interest to the text. Pictures don't just make a book attractive. They also tell a story. Study them and think about why each one has been selected by the author.

In *The American Polity*, Ladd includes the on page 357 photograph in his discussion of the presidency. Reflect on it and then answer the questions in the exercise.

| EXERCISE 11-1 | Questions on the Photograph |

1. What details in the photo make it dramatic?

_____

_____

■ The Loneliest Job—
President John F.
Kennedy in the Oval
Office

© NYT Pictures

_____

_____

2. What message does the photo send about the job of the U.S. presidency?

_____

_____

_____

_____

■ DIAGRAMS

Diagrams are drawings or illustrations that visually capture a concept or process or object under discussion. Textbooks in the sciences and social sciences rely heavily on diagrams to:

1. show and label parts of objects (plants, human cells, the arrangement of the planets), and

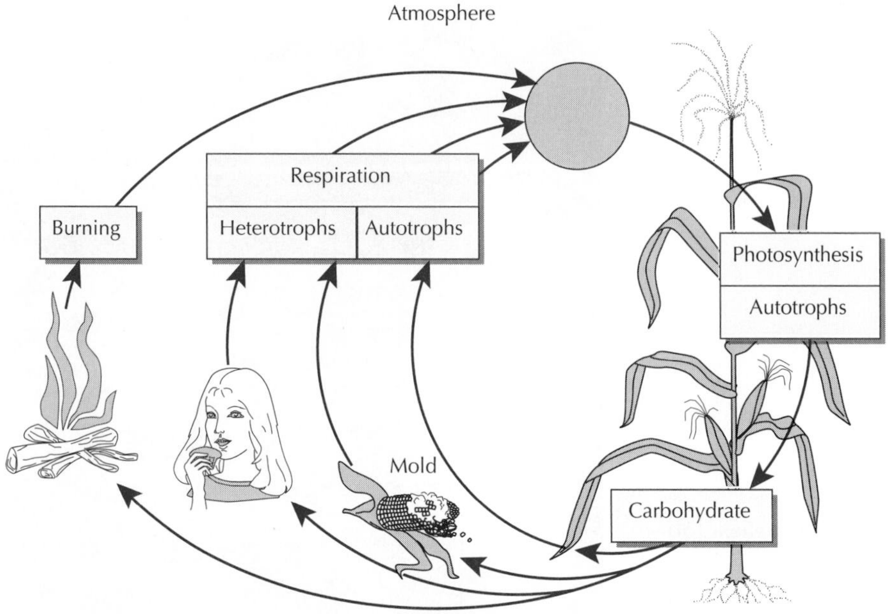

■ FIGURE 11.1 The Global Carbon Cycle

Vast amounts of carbon move through the air, soil, and water as photosynthesizing autotrophs fix carbon dioxide into organic compounds, and heterotrophs (along with nonliving combustion processes such as burning) break down those compounds and once again release carbon dioxide.

Source: Postlethwait, Hopson, and Veres, *Biology! Bringing Science to Life*

2. represent processes that are not visible, or not readily so (the process of photosynthesis, the process of sexual reproduction).

Consider, for example, the above diagram (Figure 11.1) from a biology text. The illustration creates a visual explanation of the process by which carbon moves through the air and is used by both plants and humans. The diagram helps readers to see both the complexity and the importance of the carbon cycle.

EXERCISE 11-2	**Understanding Diagrams**

Study Figure 11.2—remembering to read the accompanying explanations—and answer the questions that follow.

1. What is the diagram's subject? What process does it demonstrate?

_____

_____

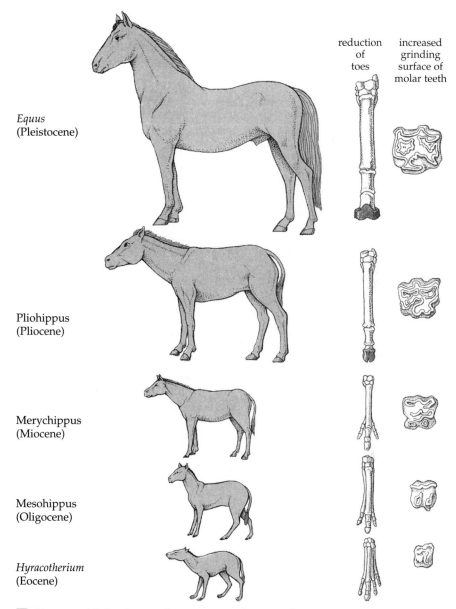

reduction
of
toes

increased
grinding
surface of
molar teeth

Equus
(Pleistocene)

Pliohippus
(Pliocene)

Merychippus
(Miocene)

Mesohippus
(Oligocene)

Hyracotherium
(Eocene)

■ **FIGURE 11.2 The Modern Horse and Some of Its Ancestors**
Only one of the several branches represented in the fossil record is shown. Over the past 60 million years, small several-toed browsers, such as *Hyracotherium*, were replaced in gradual stages by members of the genus *Equus*, characterized by, among other features, a larger size; broad molars adapted to grinding coarse grass blades; a single toe surrounded by a tough, protective keratin hoof; and a leg in which the bones of the lower leg had fused, with joints becoming more pulleylike and motion restricted to a single plane.

Source: Illustration by Shirley Baty in Curtis and Barnes, *An Invitation to Biology*, 4th ed.

_____

_____

2. What three changes in the development of *Equus* are illustrated?

_____

_____

_____

_____

3. Merychippus comes from what paleontological period?

_____

_____

_____

_____

4. How many years passed between the period of *Hyracotherium* and the period of *Equus?*

_____

_____

_____

_____

MAPS

Maps show geographical areas. Some maps show the entire surface of the Earth. Others show differences in types of land mass, such as mountains and deserts. Many maps focus on one part of the world and show changes or trends—something about that part of the world at a particular time.

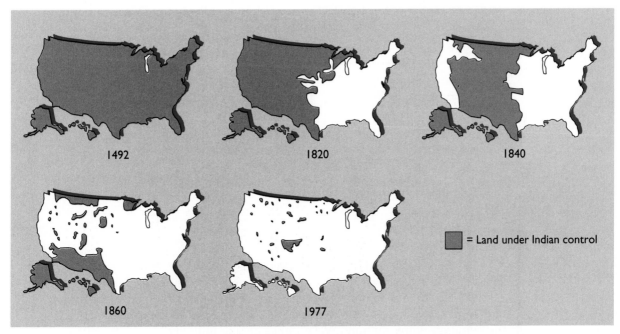

FIGURE 11.3 Indian Land within the United States, 1492–1977

Sources: Adapted from Weyler, 1982:65. Curran and Renzetti, *Social Problems*, 4th ed.

| EXERCISE 11-3 | **Reading Maps** |

Study the map in Figure 11.3 and answer the questions that follow.

1. What is the map's subject?

_____

2. Why is the first map (1492) included? What are we being asked to remember?

_____

3. What key difference do you see between the 1820 and 1840 maps? What was happening to account for the change?

_____

_____

4. What are the separate pieces of land shown at the bottom? Why are they included? What do we learn from them?

_____

_____

5. What is your reaction after studying these maps?

_____

_____

◼ TABLES

As you saw in Table 11.1, a table presents information, in columns, on a given subject. By using columns, tables summarize and focus the information.

When reading the numbers in tables, be sure that you know what the numbers represent. That is, are the numerals showing the actual numbers, or do the numerals represent hundreds or thousands or millions? Or, are the numerals percentages rather than whole numbers? The numerals in Table 11.1 are actual numbers of federal employees.

| EXERCISE 11-4 | Reading Tables |

Study Table 11.2 on the next page; then answer these questions.

1. What is the table's subject?

_____

2. What five types of products containing caffeine are covered?

_____

_____

3. What do the numbers in the table represent?

_____

4. Which food or drink product contains the most caffeine?

_____

TABLE 11.2   **Caffeine Content of Various Products**

Product	Caffeine Content (average mg per serving)	Product	Caffeine Content (average mg per serving)
COFFEE (5-oz. cup)		Coca-Cola	46
Regular brewed	65–115	Pepsi-Cola	36–38
Decaffeinated brewed	3	CHOCOLATE	
Decaffeinated instant	2	1 oz. baking chocolate	25
TEA (6-oz. cup)		1 oz. chocolate candy bar	15
Hot steeped	36	½ cup chocolate pudding	4–12
Iced	31	OVER-THE-COUNTER DRUGS	
SOFT DRINKS		No Doz (2 tablets)	200
(12-oz. servings)		Excedrin (2 tablets)	130
Jolt Cola	100	Midol (2 tablets)	65
Dr. Pepper	61	Anacin (2 tablets)	64
Mountain Dew	54		

Source: Donatelle and Davis, *Access to Health*, 4th ed.

5. Which cola drink would seem to be most appropriately named?

_____

6. According to this table, what is the best drink if you want to limit caffeine intake?

_____

7. What are some other drinks low in caffeine that are not included in this table?

_____

8. Is taking No Doz likely to cause sleeplessness? _____

GRAPHS AND CHARTS

Graphs show relationships and emphasize comparisons between two or more related items. Some people prefer to use the term *graph* to refer only to line graphs, and to use *chart* for pie, bar, and flowcharts. Let's look at each type separately.

Pie Charts

The pie chart is probably the easiest to draw and to read. It is a circle divided into segments to show the relative portion of each part to the whole. You can use pie charts only when you are examining a whole, a complete category. For example, you can divide *all* students at your college by age, or by race, or by parents' income. If you did all three, you would make three separate pie charts.

EXERCISE 11-5	**Reading Pie Charts**

Study the three pie charts in Figure 11.4 and then answer the questions that follow.

1. What is the subject of the charts?

   _____

2. In addition to the information within the pie charts, what other information is provided?

   _____

3. How would you account for the small but steady increase in the percentage of African Americans from 2000 to 2050?

   _____

   _____

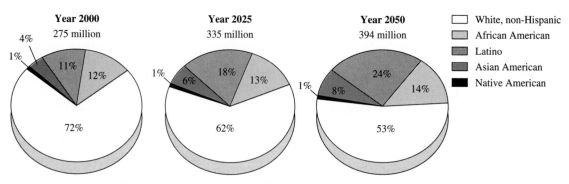

■ Figure 11.4 **The Shifting of U.S. Racial-Ethnic Mix**

Sources: U.S. Bureau of the Census. *Current Population Reports* P25:1130, 1996 James Henslin. *Sociology: A Down-to-Earth Approach,* 5th ed.

4. Which group increases by the greatest relative amount? And, how would you account for that increase?

_____

_____

5. Which figure surprises you the most? Why?

_____

_____

■ ■ ■ ■ ■

Bar Charts

Bar charts are used to show relative proportions in a visually effective way. Bars can extend from either the bottom of the chart or the left side of the chart. Colors or shadings are often used to distinguish among the items. Again, be sure to understand what each chart is showing and what the numbers represent.

EXERCISE 11-6	Reading Bar Charts

Study the chart in Figure 11.5 on the next page; and then answer the questions that follow.

1. What is the definition of adolescents used in this chart?

_____

2. Which unhealthy behavior is most frequently found among adolescents?

_____

3. Which is the unhealthy behavior that females participate in significantly more than males?

_____

4. Which is the unhealthy behavior that males participate in significantly more than females?

_____

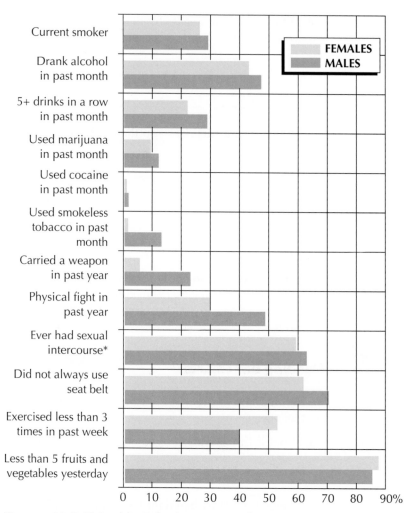

■ FIGURE 11.5 Unhealthy Behavior Among Adolescents*

*Ages 14 to 21 and never married.

Source: National Center for Health Statistics

5. Which figure surprises you the most? Why?

_____

_____

_____

■ ■ ■ ■ ■

Line Graphs

Line graphs are ideal for showing trends or changes over time or for showing a frequency distribution—a distribution relationship of two variables, such as the number of airline passengers in various age groups. Line graphs can also compare two or more trends on the same chart. Be sure to understand what the horizontal line and the vertical line represent.

EXERCISE 11-7	**Understanding Line Graphs**

Study the graph (Figure 11.6) and then answer the questions that follow.

1. What two subjects are treated by the graph?

_____

2. In 1985, what was the average annual income for men?

_____

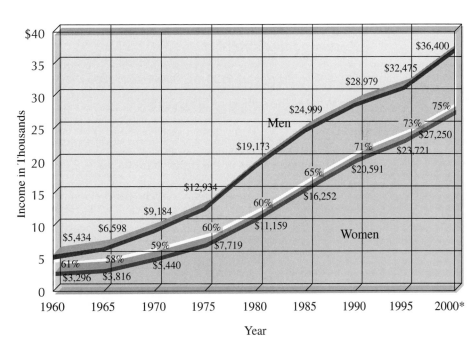

* Author's estimate

■ FIGURE 11.6 **The Gender Pay Gap Over Time: The Annual Income of Full-Time Workers and the Percentage of the Men's Income Earned by Women**

Sources: Beeghley 1989:239; Statistical Abstract 1995: Table 739. James M. Henslin, *Sociology*, 3rd ed.

3. What percent of men's income in 1985 was earned by women?

_____

4. During which five-year period did men's incomes increase by the greatest amount?

_____

5. Does the author's prediction for the year 2000 suggest that income equality for women will take place?

_____

■ ■ ■ ■ ■

Flowcharts

Flowcharts show qualitative rather than quantitative relationships. They are useful for showing steps in a process or a sequence of events or ideas. Usually flowcharts provide a visual summary that reinforces a detailed explanation in the text. They are helpful guides to reviewing for tests.

| EXERCISE 11-8 | **Reading Flowcharts** |

Study the chart (Figure 11.7) and then answer the questions that follow.

1. What is the subject of the chart?

_____

2. How many steps in the process are there? _____

3. What event helped bring about the third stage of development?

_____

4. Why is the arrow between Industrial society and Postindustrial society not a solid line?

_____

5. Although the chart shows social, not political, changes, why is it appropriate to use the word *revolution?*

_____

_____

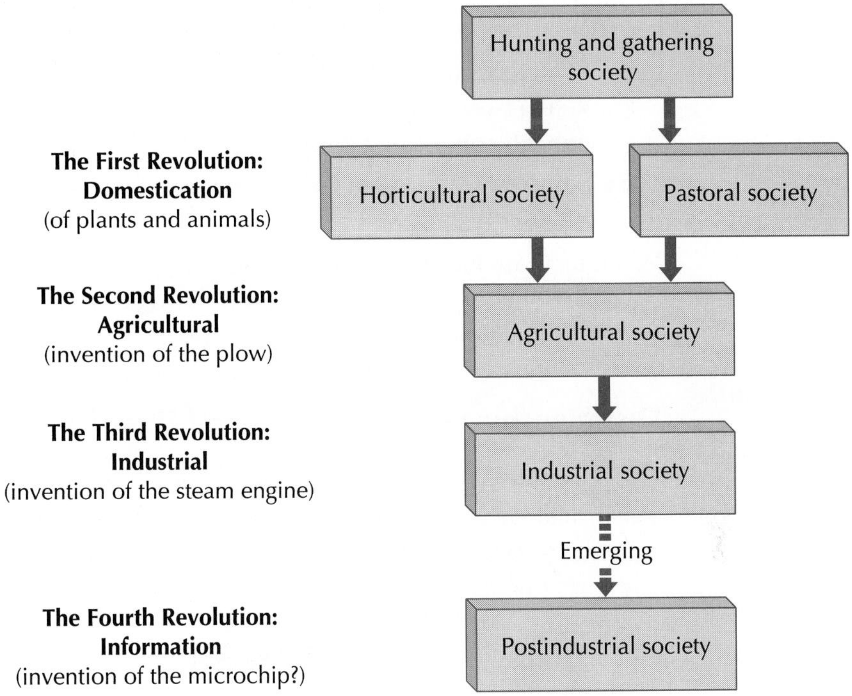
Hunting and gathering society
The First Revolution: Domestication (of plants and animals)
Horticultural society
Pastoral society
The Second Revolution: Agricultural (invention of the plow)
Agricultural society
The Third Revolution: Industrial (invention of the steam engine)
Industrial society
Emerging
The Fourth Revolution: Information (invention of the microchip?)
Postindustrial society

FIGURE 11.7 The Social Transformations of Society

Source: James M. Henslin, *Sociology*, 2nd ed.

DISTINGUISHING FACT FROM OPINION

What do these statements have in common?

> My reading class meets in 116 Gray Hall.
>
> Los Angeles is north of San Diego.
>
> The Earth is in the Milky Way galaxy.

These statements are all facts. *Facts* are verifiable. That is, we can count or measure or confirm them through observation or by turning to trusted sources. If you want to find your reading class, you check the schedule and then confirm the location by going to the classroom when the class meets. You can confirm the second fact on a map and the third one in an astronomy textbook.

In an argument over facts, one person has the facts, the other does not. Some people think they have facts, but they have misinformation instead, what we can call false facts. When reading statements that sound like facts, be alert to the possibility that the "facts" are incorrect.

Why would anyone pass on false facts?

■ Sometimes the "facts" change as we learn more about the world we live in.

■ Sometimes people pass on what they have been told without thinking critically about that "information."

■ Some writers present facts in an incomplete or distorted way to advance their own goals.

When facts are incomplete or distorted, the total impact of the writing is false. Advertisements, including political ads during elections, come to mind as examples of messages often containing false facts.

EXERCISE 11-9	Distinguishing Between Facts and False Facts

Mark each of the following statements as either F (fact) or FF (false fact). If you are unsure, indicate in the margin how you could verify the fact. If you are unsure of three or more statements, look them up in your dictionary or an encyclopedia in your library.

F   FF

_____ _____ 1. A healthy diet should include plenty of meat and eggs.

_____ _____ 2. Egg whites have no cholesterol.

_____ _____ 3. Dallas is the capital of Texas.

_____ _____ 4. The city of Kiev is in Russia.

_____ _____ 5. The majority of Americans benefiting from one or more welfare programs are white.

_____ _____ 6. HIV-infected mothers may give birth to infected babies.

_____ _____ 7. The Andromeda galaxy is larger than our galaxy.

_____ _____ 8. You can become HIV-infected by attending class with an HIV-infected person.

_____ _____ 9. The Earth is 5,000 years old.

_____ _____ 10. Over 90 percent of U.S. homes have a television set.

Critical readers remain skeptical of "facts." If a statement doesn't sound quite right to you, then check it out before accepting it as a fact.

Now, what do these statements have in common?

My reading instructor is cool.

San Diego is a nicer place to live than Los Angeles.

The Milky Way galaxy was formed about 10 billion years ago.

These statements are not facts. They are all opinions, so they are open to debate. Most writing combines facts and opinion, sometimes in the same sentence. You need to be able to tell the difference so that you can evaluate the opinions and judge whether the facts support them. Often the main idea in a paragraph or section is opinion. Authors sometimes (but not always) use signal words to distinguish between facts and opinions, so be alert to these guides to reading. The following are some of the words and phrases signalling opinions:

consequently	in conclusion
as a result	this suggests
in my view	most experts agree that

EXERCISE 11-10

Distinguishing Fact from Opinion

Mark each of the following statements as either F (fact) or O (opinion). If you are uncertain, indicate in the margin how you could confirm the fact.

F   O

_____ _____ 1. Smoking is prohibited on all flights in the continental United States.

_____ _____ 2. Many Americans have lost confidence in their elected officials.

_____ _____ 3. The best way to lose weight is to reduce the amount of fat in one's diet and to exercise regularly.

_____ _____ 4. *Tom Sawyer* was written in the 19th century.

_____ _____ 5. Americans are fascinated by movie stars and sports figures.

_____ _____ 6. The dinosaurs may have died out because of a change in climate.

_____ _____ 7. I would rather eat frozen yogurt than ice cream.

_____ _____ 8. It is discourteous to talk during a movie or lecture.

_____ _____ 9. Americans have become less courteous.

_____ _____ 10. Because of its violence, boxing should be banned.

▪ ▪ ▪ ▪ ▪

Did this exercise help you "hear" the difference between a fact and a statement of opinion? Did the exercise make you aware that opinions do not all sound the same? We need to make distinctions among several kinds of opinions because how we respond depends on the type of opinion.

"Just" an Opinion

Some people say, "That's just your opinion," as if that is a sufficient reason to reject the statement. In this context, *opinion* seems to mean a bias or prejudice—and one with which the speaker disagrees. Consider, for example, the statement that secondhand smoke is a health hazard. Is this "just" personal opinion, or is this a view held by most scientists and doctors? Smokers may wish to dismiss the opinion as prejudice against them, but smokers probably should think about the health risks to which they expose friends and family. Many opinions actually have strong factual support and cannot be easily dismissed "just" because someone prefers not to accept them.

Personal Preferences

Others—sometimes students—have been known to say, "Well, that's *my* opinion," as if that is a sufficient reason to justify the statement. Are there some opinions that you may hold without having to defend them? Yes, you do not need to defend *personal preferences*. If you prefer frozen yogurt to ice cream, that's fine. The problem comes when we turn personal preferences into debatable opinions but then refuse to defend them. If you prefer rock and roll to jazz music, that's fine, until you claim that rock and roll is a *better* kind of music than jazz. Now you have stated an opinion that can—and should—be debated. Expect jazz fans to argue with you and prepare your defense.

Judgments

Your claim about rock and roll music is a *judgment*, an opinion based on values and beliefs. Judgments are about what is good or bad, right or wrong, better or worse. Judgments can be challenged and must be defended with facts and reasons. If you say that you like to watch the Dallas Cowboys, that is your personal preference. But when you say that the Dallas Cowboys are the best football team, you must give evidence to support your judgment. The following statements are examples of judgments.

1. Jack Nicklaus is the best golfer ever to play the game.
2. The sunrise was beautiful.
3. Congress should balance the federal budget.
4. Smoking should be prohibited in all public facilities.

Inferences

There is one more type of opinion to identify: inferences. An *inference* is an opinion based on facts, or on a combination of facts and simpler inferences. You have already learned to draw inferences when you read a work with an unstated main idea.

Inferences vary from those closely tied to facts to those that are highly debatable. Here are four inferences.

1. Jack Nicklaus has been one of golf's most consistent players.
2. The sun will rise tomorrow.
3. Balancing the federal budget will result in either cutting or abolishing many popular programs.
4. Secondhand smoke is a health hazard.

Notice that these four inferences are about the same subjects as the four judgments given above, but the statements in each case are quite different. How can these inferences be supported?

1. The first inference can be supported with facts from golf records—the number of tournaments won, consistent finishes in the top ten, and so forth.
2. The second inference may sound like a fact, but until the sun actually rises, we can only assume that it will.
3. Observe that the third inference does not state whether it is good or bad to balance the budget. The sentence only asserts what the facts seem to indicate: To balance you have to cut. However, this inference is based on an assumption that can be challenged. Can you think of a way to balance the budget and not cut programs? Of course. We can raise taxes. The writer assumes a consistent tax base. Remember: Critical readers ask, "What other conclusions can be drawn? What is another way to look at the issue?" You may not think that raising taxes is a good idea, but it is an alternative to the opinion stated in the above inference.
4. The fourth inference is supported by medical research.

Opinions are found in all kinds of writing. How do we separate reasonable opinions from those with little factual or logical support? Here are some guidelines for thinking critically about opinions.

Guidelines for Evaluating Opinions

1. **Know the facts and compare sources.** The more you know, the less likely you are to accept false facts and questionable opinions. Read more than one source to see if similar views are shared.
2. **Evaluate sources.** In general, experts are likely to present facts and both label and support opinions. Be particularly wary of nonexpert Websites.

(continued on next page)

(continued from previous page)

3. **In science, distinguish between hypotheses and theories.** A hypothesis is a tentative idea that needs testing. A theory is an inference based on many facts and reasoning from those facts. Theories are supported by most experts in a field.

4. **Be alert to and evaluate unstated assumptions.** Sometimes writers assume that readers share their values and assumptions, so they don't discuss—much less defend—them. Readers need to spot the assumptions without help from writers.

5. **Be skeptical of generalizations and pay attention to wording.** Few generalizations about humans are accurate. For example: Teens are reckless drivers. A fair generalization? Of course not. What is fact is that drivers between 16 and 24 have the greatest number of accidents. That does not mean that *all* teens are reckless drivers.

6. **Analyze the evidence.** Question and debate with yourself as you read.

■ ■ ■ ■ ■

GRAPHS CAN LIE, EASY AS PIE

Boyce Rensberger

Boyce Rensberger is a staff writer for the *Washington Post*. His article on pie charts appeared in the *Post's* "Horizon" learning section on June 12, 1996.

Prepare

1. Identify the author and the work. What do you expect the author's purpose to be?

_____

_____

2. Preread to identify the subject and make predictions. What do you expect to read about?

_____

_____

3. What do you already know about the subject?

_____

_____

_____

4. Raise two questions that you expect the article to answer.

_____

_____

_____

■ ■ ■ ■ ■

1   Figures don't lie, but according to an old saying, liars figure. It's still true, and in recent years liars with axes to grind have turned to a new form of technology for help.

2   These are computer graphing programs, software into which you feed a set of figures and choose the style of graph you want—a pie chart, say, or a bar graph. Push a few keys, click the mouse a few times and instantly the computer displays your data in neatly drawn graphical form, complete with color coding and labels.

3   As a tool, graphing programs are wonderful. They are used by virtually all publishers of numerical data, from government analysts and investment brokers to high school students doing papers. Magazines and newspapers publish them in almost every issue.

4   If that were as far as it had gone, there would be no problem. We would all have a better intuitive grasp of the relative sizes of the numbers being compared. But the people who created the graphing programs took an extra step. They decided to let their customers jazz up the appearance of graphs by representing them in what is called 3-D. It isn't really three-dimensional, however, just perspective drawing. But that's not the problem.

5   The problem is that, when you tip a normally circular pie chart on its side, as is commonly done to make it look "more artistically interesting," you warp the intuitive impact of the relative sizes of the pie slices.

6   Look, for example, at Chart 1 on page 376 and try to rank the four wedges in order of size. The [gray] part is easily largest, but which is second? Most would pick the [lined] wedge, ranking the [black] a clear third in size, only a little bigger than the [white].

7   Now look at Chart 2 on page 376. It shows the same data but in an old-fashioned, straight-on, undistorted view. Now it becomes obvious that the [black] and [lined] wedges are equal, each 20 percent of the pie, and the [white] wedge is a much smaller 10 percent.

■ **Chart 1**   ■ **Chart 2**

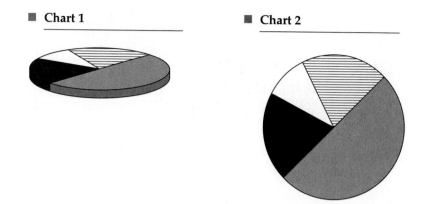

8   What happened in Chart 1 is what happens to any pie chart tipped and viewed at an oblique angle. Wedges at the top or bottom appear wider, and any wedge at the left or right will look narrower.

9   Both effects are an unavoidable result of perspective drawing, which is what the computer programs do. The numbers guiding the computer are the percentages of the pie assigned to each slice and are the same in both charts. Thus the chart maker can insist that the tipped version is accurate.

10   Might a liar use this distortion to push an unwarranted point?

11   Look at Chart 3. It shows the ethnic composition of the United States. The largest piece of the pie constitutes 76 percent of its area and represents the white, non-Latino population. African Americans, at 12 percent, constitute the second biggest group, followed by Latinos at 9 percent, Asian Americans at 3 percent and Native Americans at 1 percent. The numbers add to 101 percent because of rounding.

12   Suppose you want to promote the view that nonwhites are becoming an unduly large fraction of the American population. You could choose to put the minority groups at the top or bottom of the pie so they will benefit from the widening effect, and you would position the white majority slice so it gets as much of the squeezing effect as possible [see Chart 4].

■ **Chart 3**   ■ **Chart 4**   ■ **Chart 5**

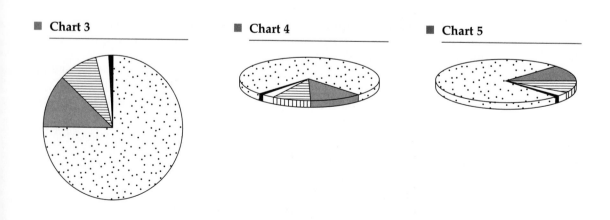

13   Now suppose you were pushing the other side, the view that minority groups really are a rather tiny segment of the population. Chart 5 shows the result of shifting them to the squeezed part of the pie.

14   Either way, the tipped pie charts are absolutely truthful representations of the facts. It's just that they have abandoned what was supposed to be the whole point of graphical representations of numerical data, making it easier for people to grasp relative sizes intuitively.

15   Next time you see tipped pie charts, be suspicious. The motive may be entirely artistic, but the point of the message may be quite distorted.

669 words

Comprehension Check

Answer the following with a, b, c, or d to indicate the phrase that best completes each statement.

_____ 1. The best statement of the essay's topic is
      a. graphics.
      b. pie charts.
      c. fun with pie charts.
      d. pie chart distortions.

_____ 2. Computer graphing programs provide
      a. pie charts.
      b. a color graphic you choose.
      c. axes to grind.
      d. false facts.

_____ 3. Computer graphing programs are frequently used
      a. by government analysts.
      b. by high school students.
      c. both a and b.
      d. hair dressers.

_____ 4. Graphics give readers
      a. a better understanding of relative sizes of comparable numbers.
      b. a better understanding of how to draw.
      c. no understanding of numbers.
      d. no understanding of life.

_____ 5. Computer graphing programs
      a. are unattractive but accurate.
      b. represent the numbers in 3-D.

     c. use perspective drawing.

     d. falsify the facts.

_____ 6. When pie charts are tipped on their sides

     a. they become inaccurate.

     b. they are more accurate.

     c. the size of each "slice" is enlarged.

     d. the relative size of each "slice" is distorted.

_____ 7. When pie charts are tipped on their sides

     a. wedges at either side appear narrower.

     b. wedges at the top and bottom appear narrower.

     c. all wedges get larger.

     d. all wedges get smaller.

_____ 8. The author asks readers to judge the relative amounts represented in Chart 1

     a. so that readers understand his point about distortion.

     b. to see if readers understand pie charts.

     c. to entertain readers.

     d. to show that the gray section is the largest.

_____ 9. Tipped pie charts are

     a. the best choice.

     b. more attractive but wrong.

     c. accurate but visually distort the numbers.

     d. distorted and inaccurate.

_____ 10. The essay's best main-idea statement is

     a. computer graphing programs lie.

     b. computer graphing programs let users present numbers in a visually attractive way.

     c. computer graphing programs miss the point of graphics because they visually distort the numbers.

     d. pie charts should not be used.

Expanding Vocabulary

*Answer with a, b, c, or d to indicate the best definition of the word in **bold** as it was used in the selection. The number in parentheses is the number of the paragraph in which the word appears.*

_____ 1. "in recent years liars with **axes to grind**" (1)
    a. axiom
    b. firings
    c. selfish aims
    d. chopping tools

_____ 2. "have a better **intuitive** grasp" (4)
    a. knowing without any apparent conscious reasoning
    b. knowing through logic and reasons
    c. invisible
    d. insidious

_____ 3. "Their customers **jazz up** the appearance" (4)
    a. make nonsense
    b. make music
    c. make more beautiful
    d. make more lively or interesting

_____ 4. "**perspective** drawing" (4)
    a. making objects look three dimensional on a two-dimensional plane
    b. making objects look larger
    c. establishing a point of view
    d. persuasive

_____ 5. "you **warp** the intuitive impact" (5)
    a. distance
    b. distort
    c. wrangle
    d. warm up

_____ 6. "straight-on, **undistorted** view" (7)
    a. undivided
    b. not distinguished
    c. not misrepresented
    d. close up

_____ 7. "viewed at an **oblique** angle" (8)
    a. slanted
    b. obliterated
    c. observed
    d. obstructed

_____ 8. "to push an **unwarranted** point" (10)

    a. unwavering

    b. groundless

    c. great

    d. unskilled

_____ 9. "an **unduly** large fraction" (12)

    a. expectantly

    b. understandably

    c. uneasily

    d. excessively

_____ 10. "a rather tiny **segment**" (13)

    a. secret

    b. sect

    c. part; section

    d. panel

Reflection and Discussion

1. Did you learn something new about the distortion of perspective drawing? If so, what is your reaction to what you have learned?

2. Should readers be protected in some way from distortions—both visual and in word choice? What is the best protection against manipulation by writers, graphic artists, or advertisements?

■ ■ ■ ■ ■

A CHANCE EVENT OR NOT? ANECDOTE, COMMON SENSE, AND STATISTICS IN SCIENCE

David Krogh

This selection comes from his text, *Biology: A Guide to the Natural World* (2000).

Prepare

1. Identify the author and the work. What do you expect the author's purpose to be?

_____

_____

2. Preread to identify the subject and make predictions. What do you expect to read about?

_____

_____

3. What do you already know about the subject?

_____

_____

_____

4. Raise two questions that you expect the article to answer.

_____

_____

_____

■ ■ ■ ■ ■

1   Valuable as they are, experimental and observational tests often are not enough to provide answers to scientific questions. In countless instances, scientists employ an additional tool in coming to comprehend reality—a mathematical tool—as you'll see in the following example.

2   The evidence that cigarette smoking causes lung cancer (and heart disease and emphysema and on and on) has been around for so long that most people have no idea why smoking was looked into as a health hazard in the first place. You might think that scientists were suspicious of tobacco decades ago and thus began experimenting with it in the laboratory, but this wasn't the case. Instead, the trail that led to tobacco as a health hazard started with a mystery about disease.

3   When the lung-cancer pioneer Alton Ochsner was in medical school in 1919, his surgery professor brought both the junior and senior classes in to see an autopsy of a man who had died of lung cancer. The disease was then so rare that the professor thought the young medical students might never see another case during their professional lifetimes. Prior to the 1920s, lung cancer was among the rarest forms of cancer, because cigarette smoking itself was rare before the twentieth century. It did not become the dominant form of tobacco use in the United States until the 1920s. This made a difference in lung-cancer rates because cigarette smoke is inhaled, while pipe and cigar smoke generally are not.

4   If you look at Figure 11.8 on page 382 you can see the rise in lung-cancer mortality in U.S. males from 1930 forward. A graph for women would show a later

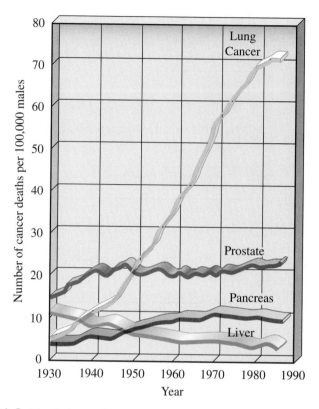

■ FIGURE 11.8 **Rise in Lung-Cancer Mortality in U.S. Males from 1930 Forward**

rise in lung-cancer deaths, because women started smoking *en masse* later. Nevertheless, this trend resulted in lung cancer becoming the most deadly form of cancer among women—a distinction that it retains to this day. (More women contract breast cancer, but more women die of lung cancer.)

5   Given the lung-cancer trends that were apparent by the 1930s, the task before scientists was to explain the alarming increase in this disease. What could the cause of this scourge be, medical detectives wondered. The effects of men being gassed in World War I? Increased road tar? Pollution from power plants? Through the 1940s, cigarette smoking was only one suspect among many.

6   Laboratory experiment eventually would play a part in fingering tobacco as the lung-cancer culprit, but the original indictment of smoking was written in numbers—in statistical tables showing that smokers were contracting lung cancer at much higher rates than nonsmokers.

7   It has sometimes been said that "science is measurement," and the phrase is a marvel of compact truth. For centuries, people had an idea that smoking might be causing serious harm, but this information fell into the realm of guessing or of anecdote, meaning personal stories. The problem with anecdote is that there is no measurement in it; there is no way of judging the validity of one story as

opposed to the next. Related to anecdote is the notion of "common sense," which is valuable in many instances, but which also had us believing for centuries that the sun moved around the Earth. In the case of smoking, it took the extremely careful measurement provided by science—through a discipline called *epidemiology*—to separate truth from fiction....

8   The importance of probability and statistics to science can hardly be overstated: These tools are used frequently in nearly every scientific discipline.

575 words

Comprehension Check

Answer the following with a, b, c, or d to indicate the phrase that best completes each statement.

_____   1. The best statement of the selection's topic is
   a. science.
   b. the role of statistics in science.
   c. smoking and lung cancer.
   d. common sense.

_____   2. To understand the world, scientists use
   a. only experiments and observation.
   b. only common sense.
   c. statistical analysis and probability theory.
   d. anecdotes

_____   3. At the beginning of the 20th century, lung cancer was
   a. rare.
   b. a major disease.
   c. not caused by smoking.
   d. unheard of.

_____   4. Cigarettes became the main form of tobacco use in the
   a. 19th century.
   b. 1920s.
   c. 1950s.
   d. 1990s.

_____   5. The notable rise in lung-cancer mortality begins in the
   a. 21st century.
   b. 1900s.
   c. 19th century.
   d. 1930s.

_____   6. The leading form of cancer deaths for women is
       a. ovarian cancer.
       b. colon cancer.
       c. breast cancer.
       d. lung cancer.

_____   7. Scientists determined that smoking was the primary cause of lung cancer by
       a. statistical probability.
       b. common sense.
       c. lab experiments with tobacco.
       d. anecdote.

_____   8. The author uses the example of believing that the sun revolves around the earth to show that
       a. common sense is the best guide to understanding reality.
       b. common sense does not always lead to scientific truths.
       c. smoking causes lung cancer.
       d. anecdotes are more helpful than common sense.

_____   9. Statistical studies and probability are
       a. rarely used by scientists.
       b. used in most scientific disciplines.
       c. less important than experimentation.
       d. cannot lead to scientific truths.

_____   10. The best statement of the selection's main idea is
       a. science doesn't need statistics.
       b. smoking is the leading cause of lung cancer.
       c. statistical studies are important to science.
       d. more men than women die from lung cancer.

Expanding Vocabulary

*Answer with a, b, c, or d to indicate the best definition of the word in **bold** as it was used in the selection. The number in parentheses is the number of the paragraph in which the word appears.*

_____   1. "Smoking causes . . . **emphysema**" (2)
       a. disease related to breast cancer
       b. disease of the lungs leading to breathing difficulty
       c. emotional distress
       d. epidemics

_____ 2. "a health **hazard**" (2)

    a. possible source of danger

    b. unlikely source of danger

    c. haze

    d. headache

_____ 3. "to see an **autopsy**" (3)

    a. authoritative answer

    b. authentic example

    c. examination of cancer cells

    d. examination of a dead body

_____ 4. "the **dominant** form of tobacco use" (3)

    a. domestic

    b. most common

    c. dangerous

    d. most unusual

_____ 5. "the rise in lung-cancer **mortality**" (4)

    a. deaths

    b. disease

    c. markers

    d. measurement

_____ 6. "started smoking *en masse*" (4)

    a. at parties

    b. two by two

    c. in small numbers

    d. all together

_____ 7. "the lung-cancer **trends**" (5)

    a. traumas

    b. trendiness

    c. general tendencies, patterns

    d. traps

_____ 8. "the cause of this **scourge**" (5)

    a. source of great suffering

    b. source of great pleasure

    c. scorn

    d. scrape

_____ 9. "as the lung-cancer **culprit**" (6)

    a. guard

    b. crush

    c. cult

    d. guilty party

_____ 10. "the original **indictment**" (6)

    a. indignation

    b. formal charge of guilt

    c. guess

    d. indulgence

Reflection and Discussion

1. What is the most important idea you learned from this passage? Why is it important?

2. What does the author gain from using the one long example of lung cancer rather than several short examples?

3. How would you explain to another reader why he or she should not think that this selection is about smoking and lung cancer?

MAKING CONNECTIONS

1. What, for you, is the most important point to remember when you read statistical information—in essay or in graphic form? Why?

2. On your own or with your class partner develop a list of key points about reading and understanding statistical information. Your audience will be other students.

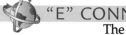

WORKSHOP

"E" CONNECTIONS

The federal government keeps lots of statistics on population change. Conduct a search to learn population figures for 2000 and projections up to 2050—by gender, age, and race/ethnic groups. Do some math: What is the percentage breakdown in 2000 by race/ethnic groups? What is this percentage projected to be in 2050? What percentage of total increase in citizens is projected for 2050? One good site to visit:

<http://www.fedstats.gov>.

WORD POWER 10
Knowing Some Common Scientific Terms

The following words, although associated with science and mathematics, appear often in books and articles. Study the following words and their meanings. Note the singular and plural forms of some of the words. Then select the correct word to complete each of the sentences below.

---

correlation complimentary, parallel, or reciprocal relationship; not a causal relationship

criteria (pl. sing.: criterion) standards on which a judgment can be based

data (pl. sing.: datum; data is also used as a singular noun) factual information, especially information organized for analysis

hypothesis tentative explanation of a set of facts that need further study

demographics characteristics of human population segments

probability likelihood that a specific event will occur

statistics (pl.; singular form means the study of numerical data) numerical data

theory systematically organized knowledge

trends general tendencies or movement

law generalization based on observed phenomena or consistent experience, for example, the law of falling bodies

---

1. The Big Bang _____ (*trends/theory*) explains the development of the universe.

2. Most students can benefit from a course in _____ (*statistics/criteria*).

3. Scientists still have observing or testing to do with explanations they have labeled _____ (*laws; hypotheses*).

4. Initial observations that smokers seemed to get lung cancer more often than nonsmokers showed a _____ (*theory/correlation*).

5. Doctors get important _____ (data/criteria) about diseases by asking all patients the same list of questions.

6. _____ (Probability/statistics) theory is essential to scientists seeking causes of major diseases such as AIDS or cancer.

7. Some scientific _____ (correlations/laws) are based on mathematical proofs; others are demonstrated by experiments that give the same results every time.

8. _____ (Criteria/Demographics) provide useful information for those planning an advertising campaign.

9. Sociologists begin by observing _____ (trends/theories) in society, but they must develop a objective study to move beyond a hypothesis.

10. Part of studying in the sciences is learning the _____ (data/criteria) for objective and thorough research plans.

CHAPTER REVIEW

1. *Graphics* refers to:

_____

_____ .

2. Two uses of graphics include:

_____

_____ .

3. To understand what a table, graph, or chart is showing, it is important to understand

_____ .

_____ .

4. A *fact* is a statement that can be _____ .

5. An *inference* is an opinion _____ .

Take a Reading Road Trip!

For additional practice with your reading skills, use the Reading Road Trip CD-ROM or visit Reading Road Trip on the Web at <http://www.ablongman.com/readingroadtrip> (password required).

CHAPTER 12	Reading and Studying for College Classes

LEARNING OBJECTIVES:

■ To get the most out of your textbook reading

■ To outline, map, and take notes on your reading

■ To skim and scan

■ To get the most out of classroom learning

■ To prepare for testing

PREPARE TO READ

Read and reflect on the chapter's title and objectives. Glance through the chapter, observing headings, to see what is covered. Now answer these questions:

1. What do you expect to learn from this chapter?

   _____

   _____

2. What do you already know about the chapter's topics?

   _____

   _____

3. What two or three questions do you want answered from reading this chapter?

   _____

   _____

_____

_____

You are probably using this book because you want to improve your reading skills to do well in college classes. And that means reading and learning from college textbooks, books that are often large and rather imposing looking. It also means showing your knowledge both in the classroom and on tests. How do you cope? You apply the new skills you are learning to reading textbooks.

 ## READING TEXTBOOKS

As you practice your **Prepare–Read–Respond** strategy with the following sections from several textbooks, we will also establish additional guidelines for successful reading and learning.

Prepare

This step in the reading process includes (1) prereading to make predictions, (2) identifying your previous knowledge, and (3) raising questions. When prereading a textbook chapter, remember to:

1. read and think about the chapter title,
2. read the opening and concluding paragraphs, or read the chapter objectives and chapter summary,
3. look through the chapter to observe headings and subheadings, and
4. look at any graphics to get a sense of what the chapter is about.

Consider the third guideline in particular. Most chapters contain major headings and at least one level of subheading. Often, you will find a second level of subheadings. All major headings will use the same type and perhaps be in color. All first-level subheadings will be in the same type but somewhat smaller than major headings. All second-level subheadings will be in the same type but smaller or in some other way less distinguished than first-level subheadings. For example:

MAJOR HEADING
First-level subheading
Second-level subheading

The various headings provide a clear structure for the material and are aids to learning.

Look back to pages 11–12 at the outline of a chapter on listening. Examine the various headings and then answer the following questions.

1. How many major headings does the chapter have? _____

2. In the last major section, how many subheadings are there? _____

3. How many second-level subheadings are there? _____

Read

Active reading includes annotating as you read and monitoring comprehension. One advantage of annotating is that you can put questions in the margin next to passages that are confusing. Here are additional guidelines for reading a textbook chapter.

1. Do not feel that you must read an entire chapter at one time. Some textbook chapters are quite lengthy and dense with information.

2. Do *always* read a complete section at one time. If you read only a paragraph or two at a time, you will have trouble seeing how the chapter holds together or what is most important to learn.

3. Look for definitions, lists, and other structures as guides to organizing the information in your own mind.

4. Try to predict what is coming. Think about what the section (or the chapter) will have to include to complete its treatment of the topic.

5. Note key examples. (They sometimes appear on tests.)

EXERCISE 12-1	**Reading a Textbook Section**

Read and annotate the following section from the chapter "Listening" from Mastering Public Speaking, 2nd ed., by Grice and Skinner. Then answer the questions that follow.

LISTENING VERSUS HEARING

1   Has the following ever happened to you? You are watching *The Late Show with David Letterman*, listening to a new Anita Baker tape, or doing economics homework when one of your parents walks by and tells you to put out the trash. Fifteen minutes later, that person walks back to find you still preoccupied with television, music, or homework, and the trash still sitting by the door. Your parent asks, "Didn't you hear me?" Well, of course you did. You *heard* the direction to put out the trash just as you heard Letterman joking with Paul Shaffer, Anita Baker harmonizing, the dog barking at a passing car, and the air conditioner clicking on in the hall. You heard all of these things, but you might not have been *listening* to any of them.

2   What is the difference between **listening** and **hearing?** Listening differs from hearing in at least four important ways.

3   **Listening Is Intermittent.** Listening is not a continuous activity, but occurs only from time to time when we choose to focus and respond to stimuli around us.

Hearing, on the other hand, is a continuous function for a person having normal hearing ability.

4   **Listening Is a Learned Skill.** Listening must be taught and learned. Unless you were born with a hearing loss, however, hearing is a natural capacity for which you need no training. We hear sounds before we are born; fetuses grow accustomed to certain voices, noises, and music. For this reason, pediatricians advise new parents not to tiptoe or whisper around the infant they have just brought home from the hospital. The child is already used to a lot of noise and must grow accustomed to the rest of it. Throughout our lives, we hear sounds even as we sleep.

5   **Listening Is Active.** Hearing means simply receiving an aural stimulus. The act of hearing is passive; it requires no work. Anytime the tiny bones of the inner ear are set in vibration, we are hearing something, and the activity requires no expenditure of energy. We can limit hearing only by trying to reduce or eliminate the sources of sound in the environment or by covering our ears.

6   Listening, in contrast, is active. It requires you to concentrate, interpret, and respond—in short, to be involved. You can hear the sound of a fire engine as you sit at your desk working on your psychology paper. You listen to the sound of the fire engine if you concentrate on its sound, identify it as a fire engine rather than an ambulance, wonder if it is coming in your direction, and then turn back to your work as you hear the sound fade away.

7   **Listening Implies Using the Message Received.** Audiences assemble for many reasons. We choose to listen to gain new information; to learn new uses for existing information; to discover arguments for beliefs or actions; to assess those arguments; to laugh and be entertained; to provide emotional support for a speaker; to celebrate a person, place, object, or idea; and to be inspired.

8   We are attracted to novel ideas and information just because we may have some future use for that data. There are literally thousands of topics you could listen to; for example, characteristics of gangsta rap, converting to electronic currency, the history of blue jeans, adapting Japanese management style to American businesses, the ethics of criminal entrapment, preparing lemon-grass chicken, fantasy league football and baseball, the history of the National Cathedral, and the life of Arthur Ashe. Some of these topics might induce you to listen carefully. Others might not interest you, so you choose not to listen. The perceived usefulness of the topic helps determine how actively you will listen to a speaker. Listening implies a choice; you must choose to participate in the process of listening.

1. What two key terms does the section define?

_____

2. What two key structures are used to define *listening?*

_____

3. In your own words, what are the characteristics of *listening* and how do they differ from *hearing*?

_____

_____

_____

_____

_____

_____

Respond

Responding consists of both review and reflection. Reflecting on what you have read helps the review process because it makes what you have studied more personally your own. Reflecting may also help your studies by leading you to see connections with other sections or chapters in the textbook. Still, when you are reading to learn from a textbook, serious review is essential to "fixing" the information in your memory.

One way to review is to read over your annotations. Then, close the book and see if you can recite the key ideas of the section. Open to the section to see if you left out any key ideas.

EXERCISE 12-2	Prepare–Read–Respond

Read the following first section of the chapter "Addictions and Addictive Behavior" from Access to Health, 4th ed., by Donatelle and Davis. Annotate, review your annotations, and then answer the questions that follow.

DEFINING ADDICTION

1 **Addiction** is an unhealthy, continued involvement with a mood-altering object or activity that creates harmful consequences. Addictive behaviors initially provide a sense of pleasure or stability that is beyond the addict's power to achieve otherwise. Eventually, the addictive behavior is necessary to give the addict a sense of normalcy.

2 Physiological dependence is only one indicator of addiction. Psychological dynamics play an important role, which explains why behaviors not related to the use of chemicals—gambling, for example—may also be addictive. In fact, psy-

chological and physiological dependence are so intertwined that it is not really possible to separate the two. For every psychological state, there is a corresponding physiological state. In other words, everything you feel is tied to a chemical process occurring in your body. Thus, addictions once thought to be entirely psychological in nature are now understood to have physiological components.

3   To be addictive, a behavior must have the potential to produce a positive mood change. Chemicals are responsible for the most profound addictions, not only because they produce dramatic mood changes, but also because they cause cellular changes to which the body adapts so well that it eventually requires the chemical in order to function normally. Yet other behaviors, such as gambling, spending, working, and sex, also create changes at the cellular level along with positive mood changes. Although the mechanism is not well understood, all forms of addiction probably reflect dysfunction of certain biochemical systems in the brain.

4   Traditionally, diagnosis of an addiction was limited to drug addiction and was based on three criteria: (1) the presence of an abstinence syndrome, or **withdrawal**— a series of temporary physical and psychological symptoms that occurs when the addict abruptly stops using the drug; (2) an associated pattern of pathological behavior (deterioration in work performance, relationships, and social interaction); and (3) **relapse,** the tendency to return to the addictive behavior after a period of abstinence. Furthermore, until recently, health professionals were unwilling to diagnose an addiction until medical symptoms appeared in the patient. Now we know that although withdrawal, pathological behavior, relapse, and medical symptoms are valid indicators of addiction, they do not characterize all addictive behavior.

Habit Versus Addiction

5   What is the distinction between a harmless habit and an addiction? The stereotypical image of the addict is of someone desperately seeking a fix 24 hours a day. Conversely, people have the notion that if you aren't doing the behavior every day, then you're not addicted. The reality is somewhere between these two extremes.

6   Addiction certainly involves elements of **habit,** which is a repetitious behavior in which the repetition may be unconscious. A habit can be annoying, but it can be broken without too much discomfort by simply becoming aware of its presence and choosing not to do it. Addiction also involves repetition of a behavior, but the repetition occurs by compulsion and considerable discomfort is experienced if the behavior is not performed. While many people consider compulsive eating an addiction, current research shows that it is actually more of a habit.

1. For a behavior to be addictive, what must it have the potential to do?

_____

2. Addictions involve both physiological dependence and

_____

3. What is the difference between a habit and an addiction?

_____

_____

4. What are four common symptoms of addiction?

_____

_____

_____

SKIMMING AND SCANNING FOR READING EFFICIENCY

So far this text has stressed reading actively for full comprehension. Sometimes, though, you may be able to speed up your reading and still achieve your reading purpose. Two other reading strategies that are appropriate at times are skimming and scanning.

Skimming

Skimming is a way to get an overview of a reading selection. When your goal is to get the "gist" or main ideas of a selection, you want to skim. The most common use of skimming is what you already do as a part of your prereading strategy. You read the title and opening paragraph and look through the work, noting headings and visuals, to get a sense of what the work is about. You can also use skimming for assigned pages when your instructor requests only a general knowledge of that material. You can skim research materials, including those on the Internet, as you look for works that will be useful to you. You can skim newspaper and magazine articles to keep up with the news or a personal interest. Just remember: Recognize how the work is organized and let that awareness help you to run your eyes quickly over the pages or down the screen. Remember as well: You can always stop to read an important section all the way through.

Scanning

Scanning involves searching for a particular piece of information. Instead of reading every word, you let your eyes move quickly, searching for what you need. To be an efficient reader, when scanning focus on finding just what you are looking for. Here are some guidelines to follow to scan effectively.

Guidelines for Scanning

1. **Understand the organization of the material.** Is the material organized in columns (dictionaries; tables)? Is it alphabetical (dictionaries; glossaries; indexes)? Are there section headings and subheadings to guide you (most textbooks)? Be clear about the organizational pattern before beginning your search.

2. **Stay focused on what you are looking for.** When scanning material in columns, do not read; run your eyes down the columns. When scanning prose materials, either focus on a key term or phrase or ask a question and then scan to find the answer. Visualize the term; hold it in your mind's eye so that you search only for that term and nothing else.

3. **Use whatever clues are available to speed your search.** Section headings are in large print. Key terms are often in *italic* or **bold** type. At the top of each page of a dictionary are the words that begin and end that page.

4. **Confirm your information.** Scan aggressively, but once you think you have found what you are looking for, take time to confirm the information. When looking for information in tables or charts, be sure to understand how the information is presented so that you can word the information correctly when you use it.

The following exercises will give you practice scanning different kinds of materials.

EXERCISE 12-3	**Scanning Indexes and Tables**

I. Scan the index page shown in Figure 12.1 on page 398 to answer the following questions about the text Patterns of Reflection. *Try to complete the questions in less than one minute.*

1. On what pages can you find a discussion of steps to active reading?

   _____

2. On what pages will you find "The Story of an Hour"?

   _____

3. Is Mrs. Zajac a person or the title of a work? _____ How do you know?

   _____

■ FIGURE 12.1

Source: Index Page from *Patterns of Reflection*, 4th ed.

4. On what pages will you find information about organization?

_____

II. Assume that you are writing a research paper on the costs of political campaigning. Scan Table 12.1 to answer the following questions. Try to complete the questions in less than one minute.

1. The table shows a typical budget for what kind of candidate?

_____

2. The largest portion of a candidate's funds comes from what source?

_____

TABLE 12.1 **Campaign for the U.S. Senate, 2000: A "Typical" Candidate's Budget of $7 Million**

Funds from	Total $	% of Total
Political action committees (PACs)	$1,540,000	22%
Contributions from individuals	4,200,000	60
Political party	1,050,000	15
Candidate's own money (including family loans)	210,000	3
TOTAL	$7,000,000	100%
Are Spent on		
Television (and radio) advertising	$2,660,000	38%
Staff salaries and consultant fees	1,400,000	20
Polling	280,000	4
Print media (literature, mail, buttons, etc.)	210,000	3
Canvassing/get-out-the-vote efforts	420,000	6
Office rent, equipment, and travel	1,050,000	15
Fund-raising expenses	700,000	10
Legal and accounting services	140,000	2
Internet sites/campaigning	140,000	2%
Total	$7,000,000	100%

Source: O'Connor and Sabato, *American Government: Roots and Reform,* 2002.

3. What percent of a typical candidate's funds is obtained from PACs?

_____

4. What is the single largest expenditure in the campaign budget?

_____

EXERCISE 12-4	**Scanning Prose Materials**

Assume that you are doing a research project on problems with U.S. elections. Your textbook contains the box insert shown in Figure 12.2 below. Scan the material to answer the following questions. Do not read the passage; search aggressively to answer only the questions. Try to answer the questions in less than one minute.

The voter turnout for the presidential election of 1988 was around 50 percent of those registered to vote. Some critics argue that the problem rests with the way U.S. elections are organized and the process of voter registration. Can changes be made to improve voter turnout? Here are the models used by some other countries that have produced better voter activity.

Italy—88.8 Percent Turnout
While voting is not compulsory, the system allows for the public disclosure of who votes and who does not. All parties receive campaign funding from the government. In addition, the government provides each party television time on state stations; time is allocated based on party membership. A party can purchase unlimited time on commercial television.

West Germany—84.4 Percent Turnout
Campaigning is limited to the ten-month period prior to election day. There is no limit on campaign spending and the primary sources of money are party members and the state. The parties are allocated paid television time on government stations; the amount of time is determined by the number of legislative seats held by the particular party.

Israel—79 Percent Turnout
In most cases, the duration of campaigns is between three and four months. Each of the parties is provided state campaign funds proportionally to representative seats, but overall spending is not limited. Television time is also allocated according to the number of seats a party holds.

Britain—75 Percent Turnout
Once it is decided that an election will be called, campaigning is usually limited to a three-week period. In national elections, campaign spending is not limited and free radio and television time is provided based on the last election performance.

Japan—71.4 Percent Turnout
Virtually all citizens are registered voters, since at the age of twenty, those who register at ward offices for social benefits (including education) are automatically made eligible. There are strict guidelines on spending with the amount being determined by district size. All candidates are allocated five free six-minute television appearances and three six-minute segments on radio.

■ FIGURE 12.2   **Getting a Better Turnout: How Other Nations Run Their Elections**

Sources: Adapted from the _New York Times,_ 13 November 1988:E1, E3. Curran and Renzetti, _Social Problems,_ 3rd ed.

1. What was the percentage of voter turnout in the 1988 U.S. presidential election? _____

2. What is the percentage of voter turnout in Japan? _____

3. What is the length of time of campaigns before an election in Britain?

_____

4. Are campaigns given paid television time in Germany? _____

WRITING-TO-LEARN STRATEGIES

For many students, reviewing their textbook annotations is not enough to help them learn difficult material. It is a good idea to have several strategies for studying and then to choose the best method for each course. You have learned to annotate and to write summaries. Strategies, in addition to annotating and summarizing, include outlining, mapping, and note taking.

Outlining

Effective outlining depends on your recognizing main ideas and levels of specificity under the main ideas. Outlining is a good choice when:

- you cannot annotate because you do not own the book,
- your text has narrow margins so you cannot do enough annotating, or
- you learn better by seeing how the material is organized.

The formal outline depends on a specific pattern of numbers, letters, and indenting to show the relationship of ideas. Here is the pattern:

I. Main idea
   A. Supporting idea
   B. Supporting idea
II. Main idea
   A. Supporting idea
   B. Supporting idea
     1. Major detail
     2. Major detail
       a. Minor detail
       b. Minor detail
III. Main idea
   A. Supporting idea
   B. Supporting idea

Whenever you are required to turn in an outline, be sure to follow the formal pattern shown here. Your instructor will evaluate the format as well as the content.

Some works are easier to outline than others. At times, when you are outlining to help yourself learn, you may want to prepare a more informal outline to meet your study needs. Even an informal outline, though, needs to show the relationship among main ideas and details. Reread the selection on addiction and think about how you would outline it. Then compare your outline with the following:

Outline: Defining Addiction
  I. Definition of Addiction
    A. Basic characteristics
        1. Unhealthy
        2. Continued over time
        3. Initial pleasure
        4. Becomes essential to feel normal
    B. Effects
        1. Physiological } both affected closely connected
        2. Psychological
  II. Traditional Criteria Used in Diagnosis
    A. Withdrawal when person stops
    B. Causes pathological behavior } Modern view—not all addicts
    C. Relapse often occurs   have symptoms.
    D. Medical symptoms develop
  III. Contrast Between Habit and Addiction
    A. Habit
        1. Repetitive behavior can be stopped
        2. Habits are result of choice
    B. Addiction
        1. Repetitive behavior is compulsive; discomfort results when
           stopped
        2. Addiction not result of choice

Notice that the outline follows the basic formal pattern, but notes have been added. Also notice the main headings that have been created to organize the selection's ideas. Follow these guidelines for making outlines.

Guidelines for Outlining

1. Items of the same level (e.g., A and B) are lined up evenly. Use a ruler if necessary (or tab settings if you are typing).

2. Each subdivision needs at least two parts. That means you cannot have an A without a B, or a 1 without a 2.

3. Any subsection can have more than two parts and some sections may not be divided at all.

4. Use your knowledge of writing patterns to help you distinguish between main ideas and supporting details. Pay attention to signal words that announce a list, or steps in a process, or contrast.

5. If you seem to be just making a list, look at what you have written to see how to reorganize the material. You may need to create some headings under which to group points.

6. Add notes to your study outlines when helpful.

EXERCISE 12-5

Preparing an Outline

Read either Spielvogel's "The Pyramids" (pp. 201–203) or Scott's "In the Rain Forest" (pp. 134–138) and then prepare an outline in the following space.

_____

_____

_____

_____

_____

_____

_____

_____

_____

_____

_____

_____

_____

_____

_____

_____

_____

Mapping

An alternative to outlining is mapping. Mapping, like outlining, shows the relationships between main ideas and supporting details. Mapping differs by using a visual pattern. Some people learn more easily from visuals than from text. If you learn best this way, use mapping to make your own diagrams from which to study.

Probably the most popular map style is one with spokes coming out of a center circle that contains a statement of the topic (see Figure 12.3). But this isn't the only useful style for mapping. You can also use a "flowchart" type of pattern (Figure 12.4) or other possibilities that you create.

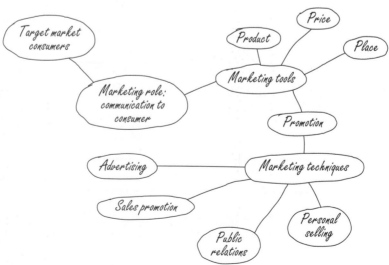

■ FIGURE 12.3   **Mapping (with spokes)**

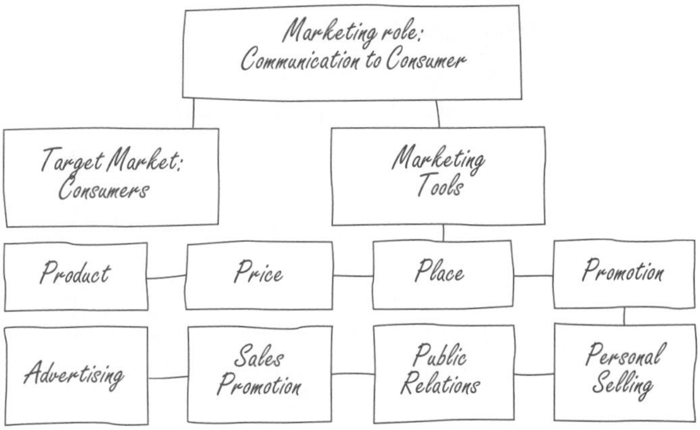

■ FIGURE 12.4   Mapping (flowchart)

Read the following paragraph on advertising and then observe how the information in this paragraph has been mapped in two different patterns in figures 12.3 and 12.4.

The Marketing Role

Marketing is the strategic process a business uses to satisfy consumer needs and wants through goods and services. The particular consumers at whom the company directs its marketing effort constitute the *target market.* The tools available to marketing include the product, its price, and the means used to deliver the product, or the place.

Marketing also includes a mechanism for communicating this information to the consumer, which is called *marketing communication,* or promotion. These four tools are collectively referred to as the *marketing mix* or the *4 Ps.* Marketing communication is further broken down into four related communication techniques: advertising, sales promotion, public relations, and personal selling. Thus advertising is only one element in a company's overall marketing communication program, although it is the most visible.

Wells, Burnett, and Moriarty, *Advertising: Principles and Practice*, 3rd ed.

Experiment with different patterns. Use the following guidelines to help you create maps from which you can learn.

Guidelines for Mapping

1. Decide on the selection's main topic and write it, in a word or phrase, within a circle or box, at the center or at the top of your paper.
2. Place each main idea on a line radiating out from the main circle or box.

(continued on next page)

(continued from previous page)

3. Use as many levels of lines or boxes as needed to include the information you want to learn.

4. Draw your map so that you can read each item without having to turn the paper around.

5. Give yourself enough room so that you can write out the information you need to learn and so that you can read what you have written. (Mapping may not work if the information is too complicated. Know when to choose outlining or note taking instead.)

6. Experiment with different patterns.

| EXERCISE 12-6 | **Mapping** |

On separate sheets of paper, prepare a map for both "Listening versus Hearing," pp. 392–393 and "Defining Addiction," pp. 394–395.

▞ NOTE TAKING: THE CORNELL METHOD

There are times when neither outlining nor mapping seems the best choice for learning. At these times note taking note taking may be the strategy to choose. For many students, it is their favorite strategy. The notes they take on assigned readings can be placed in the same notebook they use for class notes. That way, all notes are together when it's time to study for tests.

The Cornell Method is just one way of putting notes on paper so that you have a good study tool when you finish. It was devised at Cornell University and has worked well for many students.

Guidelines for the Cornell Method of Notes

1. Use 8½" by 11" lined paper that will fit into a three-ring notebook. With a ruler, draw a line from top to bottom on each page 2½" from the left margin.

2. Write your notes down the page in the 6" section to the right of the line you have drawn. Although the Cornell Method recommends using complete sentences, many students use phrases sometimes.

3. After you finish taking notes on a particular assignment, read through your notes, underlining key words.

4. Write the key words next to the notes on that topic in the smaller space to the left of the line you have drawn. Later, you can cover the notes and use the key words as a way to review.

Reread the paragraph on marketing (p. 407) and then take notes on it using the Cornell Method. Compare your note taking to the sample page of notes that follows.

Notes on the Marketing Role

Marketing-def.	<u>Marketing</u>: planned process to get goods and services to consumers.
Target market	<u>Consumers</u> represent <u>target market</u>.
Marketing tools-4	<u>Marketing tools</u> include: product, price, place, and promotion. These are the <u>4 Ps</u>.
Promotion	<u>Promotion</u>—manner of communication.
techniques-4	Can include: advertising, sales promotion, public relations, personal selling
Advertising—visible	<u>Advertising</u>—most <u>visible form</u> of marketing

■ LEARNING FROM THREE TEXTBOOK SECTIONS

Let's now put your reading and note-taking strategies to work. As you first look over each selection, you may feel that the reading will be difficult. But, if you apply your reading strategy, take notes, and answer the questions that will guide your study, you will be successful.

THE SIGNS OF LIFE

Helena Curtis and N. Sue Barnes

The following selection is an excerpt from the introduction to *An Invitation to Biology*, 4th ed. Both authors are college professors who have written other books in their field of biology.

Prepare

Use prereading strategies and then answer the following questions.

1. What do you expect to read about?

_____

_____

2. What appears to be the primary organizational strategy of the passage?

_____

Read

First read and annotate the selection. Then respond to the questions that follow.

1   The first characteristic of living things is that they are highly organized. In living things, atoms—the particles of which all matter, both living and nonliving, is composed—are combined into a vast number of very large molecules called macromolecules. Each type of macromolecule has a distinctive structure and a specific function in the life of the organism of which it is a part. Some macromolecules are linked with other macromolecules to form the structures of which the organism's body is composed. Others do not have a structural role but instead participate in the dynamic processes essential for the continuing life of the organism; among the most significant are the large molecules known as enzymes. Enzymes, with the help of a variety of smaller molecules, regulate virtually all of the processes occurring within living matter. The complex organization of both structures and processes is one of the most important properties by which an object can be identified as living.

2   The second characteristic is closely related to the first: living systems maintain a chemical composition quite different from that of their surroundings. The atoms present in living matter are the same as those in the surrounding environment, but they occur in different proportions and are arranged in different ways. Although living systems constantly exchange materials with the external environment, they maintain a stable and characteristic internal environment. This important property is called homeostasis, which means simply "staying the same."

3   A third characteristic of living things is the capacity to take in, transform, and use energy from the environment. For example, in the process of photosynthesis, green plants take light energy from the sun and transform it into chemical energy stored in complex molecules formed from water and the carbon dioxide in the air. The energy stored in these molecules is used by plants to power their life processes and to build the characteristic structures of the plant body. Animals, which can obtain this stored energy by eating plants, change it into still other forms, such as heat, motion, electricity, and chemical energy stored in the characteristic structures of the animal body.

4   Fourth, living things can respond to stimuli. Bacteria move toward or away from certain chemical substances; green plants bend toward light; mealworms congregate where it is damp; cats pounce on small moving objects. Although different organisms respond to widely varying stimuli, the capacity to respond is a fundamental and almost universal characteristic of life.

5   Fifth, and most remarkably, living things have the capacity to reproduce themselves so that, generation after generation, organisms produce more organisms like themselves. In each generation, however, there are slight variations between par-

ents and offspring and among offspring. As we shall see, the slight variations between parents and offspring provide the raw material for evolution.

6   Some living things, primarily very small organisms such as bacteria, amoebas, and some types of algae, reproduce by simply dividing in two. The offspring are usually identical to the parent. Most organisms, however, have a sixth characteristic: they grow and develop. For example, before hatching, the fertilized egg of a frog develops into the complex, but still immature, form that we recognize as a tadpole; after hatching, the tadpole continues to grow and undergoes further development, becoming a mature frog. Throughout the world of living things, similar striking patterns of growth and development occur.

7   A seventh characteristic of living things is that they are exquisitely suited to their environments. Moles, for instance, are furry animals that live underground in tunnels shoveled out by their large forepaws. Their eyes are small and almost sightless. Their noses, with which they sense the worms and other small animals that make up their diet, are fleshy and enlarged. This most important characteristic of living things is known as adaptation.

8   These characteristics of living things are intimately interrelated, and each depends, to a large extent, on the others. At any given moment in its life, an organism is organized, maintains a stable internal environment, transforms energy, responds to stimuli, and is adapted to its external environment; the organism may or may not be reproducing, growing, and developing, but it possesses the capacity to do so.

689 words

Questions on "The Signs of Life"

1. What is the dominant organizational strategy used by the authors?

_____

2. How many characteristics of living things are there?

_____

3. Which characteristic is the most remarkable?

_____

4. How are the characteristics connected to one another?

_____

5. What is an atom?

_____

_____

6. What is a macromolecule?

_____

_____

7. What are enzymes?

_____

_____

■ ■ ■ ■ ■

Answering these questions will help you take good notes on the passage. Now complete the page of notes started for you.

The Signs of Life—Characteristics of Living Things

1st char.	1. Living things highly <u>organized.</u>
Defs–key terms	atoms: _____
	macromolecules: _____
	enzymes: _____
	Both structures and processes—complex. ____
	2. _____
	_____
	3. _____
	_____
Def.	photosynthesis: _____
	_____
	4. _____
	_____

5. _____

_____

_____

Evolution _____

_____

6. Most organisms _____

_____

7. _____

_____

Def.   adaptation: _____

_____

Charac. of living things are _____.

■ ■ ■ ■ ■

DOMESTIC VIOLENCE

Rebecca J. Donatelle and Lorraine G. Davis

The following is one section from the chapter "Violence and Abuse" in *Access to Health*, 5th ed. Professor Donatelle is at Oregon State University and Professor Davis is at the University of Oregon.

Prepare

Use prereading strategies and then answer the following questions.

1. What do you expect to read about?

_____

_____

2. How many major headings are there?

_____

3. Why do you think that the "Women as Victims" section precedes the "Men as Victims" section and is longer?

_____

_____

4. A section this long probably contains several writing strategies. What two strategies do you expect to find in a textbook section on this subject?

_____

Read

First read and annotate the selection. Then respond to the questions that follow.

1   During the last decade, the subject of domestic violence has finally grabbed our attention. The Lorena Bobbitt, O. J. Simpson, and Susan Smith cases—as well as many less prominent ones—have brought the truth about domestic violence into the open.

Spousal Abuse

2   Contrary to common perception, domestic violence does not only happen to people of lower socioeconomic status and to women. It is a widespread social problem affecting all races, ethnic groups, economic classes, and both sexes. By most estimates, it is the most common and least reported crime in the United States today. **Domestic violence** refers to the use of force to control and maintain power over another person in the home environment; it includes both actual harm and the threat of harm. It can involve emotional abuse, verbal abuse, threats of physical abuse, and actual physical violence ranging from slapping and shoving to bone-breaking beatings, rape, and homicide.

Women as Victims

3   While young men are more apt to become victims of violent acts perpetrated by strangers, women are much more likely to become victims of violent acts perpetrated by spouses, lovers, ex-spouses, and ex-lovers. In 1995, nearly 5 million women were victims of assault. In fact, 6 of every 10 women in the United States will be assaulted at some time in their lives by someone they know. Every year, approximately 12 percent of married women are the victims of physical aggression perpetrated by their husbands, according to a national survey. These acts of aggression are committed in anger and often include pushing, slapping, and shoving.

4   Some women experience much more severe acts of aggression. About 4 percent of married women each year are the victims of violence that takes the form

of beating and/or threats of or actual harm caused by use of a knife or a gun. In fact, acts of aggression by a husband or boyfriend are one of the most common causes of death for young women, and roughly 2,000 women in the United States are killed each year by their partners or ex-partners. Over a recent 10-year period, according to the National Crime Survey, on average, more than 2 million assaults on women occurred each year. More than two-thirds of these assaults were committed by someone the woman knew.

5   The following United States statistics indicate the seriousness of this long-hidden problem:

- Every 15 seconds, someone batters a woman.
- Only 1 in every 250 such assaults is reported to the police.
- More than a third of women victims of domestic violence are severely abused on a regular basis.
- About five women are killed every day in domestic violence incidents.
- Three of every four women murdered are killed by their husbands.
- Domestic violence is the single greatest cause of injury to women, surpassing rape, mugging, and auto accidents combined.
- About 25 to 45 percent of all women who are battered are battered during pregnancy.
- One-quarter of suicide attempts by women occur as a result of domestic violence.

6   How many times have you heard of a woman who is repeatedly beaten by her partner or spouse and asked, "Why doesn't she just leave him?" There are many reasons why some women find it difficult, if not impossible, to break their ties with their abusers. Many women, particularly those having small children, are financially dependent on their partners. Others fear retaliation against themselves or their children. There are women who hope that the situation will change with time (it rarely does), and others who stay because their cultural or religious beliefs forbid divorce. Finally, there are women who still love the abusive partner and are concerned about what will happen to him if they leave.

7   **Cycle of Violence Theory.** Psychologist Lenore Walker has developed a theory known as the "cycle of violence" to explain how women can get caught in a downward spiral without knowing what is happening to them. The cycle has several phases:

- *Phase One: Tension Building.* In this phase, minor battering occurs, and the woman may become more nurturant, more pleasing, and more intent on anticipating the spouse's needs in order to forestall another violent scene. She assumes guilt for doing something to provoke him and tries hard to avoid doing it again.
- *Phase Two: Acute Battering.* At this stage, pleasing her man doesn't help and she can no longer control or predict the abuse. Usually, the spouse is trying to "teach her a lesson," and when he feels he has inflicted enough pain, he'll stop. When the acute attack is over, he may respond with shock and denial

about his own behavior. Both batterer and victim may soft-peddle the seriousness of the attacks.

- *Phase Three: Remorse/Reconciliation.* During this "honeymoon" period, the batterer may be kind, loving, and apologetic, swearing he will never act violently toward the woman again. He may "behave" for several weeks or months, and the woman may come to question whether she overrated the seriousness of past abuse. Then the kind of tension that precipitated abusive incidents in the past resurfaces, he loses control again, and he once more beats the woman. Unless some form of intervention breaks this downward cycle of abuse, contrition, further abuse, denial, and contrition, it will repeat again and again—perhaps ending only in the woman's, or rarely, the man's, death.

8   It is very hard for most women who get caught in this cycle of violence (which may include forced sexual relations and psychological and economic abuse as well as beatings) to summon up the courage and resolution to extricate themselves. Most need effective outside intervention.

Men as Victims

9   Are men also victims of domestic violence? The answer is yes. Clearly, some women do abuse and even kill their partners. Approximately 12 percent of men reported that their wives engaged in physically aggressive behaviors against them in the past year—nearly the same percentage as women. The difference between male and female batterers is twofold. First, although the frequency of physical aggression may be the same, the impact of physical aggression by men against women is drastically different: women are typically injured in such incidents two to three times more often than are men. These injuries tend to be more severe and have resulted in significantly more deaths. Women do engage in moderate aggression, such as pushing and shoving, at rates almost equal to men. But the severe form of aggression that is likely to land the victim in the hospital is almost always a male-against-female form of aggression. Second, a woman who is physically abused by a man is generally intimidated by him: she fears that he will use his power and control over her in some fashion. Men, however, generally report that they do not live in fear of their wives.

Causes of Domestic Violence

10   There is no single explanation for why people tend to be abusive in relationships. Although alcohol abuse is often associated with such violence, marital dissatisfaction seems to predict physical abuse better than does any other variable. Numerous studies also point to differences in the communication patterns between abusive relationships and nonabusive relationships. While some argue that the hormone testosterone is the cause of male aggression, recent studies have failed to show a strong association between physical abuse in relationships and this hormone. Many experts believe that men who engage in severe violence are more likely than other men to suffer from personality disorders.

11   Regardless of the cause, or of who should shoulder the greatest amount of blame, it is important to remember that it is the dynamics that both people bring to a relationship that result in violence and allow it to continue. Obtaining help from community support and counseling services may help determine the underlying basis of the problem and may help the victim and the batterer come to a better understanding of the actions necessary to stop the cycle of abuse.

1309 words

Questions on "Domestic Violence"

1. Who is affected by domestic violence?

_____

2. What does the term *domestic violence* mean?

_____

_____

3. What are the phases in the "cycle of violence"?

_____

_____

4. What are two differences in domestic violence when women are the victims rather than men?

_____

_____

5. What situation most often predicts domestic violence?

_____

_____

■ ■ ■ ■ ■

Answering these questions will help you take good notes on the section. Now complete the notes started for you.

Domestic Violence

Def.

Domestic violence: _____

_____

_____

_____

Some statistics
about women

Women victims: _____

_____

_____

_____

_____

_____

Cycle of violence theory:

Note steps
of cycle of
violence—

Phase 1 _____

_____

Phase 2 _____

_____

Phase 3 _____

_____

Breaking cycle—Most women need help.

Male victims: _____

_____

_____

Differences bet. men and women as victims:

Men & Women:
Differences

1. _____

_____

_____

2. _____

_____

_____

Experts
uncertain
about causes

Causes _____

_____

_____

_____

_____

_____

_____

■ ■ ■ ■ ■

DEMOCRATIC GOVERNMENT IN THE UNITED STATES

Karen O'Connor and Larry J. Sabato

The following sections come from *American Government: Continuity and Change,* the 1997 edition. Professor O'Connor teaches at American University and Larry J. Sabato is the Robert Kent Gooch Professor of Government and Foreign Affairs at the University of Virginia.

Prepare

Use prereading strategies and then answer the following questions.

1. What do you expect to read about?

_____

_____

2. How many major headings are there?

_____

3. Based on what you can *see*, what writing strategy do you expect to find throughout the sections?

_____

4. What writing strategy do you expect to find in the second section?

_____

Read

First read and annotate the selection. Then respond to the questions that follow.

The Theory of Democratic Government

1   As evidenced by the early creation of the Virginia House of Burgesses in 1619, and its objections to "taxation without representation," the colonists were quick to create participatory forms of government in which most men (subject to some landowning requirements) were allowed to participate. The New England town meeting . . . , where all citizens gather to discuss and decide issues facing the town, today stands as a surviving example of a **direct democracy,** such as was used in ancient Greece when all free, male citizens came together periodically to pass laws and "elect" leaders by lot.

2   Direct democracies, however, soon proved unworkable in the colonies. Although Rousseau argued that true democracy is impossible unless *all* citizens participate in governmental decision-making, as more and more settlers came to the New World, many town meetings were replaced by a system called **indirect** or **representative democracy.** Ironically, this system of government, in which representatives of the people are chosen by ballot, was considered undemocratic by ancient Greeks, who believed that all citizens must have a direct say in their governance.

3   Representative or indirect democracies, which call for the election of representatives to a governmental decision-making body, were formed first in the colonies and then in the new Union. Many citizens were uncomfortable with the term "democracy" and used the term **republic** to avoid any confusion between the system adopted and direct democracy. Even today, representative democracies are more commonly called "republics" and the words "democracy" and "republic" often are used interchangeably. Historically, the term "republic" implied a system of government in which the interests of the people were represented by more educated or wealthier citizens. In the early days of America, for example, only those who owned land could vote. But today, those barriers no longer exist.

What Are the Characteristics of American Democracy?

4   The United States is an indirect democracy with several distinguishing characteristics. Tremendous value is placed on the individual. All individuals are deemed rational and fair, and endowed, as Thomas Jefferson proclaimed in the Declaration of Independence, "with certain unalienable rights." And the individual is deemed more important than the state.

5   Another key characteristic of our democracy is the American emphasis on political equality, the definition of which has varied considerably over time. The importance of political equality is another reflection of American stress on the importance of the individual. Although some individuals clearly wield more political clout than others, the adage "one man, one vote" implies a sense of political equality for all.

6   **Popular consent**, the idea that governments must draw their powers from the consent of the governed, is another distinguishing characteristic of American democracy. Derived from social contract theory, the notion of popular consent was central to the Declaration of Independence and its underlying assumption that governments *must* derive their powers from the consent of the governed. A citizen's willingness to vote is thus an essential premise of democracy.

7   **Majority rule** and the preservation of minority rights are two additional facets of American democracy. Majority rule implies that only policies supported by most of the population will be made into law. This right of the majority to govern themselves is summed up by the term **popular sovereignty**. This term, however, did not come into wide usage until pre–Civil War debates over slavery. At that time, supporters of popular sovereignty argued that the citizens of new states seeking admission to the Union should be able to decide whether or not their states would allow slavery within their borders.

8   Today, emphasis on majority rule also usually stresses concern with minority rights, although tension between the two concepts still exists. One example of that tension is illustrated by the issues and controversy generated over President Bill Clinton's nomination of his longtime friend and former law school classmate Lani Guinier, a University of Pennsylvania Law School professor, to head the Civil Rights Division of the U.S. Justice Department. When her position on the respective roles of the majority and the minority became public, the controversy was such that Clinton was forced to withdraw her nomination. In a 1991 *Michigan Law Review* article, Guinier attacked a "hostile permanent (white) majority" often unwilling to give minorities in legislatures their share of power. Thus Guinier proposed, among other things, a "minority veto" to allow black legislators the ability to veto measures passed by majorities in cases where minority legislators were unable to make inroads. Once he read her work, even Clinton was unwilling to accept Guinier's ideas or defend them, noting, "I cannot fight a battle . . . if I do not believe in the ground of the battle."

9   **Personal liberty** is perhaps the single most important characteristic of American democracy. The Constitution itself was written to assure "life" and "liberty." Over the years, our concepts of liberty have changed. Liberty was first considered to be freedom "from." Thus, Americans were to be free from governmental

infringements on freedom of religion and speech, from unreasonable search and seizure, and so on…. The addition to the Constitution of the Fourteenth Amendment and its emphasis on equal protection of the laws and subsequent passage of laws guaranteeing civil rights, however, expanded Americans' concept of liberty to include demands for "freedom to" be free from discrimination. Debates over how much the government should do to guarantee these rights or liberties illustrate the conflicts that continue to occur in our democratic system.

898 words

Questions on American Government

1. What are two types of *democracy?*

_____

_____

_____

2. Why is the term *republic* appropriate for representative democracies?

_____

_____

3. *Political equality* stems from what American value?

_____

4. What characteristics of American democracy are in tension?

_____

_____

_____

_____

■ ■ ■ ■ ■

Answering these questions will help you take good notes on American government. Now complete the page of notes started for you.

Theory of democratic government: _____

direct   _____

                          _____

indirect   _____

                          _____

democracy   _____

                          _____

republic   _____

                          _____

Characteristics of American democracy: _____

individualism   _____

political equality   _____

majority rule   _____

                          _____

                          _____

minority rights   _____

                          _____

                          _____

                          _____

Respond

The last step in your reading strategy is to respond by reviewing and reflecting on the material you have read. You will need to review your notes to answer possible test questions later in this chapter. Before continuing to read, reflect on the section on domestic violence. Here is one question to aid your reflection: What is the most significant new idea you have learned about domestic violence, and why is it important to you?

_____

_____

_____

_____

_____

_____

REINFORCING LEARNING IN CLASS

One of the best methods for becoming successful in some activity is to copy the methods of successful people. Here are the methods of successful students.

Preparing for Class

Good students almost never miss class, and they go to class prepared. Some students go to class hoping that the instructor will teach them what they need to know so that they will not have to read the textbook. These students have the process backwards. Class lectures and discussions should clarify what you have already read.

Participating in Class

Good students participate in class. Active engagement in class includes the following activities.

1. **Sit near the front of the class.** From here you can see the board clearly. You also signal your instructor that you want to learn.

2. **Come with the appropriate materials.** Have needed materials assembled before the instructor begins class. *Good students do not walk in late and then further disrupt class by asking a neighbor what's happening.*

3. **Listen.** Intend to learn. Pay attention to signal words that announce a list or definition or contrast, the same signal words you find in written materials. Really listen to signal words that announce important material (because it will be on the next test!). Some of these signals include: "This is really important," "I want you all to be clear on this," and "Let me emphasize...."

4. **Participate in class discussions, question periods, and group activities.** Come to class with questions about the reading assignment or the last class lecture. Speak up in class discussions, even if you are shy, because putting the ideas in your own words is an important strategy for learning. Students who are not participating are being graded—down.

5. **Take notes.** The Cornell Method of note taking is also ideal for class notes. Take your notes in the space to the right of the vertical line on each page. Add key words and phrases down the left column after class. Label reading notes and class notes at the top of each page and keep them in the same three-ring binder notebook.

   When taking notes, listen for main ideas and get down complete definitions of key terms. Be certain to copy *everything* that is put on the board. Include signal words in your notes: the *causes* of the Civil War or the *differences between* the First and Second World Wars.

6. **Review notes immediately.** You want to fix in your memory as much of the class discussion as possible, so review your notes and add key words as soon as class is finished

PREPARING FOR TESTING

The best way to prepare for testing is to learn the material as you go. You learn the material by applying your reading strategy to the textbook, by participating in class, and by reviewing your notes every week.

Keep your focus on the task of learning. Successful students spend their time and energy doing the work of the course. Unsuccessful students spend more time thinking about their anxieties and past performances.

Most instructors describe the format of tests either in class or on the course syllabus. So you will know if a given test will be multiple-choice, fill-in-the-blank, short-answer, or essay format. Remember that any of the short-answer formats will demand knowledge of details. You will not be able to "shoot the breeze" or give personal responses to the material. Short-answer formats may test ideas and inferences as well as facts, though, so you still need to reflect on the subject matter, just as you will need to do for essay testing. First, here are some guidelines for preparing for short-answer forms of testing.

Guidelines for Short-Answer Testing

1. **Study from thorough notes.** Make certain that both class notes and reading notes are detailed and complete. Be sure to include key terms and their definitions. You may want to make vocabulary flash cards for key terms.

(continued on next page)

(continued from previous page)

2. **Concentrate on material the instructor has emphasized in class.** Your class notes should reveal what has been stressed in class. Know this material "cold."

3. **Use chapter review questions or study problems as ways to prepare.** Be sure you can answer all the review questions and also work any additional problems at each chapter's end as a way to review and test yourself.

4. **Do not overlook historical elements in your texts.** Many instructors care about the history of their field of study and expect students to learn some of that history. Be prepared for such questions as "Who was the father of psychoanalysis?" in your psychology class.

5. **Practice naming parts, reciting steps in processes, recounting key examples.** Talk through the material, either to yourself or with a study partner. Cover a page of notes and recite the material. Then check yourself for accuracy.

6. **Be able to spell key terms correctly.** For any test format other than multiple choice, you will need to write. So, practice spelling along with definitions of key terms. Instructors will forgive misspellings of minor words more readily than misspellings of key terms. Can you spell *addiction?*

7. **Anticipate the questions.** As you study, ask yourself what questions you would use to test someone. Listening in class and using the text's summaries or review questions should help you figure out most of what's coming on the test.

Here are some possible short-answer questions on the textbook sections you just studied. Review your reading notes and then see how well you would do with these test questions.

Multiple Choice

_____ 1. The seven characteristics of living things

    a. do not apply to some animals.

    b. are interrelated.

    c. are simple traits.

    d. are the same as found in nonliving things.

Always begin by looking for the words that best complete the thought. Do not try to second-guess the test or assume that there is a trick to the question. If you are unsure, consider each possibility to try to eliminate what is not correct. The characteristics are what we find in all living things, so (a) cannot be correct. Adaptability and reproduction traits are certainly complex, so (c) cannot be right. And, stones do not reproduce, so (d) cannot be right either. Thus, (b) is the correct answer.

Fill in the Blank

1. The single greatest cause of injury to women comes from

_____

Notice that this test item is more difficult than the multiple-choice item. You have to write an answer, not just select one.

True/False

                                        T   F

1. American democracy functions entirely on the concepts of political equality and majority rule.   ____ ____

When taking true/false tests, keep in mind that a statement must be *completely* true or it is false. Read each statement carefully before deciding how to mark it. The statement above is false because American democracy *also* functions on the concept of protecting minority rights. Be alert to words such as *entirely*. They often signal a false statement.

Short Answer

1. Briefly explain the phases in the "cycle of violence" theory.

_____

_____

_____.

With short-answer topics, write to the point, using just a few carefully worded sentences. You can respond to the preceding topic from your reading notes. Devote one sentence to each phase.

Guidelines for Essay Tests

To write a good essay answer, you need the same information for short-answer tests, but you also need to make connections and understand larger issues. In addition, you need to organize your thoughts in a short period of time. Here are some guidelines for coping with essay tests.

1. **Follow the seven guidelines given above for short-answer testing.** Do not think that you can just "write off the top of your head." You still need to know the subject matter and be able to spell key terms.

2. **Anticipate essay questions.** Review your class notes to see how the instructor organized the subject matter and made connections within the chapter and to other parts of the course. Make up some essay questions that *you* would ask about the material.

3. **Read the essay topic carefully and understand what you are asked to write about before you start an answer.** Too many students end up writing off the subject because they start to write everything they know without focusing on the specific topic. Use these strategies to understand essay topics.

   a. Turn the statement into a question that you then answer. For example, suppose you read this topic: Discuss the ideas of Locke that helped shape the American system of government. Ask yourself, "What were the key ideas of Locke?" Jot down key points and then think about how they were used by the Founders of our government.

   b. Pay attention to direction words. *Examine, discuss,* and *explain* call for an organized presentation of information. *Interpret* and *evaluate* ask you to make judgments and include your views. *Relate* asks you to make connections, *compare* to note similarities or differences, *trace* to use a time sequence to examine causes or steps in a process.

4. **Organize your answer before writing.** Take time to collect your thoughts and select an organization. Use one sheet of paper or the back of the test to jot down some points in the order you want to discuss them.

5. **Learn from doing.** Study each test when it is returned to you. Note any questions you did not anticipate. Compare your test to a classmate's to see why you lost points. Did you leave out a key point? Did your essay lack a clear organization? Apply the knowledge you gain to your study for the next test.

PLATE TECTONICS AND THE BREAKUP OF PANGAEA

Adapted from Helena Curtis and N. Sue Barnes

The following selection is adapted from Curtis and Barnes's textbook, *An Invitation to Biology* (4th ed., 1985). Both authors are college professors who have written other books in addition to *An Invitation to Biology*.

Prepare

1. Identify the author and work. What do you expect the author's purpose to be?

   _____

   _____

2. Preread to identify the subject and make predictions. What do you expect to read about?

   _____

   _____

3. What do you already know about the subject?

   _____

   _____

   _____

   _____

4. Raise two questions that you expect the article to answer.

   _____

   _____

   _____

   _____

■ ■ ■ ■ ■

1   Most scientists now accept the theory of plate tectonics. According to plate tectonics, the outer layer of the earth is divided into a number of sections, or plates. The continents rest on the plates, but the plates are not stationary. They slide around the surface of the earth, moving in relation to one another.

2   Sometimes the moving plates collide. Where plates bump into each other, volcanic islands may be formed. Also, mountain ranges such as the Andes or the Himalayas are created. At the boundaries where plates are separating, volcanic material wells up to fill the space. Plates may also move along their boundaries but in opposite directions, or in the same direction but at different speeds. These actions lead to earthquakes.

3   About 200 million years ago, all the major continents were locked together in one supercontinent called Pangaea. Several drawings of Pangaea have been suggested. One is shown below. Scientists generally agree that Pangaea began to break up about 190 million years ago. This is about the same time that the dinosaurs were dominating the earth and the first mammals began to appear. First, the northern group of continents, called Laurasia, split apart from the southern group (Gondwana). Later, Gondwana broke into three parts: Africa–South America, Australia–Antarctica, and India. India drifted northward and bumped into Asia (the part of Laurasia to the right). This collision started the uplift of the Himalayan mountains. These continue to rise today as India continues to push northward into Asia.

4   About 65 million years ago, South America and Africa separated enough to form half of the South Atlantic Ocean. Also, Europe, North America, and Greenland began

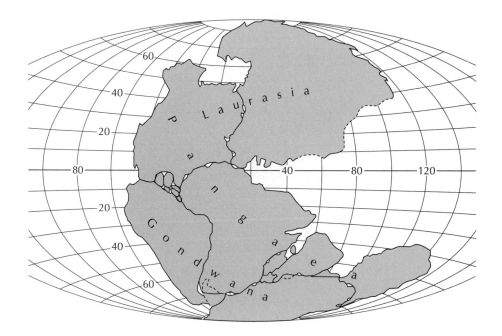

to drift apart. However, final separation between Europe and North America–Greenland did not occur until about 43 million years ago. At this same time, Australia finally split from Antarctica and moved northward to its present location. Later North and South America were joined at Panama, which was created by volcanic action.

5   One of the earliest and most convincing pieces of evidence supporting continental drift was the discovery of fossils of the same reptile (*Mesosaurus*) along the coasts of both Brazil and South Africa but nowhere else. Also, in 1982, scientists found the first fossil of a land mammal—a marsupial—in Antarctica. This supports the theory that marsupials migrated by land from South America (still home of the opossum) across Antarctica to Australia before the two continents separated, about 55 million years ago. The best known marsupials living in Australia today are the kangaroos.

417 words

Comprehension Check

Answer the following with a, b, c, or d to indicate the phrase that best completes each statement.

_____ 1. The theory of plate tectonics is that
   a. the outer layer of the moon is composed of moving plates.
   b. the inner layer of the Earth is composed of moving plates.
   c. the outer layer of the Earth is composed of moving plates.
   d. Greenland and Europe are joined.

_____ 2. Colliding plates may cause
   a. volcanic islands and mountains.
   b. big continents.
   c. marsupials.
   d. early mammals.

_____ 3. Plates moving in opposite directions or at different speeds
   a. create new continents.
   b. cause earthquakes.
   c. happened only 200 million years ago.
   d. gave rise to the dinosaurs.

_____ 4. The supercontinent is called
   a. Pangaea.
   b. Gondwana.
   c. Asia.
   d. Antarctica.

_____   5. The supercontinent began to break up when

  a. mammals dominated the Earth.

  b. the dinosaurs dominated the earth.

  c. the dinosaurs died out.

  d. only one-celled animals lived.

_____   6. When India broke off, it moved northward and bumped into

  a. Australia.

  b. South America.

  c. Asia.

  d. Antarctica.

_____   7. North and South America were joined at Panama as a result of

  a. South America bumping into North America.

  b. earthquakes.

  c. volcanic action.

  d. Greenland separating from Europe.

_____   8. To support plate tectonics theory, fossils of the same reptile have been found in

  a. both Brazil and South Africa.

  b. both Panama and Greenland.

  c. both Antarctica and North America.

  d. Brazil only.

_____   9. Marsupials

  a. live in South America.

  b. live in Australia.

  c. include kangaroos.

  d. all of the above.

_____   10. The best main-idea statement of this selection is

  a. the theory of plate tectonics is doubted by scientists.

  b. plate tectonics defines marsupials.

  c. plate tectonics explains the movement of continents and events such as volcanoes.

  d. plate tectonics explains how India hit Asia and made the Himalayan mountains.

Preparing for Testing

Create the following types of test questions on this selection.

1. True/False: _____

_____

2. Fill in the Blank: _____

_____

3. Fill in the Blank: _____

_____

4. Short Answer: _____

_____

_____

5. Short Answer: _____

_____

_____

MAKING CONNECTIONS

1. What is the most important new idea or fact for you in this selection? Why do you find it important?

2. Why is it important to understand how the universe works?

"E" CONNECTIONS

Learn about a scientific term or concept. Be able to explain the concept, as simply as possible, to classmates. Try to think of one comparison to or example from ordinary life to use in your explanation. Some possible terms include: gravity, black holes, the Big Bang, quarks, and white dwarfs. You may want to start your search at:

<http://www.HowStuffWorks.com> or <http://www.refdesk.com>.

Be sure to identify all Websites used.

WORD POWER 11
Reviewing Words Found in Testing

One way to be a good test taker is to understand what you are being asked to do in a test question. Here are some key words to be sure to know. Review them on your own or with your class partner by writing a brief definition for each word. Then select the correct term to complete each of the sentences that follow.

compare _____

_____

describe _____

_____

evaluate _____

_____

explain _____

_____

identify _____

_____

list _____

_____

summarize _____

_____

trace _____

_____

1. _____ *(Summarize/Compare)* the main ideas that make up the theory of plate tectonics.

2. _____ *(Identify/Explain)* how the process of photosynthesis works.

3. _____ *(Compare/Trace)* the steps in the process by which a bill becomes a law in the U.S. Congress.

4. _____ (*Compare/Trace*) the psychological theories of Freud and Watson.

5. _____ (*Identify/Summarize*) each of the following titles by providing the author and indicating what type of work it is.

6. _____ (*Evaluate/List*) the seven characteristics of living things.

7. _____ (*Evaluate/List*) President Reagan's economic policies.

8. _____ (*Summarize/Describe*) the painting styles of two French Impressionists.

CHAPTER REVIEW

Complete each of the following.

1. To get the most out of classroom learning, be sure to:

   a. _____

   b. _____

   c. _____

2. Mapping differs from outlining by

   _____

   _____

Answer the following questions on the three textbook selections you have studied in this chapter.

_____ 3. The process by which plants take in and change the sun's energy is called
   a. photosynthesis.
   b. homeostasis.
   c. enzymes.
   d. macromolecules.

_____ 4. Women are most likely to be victims of violence from
   a. their parents.
   b. their children.
   c. men they know.
   d. men who are strangers.

5. The United States has an _____ democracy.

6. Two concepts in American democracy are creating some tension in society

today; these two concepts are _____

_____

7. Briefly explain how domestic violence differs for male victims and female victims.

_____

_____

_____

_____

	T	F
8. Living things have a chemical makeup that is different from their environment.	____	____
9. Domestic violence is a minor problem for women.	____	____
10. Personal liberty is the most important characteristic of American democracy.	____	____

Take a Reading Road Trip!

For additional practice with your reading skills, use the Reading Road Trip CD-ROM or visit Reading Road Trip on the Web at <http://www.ablongman.com/readingroadtrip> (password required).

Additional Readings

The following selections may be assigned by your instructor or read for your own pleasure and practice. You may also use them to practice timed readings—after you study Appendix B and learn how to calculate your reading speed. Remember: your reading rate must always be connected to comprehension. Reading faster without understanding accomplishes nothing. So, always complete the comprehension check after reading the selection. Vocabulary work and questions for reflection are also provided.

IT'S A WONDERFUL NIGHT

Jess Tirado as told to Susan Burton

The following brief article appeared, with the accompanying photograph, in the Sunday Magazine section of the *New York Times* on December 23, 2001. The photo and the date are both important to this article.

Prepare

1. Identify the author and the work. What do you expect the author's purpose to be?

   _____

   _____

2. Preread to identify the subject and make predictions. What do you expect to read about?

   _____

   _____

3. What do you already know about the subject?

_____

_____

_____

4. Raise two questions that you expect the article to answer.

_____

_____

_____

_____

■ ■ ■ ■ ■

1   I was 17 when I moved to New York from Puerto Rico in 1990. I never really knew much about Rockefeller Center. I knew about the tree lighting because we had cable, so you could see it when it was shown on NBC. But I thought Rockefeller Center was a private place where people had to pay lots of money to skate. One night, I decided to take a walk. I didn't know anyone in New York. I was just following people, friendly faces, and I got to Rockefeller Center. I was mesmerized, just watching people skating around. At home, there weren't indoor or outdoor rinks. The next thing you know, I was there for two hours. Then I started going every night, skating sometimes.

2   I began as an attendant in 1992, and now I manage the rink and drive the Zamboni. Actually, it's not a Zamboni; it's an Olympia. Zamboni is like Kleenex, just a name. Our rink is so small a lot of people don't realize that we actually have a Zamboni here. I have to stop saying that, because it's actually an Olympia. The Olympia's at rink level, inside a little room, on a turntable. You just open a door, and it just backs up right onto the ice. That's when you hear the clapping. Literally, children that could have been crying in line, when the machine comes out they'll quiet down and look filled with wonder. And there is always somebody who's going to shout something out. You'll hear "Yeah, Zamboni!" or "Go, Zamboni Man!" And this year I've heard "Go, America." Before we opened this year, I wasn't expecting many people to come. Then slowly it started increasing. I talk to as many people from out of state as I can to thank them for not being afraid. I mean, it could have been anyone in these buildings. You can sense the fear sometimes in people, but once they get on skates, it's forgotten.

3   During the holidays, I close at midnight. I'm usually the last one here. That is probably one of the best feelings. You go from over a thousand people in one spot

Source: Barkel Schmidt

all day long to nobody. It's quiet. It's just me and the ice. I put some good tunes on and drive the Zamboni. Once in a blue moon, you'll get somebody who will just stand there and watch you—whether it takes 40 minutes, whether it takes an hour. I know exactly how they feel. When I leave, I walk up toward the Channel Garden. There is the tree and Prometheus behind me. And I always look down at the ice on my way out. It's a huge piece of glass, a wonderful piece of glass. There aren't many moments when you can be in front of that tree by yourself. But that moment for me is at 2 o'clock in the morning. The whole magic thing, I see it every day.

Comprehension Check

Answer the following with a, b, c, or d to indicate the phrase that best completes each statement.

_____ 1. The "I" in this narrative essay is

    a. Zamboni.

    b. Jess Tirado.

    c. Susan Burton.

    d. Prometheus.

_____   2. When he was 17, Jess moved from
  a. Puerto Rico to Rockefeller Center.
  b. New York City to Puerto Rico.
  c. Puerto Rico to New York City.
  d. Puerto Rico to Channel Garden.

_____   3. When Jess saw the Rockefeller Center ice rink, he
  a. was mesmerized.
  b. was shocked.
  c. walked away quickly.
  d. went to another rink.

_____   4. To be mesmerized means that he was
  a. engrossed in and enchanted by the scene.
  b. unhappy by what he saw.
  c. made homesick.
  d. shocked and astounded by the scene.

_____   5. Jess's job includes
  a. making ice machines.
  b. driving the ice machine.
  c. filling ice machines.
  d. ice skating.

_____   6. When they see the Olympia ice machine, people watching or waiting to skate
  a. complain about having to wait longer.
  b. leave the ice rink.
  c. keep crying.
  d. are amazed and become quiet.

_____   7. Jess really likes
  a. to be the last one at the rink.
  b. the quiet of closing time.
  c. having maybe one person watching his last ride on the "Zamboni."
  d. all of the above.

_____   8. Late at night, when it's quiet and Jess leaves the rink, it is
  a. scary.
  b. dark.
  c. magical.
  d. boring.

_____ 9. When he writes of thanking people for coming to New York City, Jess is referring to

a. the expense of visiting New York City.

b. the crowded conditions at the rink.

c. how friendly and outgoing he is.

d. the fear of traveling after 9/11.

_____ 10. The primary purpose of this essay is to

a. ridicule New York City.

b. inform readers about ice skating.

c. persuade readers to believe in the magic of New York City.

d. persuade readers to take up ice skating.

Reflection and Discussion

1. Have you been to Rockefeller Center? If so, did you find it enchanting? If not, are you now eager to go?

2. Is there a specific place you feel is special? If so, where is it and why is it special to you?

3. What is special about Jess's story?

■ ■ ■ ■ ■

SPEAKING TWO LANGUAGES, BOTH ENGLISH

William Raspberry

William Raspberry began his career in journalism in Indiana before joining the *Washington Post*. He now writes both local and syndicated columns each week, usually focusing on urban or race problems or issues regarding the poor. The following column appeared on August 20, 2001.

Prepare

1. Identify the author and the work. What do you expect the author's purpose to be?

_____

_____

2. Preread to identify the subject and make predictions. What do you expect to read about?

_____

_____

3. What do you already know about the subject?

_____

_____

_____

4. Raise two questions that you expect the article to answer.

_____

_____

_____

▪ ▪ ▪ ▪ ▪

1   Can it be that one of the reasons why inner-city children tend to do poorly in school is bilingual education?

2   No, not bilingual as in English and Spanish. I mean bilingual as in standard English and the nonstandard English that poor children often bring to school.

3   The first sort we recognize as a deliberately chosen approach to teaching. Youngsters whose home language is Spanish are, under the bilingual-ed theory, first taught in Spanish for beginning reading, arithmetic, early social studies and so on. Then, as they master content, they are gradually switched to English. The idea, at least in part, is to honor and build on what the children already know.

4   I suspect something like that is going on in many inner-city schools, where teachers, fearing to make children ashamed of themselves and their families, accept the language they bring to school and try to use it as a base for their teaching. I doubt that this second sort of bilingual ed involves much pedagogical theorizing. It probably has more to do with the feeling that these youngsters have it tough enough already without the added indignity of forcing them to "talk white."

5   But whether conscious theory or sympathetic practice, bilingual ed may not be the best approach to helping children who don't speak standard English to become successful in school.

6   My doubts on this score were confirmed a year ago in a newspaper article written by Ken Noonan, superintendent of schools in Oceanside, Calif., but more relevantly, a former bilingual teacher who was a spirited campaigner against California's Proposition 227 forbidding bilingual ed in the state.

7   When the proposition passed, Noonan at first resisted implementing it, but finally—reluctantly—gave in. Then:

8   "At the end of the first year, I was amazed by the results. State tests showed dramatic academic gains for Spanish-speaking students in reading and writing—especially in the early grades, where we had reduced class size to 20 or fewer students and implemented phonics reading instruction. . . . Without 227, we would have been teaching these students in Spanish; they would certainly have performed poorly on the state tests, which are administered in English. And we never would have seen how quickly and how early they could learn to read English."

9   Something similar could happen for urban and rural poor children—if we could see the similarity to bilingual education in the present approach. The difficulty is that the language these children speak is sufficiently close to the standard English of the educated classes that we think of it not in terms of a different language but as a marker for class or race. We don't see the urgency of switching these kids to (standard) English because we think they already speak English.

10   But the English they speak is usually not the English of their texts—or of their tests. We tell ourselves that because they speak the language well enough to be understood, it's better to get them used to expressing their thoughts—in whatever dialect—than to shame them into silence. Or we say we'll teach them proper English later, after they've gained confidence in their ability to learn. And we let them go on using their "home" language in a sort of unintended bilingual ed.

11   Wouldn't it be fascinating to see what would happen if an inner-city school decreed an end to bilingual education, instituting instead a requirement that only standard English would be used in the classroom?

12   Would the children clam up, or would they take to the "new" language with the alacrity of California's Hispanic kids? And if it started in first grade and remained consistent, would they internalize the language we associate with smart people?

13   And isn't the likelihood that the results would show up, not only on the standardized tests that everybody seems to be pushing these days but also in the children's confidence of expression, in their ability to glean meaning from the printed page and in their ability to impress others with their intelligence?

14   A voluntary Prop 227 won't fix everything. Smaller class sizes, phonics and other reforms played a part in California. But ending bilingual ed helped, too. Won't some inner-city principal be bold enough to try it?

693 words

Comprehension Check

Answer the following with a, b, c, or d to indicate the phrase that best completes each statement.

_____ 1. Raspberry's topic is
   a. bilingual education.
   b. the nonstandard English of poor children.
   c. Proposition 227.
   d. phonics reading instruction.

_____ 2. Raspberry asserts that
   a. many poor children speak Spanish.
   b. bilingual education is a bad idea.
   c. many poor children speak nonstandard English.
   d. bilingual education is the best way to teach children whose English is nonstandard.

_____ 3. When children are allowed to continue to use nonstandard English the result is
   a. the children do well in school.
   b. teachers will be fired.
   c. these children will automatically change to standard English.
   d. a second type of bilingual education.

_____ 4. Raspberry believes that nonstandard English is not corrected by teachers because the
   a. teachers don't know how to correct students.
   b. teachers don't want the children to feel bad.
   c. students will learn without correction.
   d. teachers don't think it matters.

_____ 5. Raspberry refers to an article by a California educator to show
   a. how well Hispanic students did when bilingual education was forbidden.
   b. how poorly Hispanic students did when bilingual education was forbidden.

c. that Proposition 227 should not have passed in California.

d. that Californians always do things differently.

_____ 6. The author suspects that we continue to allow nonstandard English in schools because

a. we don't see this as a type of bilingual education.

b. we don't feel any urgency to change students because they are speaking a form of English.

c. we are sensitive to class and race issues.

d. all of the above.

_____ 7. Raspberry believes that if only standard English was used in the classroom students would

a. refuse to speak standard English.

b. learn standard English and do better in school.

c. not be willing to talk in class.

d. fail standardized tests.

_____ 8. By "a voluntary Prop 227" Raspberry means

a. a national law eliminating bilingual education.

b. a state-by-state choice to end bilingual education.

c. a decision to make standard English the language of the class-room.

d. students can speak any dialect they choose.

_____ 9. The best main-idea statement of this essay is

a. schools should choose to use standard English only in the classroom.

b. all bilingual education is bad for students.

c. California was wrong to reject bilingual education.

d. schools should let students use their home language.

_____ 10. Raspberry's primary purpose in writing it to

a. inform.

b. amuse.

c. persuade.

d. share feelings.

Expanding Vocabulary

Answer the following with a, b, c, or d to indicate the best definition of the word in **bold** *as it was used in the selection. The number in parentheses is the number of the paragraph in which the word appears.*

_____ 1. "**pedagogical** theorizing" (4)

    a. pedantic

    b. executive

    c. educational

    d. pedestrian

_____ 2. "pedagogical **theorizing**" (4)

    a. formulating principles

    b. formulating therapies

    c. theatrics

    d. themes

_____ 3. "the added **indignity**" (4)

    a. downtime

    b. indictment

    c. indirectness

    d. degrading treatment

_____ 4. "but more **relevantly**" (6)

    a. controllingly

    b. connected to the current issue

    c. relentlessly

    d. remorsefully

_____ 5. "at first resisted **implementing** it" (7)

    a. engaging

    b. implanting

    c. imploring

    d. enforcing

_____ 6. "implemented **phonics** reading instruction" (8)

    a. phraseology

    b. phonographic

    c. method of teaching reading using phonetics

    d. method of teaching reading using philosophy

_____ 7. "We don't see the **urgency**" (9)

    a. compelling nature

    b. usefulness

    c. urbanity

    d. cause

_____ 8. "if an inner-city school **decreed**" (11)

    a. reprimanded

    b. required

    c. debated

    d. desired

_____ 9. "with the **alacrity** of California's Hispanic kids" (12)

    a. aimlessness

    b. slowness

    c. unwillingness

    d. enthusiastic speed

_____ 10. "their ability to **glean** meaning" (13)

    a. gather

    b. glamorize

    c. goad

    d. grade

Reflection and Discussion

1. Were you encouraged/required to speak standard English in school? If yes, was this a good idea in the long run? If no, are you glad or sorry? Explain.

2. Has Raspberry convinced you of his proposal? Why or why not?

3. What are the advantages of knowing standard English?

■ ■ ■ ■ ■

M&Ms' NEW COLOR? IT'S JUST A THIN CANDY SHELL GAME

Ana Veciana-Suarez

Cuban-born, Ana Veciana-Suarez lives in Miami, has published a novel and a collection of her nonfiction writing, and writes a popular column for the _Miami Herald_. The following column appeared February 25, 2002.

Prepare

1. Identify the author and the work. What do you expect the author's purpose to be?

   _____

   _____

2. Preread to identify the subject and make predictions. What do you expect to read about?

   _____

   _____

3. What do you already know about the subject?

   _____

   _____

   _____

4. Raise two questions that you expect the article to answer.

   _____

   _____

   _____

   _____

Vocabulary Alert: Do You Know These Words?

Here are five words that you need to know to read the following selection with understanding.

shell game con game using nut shells moved quickly over a pea. The conned bet they can guess the location of the pea.

palette range of colors on a artist's board

ghouls children in Halloween costumes

scarf down eat a lot of

gratuitous unnecessary and unwanted

▪ ▪ ▪ ▪ ▪

1   They're doing it again. Adding, subtracting, changing, switching. Don't they have anything better to do? Can't they leave well enough alone?

2   Maybe you've heard. Masterfoods USA, the Mars Inc. subsidiary that makes M&Ms, wants us to decide on a new color for the candy-covered chocolate: purple, pink or aqua. The company is advertising in 78 countries and taking votes on its Web site from March to May, with plans to add the winning color to its rainbow by August.

3   The potential new colors might sound like a Martha Stewart Easter palette, but the choices are actually based on the company's market research. Those shades were consumers' top choices to add to the red, green, blue, brown, yellow and orange that already melt in our mouths and not in our hands. While the color scheme sounds interesting, what I really want to know is if the new color will taste different and if we will get more purples, say, and not fewer of another color.

4   I love M&Ms. I've been gorging on them since I can remember. I take my junk food seriously. It is the only vice I indulge in—or will admit to, anyway. When I buy Halloween candy, I get their snack packs and hope no little ghouls or goblins come to my door, so I can scarf them down all by myself. I also have a thing for Milky Way bars and those dark chocolate Dove candies. Paradise is made of this, I'm sure.

5   Still, M&Ms have changed frequently enough for me to suspect that these reinventions have little to do with quality and everything to do with marketing. As in a sneaky but successful marketing ploy devised by the company to get free press from people like me. It wasn't that long ago—a year or two, in fact—when the company brought out its *dulce de leche* candies, a blatant but politically correct move to attract Latinos. And, of course, in 1995 blue kicked out tan, which I haven't quite gotten over because the tan ones made great eyes when I was making faces on cupcakes and other baked goods.

6   Masterfoods is not the only company forever tinkering with its products, much like Madonna refashioned herself every so often in her heyday. Last year, Barnum's Animal Crackers announced it was caging a new cracker creature for its centennial. We got to pick from among the walrus, penguin, koala and cobra. Barnum has had 53 different animals prowling around in the little red box, with only four enjoying continuous production.

7   Sometimes changes are minor, sometimes ridiculous. If there's a way of making what we eat different, catchier, somebody will think it up and take it to market. The accompanying hype is usually the way food companies revive a product whose sales have plateaued.

8   But this type of modification isn't an improvement, only a gimmick for our taste buds. Blue didn't taste any different than tan in the M&Ms' bag. Pink—my vote—probably won't, either. And hyena animal crackers were, if I remember correctly, as tasty as the rhinoceroses.

9   So in my hungry, humble opinion, food companies should rethink their strategy of senseless, gratuitous modifications and instead concentrate on what really matters: Give us more, not different—more candies, more crackers—in the same package. It's an idea that won't need any advertising.

555 words

Comprehension Check

Answer the following with a, b, c, or d to indicate the phrase that best completes each statement.

_____ 1. The author's topic is
   a. change in foods.
   b. M&Ms' colors.
   c. changing products for marketing purposes.
   d. Animal Crackers.

_____ 2. To select a new color, the makers of M&Ms
   a. asked Martha Stewart.
   b. advertised their color choice.
   c. eliminated tan.
   d. asked consumers to vote on their Web site.

_____ 3. The author's preferred new color is
   a. purple.
   b. pink.
   c. aqua.
   d. blue.

_____ 4. Veciana-Suarez says that she loves
   a. M&Ms.
   b. Milky Way bars.
   c. dark chocolate Dove candy.
   d. all of the above.

_____ 5. When the author writes that she loves M&Ms, she wants readers to understand that
   a. she is not opposed to candy or junk food in general.
   b. M&Ms are her favorite candy.
   c. she owns stock in Mars, Inc.
   d. we should not eat junk food.

_____ 6. Veciana-Suarez believes that the M&Ms company made *dulce de leche* candy to
   a. attract Latino consumers.
   b. attract French consumers.
   c. draw attention to M&Ms' new color.
   d. compete with Milky Way candy.

_____ 7. The author thinks that
    a. changes are good.
    b. hyena Animal Crackers taste better than the others.
    c. changes in color or animal shapes are important.
    d. changes in color or animal shapes are marketing gimmicks.

_____ 8. The author would like to see
    a. purple as the M&Ms new color.
    b. more candy in the same package.
    c. bigger and better packaging.
    d. more penguin Animal Crackers.

_____ 9. The author's purpose is to
    a. inform readers of the vote for a new color.
    b. persuade readers not to eat M&Ms.
    c. amuse readers with a tale about junk food.
    d. persuade readers, using some humor, not to be taken in by advertising gimmicks.

_____ 10. The best main-idea statement for this essay is
    a. Masterfoods is not the only company using gimmicks.
    b. Food companies should not use minor changes as a marketing strategy.
    c. M&Ms' company should select pick as the new color.
    d. M&Ms are a great candy.

Expanding Vocabulary

Answer the following with a, b, c, or d to indicate the best definition of the word in **bold** _as it was used in the selection. The number in parentheses is the number of the paragraph in which word appears._

_____ 1. "the Mars Inc. **subsidiary**" (2)
    a. substitute
    b. company owned by another company
    c. company for sale
    d. subsistence

_____ 2. "I've been **gorging** on them" (4)
    a. stuffing a turkey
    b. gouging
    c. gossiping
    d. stuffing oneself with food

_____ 3. "is the only **vice** I indulge in" (4)

    a. wickedness

    b. verve

    c. viciousness

    d. wilderness

_____ 4. "is the only vice I **indulge** in" (4)

    a. grapple

    b. inflate

    c. gratify

    d. indicate

_____ 5. "successful marketing **ploy**" (5)

    a. strategy designed to gain an advantage

    b. strategy designed to please

    c. plod

    d. plug

_____ 6. "a **blatant**...move to attract Latinos" (5)

    a. bland

    b. blasting

    c. pleasantly bashful

    d. unpleasantly obvious

_____ 7. "refashioned herself ... in her **heyday**" (6)

    a. period of greatest success

    b. gap in time

    c. hierarchy

    d. hideout

_____ 8. "for its **centennial**" (6)

    a. centimeter

    b. hundredth anniversary

    c. central

    d. fiftieth anniversary

_____ 9. "whose sales have **plateaued**" (7)

    a. pickled

    b. plastered

    c. left out

    d. leveled out

_____ 10. "accompanying **hype**" (8)

    a. hyper

    b. essential information

    c. excessive claims made

    d. hyphen

Reflection and Discussion

1. Find examples—in both language and statements—that add humor to this essay.
2. Do you agree that Veciana-Suarez has a good point to make? Can you think of other products that have used the same kind of advertising ploy?
3. What are the chances that we will get more candy in the same package?

■ ■ ■ ■ ■

THE GREATNESS GAP

Charles Krauthammer

A syndicated columnist, Charles Krauthammer is a regular participant on the TV political talk show *Inside Washington*. The following essay was published in *Time* magazine on July 1, 2002.

Prepare

1. Identify the author and the work. What do you expect the author's purpose to be?

    _____

    _____

2. Preread to identify the subject and make predictions. What do you expect to read about?

    _____

    _____

3. What do you already know about the subject?

_____

_____

_____

4. Raise two questions that you expect the article to answer.

_____

_____

_____

Vocabulary Alert: Do You Know These Words?

Here are five words you need to know to read the following article with understanding.

cosmic vast, limitless, beyond this Earth

transcendent to exist above and beyond the rest

deities gods

racked up accumulated

pantheon The collection of gods—or heroes—of a culture

■ ■ ■ ■ ■

1   There is excellence, and there is greatness—cosmic, transcendent, Einsteinian. We know it when we see it, we think. But how to measure it? Among Tiger Woods' varied contributions to contemporary American life is that he shows us how.

2   As just demonstrated yet again at the U.S. Open, Woods is the greatest golfer who ever lived. How do we know? You could try Method 1: Compare him directly with the former greatest golfer, Jack Nicklaus. For example, take their total scores in their first 22 major championships (of which Nicklaus won seven, Woods eight). Nicklaus was 40 strokes over par; Tiger was 81 under—an astonishing 121 strokes better.

3   But that is not the right way to compare. You cannot compare greatness directly across the ages. There are so many intervening variables: changes in technology, training, terrain, equipment, often rules and customs.

4   How then do we determine who is greatest? Method 2: The Gap. Situate each among his contemporaries. Who towers? Who is, like the U.S. today, a hyperpower with no second in sight?

5   The mark of true transcendence is running alone. Nicklaus was great, but he ran with peers: Palmer, Player, Watson. Tiger has none. Of the past 11 majors,

Woods has won seven. That means whenever and wherever the greatest players in the world gather, Woods wins twice and the third trophy is distributed among the next, oh, 150.

6   In 2000–01, Woods won four majors in a row. The *Washington Post's* Thomas Boswell found that if you take these four and add the 2001 Players Championship (considered the next most important tournament), Tiger shot a cumulative 1,357 strokes—55 strokes better than the next guy.

7   To find true greatness, you must apply the "next guy" test. Then the clouds part and the deities appear. In 1921 Babe Ruth hit 59 home runs. The next four hit 24, 24, 23 and 23. Ruth alone hit more home runs than half the teams in the major leagues.

8   In the 1981–82 season, Wayne Gretzky scored 212 points. The next two guys scored 147 and 139. Not for nothing had he been known as the Great One—since age 9.

9   Gaps like these are as rare as the gods that produce them. By 1968, no one had ever long-jumped more than 27 ft. 4¾ in. In the Mexico City Olympics that year, Bob Beamon jumped 29 ft. 2½ in.—this in a sport in which records are broken by increments of a few inches, sometimes fractions. (Yes, the air is thin in Mexico City, but it was a legal jump and the record stood for an astonishing 23 years.)

10   In physics, a quantum leap means jumping to a higher level without ever stopping—indeed, without even traveling through—anywhere in between. In our ordinary understanding of things, that is impossible. In sports, it defines greatness.

11   Not only did Michael Jordan play a game of basketball so beautiful that it defied physics, but he racked up numbers that put him in a league of his own. Jordan has averaged 31 points a game, a huge gap over the (future) Hall of Famers he played against (e.g., Karl Malone, 25.7; Charles Barkley, 22.1).

12   The most striking visual representation of the Gap is the photograph of Secretariat crossing the finish line at the Belmont Stakes, 31(!) lengths ahead of the next horse. You can barely see the others—the fastest horses in the world, mind you—in the distance.

13   In 1971, Bobby Fischer played World Championship elimination rounds against the best players on the planet. These were open-ended matches that finished only when one player had won six games. Such matches could take months, because great chess masters are so evenly matched that 80% of tournament games end in draws. Victories come at rare intervals; six wins can take forever. Not this time. Fischer conducted a campaign unrivaled since Scipio Africanus leveled Carthage. He beat two challengers six games in a row, which, combined with wins before and after, produced a streak of 20 straight victories against the very best—something never seen before and likely never to be seen again.

14   That's a Gap. To enter the pantheon—any pantheon—you've got to be so far above and beyond your contemporaries that it is said of you, as Jack Nicklaus once said of Tiger Woods, "He's playing a game I'm not familiar with."

15   The biologist and philosopher Lewis Thomas was asked what record of human achievements he would launch into space to be discovered one day by some transgalactic civilization. A continual broadcast of Bach would do, Thomas suggested, though "that would be boasting."

16   Why not make it a music video? A Bach fugue over Tiger hitting those mirac-
ulous irons from the deep rough onto the greens at Bethpage Black. Nah. The aliens
will think we did it all with computer graphics.

Comprehension Check

*Answer the following with a, b, c, or d to indicate the phrase that best completes each
statement.*

_____ 1. Krauthammer's topic is
   a. Tiger Woods.
   b. golf.
   c. the meaning of greatness.
   d. greatness.

_____ 2. One way possibly to judge Wood's greatness is to compare him to
   a. Jack Nicklaus.
   b. Wayne Gretzky.
   c. Sam Snead.
   d. Larry Bird.

_____ 3. Krauthammer says that "Method 1" does not work because
   a. it doesn't show how great Woods is.
   b. it works only for golf.
   c. there are too few differences from one time to another.
   d. there are too many differences from one time to another.

_____ 4. Krauthammer labels Method 2
   a. transcendence.
   b. Einsteinian.
   c. greatness.
   d. the Gap.

_____ 5. Method 2 determines greatness by
   a. how far a player can jump.
   b. how many goals a player gets.
   c. measuring how much better a player is than his or her competitors.
   d. measuring how bad most players are.

_____ 6. The truly great players in any sport
   a. are much, much better than those they are competing against.
   b. are deities, not human.

c. are "next guy" types.

d. make clouds part.

_____ 7. Krauthammer says that the best *visual* indicator of the Gap concept is

a. Michael Jordan averaging 31 points a game.

b. Secretariat finishing 31 lengths ahead of the other horses.

c. Bobby Fischer playing chess.

d. Scipio leveling Carthage.

_____ 8. When Krauthammer concludes that aliens/ETs would not believe a music video of Woods hitting irons to a Bach fugue, he is

a. saying that ETs only understand computers.

b. ridiculing Bach and Woods.

c. saying that Bach and Woods are amazingly great.

d. ridiculing ETs.

_____ 9. Krauthammer's primary purpose is to

a. define greatness.

b. give examples of athletes.

c. discuss aliens and deities.

d. write a biography of Woods.

_____ 10. The best main-idea statement of this essay is

a. Tiger Woods is a great golfer.

b. Tiger Woods is a better golfer than Jack Nicklaus.

c. Tiger Woods is as great as Michael Jordan.

d. Tiger Woods's greatness helps us understand how to recognize greatness.

Expanding Vocabulary

Answer the following with a, b, c, or d to indicate the best definition of the word in **bold** *as it was used in the selection. The number in paratheses is the number of the paragraph in which the word appears.*

_____ 1. "so many **intervening** variables" (3)

a. intermediate

b. coming between two things

c. coming after something else

d. intimidating

_____ 2. "so many intervening **variables**" (3)
   a. quantities taking on any set of values
   b. vanities
   c. vehicles
   d. veins

_____ 3. "changes in . . . **terrain**" (3)
   a. ground
   b. terms
   c. terror
   d. grasses

_____ 4. "**Situate** each among his contemporaries" (4)
   a. saddle
   b. size up
   c. place in an awkward location
   d. place in a particular spot

_____ 5. Tiger shot a **cumulative** 1,357 strokes" (6)
   a. cunning
   b. crushing
   c. added up, total
   d. awful

_____ 6. "records are broken by **increments**" (9)
   a. incredulous
   b. series of indecisions
   c. series of regular, small additions
   d. inconstants

_____ 7. "it **defied** physics" (11)
   a. boldly resisted
   b. delighted
   c. disgraced
   d. regulated

_____ 8. "he would **launch** into space" (15)
   a. sanction
   b. lead

c. lean

d. set into motion

_____ 9. "by some **transgalactic** civilization" (15)

a. across glaciers

b. across galaxies

c. transitional

d. transmuting

_____ 10. "A Bach **fugue**" (16)

a. fumble

b. complex function

c. complex musical composition

d. fugitive

Reflection and Discussion

1. Which of Krauthammer's examples do you admire the most? Why?

2. Krauthammer uses several clever expressions and comparisons to describe how different the truly great are from the rest. Look at these expressions again and then select the one you like the most. Explain why you chose it.

3. Who are your heroes? Why did you choose them?

■ ■ ■ ■ ■

AN IMMODEST PROPOSAL

Lisa Mundy

Lisa Mundy is a staff writer and columnist for the *Washington Post*. She publishes a column, "PostModern," regularly in the *Post*'s Sunday Magazine. This column appeared March 2, 2002.

Prepare

1. Identify the author and the work. What do you expect the author's purpose to be?

_____

_____

2. Preread to identify the subject and make predictions. What do you expect to read about?

_____

_____

3. What do you already know about the subject?

_____

_____

_____

4. Raise two questions that you expect the article to answer.

_____

_____

_____

_____

Vocabulary Alert: Do You Know These Words?

Here are four words you need to know to read the following selection with understanding.

headhunter someone who recruits high-level professionals
sexism discrimination against women
high-wire act risky job or operation
millennium span of 1,000 years

■ ■ ■ ■ ■

1   "Hi, honey. I know you've got your own established career and I know we've got two kids in school and that our family is very, you know, rooted in this area, but I've been offered this really, well, this really risky position running a company you've never heard of. It does something no other company does, in a field that no one is sure will work out. And I think that's an exciting opportunity. So what I'd like to do is, I'd like to quit my current job, and I'd like you to quit your current job, too, and I'd like to take our kids out of school, and I'd like to move our entire

household from the East Coast to the West, and you can look for a new job there while I throw myself into this iffy venture. Okay? Great! Thanks!"

2   How often does a wife get away with a proposal like that?

3   Not very often. At least, I think it's fair to say that in many—heck, let's go out on a limb here and say most—American households, a wife making a suggestion like that would produce some riveting domestic conversations.

4   But at least one woman did make such a proposal. Her name is Meg Whitman and four years ago she was sitting in her office at Hasbro, overseeing the health and longevity of classic boomer toys like Play-Doh and Mr. Potato Head. Out of the blue, a headhunter called and asked if she would like to give up that exceedingly safe position in order to run an obscure Internet venture called Auction Web. How obscure was Auction Web? So obscure that its Web site was black and white; so obscure that it had only 19 employees; so obscure that it started out as a trading site for Pez candy dispensers. Whitman, whose husband was head of neurosurgery at Massachusetts General Hospital, would later describe herself as reluctant to move her household for the sake of a "no-name Internet company." So she said no.

5   But she did fly out and talk to the founder, and then she said yes.

6   Since then, Auction Web has been renamed eBay, and in the four years since Whitman became its president and CEO, eBay has become one of the iconic Internet companies. One of the few Internet start-ups to be consistently profitable, it has seen stock growth of some 2,000 percent. In the process, Meg Whitman has become one of the richest self-made women in the world, with an estimated worth between $700 million and $1.2 billion. *Salon* magazine describes her as the "most successful Internet executive"; one might add that her rise marks one of the smartest household compromises any American husband has ever made.

7   That compromise is what's intrigued me ever since I read about her in *Salon*, one of the few general-interest magazines to have written anything of length about Whitman, who does not receive nearly so much attention as the men (AOL's Steve Case, MicroStrategy's Michael Saylor, Amazon.com's Jeff Bezos) who make up the rest of the Internet pantheon. Mostly I've been wondering what she did say, exactly, to persuade her family to move. Were there arguments? Scenes? Did the fact that her husband's career was formidably well-established make it easier, or harder, to get him to relocate? And what did they tell their two sons, whom Whitman—this interests me, too—had relatively young? (She started a family in her twenties, a time when many ambitious professional women don't feel secure enough in their careers to have kids.) Was it all unbelievably easy? Did her family just say, "Oh, sure, we'll gladly uproot our own lives so Mom can take a flier on the Internet?"

8   And what was it like once they got there? During those early days of massive growth, eBay suffered a couple of hair-raising outages as users overwhelmed the Web site's capacity; Whitman had to put an enormous amount of energy into refining the technology, enlarging the operations, e-mailing customers to apologize. Who was holding the family together while she was holding the company together? How is it that she emerged with a marriage intact, and sons who apparently still like her: Her current hobby is fly-fishing with them with equipment they bought off, yes, eBay.

9   Far from feeling jealous, I feel heartened just knowing about her: heartened that there is, unbeknownst to most of us, a woman whose family bet on her and who quite literally paid them back. I think the reason we don't read more about her is not so much sexism, probably, as the fact that when it comes to the Internet, the publishing world is more attracted to risky high-wire acts and spectacular failures than it is to quiet successes, even extraordinary ones. Recently, though, Whitman gave $30 million to Princeton University to expand its enrollment. Maybe when the name "Whitman" is chiseled on a new Ivy League dorm—taking its place among buildings bearing names like Rockefeller and Firestone—people will recognize that hers is a story of our millennium, as much as those of Bezos and Saylor and Case: a story of the way in which behind every professional success there are some dramatic personal choices, and that this is true for women as for men.

Comprehension Check

Answer the following with a, b, c, or d to indicate the phrase that best completes each statement.

_____ 1. Mundy's topic is
   a. moving to the West Coast.
   b. "Hi Honey."
   c. Whitman's move to eBay.
   d. Mr. Potato Head.

_____ 2. Meg Whitman asked her family to
   a. move to Boston.
   b. support her move to run an obscure Internet business.
   c. join her husband's move to the West Coast.
   d. let her work at Hasbro.

_____ 3. When Mundy writes that Whitman was overseeing boomer toys such as Play-Doh, she is referring to.
   a. toys that the baby-boomer generation played with.
   b. toys that go boom.
   c. the fact that Play-Doh explodes.
   d. the toys the "Bloomers" played with.

_____ 4. Whitman's husband was
   a. unemployed and eager to move.
   b. also asked to move to the West Coast.
   c. head of neurosurgery at Mass. General Hospital.
   d. head of the toy company Hasbro.

_____ 5. The Internet company Whitman was asked to head was so little known that

    a. Whitman couldn't find the office.

    b. it had only two employees.

    c. it didn't have a name.

    d. its Website was in black and white.

_____ 6. Four years after Whitman became CEO

    a. eBay changed its name.

    b. Whitman has become one of the world's richest women.

    c. eBay still fails to make money.

    d. eBay remains obscure.

_____ 7. Mundy observes that

    a. eBay was easy to run and make successful.

    b. Whitman's success has made her well known.

    c. Whitman does not get as much attention as male CEO's of other Internet companies.

    d. Whitman's family must have been unhappy with her.

_____ 8. Mundy wonders

    a. who held her family together while Whitman was working hard to be successful.

    b. why Whitman's boys don't like their mother.

    c. why the Whitmans like to fish.

    d. why Whitman's husband stayed in Boston.

_____ 9. Mundy sees Whitman as

    a. a lucky woman.

    b. a heartening example of what women with supportive families can achieve.

    c. someone who makes Mundy jealous.

    d. not as successful as her press suggests.

_____ 10. The author wants readers to

    a. understand that important personal choices stand behind most professional successes.

    b. be entertained by a cute story.

    c. learn about eBay.

    d. realize that success lies on the West Coast.

Expanding Vocabulary

*Answer the following with a, b, c, or d to indicate the best definition of the word in **bold** as it was used in the selection. The number in parentheses is the number of the paragraph in which the word appears.*

_____ 1. "throw myself into this **iffy** venture" (1)

     a. instant

     b. exciting

     c. uncertain

     d. fancy

_____ 2. "some **riveting** . . . conversations" (3)

     a. wretched

     b. engrossing

     c. reckless

     d. rolling

_____ 3. "**longevity** of . . . boomer toys" (4)

     a. long duration

     b. length

     c. width

     d. weight

_____ 4. "an **obscure** Internet venture" (4)

     a. obtuse

     b. well known

     c. not well known

     d. obligatory

_____ 5. "an obscure Internet **venture**" (4)

     a. undertaking assured of making money

     b. version

     c. adventure

     d. undertaking with an uncertain outcome

_____ 6. "**iconic** Internet companies" (6)

     a. idiomatic

     b. identical

     c. significant model

     d. identified

_____ 7. "what's **intrigued** me" (7)

    a. fascinated

    b. surprised

    c. invited

    d. frightened

_____ 8. "the Internet **pantheon**" (7)

    a. panel

    b. pantheism

    c. gods

    d. gophers

_____ 9. "**formidably** well-established" (7)

    a. awe-inspiringly

    b. formerly

    c. forthrightly

    d. ambitiously

_____ 10. "**unbeknownst** to most of us" (9)

    a. unbecoming

    b. not known

    c. unbroken

    d. not appreciated

Reflection and Discussion

1. How would you explain to someone else what is most important to Mundy about Whitman's success story? Why is Mundy so intrigued by Whitman?

2. Why should we be heartened by Whitman's story rather than jealous of her success? What is encouraging to all of us?

3. How willing are you to move and take a chance on a new job? How willing would you be with a spouse and children? Explain your views.

Take a Reading Road Trip!

For additional practice with your reading skills, use the Reading Road Trip CD-ROM or visit Reading Road Trip on the Web at **<http://www.ablongman.com/readingroadtrip>** (password required).

| # Efficient Reading

You are studying to become a better reader, not a faster reader. Comprehension, not speed, is your primary goal. Still, if you can maintain comprehension *and* use your reading time more efficiently, that is a double benefit. What can you do to read more efficiently?

IMPROVE VISUAL SKILLS

Several problems that are primarily visual problems can slow you down. One problem is called regression. *Regression* occurs when readers complete a sentence or two, realize they do not know what they have read, and go back to reread. For some, regression has become a bad habit. Improving your concentration as you read solves the problem of regression.

Vocalization and subvocalization also slow you down. *Vocalization* occurs when readers continue to move their lips as they read, even though they are not saying the words aloud. Most readers stop vocalization but continue to say the words to themselves. This is called *subvocalization*. Both lip movements and sounding the words in your head are habits that slow readers down. The first goal is to stop lip movements. An important second goal is to reduce subvocalization and let your eyes and brain do the reading. The following drills will help you see if you have any of these problems, and they can help you to reduce any that you have.

EXERCISE B-1	Rapid Word Recognition

*Move your eyes quickly across each line. Make a check over each word that is the same as the first word in **bold** type. Use a stopwatch or a clock with a second hand to time each set. Do not look back over a line. Look only from left to right. Try not to say the words. Just look for each repetition of the word in **bold.***

Set I   Begin timing.

1. **height**	high	heft	height	height	fight
2. **charge**	charge	change	cage	charge	cage
3. **trend**	tend	trend	tanned	spend	trend
4. **remain**	remiss	remark	ramble	remain	remake
5. **withdraw**	withdraw	withdrawn	withdrew	withdraw	withheld
6. **scarce**	scope	scan	scarce	scarce	scrape
7. **lately**	lazy	largely	lily	lately	lately
8. **clamp**	chomp	clamp	clamp	close	chomp
9. **soften**	sifter	soften	solve	soften	safety
10. **reality**	realty	regular	reality	reaching	reality
11. **ignite**	ignoble	ignite	inch	igloo	ignite
12. **command**	compote	command	common	demand	common
13. **distrust**	dismay	disease	distress	disdain	dismal
14. **informed**	inform	informed	informal	inflame	inform
15. **brave**	brave	bravely	brave	bravo	brace

End timing. Your time: _____   Number checked: _____

Set II   Begin timing.

1. **dismiss**	dismal	remiss	dismiss	dismiss	dismay
2. **worry**	marry	wormy	worry	wary	worry
3. **position**	position	positive	propose	pretense	posit
4. **message**	massage	message	message	massage	manage
5. **station**	sanction	stoppage	stopping	station	station
6. **verbal**	verbatim	verbal	herbal	verbal	vacant
7. **identity**	intensely	identify	identity	identity	indent
8. **million**	trillion	million	malady	million	missile
9. **human**	human	humane	humble	hopeful	humane
10. **lethal**	legal	lethal	legal	legal	lethal
11. **dinner**	dinner	diner	donor	dinner	diner
12. **vision**	version	vision	revision	visual	vision
13. **poison**	passion	poison	poison	passive	passion
14. **noise**	nose	noisome	nasal	noose	noise
15. **muddle**	middle	waddle	muddle	middle	muddle

End timing. Your time: _____   Number checked: _____

Set III   *Begin timing.*

1. **council**	council	counsel	counsel	consult	council
2. **trample**	tremble	trample	treble	topple	trample
3. **wretch**	wrest	witch	wrench	wretch	witch
4. **ponder**	pander	ponder	ponder	poacher	pander
5. **candid**	candid	cancel	corded	candid	cordial
6. **nature**	nurture	nature	nature	natural	nurture
7. **smash**	small	smoke	smash	smack	smash
8. **reduce**	remiss	renown	reduce	deduce	remiss
9. **forgive**	forgave	forgiven	forgave	forgiven	forfeit
10. **effort**	effort	effect	affect	effort	effete
11. **anger**	angle	ranger	anger	anger	ankle
12. **proud**	prod	prank	proudly	proud	prod
13. **frank**	frank	fraught	frank	fork	fraught
14. **easily**	easy	easily	messily	eerily	easy
15. **stake**	stoke	stack	stake	stake	stoke

End timing. Your time: _____   **Number checked:** _____

Set IV   *Begin timing.*

1. **lightly**	lightly	likely	loosely	likely	lightly
2. **wince**	whence	quince	win	wince	wrench
3. **manage**	manger	manage	meager	manage	manger
4. **bribe**	bribe	bride	bread	bribe	bride
5. **witch**	wench	which	witch	witch	which
6. **teacher**	teacher	preacher	thicker	toaster	teacher
7. **dinner**	diner	dinner	damper	dinner	diner
8. **sleeper**	sleepy	sleeping	sleeper	sleeping	sleepy
9. **bought**	bought	bought	brought	brought	boater
10. **opting**	opening	option	optical	opting	option
11. **ageless**	eyeless	ageless	aging	absence	ageless
12. **include**	incline	include	insane	incline	include
13. **clause**	cause	clause	close	clause	close
14. **rapid**	vapid	roped	razor	rapid	rabid
15. **umpire**	uphill	vampire	umpire	umpire	vampire

End timing. Your time: _____   **Number checked:** _____

| EXERCISE B-2 | **Word Meaning Recognition** |

*In the following sets you are looking for a word similar in meaning to the word in **bold** type. Move your eyes quickly across each line. Make a check over the word that has a meaning similar to the word in bold. Do not look back over the line; keep your eyes moving from left to right. Time yourself as you did in the previous exercise.*

Set I   *Begin timing.*

1. **glance**	glower	shine	grope	look	linger
2. **tired**	famous	fatigued	loud	trained	trite
3. **walk**	wrangle	wink	stole	stroll	wash
4. **aide**	aid	aisle	hope	angel	helper
5. **coat**	wrap	rope	cap	write	cross
6. **help**	hope	cope	aid	keep	heap
7. **giving**	gracious	going	graze	generous	grave
8. **sympathy**	servile	compassion	compete	symphony	pathos
9. **conclude**	concede	impede	question	conscious	infer
10. **twine**	twist	swing	sting	twit	string
11. **direct**	guide	leaden	divine	great	grant
12. **incorrect**	connect	interject	correct	false	facile
13. **vulgar**	vinegar	crude	vocal	crisp	vicious
14. **habitat**	habit	hopeful	dwelling	deception	drapery
15. **likely**	likeable	probable	laughable	possible	probate

End timing. Your time: _____   **Number checked:** _____

Set II   *Begin timing.*

1. **conflict**	courage	struggle	strength	conflate	course
2. **defeat**	distance	conquest	coast	conquer	deafen
3. **strange**	stranger	unusual	strangle	unlikely	strong
4. **worried**	wondered	worship	able	wrangled	anxious
5. **climb**	ascend	run	attest	lengthen	claim
6. **refill**	remake	replenish	filler	restore	falter
7. **hinder**	hidden	unhappy	thwart	thought	threw
8. **discourteous**	disguise	disrobe	ridicule	rude	religious
9. **right**	regular	correct	remake	connect	relate
10. **irregular**	erotic	erratic	regular	rational	usual

11. **declare**	proclaim	protect	decorate	babble	bashful
12. **alter**	altar	active	charge	change	twist
13. **fire**	force	dismal	failure	discharge	heed
14. **feeling**	sadness	sentiment	forceful	faith	fierce
15. **clamor**	claim	coax	noise	noose	stage

End timing. Your time: _____ Number checked: _____

Rapid Phrase Recognition

Your eyes can read the words on the page only when they stop to look at the words. Each stop is called a "fixation." One way to increase reading speed is to make each fixation as brief as possible to take in the visual information—the printed word. Another way to increase reading speed is to see more words at each fixation. When you read the word *individual*, your eyes take in the whole word in one fixation. Of course when you first learned the word, you probably sounded out each syllable, but now you can take in the word all at once because you know it. Look at how much your eyes can now take in:

in / di / vid / u / al

If you can read five syllables with one fixation, why couldn't you read a phrase in one fixation? This phrase, for example,

when / to / re / spond

has fewer syllables than the word *individual*. You can increase your reading speed without losing comprehension if you will practice expanding the number of words you take in with each fixation. Let your eyes "collect" two or three words that make up a unit of thought and read them at one stop. The following exercises will help you practice expanding fixation.

EXERCISE **B-3**	**Rapid Phrase Recognition**

Read from left to right across each line, looking for each repetition of the key phrase. Mark the key phrase each time it appears. Do not go back over any line. Try not to sound out any of the words; just look at each phrase to see if it is the key phrase to be marked.

Set I	*Key phrase: when to respond*	*Begin timing.*
when to go	when to dance	what a delight
wet your whistle	waiting for dark	when in doubt
wondering out loud	what's happening	when to respond
what's happening	when in doubt	washing the window
when in doubt	when to respond	wondering out loud
when to respond	wager a bet	when to respond

wet your whistle	wondering out loud	winter wonderland
waiting for dark	when to respond	when in doubt
washing the window	winter wonderland	when to respond
wet your whistle	wondering out loud	wager a bet

End timing. Your time: _____

Number of key phrases marked: _____ **out of 6**

Set II   *Key phrase: coping with stress*   *Begin timing.*

climbing the tree	coping with crime	careful with sticks
coping with anger	coping with stress	charging ahead
caring for pets	charging ahead	concern for others
coping with stress	challenging others	coping with stress
climbing the tree	coping with stress	caring for pets
concern for others	coping with stress	challenges ahead
cereal to eat	climbing the tree	coping with anger
caring for pets	climbing the tree	coping with stress
careless whispers	caring for pets	challenging others
coping with stress	cereal to eat	coping with anger
coping with crime	careless whispers	coping with stress

End timing. Your time: _____

Number of key phrases marked: _____ **out of 8**

Set III   *Key phrase: better and faster*   *Begin timing.*

bargain basement	better with cream	bridges with lights
brighter and faster	bigger and faster	better and faster
better and faster	bridges with lights	butter with bread
baskets of fruit	better and faster	better than others
butter with bread	better than others	bigger than life
better and faster	bargain basement	bridges with lights
brains and heart	better with cream	brighter and faster
bowls and cups	bigger than life	better and faster
best and brightest	butter with bread	better than others
better and faster	bigger and faster	baskets of fruit
best and brightest	better with cream	better and faster

End timing. Your time: _____

Number of key phrases marked: _____ **out of 7**

Set IV	*Key phrase: a safe place*	*Begin timing.*
a soft spot	a safe haven	a safe place
a softer place	a sandy spot	a shady place
a silly idea	a safe place	a soft spot
a silk purse	a safe peace	a safe haven
a strong peace	a sandy spot	a salt lick
a safe place	a solid plank	a shady place
a softer place	a sandal strap	a soft spot
a silly idea	a silk purse	a safe place
a showy piece	a strong peace	a safe haven
a safe place	a shady place	a sandy spot
a silk purse	a safe place	a sandal strap

End timing. Your time: _____

Number of key phrases marked: _____ **out of 6**

◼ EFFICIENT READING THROUGH AGGRESSIVE READING

How fast you can read *and* comprehend depends in part on your vocabulary and knowledge of the subject. But you can also practice reading faster. If you practice, you will pick up the pace of your reading without losing comprehension. To practice, you need to read aggressively. Think of yourself as attacking the book or magazine. Do not let your eyes leave the page or your mind leave the subject. Do not let anything interrupt your concentration until you finish. The following reading selection will give you practice.

Directions: Take no more than 30 seconds to skim the selection. Now answer these questions.

1. What do you expect the article to be about?

   _____

2. The driver of the four-wheel-drive vehicle called the author:

   _____

Now begin timing and read aggressively to the end of the selection.

Starting time: _____ **min.** _____ **sec.**

THE RUDE AWAKEN

Jeanne Marie Laskas, the Washington Post, *February 4, 1996*

1 God forbid you should make a mistake. To err these days is subhuman.

2 I was driving late one night alone. This was not easy. My car is not good in the snow. The heck with what lane I was in. I was just trying to keep my car pointed forward.

3 A guy behind me in a fancy four-wheel-drive vehicle began flashing his head-lights. I figured he knew something I didn't—that some danger was ahead, or that something was wrong with my car. So I slowed down. He kept flashing. I slowed down some more. He pulled up beside me, craned his neck to get a look at me. I could tell from the way he was trying to talk through the car windows that he had something really, really important to say. So I stopped and rolled down the pas-senger-side window.

4 "DON'T YOU KNOW HOW TO USE A TURN SIGNAL?" he said, spitting his words into the crisp winter air.

5 My weenie impulse was to answer him with a pathetic, "Yes."

6 "WHAT ARE YOU, STUPID?" he said. "WHAT ARE YOU, AN IDIOT?" Then he used a lot of curse words to characterize my driving, my heritage and my sex-ual history. He was still yelling when I rolled my window up and drove off.

7 I wished I hadn't bolted like a scared cat. I wished I had stayed and hissed at him. Then again, he seemed like the type to hoard firearms.

8 I was worked up the whole way home. Yes, I know tempers flare in winter—especially with two feet of snow on the ground. And I know that some people are, in fact, so breathtakingly important that their lives cannot be interrupted by some wacky indulgence on the part of Mother Nature. And yes, I know humans have a need to feign powerfulness when they are faced with their own powerlessness.

9 But please. Isn't there some jail we can put rude people in?

10 No, there isn't. And this is why the rude people are taking over.

11 I am not talking about just one jerk on a snowy highway. I am talking about the jerks you run into more and more often and in more and more places. I am talk-ing about the jerk my friend Michelle met in a department store.

12 It has been Michelle's personal challenge this winter to survive with a broken ankle. Imagine. Okay, so recently she went on her first shopping expedition, and there she was, balanced on crutches, looking through a rack of dresses. She felt some pressure. She felt a push. She looked up to see a woman at the same rack, nudging her out of the way.

13 "Um," said Michelle, "I think there's room for both of us here?"

14 The lady looked at her. The lady said: "Get out of my way unless you want your other leg broken."

15 What does a normal courteous person do in a situation like this? Michelle's impulse was not to hiss, nor to run away. Instead, she reported the incident to the store manager, pointing out that the store was about to lose a good customer on account of this bully. She said people like this should be kicked out of the store.

16   The manager said there was nothing she could do. Not unless there was actual physical contact and a store employee witnessed it. "Store policy," she told Michelle. "Rude people like that are just the type to sue."

17   Suing. Shooting. The rude people seize all the power. The normal courteous people get none. This is what Michelle and I were concluding as we tried to think of a way to combat the bullies. "Solidarity!" we were saying. Take back the public places! Take back the stores, the buses, the parking spaces, the crisp winter air!

18   We imagined laws against rudeness. We considered mandatory Valium prescriptions for rude people. We envisioned support groups for the victims of rudeness. We wondered: Are we getting old?

19   For a while I walked around thinking that's probably it. You're supposed to think the world is getting uglier as you age.

20   Later I went over to a friend's house where a lot of neighborhood boys were playing. Most were about 9 years old, and they were playing rough, as boys do. But one was different. A rude person in training. For no apparent reason, this kid kicked my friend's dog, then made an obscene gesture at it. I looked at Tom, my 14-year-old nephew. "Kids are getting meaner," Tom said. "Definitely." He said maybe we should go upstairs and get a hot dog.

21   Just then, Katie, my 3-year-old niece, finished twirling around in her own personal time of glee and plopped down in the rude kid's seat. She didn't know it was his seat.

22   "Get up, bitch," the boy said, "before I kick you, too."

23   I looked at Katie. I wanted to scoop her up, carry her away. I wanted to shield her forever from the generations of bullies her future held.

24   But Katie straightened her back. She folded her arms. She looked the boy square in the eye. She said: "You are rude."

25   The room went quiet. The boy retreated.

26   I'm telling you, it's a start. Try it. All together now: "You are rude."

886 words

Finishing time: _____ min. _____ sec.

Starting time: _____ min. _____ sec. (subtract)

Reading time: _____ min. _____ sec. = _____ sec.

No. of words ÷ reading time (in seconds) x 60 = _____ wpm

Comprehension Check

Select the letter of the phrase that best completes the statement.

_____ 1. The best main-idea statement is:

    a. Rude people should be told they are rude and not be allowed to get away with bullying others.

    b. Older people always think young people are rude.

    c. Rude people should be put in jail.

_____ 2. The writer's friend Michelle experienced rudeness while

    a. she was visiting a friend.

    b. she was shopping on crutches.

    c. she was driving in snow.

_____ 3. We are to infer that the author

    a. believes that her age explains her sense of more rude people.

    b. does not believe that her age explains her sense of more rude people.

    c. believes that nothing can be done about rudeness.

_____ 4. The author believes that

    a. rude people are bullies.

    b. rudeness starts in childhood and continues unless corrected.

    c. both (a) and (b).

_____ 5. The author wants

    a. rude people sent to jail.

    b. courteous people to tell rude people they are being rude.

    c. rude people to take Valium.

Comprehension score: **# right x 20** = _____ %

Take a Reading Road Trip!

For additional practice with your reading skills, use the Reading Road Trip CD-ROM or visit Reading Road Trip on the Web at <http://www.ablongman.com/readingroadtrip> (password required).

Glossary

Analysis Dividing a work or a topic into its parts.

Annotating A combination of underlining and marginal notes used to guide one's study of written material.

Bias The position or viewpoint of the author, as revealed in the way facts are presented and strategies are used to create tone.

Cause and effect An organizational strategy in which one or more items are shown to produce one or more consequences.

Chronology The arrangement of events in time sequence. A narrative or historical account organizes events in chronological order. A process analysis explains steps in their appropriate chronology.

Cognition The process of knowing or learning.

Commitment An active desire to do something well.

Comparison A structuring of information to show similarities between two items.

Concentration An active attention given to a task.

Connotation The associations and emotional overtones suggested by a word.

Context clues The language environment that gives information about the meaning of words within that environment.

Contrast A structuring of information to show differences between two items.

Cornell Method A method of taking notes from reading or from lectures. A vertical line divides each page into two parts, the left part one-third of the page and the right part two-thirds. Notes are taken to the right of the line, and key words and topics are placed to the left.

Critical thinking An organized, purposeful study of information and ideas to evaluate their usefulness.

Definition Explanation of a word's meaning or meanings. It can be provided in a sentence or expanded into an essay.

Denotation The meanings of a word, often referred to as a word's dictionary definitions.

Description Details appealing to the five senses that help readers to "see" the writer's subject.

Details Specific pieces of information that range from descriptions of people and places to statistical data and that are used by writers to illustrate and support ideas and general points.

Evidence Facts and examples used to support the main idea of an argument.

Example A specific illustration used to develop a main idea.

Expository writing Writing primarily designed to provide information (e.g., reporting and textbook writing).

Expressive writing Writing designed to produce an emotional as well as intellectual response to the subject discussed and to generate reflection on human life and experiences.

474

Fact A statement that is verifiable by observation, measurement, experiment, or use of reliable reference sources such as encyclopedias.

Fiction An imagined narrative; a story.

Figurative language Language containing figures of speech (e.g., metaphors) that extend meaning beyond the literal.

Flowchart A type of graph best used to depict steps in a process, or a sequence of events or ideas.

Graphics Methods of presenting information visually, such as graphs, maps, charts, or diagrams.

Highlighting The use of colored markers to make some lines of a text stand out, as an aid to studying the text.

Inference A conclusion drawn from related information on a given subject.

Irony The expression of some form of discrepancy between what is said and what is meant, what we expect to happen and what actually happens, or what a character says and what we understand to be true.

Main idea The central point of a passage or work.

Mapping A writing-to-learn strategy that displays main ideas and shows their relationships graphically.

Metaphor A figure of speech in which a comparison is either stated or implied between two basically unlike items (e.g., Love is compared to red roses.).

Monitoring Regular, purposeful checking of one's work to maintain ideal performance of a task.

Note taking Paraphrasing and summarizing main ideas and key points in assigned readings as a strategy for studying the readings.

Opinion Statements of inference or judgment, in contrast to statements of fact.

Organization The structure or pattern of development of a work.

Outlining A strategy for summarizing and indicating the relationships of a work's main ideas, main details, and minor details by using a pattern of Roman numerals, letters, and Arabic numerals and indentation.

Personification A comparison that gives human qualities to something not human (e.g., "The daffodils tossed their heads.").

Persuasive writing Writing primarily designed to support a position on an issue or beliefs about a given subject.

Point of View The perspective from which a story is told.

Preread A step in preparing to read that involves getting an overview by reading only key parts of a work.

Purpose The reason or reasons a writer chooses to write a particular work.

Scanning A method of quick reading that focuses on finding just the information needed from the reading material.

Signal words Words or phrases that make clear a passage's structure.

Simile A comparison between two basically unlike things stated explicitly through a connector such as *like* or *as* (e.g., "My love is like a red, red rose.").

Skimming A reading strategy that focuses on obtaining an overview or "gist" of a work by searching for main ideas and skipping most details.

Style A writer's choice of words and sentence patterns.

Subvocalization Practice of sounding words in one's head as one reads.

Summary A condensed, objective restatement in different words of the main points of a passage or work.

Thesis The main idea of an essay, article, or book; what a writer asserts about his or her subject.

Tone The way the writer's attitude is expressed (e.g., playful, sarcastic.).

Topic The subject of a piece of writing.

Topic sentence The sentence in a paragraph that states the paragraph's main idea. (In some paragraphs, the main idea is not stated but implied.)

Vocalization Practice of moving one's lips or saying words aloud as one reads.

Credits

Amelia Earhart in training plane photo. Reprinted with permission of Institute for Advanced Study, Harvard University.

Anne-Marie Ambert, from *Families in the New Millennium*, copyright © 2001 by Allyn & Bacon.

Copyright © 1994 by Houghton Mifflin Company. Adapted and reproduced by permission from *The American Heritage Dictionary, Third Paperback Edition*.

Cecelie Berry, "It's Time We Rejected Litmus Test." From *Newsweek*, February 7, 2000. Copyright © 2000 Newsweek, Inc. All rights reserved. Reprinted by permission.

Bishop and Aldanda, *Step Up to Wellness: A Stage-Based Approach*. Copyright © 1998 by Pearson Education. Reprinted by permission.

Suzanne Britt, "Neat People vs. Sloppy People." Reprinted by permission of the author.

Dik Browne, cartoon: "Hagar the Horrible." Copyright © 1996. Reprinted with special permission of King Features Syndicate.

"It's A Wonderful Night," by Susan Burton. Copyright © 2001 by Susan Burton. Distributed by The New York Times Special Features.

Elizabeth Castor, "Frozen in Time." Copyright © 2002, The Washington Post, reprinted with permission.

Curtis and Barnes, excerpts from Helena Curtis and N. Sue Barnes, *An Invitation to Biology*, Fourth Edition, pp. 1-4, 55, 553; adaptation of "The Breakup of Pangaea" map. Copyright © 1992 Worth Publishers, New York. Reprinted and adapted with permission.

Thomas V. DiBacco, "Dr. Franklin's Tips for Staying Well," from *The Washington Post*, January 30, 1996. Reprinted with permission of the author.

Davis, excerpt from *Computer Information Systems: An Introduction*. Copyright © 1997 by Thomson Learning. Reprinted by permission.

Donatelle and Davis, excerpts from *Access to Health*, Fourth Edition, pp. 84, 107, 195, 288, 599; table, p. 365; figure, p. 63. Copyright © 1996 by Allyn & Bacon. Reprinted by permission.

Donatelle and Davis, excerpt from *Access to Health*, Fifth Edition, pp. 93-98. Copyright © 1998 by Allyn & Bacon. Reprinted by permission.

From William DuBois and R. Dean Wright, *Applying Sociology: Making a Better World*. Published by Allyn & Bacon, Boston, MA. Copyright © 2001 by Pearson Education. Reprinted by permission of publisher.

Joel R. Evans and Barry Berman, material from *Marketing*, Sixth Edition, Copyright © 1993 by Allyn & Bacon. Reprinted by permission.

From Jean Folkerts & Stephen Lacy, *Media In Your Life: An Introduction To Mass Communication*, Second Edition. Published by Allyn & Bacon, Boston, MA. Copyright © 2001 by Pearson Education. Reprinted by permission of the publisher.

Index